UNITED STATES GOVERNMENT

Policy and Supporting Positions

Committee on Oversight and Government Reform

U.S. House of Representatives

112th Congress, 2d Session

DECEMBER 1, 2012

U.S. GOVERNMENT PRINTING OFFICE

WASHINGTON, D.C. : 2012

COMMITTEE ON OVERSIGHT AND GOVERNMENT REFORM

DARRELL E. ISSA, California, *Chairman*

DAN BURTON, Indiana
JOHN L. MICA, Florida
TODD RUSSELL PLATTS, Pennsylvania
MICHAEL R. TURNER, Ohio
PATRICK T. McHENRY, North Carolina
JIM JORDAN, Ohio
JASON CHAFFETZ, Utah
CONNIE MACK, Florida
TIM WALBERG, Michigan
JAMES LANKFORD, Oklahoma
JUSTIN AMASH, Michigan
ANN MARIE BUERKLE, New York
PAUL A. GOSAR, Arizona
RAÚL R. LABRADOR, Idaho
PATRICK MEEHAN, Pennsylvania
SCOTT DesJARLAIS, Tennessee
JOE WALSH, Illinois
TREY GOWDY, South Carolina
DENNIS A. ROSS, Florida
BLAKE FARENTHOLD, Texas
MIKE KELLY, Pennsylvania
VACANCY

ELIJAH E. CUMMINGS, Maryland,
    Ranking Minority Member
EDOLPHUS TOWNS, New York
CAROLYN B. MALONEY, New York
ELEANOR HOLMES NORTON, District of
    Columbia
DENNIS J. KUCINICH, Ohio
JOHN F. TIERNEY, Massachusetts
WM. LACY CLAY, Missouri
STEPHEN F. LYNCH, Massachusetts
JIM COOPER, Tennessee
GERALD E. CONNOLLY, Virginia
MIKE QUIGLEY, Illinois
DANNY K. DAVIS, Illinois
BRUCE L. BRALEY, Iowa
PETER WELCH, Vermont
JOHN A. YARMUTH, Kentucky
CHRISTOPHER S. MURPHY, Connecticut
JACKIE SPEIER, California

LAWRENCE J. BRADY, *Staff Director*
JOHN D. CUADERES, *Deputy Staff Director*
ROBERT BORDEN, *General Counsel*
LINDA A. GOOD, *Chief Clerk*
DAVID RAPALLO, *Minority Staff Director*

FOREWORD

Every four years, just after the Presidential election, the "United States Government Policy and Supporting Positions," commonly known as the *Plum Book,* is published, alternately, by the Senate Committee on Homeland Security and Governmental Affairs and the House Committee on Oversight and Government Reform.

This publication contains data (as of June 30, 2012) on over 8,000 Federal civil service leadership and support positions in the legislative and executive branches of the Federal Government that may be subject to noncompetitive appointment (e.g., positions such as agency heads and their immediate subordinates, policy executives and advisors, and aides who report to these officials). The duties of many such positions may involve advocacy of Administration policies and programs and the incumbents usually have a close and confidential working relationship with the agency head or other key officials.

Following are the major categories of positions listed:

- Executive Schedule and salary-equivalent positions paid at the rates established for levels I through V of the Executive Schedule;

- Senior Executive Service (SES) "General" positions;

- Senior Foreign Service positions;

- Schedule C positions excepted from the competitive service by the President, or by the Director, Office of Personnel Management, because of the confidential or policy-determining nature of the position duties; and

- Other positions at the GS–14 and above level excepted from the competitive civil service by law because of the confidential or policy-determining nature of the position duties.

See Appendix 2 for more details on SES appointments and Appendix 3 for more details on Schedule C appointments. Additional information on the positions listed and the Federal salary schedules under which they are paid is provided in the appendices. The Legend on the following page shows the codes and acronyms used in this publication.

DISCLAIMER

The information for this committee print was provided to the committee by the U.S. Office of Personnel Management [OPM] on November 1, 2012. Only grammatical and technical modifications have been made.

LEGEND

Position Location (Column 1)

Listed are the cities, States/Provinces and foreign countries in which the positions are located. Countries and cities (or other subdivisions) are shown for overseas posts. Note that "Washington, DC" includes positions in the entire metropolitan area and therefore may include certain cities and counties in the States of Maryland and Virginia.

Position Title (Column 2)

Listed are the position titles and the names of the organizations in which they are located.

Name of Incumbent (Column 3)

Listed are the names of individuals serving under other than career appointments. The phrase "Career Incumbent" is shown for positions incumbered by career appointees. The term "Vacant" is shown for positions that were not occupied on June 30, 2012, the "as of" date of this publication.

Note the law requires "member" positions in certain agencies (e.g., boards, committees, and commissions) be filled on a bipartisan basis. For such positions, the following letter codes are shown in parentheses following the name of the incumbent:

(D) = Democrat   (I) = Independent   (R) = Republican

Type of Appointment (Column 4)

Listed are letter codes that denote the type of appointment under which the position incumbent is serving. Note that several categories of positions can be filled by more than one type of appointment, e.g., SES positions listed in this publication may be filled by using career, noncareer, limited emergency, or limited term appointment authorities. Therefore, no "Type of Appointment" is shown for such positions when they are vacant.

PAS	=	Presidential Appointment with Senate Confirmation
PA	=	Presidential Appointment (without Senate Confirmation)
CA	=	Career Appointment
NA	=	Noncareer Appointment
EA	=	Limited Emergency Appointment
TA	=	Limited Term Appointment
SC	=	Schedule C Excepted Appointment
XS	=	Appointment Excepted by Statute

Pay Plan (Column 5)

Listed are letter codes that denote the Federal salary schedule or pay system under which the position incumbents are going to be paid. Tables showing the salary ranges for major pay systems are contained in Appendix 4.

AD	=	Administratively Determined Rates
ES	=	Senior Executive Service
EX	=	Executive Schedule
FA	=	Foreign Service Chiefs of Mission
FE	=	Senior Foreign Service
FP	=	Foreign Service Specialist
GS	=	General Schedule
PD	=	Daily Pay Rate* (per diem)
SL	=	Senior Level
TM	=	Federal Housing Finance Board Merit Pay
VH	=	Farm Credit Administration Pay Plan
WC	=	Without Compensation*
OT	=	Other Pay Plan* (all those not listed separately)

* Although not pay plans, these codes are shown for information purposes.

Level, Grade, or Pay (Column 6)

Listed are numerical and letter codes that denote the level, grade or salary of the position incumbered:

Levels I through V of the Executive Schedule

Grades 1 through 15 of the General Schedule

Annual Salary in Dollars

Daily Pay Rate in Dollars

If there is no entry in this column, the position does not have an established level, grade, or pay rate. For example, the pay rate for Senior Executive Service and Senior Level positions is "personal," i.e., attached to the incumbent, not the position. The pay rate for each new appointee is set by the appointing authority (usually the agency head) on a case-by-case basis. Annual salary schedules and pay ranges for such positions are shown in Appendix 4.

Tenure (Column 7)

Listed are the terms or durations of the appointment in years. If there is no entry in this column, the appointment has no fixed term.

Expires (Column 8)

Listed are the expiration dates for time-limited appointments. If there is no entry in this column, the incumbent is not serving under a time-limited appointment. However, many member positions on agency advisory boards, councils, and commissions are filled initially for a fixed term, but the incumbents may (and often do) serve beyond the expiration date until they are replaced. In such cases, no expiration date is shown.

CONTENTS

APPENDICES

LEGISLATIVE BRANCH

ARCHITECT OF THE CAPITOL

Location	Position	Name of Incumbent	Type of Appt.	Pay Plan	Level, Grade, or Pay	Tenure	Expires
Washington, DC	Architect of the Capitol	Stephen T. Ayers	PAS	EX	III	10 Years	05/13/20

GOVERNMENT ACCOUNTABILITY OFFICE

Location	Position	Name of Incumbent	Type of Appt.	Pay Plan	Level, Grade, or Pay	Tenure	Expires
Washington, DC	Comptroller General of United States	Gene L. Dodaro	PAS	EX	II	15 Years	12/22/25
Do	Deputy Comptroller General	Vacant	PAS	EX	III	....	

GOVERNMENT PRINTING OFFICE

Location	Position	Name of Incumbent	Type of Appt.	Pay Plan	Level, Grade, or Pay	Tenure	Expires
	OFFICE OF THE PUBLIC PRINTER						
Washington, DC	Public Printer	Vacant	PAS	EX	II	....	
Do	Deputy Public Printer	Davita E. Vance-Cooks	XS	EX	III	....	
Do	Superintendent of Documents	Mary Alice Baish	XS	SL	....	....	
Do	Inspector General	Michael A. Raponi	XS	SL	....	....	
Do	Executive Assistant to the Public Printer	Heather M. Lawson	SC	OT	....	....	

LIBRARY OF CONGRESS

Location	Position	Name of Incumbent	Type of Appt.	Pay Plan	Level, Grade, or Pay	Tenure	Expires
Washington, DC	Librarian of Congress	James H. Billington	PAS	EX	II	....	
	TRUST FUND BOARD						
Do	Ex Officio Member, Secretary of Treasury	Timothy F. Geithner	XS	WC	....	5 Years	01/20/13
Do	Board Member	Joan W. Harris	PA	WC	....	5 Years	12/02/16
Do	......do	Vacant	PA	WC	....	....	
	PERMANENT COMMITTEE FOR THE OLIVER WENDELL HOLMES DEVISE						
Do	Committee Member	Linda K. Kerber	PA	WC	....	8 Years	06/30/19
Do	......do	Michael Les Benedict	PA	WC	....	8 Years	04/30/19
Do	......do	Rachel F. Moran	PA	WC	....	8 Years	09/30/19
Do	......do	Vacant	PA	WC	....	....	
	AMERICAN FOLKLIFE CENTER						
Do	Trustee Member	Susan Hildreth	PA	WC	....	5 Years	
Do	......do	Robert G. Stanton	PA	WC	....	5 Years	
Do	Ex Officio Member, Chairman, National Endowment for the Arts.	Rocco Landesman	XS	WC	....	5 Years	
Do	Ex Officio Member, Chairman, National Endowment for the Humanities.	James A. Leach	XS	WC	....	5 Years	
Do	Trustee Member	Vacant	PA	WC	....	....	
Do	......do	......do	PA	WC	....	....	

EXECUTIVE BRANCH

EXECUTIVE OFFICE OF THE PRESIDENT

Location	Position	Name of Incumbent	Type of Appt.	Pay Plan	Level, Grade, or Pay	Tenure	Expires
	EXECUTIVE OFFICE OF THE PRESIDENT						
	WHITE HOUSE OFFICE						
Washington, DC	Assistant to the President and Chief of Staff	Jacob J. Lew	PA	AD	....	....	
Do	Assistant to the President for Homeland Security and Counterterrorism.	John O. Brennan	PA	AD	....	....	
Do	Assistant to the President and Press Secretary.	James F. Carney	PA	AD	....	....	
Do	Assistant to the President and Deputy Chief of Staff for Planning.	Mark B. Childress	PA	AD	....	....	
Do	Assistant to the President and Deputy Chief of Staff for Policy.	Nancy-Ann M. DeParle	PA	AD	....	....	
Do	Assistant to the President and National Security Advisor.	Thomas E. Donilon	PA	AD	....	....	
Do	Assistant to the President and Director of Speechwriting.	Jonathan E. Favreau	PA	AD	....	....	
Do	Assistant to the President and Deputy National Security Advisor for International Economics.	Michael B. Froman	PA	AD	....	....	
Do	Senior Advisor and Assistant to the President for Intergovernmental Affairs and Public Engagement.	Valerie B. Jarrett	PA	AD	....	....	
Do	Assistant to the President and Cabinet Secretary.	Christopher P. Lu	PA	AD	....	....	
Do	Assistant to the President and Deputy Chief of Staff for Operations.	Alyssa M. Mastromonaco ...	PA	AD	....	....	
Do	Assistant to the President and Deputy National Security Advisor.	Denis R. McDonough	PA	AD	....	....	
Do	Assistant to the President and Director of the Domestic Policy Council.	Cecilia Muñoz	PA	AD	....	....	
Do	Assistant to the President and Director, Office of Legislative Affairs.	Robert L. Nabors II	PA	AD	....	....	
Do	Assistant to the President and Director of Communications.	Howard D. Pfeiffer	PA	AD	....	....	
Do	Assistant to the President and Senior Advisor	David A. Plouffe	PA	AD	....	....	
Do	Counselor to the President	Peter M. Rouse	PA	AD	....	....	
Do	Assistant to the President and Counsel to the President.	Kathryn H. Ruemmler	PA	AD	....	....	
Do	Assistant to the President for Economic Policy and Director of the National Economic Council.	Eugene B. Sperling	PA	AD	....	....	
Do	Assistant to the President and Chief of Staff to the First Lady.	Christina M. Tchen	PA	AD	....	....	
Do	Assistant to the President and Director of Presidential Personnel.	Nancy D. Hogan	PA	AD	....	....	
Do	Assistant to the President for Management and Administration.	Bradley J. Kiley	PA	AD	....	....	
Do	Deputy Assistant to the President and Principal Deputy Counsel to the President.	Caroline K. Cheng	PA	AD	....	....	
Do	Deputy Assistant to the President and Deputy Counsel to the President.	Steven P. Croley	PA	AD	....	....	
Do	......do	Avril D. Haines	PA	AD	....	....	
Do	......do	Leslie B. Kiernan	PA	AD	....	....	
Do	Deputy Assistant to the President and Staff Secretary.	Douglas J. Kramer	PA	AD	....	....	
Do	Deputy Assistant to the President for Health Policy.	Jeanne M. Lambrew	PA	AD	....	....	
Do	Deputy Assistant to the President for Legislative Affairs and Senate Liaison.	Jules E. Pagano	PA	AD	....	....	
Do	Deputy Assistant to the President and Deputy Director of Communications.	Jennifer M. Palmieri	PA	AD	....	....	
Do	Deputy Assistant to the President for Legislative Affairs and House Liaison.	Jonathan D. Samuels	PA	AD	....	....	
Do	Deputy Assistant to the President and Director of Intergovernmental Affairs.	David P. Agnew	PA	AD	....	....	
Do	Deputy Assistant to the President and Director of the Office of Public Engagement.	Jonathan K. Carson	PA	AD	....	....	

(2)

EXECUTIVE OFFICE OF THE PRESIDENT—Continued

Location	Position	Name of Incumbent	Type of Appt.	Pay Plan	Level, Grade, or Pay	Tenure	Expires
Washington, DC	Deputy Assistant to the President for Management and Administration.	Katy A. Kale	PA	AD	....	....	
Do	Deputy Assistant to the President, Deputy National Security Advisor for Strategic Communications and Speechwriting.	Benjamin J. Rhodes	PA	AD	....	....	
Do	Deputy Assistant to the President and Counselor to the Senior Advisor for Strategic Engagement.	Michael A. Strautmanis	PA	AD	....	....	
Do	Director of Records Management	Philip C. Droege	XS	AD	....	....	
Do	Executive Clerk	David E. Kalbaugh	XS	AD	....	....	
Do	Deputy Assistant to the President and Director of Scheduling and Advance.	Danielle M. Crutchfield	PA	AD	....	....	
Do	Deputy Assistant to the President and Director of Policy and Projects for the First Lady.	Jocelyn C. Frye	PA	AD	....	....	
Do	Deputy Assistant to the President for Energy and Climate Change.	Heather R. Zichal	PA	AD	....	....	
Do	Special Assistant to the President and Senior Counsel to the President.	Christopher D. Kang	PA	AD	....	....	
Do	Special Assistant to the President and Associate Counsel to the President.	Brian J. Egan	PA	AD	....	....	
Do	Special Assistant to the President for Legislative Affairs.	Layth S. Elhassani	PA	AD	....	....	
Do	Special Assistant to the President and Associate Counsel to the President.	Zulima L. Espinel	PA	AD	....	....	
Do	......do	Michael J. Gottlieb	PA	AD	....	....	
Do	......do	Kathleen R. Hartnett	PA	AD	....	....	
Do	Special Assistant to the President for Legislative Affairs.	Luis A. Jimenez	PA	AD	....	....	
Do	......do	Alejandro Perez	PA	AD	....	....	
Do	......do	Miguel E. Rodriguez	PA	AD	....	....	
Do	Special Assistant to the President and Special Counsel to the President.	Edward N. Siskel	PA	AD	....	....	
Do	Special Assistant to the President and Associate Counsel to the President.	Anne K. Small	PA	AD	....	....	
Do	......do	Chun-Wei J. Su	PA	AD	....	....	
Do	Special Assistant to the President for Legislative Affairs.	Anne E. Wall	PA	AD	....	....	
Do	Special Assistant to the President and Associate Counsel to the President.	Andrew M. Wright	PA	AD	....	....	
Do	Deputy Assistant to the President and Director, Office of the Chief of Staff.	Emmett S. Beliveau	PA	AD	....	....	
Do	Deputy Assistant to the President and Deputy Cabinet Secretary.	Rachana Bhowmik	PA	AD	....	....	
Do	Deputy Assistant to the President and Deputy Director of Presidential Personnel.	Jonathan D. McBride	PA	AD	....	....	
Do	Special Assistant to the President, Trip Director and Personal Aide to the President.	Marvin D. Nicholson, Jr. ...	PA	AD	....	....	
Do	Deputy Assistant to the President and Director of Advance and Operations.	Peter A. Selfridge	PA	AD	....	....	
Do	Deputy Assistant to the President and Director of Scheduling.	Jessica N. Wright	PA	AD	....	....	
Do	Special Assistant to the President and Principal Deputy Press Secretary.	Joshua R. Earnest	PA	AD	....	....	
Do	Special Assistant to the President and Chief of Staff for Presidential Personnel.	Margaret T. McLaughlin ...	PA	AD	....	....	
Do	Special Assistant to the President and Deputy Chief of Staff and Director of Operations for the First Lady.	Melissa E. Winter	PA	AD	....	....	
Do	Special Assistant to the President and White House Social Secretary.	Jeremy M. Bernard	PA	AD	....	....	
Do	Special Assistant to the President for Legislative Affairs.	Nicole M. Isaac	PA	AD	....	....	
Do	......do	Jessica A. Maher	PA	AD	....	....	
Do	Special Assistant to the President and Director of Digital Strategy.	Robert M. Phillips III	PA	AD	....	....	
Do	Special Assistant to the President and Associate Counsel to the President.	Brian H. Fletcher	PA	AD	....	....	
Do	......do	Jason G. Green	PA	AD	....	....	
Do	Special Assistant to the President and Director of Communications for the First Lady.	Kristina K. Schake	PA	AD	....	....	
Do	Deputy Director of Records Management	Paul S. Raizk	XS	AD	....	....	
Do	Special Assistant to the President for Presidential Personnel.	Teresa R. Chaurand	PA	AD	....	....	
Do	......do	Collin T. McMahon	PA	AD	....	....	
Do	......do	Amanda D. Moose	PA	AD	....	....	
Do	......do	David L. Noble	PA	AD	....	....	

EXECUTIVE OFFICE OF THE PRESIDENT—Continued

Location	Position	Name of Incumbent	Type of Appt.	Pay Plan	Level, Grade, or Pay	Tenure	Expires
Washington, DC	Special Assistant to the President for Presidential Personnel.	Kamala M. Vasagam	PA	AD	....	....	
Do	Supervisor of Search and File	Wandra E. Stone	XS	AD	....	....	
Do	Special Assistant to the President and Deputy Press Secretary.	Jamie E. Smith	PA	AD	....	....	
Do	Special Assistant to the President and Director of Presidential Correspondence.	Elizabeth H. Olson	PA	AD	....	....	
Do	Assistant Executive Clerk	William W. McCathran	XS	AD	....	....	
	OFFICE OF THE VICE PRESIDENT						
Do	Assistant to the President and Chief of Staff	Bruce N. Reed	PA	AD	....	....	
Do	Deputy Assistant to the President and Deputy Chief of Staff.	Alan L. Hoffman	PA	AD	....	....	
Do	Deputy Assistant to the President and National Security Advisor.	Antony J. Blinken	PA	AD	....	....	
Do	Counselor to the Vice President	Steven J. Ricchetti	PA	AD	....	....	
Do	Deputy Assistant to the President for Economic Policy.	Sarah A. Bianchi	PA	AD	....	....	
Do	Deputy Assistant to the President and Senior Advisor to the Vice President.	Jose Cerda	PA	AD	....	....	
Do	Deputy Assistant to the President and Counsel to the Vice President.	Cynthia C. Hogan	PA	AD	....	....	
Do	Special Assistant to the President and Assistant to the Vice President for Communications.	Shailagh J. Murray	PA	AD	....	....	
Do	Deputy Assistant to the President and Chief of Staff to Dr. Jill Biden.	Catherine M. Russell	PA	AD	....	....	
Do	Director of Operations	Elisabeth A. Hire	XS	AD	....	....	
Do	Deputy Assistant to the Vice President for National Security Affairs.	Julianne C. Smith	XS	AD	....	....	
Do	Special Assistant to the President and Assistant to the Vice President for Intergovernmental Affairs, Public Engagement and Correspondence.	Evan M. Ryan	PA	AD	....	....	
Do	Senior Advisor for Middle East Affairs	Jonathan J. Finer	XS	AD	....	....	
	OFFICE OF POLICY DEVELOPMENT						
Do	Deputy Assistant to the President and Deputy Director of the Domestic Policy Council.	Mark Zuckerman	PA	AD	....	....	
Do	Deputy Assistant to the President and Deputy Director, National Economic Council.	Brian C. Deese	PA	AD	....	....	
Do	Assistant to the President and Principal Deputy Director of the National Economic Council.	Jason L. Furman	PA	AD	....	....	
Do	Deputy Assistant to the President and Deputy Director, National Economic Council.	Danielle C. Gray	PA	AD	....	....	
Do	Special Assistant to the President for Economic Policy.	Aviva R. Aron-Dine	PA	AD	....	....	
Do	Special Assistant to the President for International Economic Affairs.	Caroline M. Atkinson	PA	AD	....	....	
Do	Special Assistant to the President for Healthcare and Economic Policy.	Elizabeth J. Fowler	PA	AD	....	....	
Do	Special Assistant to the President for Economic Policy.	Michael J. Pyle	PA	AD	....	....	
Do	......do	Matthew A. Vogel	PA	AD	....	....	
Do	Special Assistant to the President and Director, Office of Social Innovation and Civic Participation.	Jonathan A. Greenblatt	PA	AD	....	....	
Do	Special Assistant to the President for Manufacturing Policy.	Jason S. Miller	PA	AD	....	....	
Do	Special Assistant to the President and Chief of Staff of the Domestic Policy Council.	Carlos A. Monje, Jr.	PA	AD	....	....	
Do	Chief of Staff of the National Economic Council.	Gregory S. Nelson	XS	AD	....	....	
Do	Special Assistant to the President for Education Policy.	Roberto J. Rodriguez	PA	AD	....	....	
Do	Deputy Assistant to the President for Urban Affairs and Economic Mobility.	Racquel S. Russell	PA	AD	....	....	
Do	Director	Rory A. MacFarquhar	XS	AD	....	....	
	OFFICE OF ADMINISTRATION						
Do	Special Assistant to the President and Director.	Elizabeth A. Jones	PA	AD	....	....	
Do	General Counsel	Angela Ohm	XS	AD	....	....	
Do	Chief Information Officer	Brook Mickey Colangelo	XS	AD	....	....	
Do	Chief of Operation Services	Erica De Vos	XS	AD	....	....	
Do	Chief Financial Officer	Catherine G. Solomon	PA	AD	....	....	

EXECUTIVE OFFICE OF THE PRESIDENT—Continued

Location	Position	Name of Incumbent	Type of Appt.	Pay Plan	Level, Grade, or Pay	Tenure	Expires
	OFFICE OF MANAGEMENT AND BUDGET						
	Office of the Director						
Washington, DC	Director	Vacant	PAS	EX			
Do	Senior Advisor	Meaghan Kate Muldoon	SC	GS	15		
Do	Confidential Assistant	Roxana Moussavian	SC	GS	7		
Do	Deputy Director	Heather A. Higginbottom	PAS	EX	II		
Do	Confidential Assistant	Mario Jay Carroll	SC	GS	7		
Do	Executive Associate Director	Robert M. Gordon	NA	ES			
Do	Confidential Assistant	Jamal Thomas O'Neal Brown.	SC	GS	7		
Do	Intellectual Property Enforcement Coordinator.	Victoria Espinel	PAS	SL			
Do	Confidential Assistant	Robert Matthew Bassey Ikoku.	SC	GS	9		
	Deputy Director for Management						
Do	Deputy Director	Jeffrey Dunston Zients	PAS	EX	II		
Do	Senior Advisor	Adam Maxwell Cooper Neufeld.	SC	GS	15		
Do	Executive Director, Government Reorganization Initiative.	Elizabeth M. Brown	NA	ES			
Do	Senior Advisor	Lori Michelle Moore	NA	ES			
Do	Special Assistant	Eric Frank Minkove	SC	GS	15		
Do	Associate Director for Performance Management.	Shelley Hope Metzenbaum	NA	ES			
Do	Deputy Assistant Director	Career Incumbent	CA	ES			
	Management and Operations						
Do	Associate Director	......do	CA	ES			
Do	Assistant Director	......do	CA	ES			
	Economic Policy						
Do	Associate Director	Vacant		ES			
Do	Deputy Associate Director	Career Incumbent	CA	ES			
	Legislative Reference Division						
Do	Chief, Resources, Defense, International Branch.	......do	CA	ES			
Do	Chief, Health, Education, Veterans and Social Programs.	......do	CA	ES			
Do	Assistant Director, Legislative Reference	......do	CA	ES			
Do	Chief, Economics, Science and Government Branch.	......do	CA	ES			
	Office of Federal Procurement Policy						
Do	Administrator	Joseph Gerald Jordan	PAS	EX	III		
Do	Deputy Administrator	Career Incumbent	CA	ES			
Do	Associate Administrator for Acquisition Workforce Programs.	......do	CA	SL			
Do	Associate Administrator	......do	CA	ES			
Do	Confidential Assistant	Nikolis Robert Smith	SC	GS	9		
	General Counsel						
Do	General Counsel	Boris Bershteyn	NA	ES			
Do	Deputy General Counsel	Career Incumbent	CA	ES			
Do	......do	Thomas Lue	PA	SL			
	Office of Information and Regulatory Affairs						
Do	Deputy Administrator	Career Incumbent	CA	ES			
Do	Chief, Food, Health and Labor Branch	......do	CA	ES			
Do	Administrator, Office of Information and Regulatory Affairs.	Cass R. Sunstein	PAS	EX	III		
Do	Chief, Natural Resources and Environment Branch.	Career Incumbent	CA	ES			
Do	Senior Technical Analyst	......do	CA	SL			
Do	Chief, Statistical Policy Branch	......do	CA	ES			
Do	Chief, Transportation and Security Branch	......do	CA	ES			
Do	Chief, Information Policy Branch	......do	CA	ES			
Do	Counselor to the Administrator	Shayna L. Strom	SC	GS	13		
Do	Associate Administrator	Jeffrey G. Weiss	NA	ES			
	Office of E-Government and Information Technology						
Do	Administrator	Steven Lee VanRoekel	PA	EX	III		
Do	Deputy Administrator	Career Incumbent	CA	ES			
Do	Chief Architect	......do	CA	ES			
Do	Confidential Assistant	Laura E. Lynch	SC	GS	9		

EXECUTIVE OFFICE OF THE PRESIDENT—Continued

Location	Position	Name of Incumbent	Type of Appt.	Pay Plan	Level, Grade, or Pay	Tenure	Expires
	Office of Federal Financial Management						
Washington, DC	Coordinator, Partnership Fund for Program Integrity Innovation.	Gary Lee Glickman	TA	ES	....	....	02/11/13
Do	Deputy Controller	Career Incumbent	CA	ES	....	....	
Do	Controller, Office of Federal Financial Management.	Daniel I. Werfel	PAS	EX	III	....	
Do	Chief, Accountability, Performance, and Reporting Branch.	Career Incumbent	CA	ES	....	....	
Do	Confidential Assistant	David Allen Vorhaus	SC	GS	12	....	
Do	Chief, Management Controls and Assistance Branch.	Career Incumbent	CA	ES	....	....	
	Budget Review						
Do	Chief, Budget Review Branch	Vacant	....	ES	....	....	
Do	Deputy Chief, Budget Review Branch	Career Incumbent	CA	ES	....	....	
Do	Chief, Budget Analysis Branch	......do	CA	ES	....	....	
Do	Deputy Chief, Budget Analysis Branch	......do	CA	ES	....	....	
Do	Chief, Budget Concepts Branch	......do	CA	ES	....	....	
Do	Chief, Budget Systems Branch	......do	CA	ES	....	....	
Do	Assistant Director for Budget Review	......do	CA	ES	....	....	
Do	Deputy Assistant Director for Budget Review	......do	CA	ES	....	....	
	National Security Programs						
Do	Confidential Assistant	Daniel Shives Sutton	SC	GS	11	....	
Do	Associate Director for National Security Programs.	Steve Michael Kosiak	NA	ES	....	....	
	International Affairs Division						
Do	Deputy Associate Director	Career Incumbent	CA	ES	....	....	
Do	Chief, State Branch	......do	CA	ES	....	....	
Do	Chief, Economic Affairs Branch	......do	CA	ES	....	....	
	National Security Division						
Do	Chief, Operations and Support Branch	......do	CA	ES	....	....	
Do	Chief, Force Structure and Investment Branch.	......do	CA	ES	....	....	
Do	Deputy Associate Director for National Security.	......do	CA	ES	....	....	
Do	Chief, Command, Control, Communications, and Intelligence Branch.	Vacant	....	ES	....	....	
Do	Chief, Veterans Affairs and Defense Health Branch.	Career Incumbent	CA	ES	....	....	
	Health Division						
Do	Associate Director for Health	Keith J. Fontenot	NA	ES	....	....	
Do	Chief, Medicare Branch	Vacant	....	ES	....	....	
Do	Chief, Medicaid Branch	Career Incumbent	CA	ES	....	....	
Do	Chief, Health and Human Services Branch	Vacant	....	ES	....	....	
Do	Confidential Assistant	Kristin Catherine Rzeczkowski.	SC	GS	9	....	
Do	Deputy Associate Director for Health	Career Incumbent	CA	ES	....	....	
Do	Chief, Health Insurance and Data Analysis Branch.	......do	CA	ES	....	....	
Do	Chief, Public Health Branch	......do	CA	ES	....	....	
	General Government Programs						
Do	Associate Director	Dana Joy Hyde	NA	ES	....	....	
Do	Confidential Assistant	Autumn Catherine Lynch ..	SC	GS	7	....	
	Transportation, Homeland, Justice and Services Division						
Do	Chief, Justice Branch	Career Incumbent	CA	ES	....	....	
Do	Chief, Transportation Branch	......do	CA	ES	....	....	
Do	Deputy Associate Director, Transportation, Homeland, Justice and Services.	......do	CA	ES	....	....	
Do	Chief, Homeland Security Branch	......do	CA	ES	....	....	
	Housing, Treasury and Commerce Division						
Do	Chief, Treasury Branch	......do	CA	ES	....	....	
Do	Deputy Associate Director for Housing, Treasury and Commerce.	......do	CA	ES	....	....	
Do	Chief, Commerce Branch	......do	CA	ES	....	....	
Do	Chief, Housing Branch	......do	CA	ES	....	....	
	Natural Resource Programs						
Do	Associate Director	Sally C. Ericsson	NA	ES	....	....	
Do	Confidential Assistant	Aerica Banks	SC	GS	8	....	
	Natural Resources Division						
Do	Deputy Associate Director	Career Incumbent	CA	ES	....	....	

EXECUTIVE OFFICE OF THE PRESIDENT—Continued

Location	Position	Name of Incumbent	Type of Appt.	Pay Plan	Level, Grade, or Pay	Tenure	Expires
Washington, DC	Chief, Interior Branch	Career Incumbent	CA	ES	....	....	
Do	Chief, Agricultural Branch	......do	CA	ES	....	....	
Do	Chief, Environment Branch	......do	CA	ES	....	....	
	Energy, Science and Water Division						
Do	Chief, Water and Power Branch	......do	CA	ES	....	....	
Do	Chief, Energy Branch	......do	CA	ES	....	....	
Do	Chief, Science and Space Programs Branch ...	......do	CA	ES	....	....	
Do	Deputy Associate Director for Energy and Science Division.	......do	CA	ES	....	....	
	Communications						
Do	Associate Director, Strategic Planning and Communications.	Kenneth S. Baer	NA	ES	....	....	
Do	Deputy Associate Director for Communications, Management.	Moira K.M. Muntz	SC	GS	14	....	
Do	Press Assistant	Robert Sydney Friedlander	SC	GS	9	....	
	Legislative Affairs						
Do	Deputy to the Associate Director for Legislative Affairs (House).	Allie Rebecca Neill	SC	GS	15	....	
Do	Legislative Assistant	Calla Brown	SC	GS	8	....	
Do	Deputy Associate Director (Appropriations) ...	Lindsey R. Berman	SC	GS	12	....	
Do	Associate Director for Legislative Affairs	Kristen Joan Sarri	NA	ES	....	....	
	Education, Income Maintenance, Labor Management and Operations						
Do	Associate Director	Martha B. Coven	NA	ES	....	....	
Do	Confidential Assistant	Taryn Harumi Toyama	SC	GS	9	....	
Do	Deputy Associate Director	Career Incumbent	CA	ES	....	....	
Do	Chief, Education Branch	Vacant		ES	....	....	
Do	Chief, Income Maintenance Branch	Career Incumbent	CA	ES	....	....	
Do	Chief, Labor Branch	......do	CA	ES	....	....	
	COUNCIL OF ECONOMIC ADVISERS						
Do	Chairman	Alan Bennett Krueger	PAS	EX	II	....	
Do	Member	Katharine Gail Abraham ...	PAS	EX	IV	....	
Do	......do	Vacant	PAS	EX	....	....	
Do	Chief of Staff	David P. Vandivier	XS	OT	....	....	
Do	Director for Macroeconomic Forecasting	Career Incumbent	CA	ES	....	....	
	COUNCIL ON ENVIRONMENTAL QUALITY						
Do	Chairman	Nancy Helen Sutley	PAS	EX	II	....	
Do	Member	Vacant	PAS	EX	....	....	
Do	......do	......do	PAS	EX	....	....	
Do	Deputy Director and General Counsel	Gary Schoenholtz Guzy	PAS	EX	IV	....	
Do	Special Assistant (Energy/Climate Change) ...	Jesse M. McCormick	SC	GS	7	....	
Do	Special Assistant	Ann K. Hunter-Pirtle	SC	GS	5	....	
Do	Scheduler to the Chair	Rebecca R. Ferdman	SC	GS	7	....	
Do	Associate Director for Congressional Affairs ..	Trenton D. Bauserman	SC	GS	14	....	
Do	Special Assistant (Legislative Affairs)	Joshua Friedmann	SC	GS	7	....	
Do	Associate Director for Land and Water	Jay Jeffrey Jenson	XS	AD	....	....	
Do	Associate Director for Energy and Climate Change.	Vacant	XS	AD	....	....	
Do	Chief of Staff	Michael Jay Boots	XS	AD	....	....	
Do	Deputy Chief of Staff	Lowry Alexander Crook	XS	AD	....	....	
	OFFICE OF THE UNITED STATES TRADE REPRESENTATIVE						
	Office of the Ambassador						
Washington, DC	United States Trade Representative	Ronald Kirk	PAS	EX	I	....	
Do	Chief of Staff	Lisa Annette Garcia	NA	ES	....	....	
Do	Director of Scheduling and Advance	Anna Marie Rafdal	SC	GS	13	....	
Do	Special Assistant for Scheduling	Jenna Whitney Barzelay ..	SC	GS	9	....	
Do	Confidential Assistant to the Chief of Staff	Rebecca T. Rosen	SC	GS	9	....	
	Deputy United States Trade Representative (1)						
Do	Deputy United States Trade Representative ..	Demetrios James Marantis	PAS	EX	III	....	
Do	Special Assistant	Janis Paulis Lazda	SC	GS	15	....	
	Chief Agricultural Negotiator						
Do	Chief Agricultural Negotiator	Islam Ahmed Siddiqui	PAS	EX	III	....	
	Deputy United States Trade Representative (2)						
Do	Deputy United States Trade Representative ..	Miriam Elizabeth Sapiro ...	PAS	EX	III	....	
Do	Senior Advisor	David Roth	XS	AD	....	....	

EXECUTIVE OFFICE OF THE PRESIDENT—Continued

Location	Position	Name of Incumbent	Type of Appt.	Pay Plan	Level, Grade, or Pay	Tenure	Expires
	Geneva						
Geneva, Switzerland.	Deputy United States Trade Representative ..	Michael Ward Punke	PAS	EX	III	....	
Do	Deputy Chief of Mission - Geneva	Career Incumbent	CA	ES	....	....	
	Agricultural Affairs						
Washington, DC	Assistant United States Representative for Agricultural Affairs.	......do	CA	ES	....	....	
	General Counsel						
Do	Deputy General Counsel	Vacant	....	ES	....	....	
Do	Chief Counsel for Legal Affairs	Career Incumbent	CA	ES	....	....	
Do	Senior Counsel for Dispute Settlement	......do	CA	ES	....	....	
Do	General Counsel	Timothy Mark Reif	NA	ES	....	....	
	Public and Media Affairs						
Do	Assistant United States Trade Representative for Public and Media Affairs.	Carol Joy Guthrie	NA	ES	....	....	
Do	Deputy Assistant United States Trade Representative for Public and Media Affairs.	Nkenge Leian Harmon	SC	GS	15	....	
Do	Public Affairs Specialist	Andrea D. Mead	SC	GS	14	....	
	Congressional Affairs						
Do	Deputy Assistant United States Trade Representative for Congressional Affairs.	Rene Munoz	XS	AD	....	....	
Do	Assistant United States Representative for Congressional Affairs.	Jack M. Campbell	NA	ES	....	....	
Do	Director of Congressional Affairs	Dori Susan Friedberg	SC	GS	12	....	
	Special Textile Negotiator						
Do	Assistant United States Trade Representative for Textile.	Gail Wendy Strickler	XS	AD	....	....	
	Intergovernmental Affairs and Public Engagement						
Do	Assistant United States Trade Representative for Intergovernmental Affairs and Public Liaison.	Christine Leigh Turner	XS	AD	....	....	
	China Affairs						
Do	Assistant United States Trade Representative for China.	Career Incumbent	CA	ES	....	....	
	Japan, Korea and Asia Pacific Economic Cooperation Affairs						
Do	Assistant United States Trade Representative for Japan.	......do	CA	ES	....	....	
	Southeast Asia and Pacific						
Do	Assistant United States Trade Representative for Asia and the Pacific.	......do	CA	ES	....	....	
	Central and South Asian Affairs						
Do	Assistant United States Trade Representative for Central and South Asia.	......do	CA	ES	....	....	
	African Affairs						
Do	Assistant United States Trade Representative for Africa.	......do	CA	ES	....	....	
	Environment and Natural Resources						
Do	Assistant United States Trade Representative for Environment and Natural Resources.	Vacant	....	ES	....	....	
	World Trade Organization and Multicultural Affairs						
Do	Assistant United States Trade Representative for World Trade Organization and Multilateral Affairs.	Career Incumbent	CA	ES	....	....	
	Administration						
Do	Assistant United States Trade Representative for Administration.	......do	CA	ES	....	....	
	Services and Investment						
Do	Assistant United States Trade Representative for Services and Investment.	......do	CA	ES	....	....	
	Monitoring and Enforcement						
Do	Assistant United States Trade Representative for Monitoring and Enforcement.	......do	CA	ES	....	....	

EXECUTIVE OFFICE OF THE PRESIDENT—Continued

Location	Position	Name of Incumbent	Type of Appt.	Pay Plan	Level, Grade, or Pay	Tenure	Expires
	Small Business, Market Access and Industrial Competitiveness						
Washington, DC	Assistant United States Trade Representative for Industry, Market Access and Telecommunications.	Career Incumbent	CA	ES	....	....	
	Trade Policy and Economics						
Do	Assistant United States Trade Representative for Trade Policy and Economics.	......do	CA	ES	....	....	
	Intellectual Property and Innovation						
Do	Assistant United States Trade Representative for Intellectual Property and Innovation.	......do	CA	ES	....	....	
	Europe and Middle East						
Do	Assistant United States Trade Representative for Europe and the Middle East.	......do	CA	ES	....	....	
	Labor						
Do	Assistant United States Trade Representative for Labor.	......do	CA	ES	....	....	
	OFFICE OF SCIENCE AND TECHNOLOGY POLICY						
Do	Director	Vacant	PAS	EX	....	....	
Do	Chief of Staff	Frederick C. Siger	NA	ES	....	....	
Do	Deputy Chief of Staff and Assistant Director	Career Incumbent	CA	ES	....	....	
Do	Assistant to the President for Science and Technology.	John Paul Holdren	PAS	EX	II	....	
Do	Deputy Director for Policy	Thomas Amadeus Kalil	NA	ES	....	....	
Do	Assistant to the President and Chief Technology Officer.	Todd Youngsuh Park	PAS	EX	III	....	
Do	Associate Director, Environment	Vacant	PAS	EX	....	....	
Do	Associate Director, Technology	......do	PAS	EX	....	....	
Do	Associate Director, Science	......do	PAS	EX	....	....	
Do	Assistant Director, Legislative Affairs	Donna Marie Pignatelli	SC	GS	15	....	
Do	Confidential Assistant	Lauren Emily Andersen	SC	GS	7	....	
Do	Executive Assistant	Karrie Suzanne Pitzer	SC	GS	13	....	
Do	Confidential Assistant	Rebecca L. Grimm	SC	GS	7	....	
Do	......do	Vivian P. Graubard	SC	GS	7	....	
	OFFICE OF NATIONAL DRUG CONTROL POLICY						
	Office of the Director						
Washington, DC	Director	R. Gil Kerlikowske	PAS	EX	I	....	
Do	Senior Policy Advisor	Rene Hanna	SC	GS	15	....	
Do	Deputy Director, ONDCP	Vacant	PAS	EX	....	....	
Do	Chief of Staff	Regina Marie Labelle	NA	ES	....	....	
	Office of Legal Counsel						
Do	General Counsel	Jeffrey Jonathan Teitz	NA	ES	....	....	
Do	Senior Counsel to the General Counsel	Career Incumbent	CA	ES	....	....	
	Research/Data Analysis						
Do	Deputy Associate Director	......do	CA	ES	....	....	
Do	Associate Director	......do	CA	ES	....	....	
	Intergovernmental Public Liaison						
Do	Policy Analyst	Quinn Laydon Staudt	SC	GS	11	....	
Do	......do	Kathryn Ann Greene	SC	GS	12	....	
	Office of Public Affairs						
Do	Associate Directorate for Public Affairs	Rafael E. LeMaitre	SC	GS	15	....	
Do	Special Assistant for Strategic Communications.	Berit Hallberg	SC	GS	11	....	
	Office of Management and Administration						
Do	Associate Director	Career Incumbent	CA	ES	....	....	
Do	Deputy Associate Director	Vacant	....	ES	....	....	
	Office of Performance and Budget						
Do	Associate Director	Career Incumbent	CA	ES	....	....	
	Office of Demand Reduction						
Do	Deputy Director	David Kunimitsu Mineta ...	PAS	EX	III	....	
Do	Assistant Deputy Director	Career Incumbent	CA	ES	....	....	
	Office of Supply Reduction						
Do	Associate Deputy Director	......do	CA	ES	....	....	
Do	Deputy Director	Marilyn A. Quagliotti	PA	EX	III	....	

EXECUTIVE OFFICE OF THE PRESIDENT—Continued

Location	Position	Name of Incumbent	Type of Appt.	Pay Plan	Level, Grade, or Pay	Tenure	Expires
Washington, DC	Assistant Deputy Director	Career Incumbent	CA	ES	....	....	
Do	Associate Director for Intelligence	......do	CA	ES	....	....	
	State, Local, and Tribal Affairs						
Do	Deputy Director	Benjamin B. Tucker	PAS	EX	III	....	
	NATIONAL SECURITY COUNCIL						
Do	Deputy Assistant to the President for National Security Affairs, Executive Secretary and NSC Chief of Staff.	Brian McKeon	PA	EX	IV	....	

DEPARTMENTS

DEPARTMENT OF AGRICULTURE

Location	Position	Name of Incumbent	Type of Appt.	Pay Plan	Level, Grade, or Pay	Tenure	Expires
	OFFICE OF THE SECRETARY						
Washington, DC	Secretary	Thomas James Vilsack	PAS	EX	I		
Do	Deputy Secretary	Kathleen A. Merrigan	PAS	EX	II		
Do	Chief of Staff	Krysta L. Harden	NA	ES			
Do	Deputy Chief of Staff	Carole E. Jett	NA	ES			
Do	Senior Advisor to the Secretary	Anne MacMillan	NA	ES			
Do	Senior Counsel and Senior Advisor to the Secretary.	Max Holtzman	NA	ES			
Do	Senior Policy Advisor	Robert Farrell Bonnie	NA	ES			
Do	Senior Advisor	Sarah Bittleman	NA	ES			
Springdale, AR	Senior Advisor for Tribal Affairs	Janie Simms Hipp	NA	ES			
Washington, DC	Senior Advisor to the Secretary	Brandon Clark Willis	NA	ES			
Do	Chief of Staff to the Deputy Secretary	Suzanne Smith Palmieri	NA	ES			
Do	Senior Advisor	Douglas McKalip	TA	ES			02/12/13
Do	White House Liaison	Marie Williams	SC	GS	15		
Do	Director of the Office of Faith Based and Neighborhood Outreach.	Max Brady Finberg	SC	GS	15		
Do	Advisor to the Secretary for Special Projects ..	Yeshimebet Abebe	SC	GS	15		
Do	Senior Program Manager for Global Food Security.	Lona Sue Stoll	SC	GS	15		
Do	Executive Assistant to the Secretary	Lanon Baccam	SC	GS	13		
Do	Advisor to the Secretary	Todd Batta	SC	GS	15		
Do	Confidential Assistant	Charles Allen Fromstein	SC	GS	11		
Do	Special Assistant	Johnie Jones	SC	GS	9		
	Office of the Assistant Secretary for Congressional Relations						
Do	Assistant Secretary	Brian T. Baenig	PAS	EX	IV		
Do	Deputy Assistant Secretary	Ann Atkins Wright	NA	ES			
Do	Director, Intergovernmental Affairs	Jennifer M. Yezak	SC	GS	15		
Do	Confidential Assistant	Ashley Martin	SC	GS	13		
Do	....do	Callie Varner	SC	GS	13		
Do	Special Assistant	Monica Wyant	SC	GS	12		
Do	Staff Assistant	Ashlee N. Johnson	SC	GS	11		
Do	....do	Kevin Thomas Bailey	SC	GS	9		
Do	Staff Assistant (Legislative Analyst)	Ryan Caldwell	SC	GS	9		
	Office of Communications						
Do	Director	Matthew Paul	NA	ES			
Do	Deputy Director, Operations	Justin P. Dejong	SC	GS	15		
Do	Director of Advance	Timothy John Gannon	SC	GS	15		
Do	Director of Scheduling and Advance	Sally Cluthe	SC	GS	15		
Do	Press Secretary	Courtney Rowe	SC	GS	14		
Do	Advance Lead	Malcolm Xavier Eve	SC	GS	14		
Do	Deputy Director of Scheduling	Toby Snow Osherson	SC	GS	13		
Do	Speech Writer	Charles Altman Lippstreu	SC	GS	12		
Do	Deputy Press Secretary	Stephanie Catherine Chan	SC	GS	11		
	Office of the Chief Information Officer						
Do	Chief Information Officer	Vacant		ES			
Do	Deputy Chief Information Officer (Policy)	......do		ES			
Do	Associate Chief Information Officer, Cyber and Privacy and Oversight.	Career Incumbent	CA	ES			
Do	Associate Chief Information Officer, Information Technology Services.	......do	CA	ES			
Do	Associate Chief Information Officer	......do	CA	ES			
Do	Associate Chief Information Officer, International Security Operations Center, Cyber.	......do	CA	ES			
Do	Associate Chief Information Officer, Technology Planning, Architecture and E-Government.	......do	CA	ES			
	Office of the Chief Financial Officer						
Do	Chief Financial Officer	Vacant	PAS	EX			
	National Finance Center						
New Orleans, LA ...	Director	Career Incumbent	CA	ES			
Do	Director, Government Employee Services Division.	......do	CA	ES			

DEPARTMENT OF AGRICULTURE—Continued

Location	Position	Name of Incumbent	Type of Appt.	Pay Plan	Level, Grade, or Pay	Tenure	Expires
	Office of Budget and Program Analysis						
Washington, DC	Director	Career Incumbent	CA	ES	....	....	
Do	Associate Director	......do	CA	ES	....	....	
Do	Deputy Director, Budget, Legislative and Regulation Systems.	......do	CA	ES	....	....	
Do	Deputy Director for Program Analysis	......do	CA	ES	....	....	
Do	Director, Budget Control and Analysis Division.	......do	CA	ES	....	....	
	Office of the General Counsel						
Do	General Counsel	Ramona E. Romero	PAS	EX	IV	....	
Do	Deputy General Counsel	Frederick W. Pfaeffle, Esq.	NA	ES	....	....	
Do	Associate General Counsel, International Affairs, Food Assistance and Farm and Rural Programs.	Career Incumbent	CA	ES	....	....	
Do	Assistant General Counsel, International Affairs, Food Assistance, and Farm and Rural Programs.	......do	CA	ES	....	....	
Do	Associate General Counsel, General Law and Research.	......do	CA	ES	....	....	
Do	Assistant General Counsel, International Affairs, Food Assistance, and Farm and Rural Programs.	Vacant	....	ES	....	....	
Do	Assistant General Counsel, General Law and Research.	......do	....	ES	....	....	
Do	Associate General Counsel, Civil Rights, Labor, and Employment Law.	Career Incumbent	CA	ES	....	....	
Do	Assistant General Counsel, Civil Rights, Labor, and Employment Law.	......do	CA	ES	....	....	
Do	Associate General Counsel, Natural Resources and Environment.	......do	CA	ES	....	....	
Do	Assistant General Counsel, Natural Resources.	......do	CA	ES	....	....	
Do	Associate General Counsel, Marketing, Regulatory, and Food Safety.	......do	CA	ES	....	....	
Do	Assistant General Counsel, Marketing, Regulatory, and Food Safety.	......do	CA	ES	....	....	
Do	Assistant General Counsel, Marketing, Regulatory and Food Safety.	Vacant	....	ES	....	....	
San Francisco, CA	Regional Attorney	Career Incumbent	CA	ES	....	....	
Kansas City, MO ...	......do	......do	CA	ES	....	....	
Atlanta, GA	......do	......do	CA	ES	....	....	
Denver, CO	......do	......do	CA	ES	....	....	
Washington, DC	Director, Office of Ethics	......do	CA	ES	....	....	
Do	Senior Counselor	Susan B. Keith	SC	GS	15	....	
	Office of the Chief Economist						
Do	Chief Economist	Career Incumbent	CA	ES	....	....	
	Office of the Assistant Secretary for Administration						
Do	Assistant Secretary	Vacant	PA	EX	IV	....	
Do	Deputy Assistant Secretary	Oscar Gonzales, Jr.	NA	ES	....	....	
Do	......do	Career Incumbent	CA	ES	....	....	
Do	Senior Advisor	Carmen D. Jones	NA	ES	....	....	
Do	Associate Assistant Secretary	Career Incumbent	CA	ES	....	....	
Do	Chief of Staff	Gregory A. Diephouse	SC	GS	15	....	
Do	Special Assistant	Julianna E. Grogan-Brown	SC	GS	13	....	
Do	Confidential Assistant	Carlissia N. Graham	SC	GS	11	....	
	Office of Homeland Security and Emergency Coordination						
Do	Director	Career Incumbent	CA	ES	....	....	
Do	Deputy Director	......do	CA	ES	....	....	
	Office of Human Resources Management						
Do	Director	......do	CA	ES	....	....	
Do	Deputy Director	......do	CA	ES	....	....	
Do	Human Resources Transformation Project Manager.	Anita R. Adkins	TA	ES	....	....	04/15/13
	Office of Small and Disadvantaged Business Utilization						
Do	Director	Vacant	....	ES	....	....	
	Office of the Assistant Secretary for Civil Rights						
Do	Assistant Secretary	Joseph E. Leonard, Jr.	PAS	EX	IV	....	

DEPARTMENT OF AGRICULTURE—Continued

Location	Position	Name of Incumbent	Type of Appt.	Pay Plan	Level, Grade, or Pay	Tenure	Expires
Washington, DC	Deputy Assistant Secretary	Vacant	....	ES	....	....	
Do	Senior Advisor	Jenny Montoya Tansey	SC	GS	14	....	
	Office of Civil Rights						
Do	Director, Office of Adjudication and Compliance.	Career Incumbent	CA	ES	....	....	
Do	Director, Outreach and Diversity	......do	CA	ES	....	....	
	Office of the Under Secretary for Rural Development						
Do	Under Secretary	Dallas P. Tonsager	PAS	EX	III	....	
Do	Deputy Under Secretary	Cheryl Lois Cook	NA	ES	....	....	
Do	......do	Douglas John O'Brien	NA	ES	....	....	
Do	Chief of Staff	John Charles Padalino	SC	GS	15	....	
Do	Confidential Assistant	Alexander M. Jones	SC	GS	15	....	
Do	Senior Advisor	Sylvia Bolivar	SC	GS	15	....	
Do	Director, Legislative and Public Affairs Staff	David Sandretti	SC	GS	15	....	
Do	Special Assistant	Katherine Elizabeth Yocum.	SC	GS	14	....	
Do	Special Assistant for Energy Programs	Todd E. Campbell	SC	GS	12	....	
	Rural Business Service						
Do	Administrator	Judith Ann Canales	NA	ES	....	....	
Do	Chief of Staff	Curtis A. Wiley	NA	ES	....	....	
Do	Deputy Administrator, Cooperative Services ..	Career Incumbent	CA	ES	....	....	
Do	Special Assistant	Justin Sterling Hatmaker	SC	GS	14	....	
	Rural Housing Service						
Do	Administrator	Tammye Hildamar Trevino	NA	ES	....	....	
Do	Associate Administrator	Vacant	....	ES	....	....	
Do	Chief Information Officer	......do	....	ES	....	....	
Do	Deputy Administrator, Community Programs	Career Incumbent	CA	ES	....	....	
Do	Deputy Administrator, Single-Family Housing.	......do	CA	ES	....	....	
Do	Chief of Staff	Ada Cristina Chiappe	SC	GS	15	....	
Omaha, NE	Executive Director, National Food and Agriculture Council.	John J. Berge	SC	GS	15	....	
Washington, DC	Special Assistant	Lillian Elizabeth Salerno ..	SC	GS	15	....	
Do	Confidential Assistant	Ashli Palmer	SC	GS	13	....	
Do	Special Assistant	Denise Nichole Scott	SC	GS	11	....	
Montgomery, AL	State Director - Alabama	Ronald Wayne Davis	SC	GS	15	....	
Palmer, AK	State Director - Alaska	James Robert Nordlund	SC	GS	15	....	
Phoenix, AZ	State Director - Arizona	Alan J. Stephens	SC	GS	15	....	
Little Rock, AR	State Director - Arkansas	Lawrence E. McCullough ..	SC	GS	15	....	
Davis, CA	State Director - California	Glenda Lee Humiston	SC	GS	15	....	
Lakewood, CO	State Director - Colorado	James R. Isgar	SC	GS	15	....	
Dover, DE	State Director - Delaware/Maryland	John F. Tarburton	SC	GS	15	....	
Gainesville, FL	State Director - Florida/Virgin Islands	Richard Albert Machek	SC	GS	15	....	
Washington, DC	State Director - Georgia	Quinton Nigel Robinson	SC	GS	15	....	
Hilo, HI	State Director - Hawaii	Chris Jun Kanazawa	SC	GS	15	....	
Boise, ID	State Director - Idaho	Wallace E. Hedrick	SC	GS	15	....	
Champaign, IL	State Director - Illinois	Colleen Rae Callahan Burns.	SC	GS	15	....	
Indianapolis, IN	State Director - Indiana	Philip G. Lehmkuhler	SC	GS	15	....	
Des Moines, IA	State Director - Iowa	William Joseph Menner	SC	GS	15	....	
Topeka, KS	State Director - Kansas	Patricia Ann Clark	SC	GS	15	....	
Lexington, KY	State Director - Kentucky	Thomas Gene Fern	SC	GS	15	....	
Alexandria, LA	State Director - Louisiana	Clarence Willie Hawkins ...	SC	GS	15	....	
Bangor, ME	State Director - Maine	Virginia A. Manuel	SC	GS	15	....	
Amherst, MA	State Director - Massachusetts	Jonathan Lee Healy	SC	GS	15	....	
East Lansing, MI ...	State Director - Michigan	James Jeffrey Turner	SC	GS	15	....	
St. Paul, MN	State Director - Minnesota	Mary Colleen Landkamer ..	SC	GS	15	....	
Jackson, MS	State Director - Mississippi	Trina N. George	SC	GS	15	....	
Columbia, MO	State Director - Missouri	Anita J. Dunning	SC	GS	15	....	
Bozeman, MT	State Director - Montana	Matthew J. Jones	SC	GS	15	....	
Lincoln, NE	State Director - Nebraska	Maxine B. Moul	SC	GS	15	....	
Carson City, NV	State Director - Nevada	Sarah Jose Mersereau Adler.	SC	GS	15	....	
Mt. Holly, NJ	State Director - New Jersey	Howard Henderson	SC	GS	15	....	
Albuquerque, NM ..	State Director - New Mexico	Terrence Jules Brunner	SC	GS	15	....	
Syracuse, NY	State Director - New York	Bryan Clerkin	SC	GS	15	....	
Raleigh, NC	State Director - North Carolina	Randall A. Gore	SC	GS	15	....	
Bismarck, ND	State Director - North Dakota	Jasper John Schneider	SC	GS	15	....	
Columbus, OH	State Director - Ohio	John Anthony Logan	SC	GS	15	....	
Stillwater, OK	State Director - Oklahoma	David Ryan McMullen	SC	GS	15	....	
Portland, OR	State Director - Oregon	Vicki Lynn Walker	SC	GS	15	....	
Harrisburg, PA	State Director - Pennsylvania	Thomas Percy Williams	SC	GS	15	....	

DEPARTMENT OF AGRICULTURE—Continued

Location	Position	Name of Incumbent	Type of Appt.	Pay Plan	Level, Grade, or Pay	Tenure	Expires
Hato Rey, Puerto Rico.	State Director - Puerto Rico	Jose A. Otero	SC	GS	15	....	
Columbia, SC	State Director - South Carolina	Vernita F. Dore	SC	GS	15	....	
Huron, SD	State Director - South Dakota	Elsie May Meeks	SC	GS	15	....	
Nashville, TN	State Director - Tennessee	Bobby Mack Goode	SC	GS	15	....	
Temple, TX	State Director - Texas	Francisco Valentin, Jr.	SC	GS	15	....	
Salt Lake City, UT	State Director - Utah	Wilson David Conine	SC	GS	15	....	
Montpelier, VT	State Director - Vermont	Molly Patricia Lambert	SC	GS	15	....	
Richmond, VA	State Director - Virginia	Ellen Matthews Davis	SC	GS	15	....	
Olympia, WA	State Director - Washington	Mario M. Villanueva	SC	GS	15	....	
Morgantown, WV	State Director - West Virginia	Robert D. Lewis	SC	GS	15	....	
Stevens Point, WI	State Director - Wisconsin	Stan Gruszynski	SC	GS	15	....	
Casper, WY	State Director - Wyoming	Derrel Carruth	SC	GS	15	....	
	Rural Utilities Service						
Washington, DC	Administrator	Jonathan S. Adelstein	PA	EX	IV	....	
Do	Deputy Administrator	Jessica Ann Zufolo	NA	ES	....	....	
Do	Assistant Administrator, Water and Environmental Programs.	Career Incumbent	CA	ES	....	....	
Do	Assistant Administrator, Telecommunications	.....do	CA	ES	....	....	
Do	Assistant Administrator, Electric Program	.....do	CA	ES	....	....	
Do	Chief of Staff	.....do	CA	ES	....	....	
Do	Special Assistant	Sara Buettner-Connelly	SC	GS	11	....	
Do	Staff Assistant	Nita Contreras	SC	GS	7	....	
	Office of the Under Secretary for Marketing and Regulatory Programs						
Do	Under Secretary	Edward M. Avalos	PAS	EX	IV	....	
Do	Deputy Under Secretary	Rebecca Ann Blue	NA	ES	....	....	
Do	.....do	Joan L. Walsh	NA	ES	....	....	
Do	Senior Advisor	John Michael Schmidt	SC	GS	14	....	
Do	Confidential Assistant	Elanor Starmer	SC	GS	13	....	
Do	Special Assistant	Lisa Bertelson	SC	GS	11	....	
	Agricultural Marketing Service						
Do	Administrator	Career Incumbent	CA	ES	....	....	
Do	Associate Administrator	Vacant	....	ES	....	....	
Do	Chief of Staff	Sara F. Eckhouse	SC	GS	14	....	
	Animal and Plant Health Inspection Service						
Do	Administrator	Career Incumbent	CA	ES	....	....	
Do	Associate Administrator	.....do	CA	ES	....	....	
Do	Senior Invasive Species Coordinator	.....do	CA	ES	....	....	
Do	Deputy Administrator, Policy and Program Development.	.....do	CA	ES	....	....	
	Veterinary Services						
Do	Deputy Administrator	.....do	CA	ES	....	....	
Do	Associate Deputy Administrator, Regional Programs.	.....do	CA	ES	....	....	
Ames, IA	Director, National Veterinary Services Laboratories.	.....do	CA	ES	....	....	
	Plant Protection and Quarantine Service						
Washington, DC	Deputy Administrator	.....do	CA	ES	....	....	
Do	Associate Deputy Administrator	Vacant	....	ES	....	....	
	Grain Inspection, Packers and Stockyards Administration						
Do	Administrator	Lawrence W. Mitchell	NA	ES	....	....	
Do	Deputy Administrator, Packers and Stockyards.	Career Incumbent	CA	ES	....	....	
Do	Deputy Administrator, Grain Inspection	.....do	CA	ES	....	....	
Kansas City, KS	Director, Technical Services Division	.....do	CA	ES	....	....	
	Office of the Under Secretary for Food Safety						
Washington, DC	Under Secretary	Elisabeth A. Hagen	PAS	EX	III	....	
Do	Deputy Under Secretary	Brian Ronholm	NA	ES	....	....	
Do	Chief of Staff	Adela R. Ramos	SC	GS	15	....	
Do	Special Assistant	Kathryn S. Naessens	SC	GS	11	....	
	Food Safety and Inspection Service						
Do	Administrator	Career Incumbent	CA	ES	....	....	
	Office of the Under Secretary for Food, Nutrition and Consumer Services						
Do	Under Secretary	Kevin W. Concannon	PAS	EX	III	....	
Do	Deputy Under Secretary	Jane Knight Thornton	NA	ES	....	....	
Do	Senior Advisor	Jerold R. Mande	NA	ES	....	....	

DEPARTMENT OF AGRICULTURE—Continued

Location	Position	Name of Incumbent	Type of Appt.	Pay Plan	Level, Grade, or Pay	Tenure	Expires
	Food and Nutrition Service						
Alexandria, VA	Administrator	Audrey Rowe	NA	ES			
Washington, DC	Senior Advisor for SNAP Access	Lisa Jane Pino	NA	ES			
Portland, OR	Program Manager, Farm to School Program	Deborah J. Kane	TA	ES			01/14/15
Alexandria, VA	Associate Administrator, Supplemental Nutrition Assistance Program.	Career Incumbent	CA	ES			
Do	Associate Administrator, Special Nutrition Programs.	......do	CA	ES			
Washington, DC	Program Manager (Associate Administrator), Research Analysis, Communications and Strategic Support.	......do	CA	ES			
Atlanta, GA	Regional Administrator, Atlanta	......do	CA	ES			
Robbinsville, NJ	Regional Administrator, Robbinsville	......do	CA	ES			
San Francisco, CA	Regional Administrator, San Francisco	......do	CA	ES			
Dallas, TX	Regional Administrator, Dallas	......do	CA	ES			
Chicago, IL	Regional Administrator, Chicago	......do	CA	ES			
Denver, CO	Regional Administrator, Denver	......do	CA	ES			
Boston, MA	Regional Administrator - Northeast Region	......do	CA	ES			
Alexandria, VA	Chief Information Officer	Vacant		ES			
Do	Associate Deputy Administrator for Management.	......do		ES			
Do	Chief of Staff	Stacey Yolanda Brayboy	SC	GS	15		
Washington, DC	Advisor for Special Projects	Norah Ann Deluhery	SC	GS	15		
	Center for Nutrition Policy and Promotion						
Alexandria, VA	Director	Rajen S. Anand	NA	ES			
	Office of the Under Secretary Farm and Foreign Agricultural Service						
Washington, DC	Under Secretary	Michael Thomas Scuse	PAS	EX	III		
Do	Deputy Under Secretary	Darci L. Vetter	NA	ES			
Do	......do	Karis Trammel Gutter	NA	ES			
Do	Chief of Staff	Amy Reiter	SC	GS	15		
Do	Special Assistant	Jillian Semaan	SC	GS	13		
	Foreign Agricultural Service						
Do	Administrator	Career Incumbent	CA	FE			
Do	Associate Administrator	Janet A. Nuzum	NA	ES			
Do	Deputy Administrator for International Trade Policy.	Career Incumbent	CA	ES			
Do	Deputy Administrator, Trade Programs	......do	CA	ES			
Do	Minister Counselor of Agriculture	Michael Vernon Michener	SC	GS	15		
Do	Senior Advisor to the Director	Patrick F. Kerrigan, Jr.	SC	GS	15		
Do	Confidential Assistant	Jaclyn Ilene Urness	SC	GS	13		
	Farm Service Agency						
Do	Administrator	Juan M. Garcia	NA	ES			
Do	Associate Administrator for Operations and Management.	Career Incumbent	CA	ES			
Do	Deputy Administrator for Commodity Operations.	James William Monahan	NA	ES			
Do	Deputy Administrator for Farm Programs	Vacant		ES			
Do	Deputy Administrator for Field Operations	......do		ES			
Do	Deputy Administrator for Management	......do		ES			
Do	Director, Economic and Policy Analysis Staff	Career Incumbent	CA	ES			
Do	Director, Production, Emergencies and Compliance Division.	......do	CA	ES			
Do	Director, Information Technology Services Division.	......do	CA	ES			
Do	Special Assistant	Tony Jackson	SC	GS	15		
Do	Chief of Staff	Henry Todd Atkinson	SC	GS	15		
Do	Special Assistant	Rebecca J. Shively	SC	GS	9		
Montgomery, AL	State Executive Director - Alabama	Daniel Robinson	SC	GS	15		
Palmer, AK	State Executive Director - Alaska	Daniel Consenstein	SC	GS	15		
Phoenix, AZ	State Executive Director - Arizona	Robert Arthur Piceno	SC	GS	15		
Little Rock, AR	State Executive Director - Arkansas	Linda R. Newkirk	SC	GS	15		
Davis, CA	State Executive Director - California	Valente Dolcini	SC	GS	15		
Lakewood, CO	State Executive Director - Colorado	Trudy Kareus	SC	GS	15		
Tolland, CT	State Executive Director - Connecticut	Marsha B. Jette	SC	GS	15		
Dover, DE	State Executive Director - Delaware	Robert Walls	SC	GS	15		
Gainesville, FL	State Executive Director - Florida	Timothy A. Manning	SC	GS	15		
Athens, GA	State Executive Director - Georgia	Charles H. Stripling	SC	GS	15		
Honolulu, HI	State Executive Director - Hawaii	Diane Lynn Ley	SC	GS	15		
Boise, ID	State Executive Director - Idaho	Richard Rush	SC	GS	15		
Springfield, IL	State Executive Director - Illinois	Scherrie V. Giamanco	SC	GS	15		
Indianapolis, IN	State Executive Director - Indiana	Julia Ann Wickard	SC	GS	15		
Des Moines, IA	State Executive Director - Iowa	John Richard Whitaker	SC	GS	15		

DEPARTMENT OF AGRICULTURE—Continued

Location	Position	Name of Incumbent	Type of Appt.	Pay Plan	Level, Grade, or Pay	Tenure	Expires
Manhattan, KS	State Executive Director - Kansas	Adrian Polansky	SC	GS	15	....	
Lexington, KY	State Executive Director - Kentucky	John W. McCauley	SC	GS	15	....	
Alexandria, LA	State Executive Director - Louisiana	Willie F. Cooper	SC	GS	15	....	
Bangor, ME	State Executive Director - Maine	Donovan Edwin Todd III ...	SC	GS	15	....	
Annapolis, MD	State Executive Director - Maryland	Lucie Snodgrass	SC	GS	15	....	
Amherst, MA	State Executive Director - Massachusetts	Richard J. Burke	SC	GS	15	....	
East Lansing, MI ...	State Executive Director - Michigan	Christine White	SC	GS	15	....	
St. Paul, MN	State Executive Director - Minnesota	Linda K. Hennen	SC	GS	15	....	
Jackson, MS	State Executive Director - Mississippi	Michael Ray Sullivan	SC	GS	15	....	
Bozeman, MT	State Executive Director - Montana	Bruce Edward Nelson	SC	GS	15	....	
Lincoln, NE	State Executive Director - Nebraska	Daniel L. Steinkruger	SC	GS	15	....	
Reno, NV	State Executive Director - Nevada	Clinton M. Koble	SC	GS	15	....	
Concord, NH	State Executive Director - New Hampshire	James G. Phinizy	SC	GS	15	....	
Hamilton Square, NJ.	State Executive Director - New Jersey	Paul J. Hlubik	SC	GS	15	....	
Albuquerque, NM ..	State Executive Director - New Mexico	Lawrence Rael	SC	GS	15	....	
Syracuse, NY	State Executive Director - New York	James R. Barber	SC	GS	15	....	
Raleigh, NC	State Executive Director - North Carolina	Aaron A. Martin	SC	GS	15	....	
Fargo, ND	State Executive Director - North Dakota	Aaron Krauter	SC	GS	15	....	
Columbus, OH	State Executive Director - Ohio	Steven Douglas Maurer	SC	GS	15	....	
Stillwater, OK	State Executive Director - Oklahoma	Francie Kucera Tolle	SC	GS	15	....	
Tualatin, OR	State Executive Director - Oregon	Lynn E. Voigt	SC	GS	15	....	
Harrisburg, PA	State Executive Director - Pennsylvania	Billy Wehry	SC	GS	15	....	
Warwick, RI	State Executive Director - Rhode Island	Paul E. Brule	SC	GS	15	....	
Columbia, SC	State Executive Director - South Carolina	Laurie Lawson	SC	GS	15	....	
Huron, SD	State Executive Director - South Dakota	Craig D. Schaunaman	SC	GS	15	....	
Nashville, TN	State Executive Director - Tennessee	Eugene Davidson	SC	GS	15	....	
Salt Lake City, UT	State Executive Director - Utah	Arthur Louis Douglas	SC	GS	15	....	
Burlington, VT	State Executive Director - Vermont	Robert George Paquin	SC	GS	15	....	
Richmond, VA	State Executive Director - Virginia	James Calvin Parrish	SC	GS	15	....	
Spokane, WA	State Executive Director - Washington	Judith Corrine Olson	SC	GS	15	....	
Morgantown, WV ...	State Executive Director - West Virginia	Alfred J. Lewis	SC	GS	15	....	
Madison, WI	State Executive Director - Wisconsin	Brad Michael Pfaff	SC	GS	15	....	
Casper, WY	State Executive Director - Wyoming	Gregory J. Goertz	SC	GS	15	....	
	Risk Management Agency						
Washington, DC	Administrator	Career Incumbent	CA	ES	....	....	
Do	Associate Administrator	Barbara Leach	NA	ES	....	....	
Do	Deputy Administrator for Compliance	Career Incumbent	CA	ES	....	....	
Do	Director, Congressional and External Affairs	Patricia Engel	SC	GS	15	....	
Do	Special Assistant	Patrick Scates	SC	GS	15	....	
Do	Confidential Assistant	Leigh Allen	SC	GS	11	....	
	Office of the Under Secretary for Research, Education, and Economics						
Do	Under Secretary	Catherine E. Woteki	PAS	EX	III	....	
Do	Deputy Under Secretary	Career Incumbent	CA	ES	....	....	
Do	Chief of Staff	Elvis Cordova	SC	GS	15	....	
Do	Confidential Assistant	Franz J. Hochstrasser	SC	GS	12	....	
Do	Senior Advisor (Scientific Integrity)	Ramaswamy N. Gita	TA	ES	....	....	06/24/14
	Agricultural Research Service						
Do	Administrator	Career Incumbent	CA	ES	....	....	
Beltsville, MD	Director, National Agricultural Library	......do	CA	ES	....	....	
	National Institute of Food and Agriculture						
Washington, DC	Director	Sonny Ramaswamy	PA	EX	II	....	
Do	Assistant Director, Institute of Food Production and Sustainability.	Career Incumbent	CA	ES	....	....	
Do	Assistant Director, Institute of Youth, Family and Community.	......do	CA	ES	....	....	
Do	Deputy Director, Agricultural and Natural Resources.	......do	CA	ES	....	....	
Do	Deputy Director, Food and Community Resources.	......do	CA	ES	....	....	
Do	Director of Congressional Affairs for Research, Education, and Economics and National Institute of Food and Agriculture.	Venkateswar N. Neralla	SC	GS	15	....	
	Office of Under Secretary for Natural Resources and Environment						
Do	Under Secretary	Harris Sherman	PAS	EX	III	....	
Do	Deputy Under Secretary	Ann Cameron Mills	NA	ES	....	....	
Do	......do	Arthur Blazer	NA	ES	....	....	
Do	Chief of Staff	Sarah Scanlon	SC	GS	15	....	
Do	Special Assistant	Meryl L.R. Harrell	SC	GS	14	....	
Do	Staff Assistant	Yaesul Park	SC	GS	7	....	

DEPARTMENT OF AGRICULTURE—Continued

Location	Position	Name of Incumbent	Type of Appt.	Pay Plan	Level, Grade, or Pay	Tenure	Expires
	Natural Resources Conservation Service						
Washington, DC	Chief	David Clark White	NA	ES	....	....	
Do	Associate Chief	Vacant	....	ES	....	....	
Do	Chief of Staff	Jason Anthony Weller	NA	ES	....	....	
Do	Deputy Chief for Management	Vacant	....	ES	....	....	
Do	Chief Information Officer	Career Incumbent	CA	ES	....	....	
Do	Deputy Chief for Science and Technology	......do	CA	ES	....	....	
Beltsville, MD	Deputy Chief Soil Survey and Resource Assessment.	......do	CA	ES	....	....	
Washington, DC	Regional Conservationist (East)	......do	CA	ES	....	....	
Do	Regional Conservationist (Central)	......do	CA	ES	....	....	
Boise, ID	Regional Conservationist (West)	......do	CA	ES	....	....	
Davis, CA	State Conservationist, California	Vacant	....	ES	....	....	
Temple, TX	State Conservationist, Temple, Texas	Career Incumbent	CA	ES	....	....	
Washington, DC	Assistant Chief	James M. Gore	SC	GS	15	....	
Do	Special Assistant	Michael Martinez	SC	GS	14	....	
Do	......do	Yahaira Enid Lopez Ramos	SC	GS	11	....	
	Forest Service						
Do	Chief Forester	Career Incumbent	CA	ES	....	....	
Do	Associate Chief Forester	......do	CA	ES	....	....	
Do	Chief of Staff	......do	CA	ES	....	....	
Arlington, VA	Chief Information Officer	......do	CA	ES	....	....	
Washington, DC	Associate Deputy Chief, Business Operations, Policy.	......do	CA	ES	....	....	
Albuquerque, NM ..	Director, Albuquerque Service Center-Budget and Finance.	......do	CA	ES	....	....	
Arlington, VA	Director, Human Resources Management	Vacant	....	ES	....	....	
Washington, DC	Director, Strategic Planning and Budget Accountability.	Career Incumbent	CA	ES	....	....	
Arlington, VA	Director, Civil Rights Staff	......do	CA	ES	....	....	
Lakewood, CO	Director, National Job Corps	......do	CA	ES	....	....	
Washington, DC	Director, Senior Youth and Volunteer Programs.	......do	CA	ES	....	....	
Do	Advisor to the Chief on Climate Change	......do	CA	ES	....	....	
	Research						
Do	Deputy Chief, Research and Development	......do	CA	ES	....	....	
Do	Associate Deputy Chief, Research and Development.	......do	CA	ES	....	....	
	National Forest System						
Do	Deputy Chief	......do	CA	ES	....	....	
Do	Associate Deputy Chief	......do	CA	ES	....	....	
Do	......do	Vacant	....	ES	....	....	
Do	Director, Recreation and Heritage Resources	Career Incumbent	CA	ES	....	....	
	State and Private Forestry						
Do	Deputy Chief	......do	CA	ES	....	....	
Do	Associate Deputy Chief	......do	CA	ES	....	....	
Do	......do	......do	CA	ES	....	....	
	Field Units						
Missoula, MT	Regional Forester, Region 1, Northern Region	......do	CA	ES	....	....	
Lakewood, CO	Regional Forester, Region 2, Rocky Mountain Region.	......do	CA	ES	....	....	
Albuquerque, NM ..	Regional Forester, Region 3, Southwest Region.	......do	CA	ES	....	....	
Ogden, UT	Regional Forester, Region 4, Intermountain Region.	......do	CA	ES	....	....	
San Francisco, CA	Regional Forester, Region 5, Pacific Southwest Region.	......do	CA	ES	....	....	
Portland, OR	Regional Forester, Region 6, Pacific Northwest Region.	......do	CA	ES	....	....	
Atlanta, GA	Regional Forester, Region 8, Southern Region	......do	CA	ES	....	....	
Milwaukee, WI	Regional Forester, Region 9, Eastern Region	......do	CA	ES	....	....	
Juneau, AK	Regional Forester, Region 10, Juneau	......do	CA	ES	....	....	
	International Forest System						
Washington, DC	Director of International Programs	......do	CA	ES	....	....	

DEPARTMENT OF AGRICULTURE OFFICE OF THE INSPECTOR GENERAL

Location	Position	Name of Incumbent	Type of Appt.	Pay Plan	Level, Grade, or Pay	Tenure	Expires
	OFFICE OF INSPECTOR GENERAL						
Washington, DC	Inspector General	Phyllis Fong	PAS	EX	III	....	
Do	Special Assistant	Vacant	....	ES	....	....	

DEPARTMENT OF COMMERCE

Location	Position	Name of Incumbent	Type of Appt.	Pay Plan	Level, Grade, or Pay	Tenure	Expires
	OFFICE OF THE SECRETARY						
	Immediate Office						
Washington, DC	Secretary	Vacant	PAS	EX	I	....	
Do	Senior Advisor to the Secretary for NOAA	......do	....	ES	....	....	
Do	Executive Assistant to the Secretary	Erin M. Walls	SC	GS	13	....	
Do	Special Assistant	Benjamin W. Flatgard	SC	GS	12	....	
	Office of the Chief of Staff						
Do	Chief of Staff	Bruce H. Andrews	NA	ES	....	....	
Do	Deputy Chief of Staff	Katharine Lister	NA	ES	....	....	
Do	Senior Advisor to the Secretary	Steven J. Olson	SC	GS	15	....	
Do	Director of Scheduling	Michelle Shwimer	SC	GS	13	....	
Do	Director, National Export Events	Lyle Canceko	SC	GS	13	....	
Do	Deputy Director of Advance	Carly J. Montoya	SC	GS	12	....	
Do	Special Assistant	Dennis Clark	SC	GS	12	....	
Do	Deputy Director of Scheduling	Jennifer E. Murray	SC	GS	11	....	
Do	Advance Specialist	Alexander B. Baker	SC	GS	11	....	
Do	......do	Reid Rosenberg	SC	GS	11	....	
Do	Protocol Officer	Deilia Jackson	SC	GS	11	....	
Do	Special Assistant to the Chief of Staff	Aparna Paladugu	SC	GS	9	....	
Do	Confidential Assistant to the Deputy Chief of Staff.	Victoria Leung Din	SC	GS	7	....	
	Office of White House Liaison						
Do	Director	John C. Connor	NA	ES	....	....	
Do	Deputy Director	Kristin Sheehy	SC	GS	13	....	
Do	Special Assistant	Jamal Pope	SC	GS	9	....	
	Office of Executive Secretariat						
Do	Director	Latoya Murphy	NA	ES	....	....	
Do	Deputy Director	Madhura Valverde	SC	GS	13	....	
Do	Special Assistant	Brian P. Brothman	SC	GS	11	....	
Do	Confidential Assistant	Gregory M. Cuneo	SC	GS	9	....	
Do	......do	Bontu Itana	SC	GS	9	....	
	Office of Business Liaison						
Do	Director	Matthew T. McGuire	NA	ES	....	....	
Do	Deputy Director	Katina Rojas Joy	SC	GS	14	....	
Do	Senior Advisor	Ari A. Matusiak	SC	GS	14	....	
Do	Special Assistant	Jenna Dunay	SC	GS	9	....	
	Office of Policy and Strategic Planning						
Do	Counselor to the Secretary and Director	Malcolm R. Lee	NA	ES	....	....	
Do	Special Assistant	Anthony V. Lynn	SC	GS	9	....	
	Office of Public Affairs						
Do	Director	Jennifer Friedman	NA	ES	....	....	
Do	Deputy Director	Sonja Steptoe	SC	GS	15	....	
Do	Director of Speechwriting	Nathan Osburn	SC	GS	14	....	
Do	Senior Advisor for Communications and Policy.	Jennifer Berlin	SC	GS	14	....	
Do	Director of Digital Strategy	Michael Kruger	SC	GS	13	....	
Do	Deputy Press Secretary	Sarah R. Horowitz	SC	GS	11	....	
Do	Confidential Assistant	Katherine Martin	SC	GS	7	....	
Do	......do	Rachel D. Rubin	SC	GS	7	....	
	Office of the Deputy Secretary						
Do	Deputy Secretary	Rebecca M. Blank	PAS	EX	II	....	
Do	Chief of Staff to the Deputy Secretary	Justin Ehrenwerth	NA	ES	....	....	
Do	Senior Advisor for Policy and Program Integration.	Career Incumbent	CA	ES	....	....	
Do	Special Advisor	Theresa Rose Sena	SC	GS	14	....	
Do	Special Assistant	Matthew Warshaw	SC	GS	11	....	
Do	Special Assistant to the Deputy Secretary	Nnaji Campbell	SC	GS	9	....	
	Office of Legislative and Intergovernmental Affairs						
Do	Assistant Secretary	Vacant	PAS	EX	IV	....	
Do	Deputy Assistant Secretary	Rodney J. Stowers	NA	ES	....	....	
Do	Director of Intergovernmental Affairs	William A. Ramos	SC	GS	14	....	
Do	Associate Director of Legislative and Intergovernmental Affairs.	Victoria Tung	SC	GS	13	....	
Do	Associate Director of Legislative Affairs	Andrew H. Su	SC	GS	13	....	
Do	Legislative Assistant	Ashley A. Zuelke	SC	GS	9	....	
Do	......do	Emily Hildebrand	SC	GS	9	....	
Do	Confidential Assistant	David H. Talbot	SC	GS	7	....	
Do	Associate Director for Oversight	Brian C. Eiler	SC	GS	13	....	

DEPARTMENT OF COMMERCE—Continued

Location	Position	Name of Incumbent	Type of Appt.	Pay Plan	Level, Grade, or Pay	Tenure	Expires
	Office of the Chief Financial Officer and Assistant Secretary for Administration						
Washington, DC	Chief Financial Officer and Assistant Secretary for Administration.	Scott B. Quehl	PAS	EX	IV	....	
Do	Deputy Assistant Secretary for Administration.	Frederick E. Stephens	NA	ES	....	....	
Do	Senior Acquisition Strategy Advisor	Vacant	....	ES	....	....	
Do	Chief Privacy Officer and Director of Open Government.	......do	....	ES	....	....	
Do	Director, Office of Civil Rights	Career Incumbent	CA	ES	....	....	
Do	Director, Risk Management and Program Evaluation.	Vacant	....	ES	....	....	
Do	Director, Financial Management Systems	Career Incumbent	CA	ES	....	....	
	Office of the General Counsel						
Do	General Counsel	Cameron Forbes Kerry	PAS	EX	IV	....	
Do	Deputy General Counsel	Geovette E. Washington	NA	ES	....	....	
Do	Assistant General Counsel for Administration	Career Incumbent	CA	ES	....	....	
Do	Chief, Employment and Labor Law Division ..	......do	CA	ES	....	....	
Do	Chief, General Law Division	......do	CA	ES	....	....	
Do	Assistant General Counsel for Finance and Litigation.	......do	CA	ES	....	....	
Do	Assistant General Counsel for Legislation and Regulation.	......do	CA	ES	....	....	
Do	Chief Counsel for Import Administration	......do	CA	ES	....	....	
Do	Chief Counsel for International Commerce	......do	CA	ES	....	....	
Do	Chief Counsel for Economic Affairs	......do	CA	ES	....	....	
Do	Chief Counsel for Industry and Security	......do	CA	ES	....	....	
Do	Deputy General Counsel for Strategic Initiatives.	Alexander Hoehn-Saric	SC	GS	15	....	
Do	Senior Advisor	Quentin Palfrey	SC	GS	15	....	
Do	Special Advisor	Michelle Duff-Mitchell	SC	GS	13	....	
Do	Special Assistant	Nicholas Ahrens	SC	GS	11	....	
	BUREAU OF INDUSTRY AND SECURITY						
Do	Under Secretary	Eric L. Hirschhorn	PAS	EX	III	....	
Do	Deputy Under Secretary	Career Incumbent	CA	ES	....	....	
Do	Chief of Staff	Sharon Yanagi	SC	GS	15	....	
Do	Director of Congressional and Public Affairs ..	Charles Kinney	SC	GS	15	....	
Do	Senior Advisor	Daniel Meza	SC	GS	14	....	
Do	Special Assistant	Samir Jammal	SC	GS	13	....	
Do	Assistant Secretary for Export Administration.	Kevin J. Wolf	PAS	EX	IV	....	
Do	Deputy Assistant Secretary for Export Administration.	Career Incumbent	CA	ES	....	....	
Do	Director, Office of Nonproliferation and Treaty Compliance.	......do	CA	ES	....	....	
Do	Director, Office of Exporter Services	......do	CA	ES	....	....	
Do	Director, Office of National Security and Technology Transfer Controls.	......do	CA	ES	....	....	
Do	Director, Office of Strategic Industries and Economic Security.	Vacant	....	ES	....	....	
Do	Senior Advisor	Steven Emme	SC	GS	15	....	
Do	Assistant Secretary for Export Enforcement ..	David W. Mills	PAS	EX	IV	....	
	ECONOMIC DEVELOPMENT ADMINISTRATION						
Do	Assistant Secretary	Vacant	PAS	EX	IV	....	
Do	Deputy Assistant Secretary for Economic Development.	Matthew S. Erskine	NA	ES	....	....	
Do	Deputy Assistant Secretary for Regional Affairs.	Career Incumbent	CA	ES	....	....	
Do	Senior Advisor	Barry Johnson	NA	ES	....	....	
Do	Chief of Staff	Tene Dolphin	SC	GS	15	....	
Do	Director of Outreach	Angela B. Martinez	SC	GS	15	....	
Do	Director of Public Affairs	Cleve Mesidor	SC	GS	15	....	
Do	Director, Office of Innovation and Entrepreneurship.	Nishith Acharya	SC	GS	15	....	
Do	Senior Advisor	Katherine W. Dedrick	SC	GS	15	....	
Do	Special Advisor	Haley Stevens	SC	GS	13	....	
Do	Chief Counsel for Economic Development	Vacant	....	ES	....	....	
Philadelphia, PA	Philadelphia Regional Director	Career Incumbent	CA	ES	....	....	
Chicago, IL	Chicago Regional Director	......do	CA	ES	....	....	
Austin, TX	Regional Director, Austin Regional Office	......do	CA	ES	....	....	
Atlanta, GA	Regional Director, Atlanta Regional Office	......do	CA	ES	....	....	
Seattle, WA	Regional Director, Seattle Regional Office	......do	CA	ES	....	....	

DEPARTMENT OF COMMERCE—Continued

Location	Position	Name of Incumbent	Type of Appt.	Pay Plan	Level, Grade, or Pay	Tenure	Expires
Denver, CO	Regional Director, Denver Regional Office	Career Incumbent	CA	ES	....	....	
	ECONOMICS AND STATISTICS ADMINISTRATION						
Washington, DC	Under Secretary for Economic Affairs	Vacant	PAS	EX	III	....	
Do	Deputy Under Secretary for Economic Affairs	......do	....	ES		....	
Do	Associate Under Secretary for Management ...	Career Incumbent	CA	ES	....	....	
Do	Chief Economist	Mark E. Doms	NA	ES		....	
Do	Deputy Chief Economist	Career Incumbent	CA	ES		....	
	BUREAU OF THE CENSUS						
Suitland, MD	Director	Robert M. Groves	PAS	EX	IV	....	
Do	Deputy Director	Career Incumbent	CA	ES		....	
Do	Associate Director for Communications	Steven Jost	NA	ES		....	
Do	Assistant Director for Communications	Vacant	....	ES		....	
Do	Senior Advisor for Data Management	Career Incumbent	CA	ES	....	....	
Do	Chief of Congressional Affairs	Angela Manso	SC	GS	14	....	
Washington, DC	Director, Office of Faith Based and Neighborhood Partnerships.	Cedric M. Grant	SC	GS	14	....	
	INTERNATIONAL TRADE ADMINISTRATION						
Do	Under Secretary for International Trade	Francisco J. Sanchez	PAS	EX	III	....	
Do	Deputy Under Secretary	Career Incumbent	CA	ES	....	....	
Do	Chief of Staff	Adam Wilczewski	NA	ES		....	
Do	Senior Policy Advisor	Peter Kaldes	SC	GS	15	....	
Do	Senior Advisor and Director of Public Affairs	Mary L. Trupo	SC	GS	15	....	
Do	Senior Advisor	Phu Duc Huynh	SC	GS	15	....	
Do	Deputy Director of Public Affairs	Mara Nicole Lee	SC	GS	14	....	
Do	Special Advisor	Carleton B. Shephard	SC	GS	14	....	
Do	Special Assistant	Iris A. Ferguson	SC	GS	12	....	
Do	Confidential Assistant and Scheduler to the Under Secretary.	Parker D. Sheedy	SC	GS	7	....	
Do	Chief Information Officer	Career Incumbent	CA	ES	....	....	
Do	Assistant Secretary for Import Administration.	Paul Piquado	PAS	EX	IV	....	
Do	Deputy Assistant Secretary for Import Administration.	Career Incumbent	CA	ES	....	....	
Do	Special Advisor	Ryan K. Rhodes	SC	GS	14	....	
Do	Deputy Assistant Secretary for Textiles and Apparel.	Kimberly T. Glas	NA	ES		....	
Do	Deputy Assistant Secretary for Antidumping and Countervailing Duty Operations.	Career Incumbent	CA	ES	....	....	
Do	Deputy Assistant Secretary for Antidumping and Countervailing Duty Policy and Negotiations.	Lynn M. Fischer Fox	NA	ES		....	
Do	Director, Office of Policy	Career Incumbent	CA	ES		....	
Do	Special Advisor	Steven G. Glickman	SC	GS	14	....	
Do	Assistant Secretary for Market Access and Compliance.	Michael C. Camunez	PAS	EX	IV	....	
Do	Deputy Assistant Secretary for Market Access and Compliance.	Career Incumbent	CA	ES	....	....	
Do	Special Advisor	Gabriel F. Soledad	SC	GS	14	....	
Do	......do	Thomas S. Wyler	SC	GS	14	....	
Do	Deputy Assistant Secretary for Africa, the Middle East and South Asia.	Career Incumbent	CA	ES	....	....	
Do	Deputy Assistant Secretary for Asia	......do	CA	ES		....	
Do	Deputy Assistant Secretary for Europe	Matthew Murray	NA	ES		....	
Do	Deputy Assistant Secretary for Trade Agreements and Compliance.	Career Incumbent	CA	ES		....	
Do	Deputy Assistant Secretary for Western Hemisphere.	......do	CA	ES		....	
Do	Assistant Secretary for Manufacturing and Services.	Nicole Y. Lamb-Hale	PAS	EX	IV	....	
Do	Deputy Assistant Secretary for Manufacturing and Services.	Career Incumbent	CA	ES	....	....	
Do	Senior Director for Industry and Analysis	Vacant		ES		....	
Do	Deputy Director of Advisory Committees	Jennifer L. Pilat	SC	GS	12	....	
Do	Special Assistant	Todd A. Valentine	SC	GS	12	....	
Do	Deputy Assistant Secretary for Industry Analysis.	Career Incumbent	CA	ES		....	
Do	Director, Office of Competition and Economic Analysis.	......do	CA	ES		....	
Do	Deputy Assistant Secretary for Manufacturing.	Vacant		ES		....	
Do	Director, Office of Aerospace and Automotive Industries.	Career Incumbent	CA	ES		....	

DEPARTMENT OF COMMERCE—Continued

Location	Position	Name of Incumbent	Type of Appt.	Pay Plan	Level, Grade, or Pay	Tenure	Expires
Washington, DC	Deputy Assistant Secretary for Services	Kenneth Hyatt	NA	ES	....	....	
Do	Senior Director for Services	Career Incumbent	CA	ES	....	....	
Do	Director, Office of Service Industries	......do	CA	ES	....	....	
Do	Assistant Secretary of Commerce and Director General of United States Foreign Commercial Service.	Vacant	PAS	EX	IV	....	
Do	Deputy Director General	Career Incumbent	CA	ES	....	....	
Do	Executive Director for Export Policy, Promotion and Strategy.	Michael D. Masserman	NA	ES	....	....	
Do	Executive Director, SelectUSA	Vacant	....	ES	....	....	
Do	Senior Advisor, SelectUSA	......do	....	ES	....	....	
Do	Director, Office of Strategic Planning and Resource Management.	......do	....	FE	....	....	
Do	Director, Office of Strategic Partnerships	Matthew R. Kennedy	SC	GS	15	....	
Do	Special Advisor	Kevin T. Gluba	SC	GS	14	....	
Do	Executive Assistant	Jennifer Arvanitis	SC	GS	12	....	
Do	Deputy Assistant Secretary for International Operations.	Career Incumbent	CA	FE	....	....	
Do	Deputy Assistant Secretary for Domestic Operations.	Antwaun D. Griffin	NA	ES	....	....	
Do	Executive Director for Trade Promotion and Outreach.	Vacant	....	ES	....	....	
Do	National Field Director	Career Incumbent	CA	ES	....	....	
Do	Director, Advocacy Center	Bryan J. Erwin	NA	ES	....	....	
Beijing, China	Senior Commercial Officer, Beijing	Career Incumbent	CA	FE	....	....	
Shanghai, China	Principal Commercial Officer, Shanghai	......do	CA	FE	....	....	
Singapore	Senior Commercial Officer, Singapore	......do	CA	FE	....	....	
Hong Kong	Senior Commercial Officer, Hong Kong	......do	CA	FE	....	....	
Bangkok, Thailand	Senior Commercial Officer, Bangkok	......do	CA	FE	....	....	
Tokyo, Japan	Senior Commercial Officer, Tokyo	......do	CA	FE	....	....	
Do	Deputy Senior Commercial Officer, Tokyo	......do	CA	FE	....	....	
Seoul, Korea, Republic of.	Senior Commercial Officer, Seoul	......do	CA	FE	....	....	
Sydney, Australia ..	Regional Senior Commercial Officer, Sydney	......do	CA	FE	....	....	
Sao Paulo, Brazil ...	Senior Commercial Officer, Sao Paulo	......do	CA	FE	....	....	
Mexico City, Mexico.	Senior Commercial Officer, Mexico City	......do	CA	FE	....	....	
Ottawa, Ontario, Canada.	Senior Commercial Officer, Ottawa	......do	CA	FE	....	....	
Toronto, Ontario, Canada.	Principal Commercial Officer, Toronto	......do	CA	FE	....	....	
New Delhi, India ...	Senior Commercial Officer, New Delhi	......do	CA	FE	....	....	
Do	Deputy Senior Commercial Officer, New Delhi.	......do	CA	FE	....	....	
Riyadh, Saudi Arabia.	Senior Commercial Officer, Riyadh	......do	CA	FE	....	....	
Cairo, Egypt	Regional Senior Commercial Officer, Cairo	......do	CA	FE	....	....	
Ankara, Turkey	Senior Commercial Officer, Ankara	......do	CA	FE	....	....	
Washington, DC	Regional Director, ANESA	......do	CA	FE	....	....	
Johannesburg, South Africa.	Senior Commercial Officer, Johannesburg	......do	CA	FE	....	....	
Washington, DC	Commercial Officer, World Bank	......do	CA	FE	....	....	
Paris, France	Senior Commercial Officer, Paris	......do	CA	FE	....	....	
Madrid, Spain	Senior Commercial Officer, Madrid	......do	CA	FE	....	....	
Washington, DC	Regional Director, EAP	......do	CA	FE	....	....	
London, United Kingdom.	Senior Commercial Officer, London	......do	CA	FE	....	....	
Do	Commercial Officer, ERBD, London	......do	CA	FE	....	....	
Brussels, Belgium	Senior Commercial Officer, US EC, Brussels	......do	CA	FE	....	....	
The Hague, Netherlands.	Senior Commercial Officer, The Hague	......do	CA	FE	....	....	
Washington, DC	Regional Director, EUR	......do	CA	FE	....	....	
Rome, Italy	Senior Commercial Officer, Rome	......do	CA	FE	....	....	
Berlin, Germany	Senior Commercial Officer, Berlin	......do	CA	FE	....	....	
Moscow, Russia	Senior Commercial Officer, Moscow	......do	CA	FE	....	....	
Washington, DC	Regional Director, WH	......do	CA	FE	....	....	
Guangzhou, China	Principal Commercial Officer, Guangzhou	......do	CA	FE	....	....	
Washington, DC	Full Time AFSA Representative	......do	CA	FE	....	....	
Do	Training Compliment	......do	CA	FE	....	....	
	MINORITY BUSINESS DEVELOPMENT AGENCY						
Do	National Director	David A. Hinson	NA	ES	....	....	
Do	Special Advisor	Candace Jackson	SC	GS	13	....	
Do	Deputy Director	Alejandra Y. Castillo	NA	ES	....	....	

DEPARTMENT OF COMMERCE—Continued

Location	Position	Name of Incumbent	Type of Appt.	Pay Plan	Level, Grade, or Pay	Tenure	Expires
	NATIONAL OCEANIC AND ATMOSPHERIC ADMINISTRATION						
Washington, DC	Under Secretary of Commerce for Oceans and Atmosphere and NOAA Administrator.	Jane Lubchenco	PAS	EX	III	....	
Do	Assistant Secretary for Environmental Observation and Prediction.	Kathryn D. Sullivan	PAS	EX	IV	....	
Do	Assistant Secretary for Conservation and Management.	Vacant	PAS	EX	IV	....	
Do	Principal Deputy Under Secretary for Oceans and Atmosphere.	Margaret F. Spring	NA	ES	....	....	
Do	Deputy Under Secretary for Operations	Career Incumbent	CA	ES	....	....	
Do	Chief of Staff for NOAA	Ruth Renee Stone	NA	ES	....	....	
Do	Director of Communications	Ciaran M. Clayton	NA	ES	....	....	
Do	Deputy Director, Office of Communications	Career Incumbent	CA	ES	....	....	
Do	Director of Policy/Senior Policy Advisor	Sally J. Yozell	NA	ES	....	....	
Do	Associate Senior Advisor	Career Incumbent	CA	ES	....	....	
Do	Deputy Director of Policy	Christine L. Blackburn	SC	GS	14	....	
Do	Senior Policy Advisor	Karen Hyun	SC	GS	14	....	
Do	.....do	Jainey K. Bavishi	SC	GS	13	....	
Do	Special Assistant	Jacqueline N. Bray	SC	GS	12	....	
Do	.....do	Richard M. Love, Jr.	SC	GS	11	....	
Do	Deputy Assistant Secretary for International Fisheries.	Russell F. Smith	NA	ES	....	....	
Do	Deputy Assistant Secretary for International Affairs.	Career Incumbent	CA	ES	....	....	
Do	Chief Scientist	Vacant	PAS	EX	V	....	
Do	General Counsel	Lois J. Schiffer	NA	ES	....	....	
Silver Spring, MD	Deputy General Counsel for National Oceanic and Atmospheric Administration.	Career Incumbent	CA	ES	....	....	
Washington, DC	Deputy General Counsel for Atmospheric and Ocean Research and Services.	......do	CA	ES	....	....	
Do	Assistant General Counsel for Fisheries	......do	CA	ES	....	....	
Do	Director, Office of Legislative Affairs	John S. Gray III	NA	ES	....	....	
Do	Deputy Director, Office of Legislative Affairs	Amanda Greenwell	SC	GS	15	....	
Do	Assistant Administrator, Office of Program Planning and Integration.	Career Incumbent	CA	ES	....	....	
Do	Assistant Administrator for Marine Fisheries	Eric C. Schwaab	NA	ES	....	....	
Silver Spring, MD	Deputy Assistant Administrator for Regulatory Programs.	Career Incumbent	CA	ES	....	....	
Washington, DC	Director, Office of Protected Resources	Vacant	....	ES	....	....	
Woods Hole, MA	Regional Administrator, Northeast Region	......do	....	ES	....	....	
St. Petersburg, FL	Regional Administrator, Southeast Region	Career Incumbent	CA	ES	....	....	
Seattle, WA	Regional Administrator, Northwest Region	William W. Stelle, Jr.	NA	ES	....	....	
Santa Rosa, CA	Regional Administrator, Southwest Region	Career Incumbent	CA	ES	....	....	
Juneau, AK	Regional Administrator, Alaska Region	......do	CA	ES	....	....	
Honolulu, HI	Regional Administrator, Pacific Island Region	......do	CA	ES	....	....	
Washington, DC	Assistant Administrator for Ocean Services and Coastal Zone Management.	......do	CA	ES	....	....	
Charleston, SC	Director, NOAA Coastal Services Center	......do	CA	ES	....	....	
Silver Spring, MD	Director, Office of National Marine Sanctuaries.	......do	CA	ES	....	....	
Washington, DC	Director, Office of Ocean and Coastal Resource Management.	Vacant	....	ES	....	....	
Do	Assistant Administrator for National Environmental Satellite, Data and Information Services (NESDIS).	Career Incumbent	CA	ES	....	....	
Silver Spring, MD	Deputy Assistant Administrator, NESDIS	......do	CA	ES	....	....	
Suitland, MD	Director, Office of Satellite and Product Operations.	......do	CA	ES	....	....	
Washington, DC	Executive Director, Office of Space Commercialization.	Vacant	....	ES	....	....	
Silver Spring, MD	Assistant Administrator for Weather Services	Career Incumbent	CA	ES	....	....	
Washington, DC	Deputy Assistant Administrator for Weather Services.	......do	CA	ES	....	....	
Do	Assistant Administrator for Oceanic and Atmospheric Research.	......do	CA	ES	....	....	
Silver Spring, MD	Deputy Assistant Administrator for Programs and Administration.	......do	CA	ES	....	....	
	NATIONAL TELECOMMUNICATIONS AND INFORMATION ADMINISTRATION						
Washington, DC	Assistant Secretary of Commerce for Communications and Information.	Lawrence E. Strickling	PAS	EX	IV	....	
Do	Deputy Assistant Secretary for Communications and Information.	Anna M. Gomez	NA	ES	....	....	
Do	Chief of Staff	Thomas C. Power	SC	GS	15	....	

DEPARTMENT OF COMMERCE—Continued

Location	Position	Name of Incumbent	Type of Appt.	Pay Plan	Level, Grade, or Pay	Tenure	Expires
Washington, DC	Chief Counsel	Career Incumbent	CA	ES	....	....	
Do	Associate Administrator, Office of International Affairs.	......do	CA	ES	....	....	
Do	Associate Administrator for Policy Analysis and Development.	Vacant		ES	....	....	
Do	Deputy Associate Administrator for Policy Analysis and Development.	......do		ES	....	....	
Do	Associate Administrator for Spectrum Management.	Career Incumbent	CA	ES	....	....	
Do	Deputy Associate Administrator for Domestic Spectrum Management.	......do	CA	ES	....	....	
Do	Deputy Associate Administrator for International Spectrum Management.	......do	CA	ES	....	....	
Do	Associate Administrator for Telecommunications and Information Applications.	......do	CA	ES	....	....	
Do	Deputy Associate Administrator for Telecommunications and Information Applications.	Vacant		ES	....	....	
	NATIONAL INSTITUTE OF STANDARDS AND TECHNOLOGY						
Gaithersburg, MD	Under Secretary of Commerce for Standards and Technology.	Patrick D. Gallagher	PAS	EX	IV	....	
	NATIONAL TECHNICAL INFORMATION SERVICE						
Bethesda, MD	Director	Career Incumbent	CA	ES	....	....	
	U.S. PATENT AND TRADEMARK OFFICE						
Alexandria, VA	Under Secretary of Commerce for Intellectual Property and Director of the U.S. Patent and Trademark Office.	David James Kappos	PAS	EX	III	....	
Do	Deputy Under Secretary for Intellectual Property and Deputy Director of the U.S. Patent and Trademark Office.	Teresa Stenek Rea	XS	AD	....	....	
Do	Chief of Staff	Peter C. Pappas	NA	ES	....	....	
Do	Deputy Chief of Staff	Azam Brian Khan	SC	GS	15	....	
Do	Special Advisor	Vikrum D. Aiyer	SC	GS	14	....	
Do	Chief Communications Officer and Senior Advisor to the Under Secretary and Director.	Vacant		ES	....	....	
Do	Deputy Chief Communications Officer	Patrick C. Ross	SC	GS	14	....	
Do	Administrator for Policy and External Affairs	Career Incumbent	CA	ES	....	....	
Do	General Counsel	......do	CA	ES	....	....	
Do	Chief Administrative Officer	......do	CA	ES	....	....	
Do	Senior Advisor to the Commissioner for Patents.	Bradford R. Huther	TA	ES	....	....	01/24/13
Do	Chief Information Officer	Career Incumbent	CA	ES	....	....	

DEPARTMENT OF COMMERCE OFFICE OF THE INSPECTOR GENERAL

Location	Position	Name of Incumbent	Type of Appt.	Pay Plan	Level, Grade, or Pay	Tenure	Expires
Washington, DC	Inspector General	Todd J. Zinser	PAS	EX	IV	....	

DEPARTMENT OF DEFENSE

OFFICE OF THE SECRETARY OF DEFENSE

Location	Position	Name of Incumbent	Type of Appt.	Pay Plan	Level, Grade, or Pay	Tenure	Expires
	OFFICE OF THE SECRETARY						
Arlington, VA	Secretary	Leon E. Panetta	PAS	EX	I		
Do	Deputy Secretary	Ashton B. Carter	PAS	EX	II		
Do	Special Assistant to the Secretary and Deputy Secretary of Defense.	Jeremy B. Bash	NA	ES			
Do	Executive Secretary	Career Incumbent	CA	ES			
Do	Special Assistant to the Secretary of Defense	Marcel J. Lettre II	NA	ES			
Do	......do	Monica P. Medina	NA	ES			
Do	Special Assistant to the Deputy Secretary of Defense.	Wendy R. Anderson	NA	ES			
Do	Special Advisor to the Deputy Secretary of Defense.	Terence Szuplat	NA	ES			
Do	Special Assistant to the Secretary of Defense for White House Liaison.	Shelly O. Stoneman	NA	ES			
Silverdale, WA	Director, Office of the Convening Authority	Bruce E. MacDonald	TA	ES			03/06/13
Arlington, VA	Confidential Assistant	Delonnie Henry	SC	GS	15		
Do	Director, Travel Operations	James P. Eby	SC	GS	15		
Do	Special Assistant to the Deputy Secretary of Defense.	Jonathan L. Lee	SC	GS	15		
Do	Special Assistant to the Deputy Secretary	Jonathan S. Lachman	SC	GS	15		
Do	Special Assistant to the Secretary of Defense for Protocol.	Anne W. Lieberman	SC	GS	14		
Do	Confidential Assistant	Faye L. Brown	SC	GS	14		
Do	Advance Officer	Stacee N. Bako	SC	GS	14		
Do	Deputy White House Liaison	Jeffrey M. Stephens	SC	GS	13		
Do	Advance Officer	Lyndsey Toeppen	SC	GS	13		
Do	Protocol Officer	Maribel Serocki	SC	GS	13		
Do	......do	Pamela P. Wilson	SC	GS	12		
Do	Advance Officer	Marik Von Rennenkampff	SC	GS	12		
Do	Special Assistant to the White House Liaison	Valerie N. Miller	SC	GS	12		
Do	Advance Officer	Carrie A. Kagawa	SC	GS	11		
Do	Confidential Assistant	Elliot Gillerman	SC	GS	11		
	Office of the Under Secretary of Defense (Policy)						
Do	Under Secretary	James N. Miller	PAS	EX	III		
Do	Assistant Secretary of Defense (Special Operations/Low Intensity Conflict).	Michael A. Sheehan	PAS	EX	IV		
Do	Principal Deputy Under Secretary	Kathleen A. Hicks	PAS	EX	IV		
Do	Assistant Secretary of Defense (Global Strategic Affairs).	Madelyn R. Creedon	PAS	EX	IV		
Do	Assistant Secretary of Defense (International Security Affairs).	Derek Chollet	PAS	EX	IV		
Do	Assistant Secretary of Defense (Homeland Defense and Americas' Security Affairs).	Paul N. Stockton	PAS	EX	IV		
Do	Assistant Secretary of Defense (Asian and Pacific Security Affairs).	Mark W. Lippert	PAS	EX	IV		
Do	Deputy Assistant Secretary of Defense (African Affairs).	Career Incumbent	CA	ES			
Do	Principal Deputy Assistant Secretary of Defense (Special Operations/Low Intensity Conflict).	Vacant		ES			
Do	Deputy Assistant Secretary of Defense (Western Hemisphere Affairs).	Francisco O. Mora	NA	ES			
Do	Principal Deputy Assistant Secretary of Defense (Homeland Defense and Americas' Security Affairs).	Todd M. Rosenblum	NA	ES			
Do	Deputy Assistant Secretary of Defense (Rule of Law/Detainee Policy).	William K. Lietzau	NA	ES			
Do	Foreign Relations and Defense Policy Manager (Rule of Law/Detainee Policy).	Career Incumbent	CA	ES			
Do	Deputy Assistant Secretary of Defense (Nuclear and Missile Defense).	Bradley H. Roberts	NA	ES			
Do	Principal Deputy Assistant Secretary of Defense (International Security Affairs).	Career Incumbent	CA	ES			
Do	Foreign Relations and Defense Policy Manager (Homeland Defense Integration and Defense Support of Civil Authorities).	......do	CA	ES			
Do	Foreign Relations and Defense Policy Manager.	......do	CA	ES			
Do	Principal Deputy Assistant Secretary of Defense (Asian and Pacific Security Affairs).	Peter R. Lavoy	NA	ES			
Do	Deputy Assistant Secretary of Defense (East Asia).	Vacant		ES			

DEPARTMENT OF DEFENSE—Continued

OFFICE OF THE SECRETARY OF DEFENSE—Continued

Location	Position	Name of Incumbent	Type of Appt.	Pay Plan	Level, Grade, or Pay	Tenure	Expires
Arlington, VA	Deputy Assistant Secretary of Defense (South and Southeast Asia).	Vikram J. Singh	NA	ES			
Do	Deputy Assistant Secretary of Defense (Counternarcotics and Global Threats).	William F. Wechsler	NA	ES			
Do	Foreign Relations and Defense Policy Manager.	Career Incumbent	CA	ES			
Do	......do	......do	CA	ES			
Do	Deputy Assistant Secretary of Defense (Forces Development).	David A. Ochmanek	NA	ES			
Do	Deputy Assistant Secretary of Defense (Middle East).	Matthew J. Spence	NA	ES			
Do	Foreign Relations and Defense Policy Manager.	Career Incumbent	CA	ES			
Do	Deputy Assistant Secretary of Defense (Afghanistan, Pakistan and Central Asia).	David S. Sedney	NA	ES			
Do	Director, Defense Technology Security Administration.	Career Incumbent	CA	ES			
Do	Deputy Assistant Secretary of Defense (Partnership Strategy and Stability Operations).	James A. Schear	NA	ES			
Do	Foreign Relations and Defense Policy Manager (Deputy Chief of Staff for Stability Operations).	Career Incumbent	CA	ES			
Do	Foreign Relations and Defense Policy Manager.	......do	CA	ES			
Do	Deputy Assistant Secretary of Defense (Europe and North Atlantic Treaty Organization Policy).	James J. Townsend, Jr.	NA	ES			
Do	Foreign Relations and Defense Policy Manager (Chief of Staff).	Career Incumbent	CA	ES			
Do	Foreign Relations and Defense Policy Manager (Principal Director, Counternarcotics and Global Threats).	......do	CA	ES			
Do	Deputy Under Secretary of Defense (Strategy, Plans, and Forces).	Vacant		ES			
Do	Deputy Assistant Secretary of Defense (Countering Weapons of Mass Destruction).	Rebecca Hersman	NA	ES			
Do	Principal Director (Europe and North Atlantic Treaty Organization).	Vacant		ES			
Do	Deputy Assistant Secretary of Defense (Plans).	Robert M. Scher	NA	ES			
Do	Chief of Staff to the Under Secretary of Defense for Policy.	Career Incumbent	CA	ES			
Do	Foreign Relations and Defense Policy Manager (Principal Director, Special Operations and Combating Terrorism).	......do	CA	ES			
Do	Principal Deputy Assistant Secretary of Defense for Strategic Affairs.	......do	CA	ES			
Do	Deputy Assistant Secretary of Defense for Special Operations and Combating Terrorism.	......do	CA	ES			
Do	Deputy Assistant Secretary of Defense (Defense Continuity and Crisis Management).	......do	CA	ES			
Do	Principal Director, Countering Weapons of Mass Destruction.	Vacant		ES			
Do	Deputy Assistant Secretary of Defense (Russia, Ukraine and Eurasia Policy).	Evelyn Farkas	NA	ES			
Do	Principal Director, Strategy	Vacant		ES			
Do	Foreign Relations and Defense Policy Manager.	Career Incumbent	CA	ES			
Do	Deputy Assistant Secretary of Defense (Strategy).	Daniel Y. Chiu	NA	ES			
Do	Foreign Relations and Defense Policy Manager (Visiting Professor, NDU).	Career Incumbent	CA	ES			
Do	Deputy Assistant Secretary of Defense (Homeland Defense Strategy and Force Planning).	Jose S. Mayorga, Jr.	NA	ES			
Do	Senior Advisor for China Policy and Integration.	David F. Helvey	TA	ES			10/24/12
Do	Deputy Assistant Secretary of Defense for Prisoners of War (POW)/Missing Personnel Affairs and Director, Defense POW/Missing Personnel Office.	W. Montague Winfield	NA	ES			
Do	Special Assistant to the ASD (ISA)	Anna A. Makanju	SC	GS	15	3 Years	

DEPARTMENT OF DEFENSE—Continued

OFFICE OF THE SECRETARY OF DEFENSE—Continued

Location	Position	Name of Incumbent	Type of Appt.	Pay Plan	Level, Grade, or Pay	Tenure	Expires
Arlington, VA	Foreign Relations and Defense Policy Manager (Principal Director, Force Development).	Career Incumbent	CA	ES	....	....	
Do	Senior Advisor to the Under Secretary of Defense Policy (Principal Director POW/MIA and Principal Director Defense POW/ Missing Personnel Office).	......do	CA	ES	....	....	
Do	Foreign Relations and Defense Policy Manager.	Vacant	....	ES	....	....	
Do	Deputy Assistant Secretary of Defense (Space Policy).	Career Incumbent	CA	ES	....	....	
Do	Deputy Assistant Secretary of Defense Homeland Defense Integration and Defense Support of Civil Authorities and Chief of Staff.	......do	CA	ES	....	....	
Do	Deputy Assistant Secretary of Defense (Cyber Policy).	Eric Rosenbach	NA	ES	....	....	
Do	Senior Director for Defense Policy and Strategy.	Christine E. Wormuth	NA	ES	....	....	
Do	Senior Advisor to the Under Secretary of Defense for Policy.	Vacant	....	ES	....	....	
Do	Foreign Relations and Defense Policy Manager (Principal Director, Afghanistan, Pakistan and Central Asia).	Career Incumbent	CA	ES	....	....	
Do	Director, Periodic Review Secretariat	Norton C. Joerg	TA	ES	....	....	02/18/15
Do	Senior Advisor to the Under Secretary of Defense (Policy).	Career Incumbent	CA	ES	....	....	
Do	Special Advisor to Assistant Secretary of Defense (SO/LIC).	......do	CA	ES	....	....	
Do	Chief Operating Officer	......do	CA	ES	....	....	
Do	Foreign Relations Defense Policy Manager (Deputy Director, Defense Technology Security Administration).	......do	CA	ES	....	....	
Do	Foreign Relations Defense Policy Manager (Principal Director, Cyber Policy).	......do	CA	ES	....	....	
Do	Foreign Relations Defense Policy Manager (Principal Director, Russia, Ukraine and Eurasia).	......do	CA	ES	....	....	
Do	Director for Strategic Business Development	Kristopher R. Haag	TA	ES	....	....	02/28/13
Do	Director of Policy and Financial Management	Regina A. Tedla-Dubey	TA	ES	....	....	03/28/13
Do	Special Assistant to Assistant Secretary of Defense (Special Operations/Low Intensity Conflict).	Erin M. Logan	SC	GS	15	....	
Do	Staff Assistant	Shawn W. Brimley	SC	GS	15	....	
Do	Principal Director, Nuclear and Missile Defense Policy.	John F. Plumb	SC	GS	15	....	
Do	Director, Pakistan	Thomas C. Greenwood	SC	GS	15	....	
Do	Special Advisor to Deputy Assistant Secretary of Defense (Detainee Policy).	Alex Wagner	SC	GS	15	....	
Do	Special Assistant to the Deputy Assistant Secretary of Defense (East Asia).	Frank Aum	SC	GS	15	....	
Do	Senior Communications Advisor for Under Secretary of Defense (Policy).	Mark J. Ribbing	SC	GS	15	....	
Do	Special Assistant to the Deputy Assistant Secretary of Defense (Middle East).	Eric Lynn	SC	GS	15	....	
Do	Special Assistant to the Principal Deputy Under Secretary of Defense (Policy).	Jonathan Reiber	SC	GS	14	....	
Do	Special Assistant to the Deputy Assistant Secretary of Defense (Europe/NATO).	Samuel J. Brannen	SC	GS	14	....	
Do	Special Assistant to the Principal Deputy Under Secretary of Defense (Policy).	Siddharth Mohandas	SC	GS	14	....	
Do	Staff Assistant	Alice Hunt Friend	SC	GS	14	....	
Do	Special Assistant to the Assistant Secretary of Defense (Homeland Defense and Americas' Security Affairs).	Andrew D. Heighington	SC	GS	13	....	
Do	Special Assistant to the Deputy Assistant Secretary of Defense (South and Southeast Asia).	Nicholas C. Wallar	SC	GS	13	....	
Do	Special Assistant to the Assistant Secretary of Defense (Asian and Pacific Security Affairs).	Lindsey W. Ford	SC	GS	12	....	
Do	Special Assistant to the Deputy Assistant Secretary of Defense (Western Hemisphere Affairs).	Nicholas F. Zimmerman	SC	GS	12	....	

DEPARTMENT OF DEFENSE—Continued

OFFICE OF THE SECRETARY OF DEFENSE—Continued

Location	Position	Name of Incumbent	Type of Appt.	Pay Plan	Level, Grade, or Pay	Tenure	Expires
Arlington, VA	Special Assistant to the Assistant Secretary of Defense (Global Strategic Affairs).	David L. Vorland	SC	GS	12	....	
	United States Mission to the North Atlantic Treaty Organization						
Brussels, Belgium	Foreign Relations and Defense Policy Manager.	Career Incumbent	CA	ES	....	....	
Do	Defense Advisor to the U.S. Ambassador to NATO.	Robert G. Bell	NA	ES	....	....	
	Office of the Director, Operational Test and Evaluation						
Arlington, VA	Director	J. M. Gilmore	PAS	EX	IV	....	
Do	Principal Deputy Director	Career Incumbent	CA	ES	....	....	
Do	Deputy Director for Land and Expeditionary Warfare.	......do	CA	ES	....	....	
Do	Deputy Director for Air Warfare	......do	CA	ES	....	....	
Do	Deputy Director for Naval Warfare	......do	CA	ES	....	....	
Do	Deputy Director, Net-Centric Space and Missile Defense Systems.	......do	CA	ES	....	....	
Do	Special Assistant	Eric Loeb	SC	GS	15	....	
	Office of the Director, Net Assessment						
Do	Director	Andrew W. Marshall	NA	ES	....	....	
Do	Deputy Director	Career Incumbent	CA	ES	....	....	
Do	Associate Director	......do	CA	ES	....	....	
	Joint Activities						
Do	Director of Administration and Management/Comptroller, National Guard Bureau.	......do	CA	ES	....	....	
	Office of the Under Secretary of Defense (Personnel and Readiness)						
Do	Under Secretary of Defense (Personnel and Readiness).	Erin C. Conaton	PAS	EX	III	....	
Do	Principal Deputy Under Secretary of Defense (Personnel and Readiness).	Jo Ann Rooney	PAS	EX	IV	....	
Do	Assistant Secretary of Defense (Health Affairs).	Jonathan Woodson	PAS	EX	IV	....	
Do	Assistant Secretary of Defense (Readiness and Force Management).	Vacant	PAS	EX		....	
Do	Principal Deputy Assistant Secretary of Defense (Health Affairs)/Principal Deputy Director, TMA.	Karen Sue Guice	NA	ES		....	
Do	Principal Director, Requirements and Strategic Integration.	Career Incumbent	CA	ES		....	
Do	Deputy Assistant Secretary of Defense for Wounded Warrior Care and Transition Policy.	John R. Campbell	NA	ES		....	
Do	Deputy Assistant Secretary of Defense for Military Community and Family Policy.	Vacant		ES		....	
Do	Director, Personnel and Readiness, Integration and Strategic Management.	Laura D. Stubbs	NA	ES		....	
Do	Deputy Assistant Secretary of Defense (Health Budgets and Financial Policy).	Career Incumbent	CA	ES		....	
Do	Deputy Assistant Secretary of Defense (Readiness).	Laura J. Junor	NA	ES		....	
Do	Deputy Assistant Secretary of Defense (Civilian Personnel Policy).	Career Incumbent	CA	ES		....	
Do	Principal Director for Diversity Management and Equal Opportunity.	......do	CA	ES		....	
Do	Director Readiness Programming and Assessment.	......do	CA	ES		....	
Do	Principal Director (Military Community and Family Policy).	......do	CA	ES		....	
Do	Director, Personnel and Readiness Analysis ..	......do	CA	ES		....	
Do	Principal Director, DoDEA and Associate Director for Education.	Vacant		ES		....	
Do	Deputy Assistant Secretary of Defense (Military Personnel Policy).	Career Incumbent	CA	ES		....	
Do	Deputy Assistant Secretary of Defense (Force Health Protection and Readiness).	Vacant		ES		....	
Do	Deputy Assistant Secretary of Defense for Clinical and Program Policy.	Warren E. Lockette	NA	ES		....	

DEPARTMENT OF DEFENSE—Continued

OFFICE OF THE SECRETARY OF DEFENSE—Continued

Location	Position	Name of Incumbent	Type of Appt.	Pay Plan	Level, Grade, or Pay	Tenure	Expires
Arlington, VA	Principal Director, Wounded Warrior Care and Transition Policy.	Career Incumbent	CA	ES			
Do	Principal Deputy Assistant Secretary of Defense (Readiness and Force Management).	Frederick E. Vollrath	NA	ES			
Do	Principal Director (Civilian Personnel Policy)	Career Incumbent	CA	ES			
Do	Director, Accession Policy	Vacant		ES			
Do	Director, Readiness and Training Policy and Programs.	Career Incumbent	CA	ES			
Do	Principal Director, Military Personnel Policy	Vacant		ES			
Do	Director, Officer and Enlisted Personnel Management.	Career Incumbent	CA	ES			
Peachtree City, GA	Director, Domestic Dependent Elementary and Secondary Schools and the Department of Defense Dependents Schools Cuba.	......do	CA	ES			
Urazoe, Okinawa, Japan.	Director, Department of Defense Dependents Schools Pacific and Domestic Dependent Elementary and Secondary Schools Guam.	Vacant		ES			
Wiesbaden, Germany.	Director, Department of Defense Dependents Schools Europe.	Career Incumbent	CA	ES			
Arlington, VA	Director of Military Compensation	......do	CA	ES			
Do	Director, Talent Acquisition, Development and Management.	......do	CA	ES			
Do	Deputy Chief, Tricare Policy and Operations	......do	CA	ES			
Do	Program Executive Officer	......do	CA	ES			
Do	Associate Director for Financial and Business Operations.	Vacant		ES			
Do	Director, Quadrennial Review of Military Compensation.	Career Incumbent	CA	ES			
Do	Deputy Director, Force Health Protection and Readiness Programs.	......do	CA	ES			
Do	Principal Advisor, Portfolio Management Project Office.	George Chambers	TA	ES			07/20/13
Do	Special Assistant and Senior Advisor to Under Secretary of Defense and Principal Deputy Undersecretary of Defense (Personnel and Readiness).	Vacant		ES			
Do	Special Assistant and Senior Advisor to the Under Secretary of Defense and Principal Under Secretary of Defense (Personnel and Readiness).	Career Incumbent	CA	ES			
Do	Director, Resource and Financial Management.	......do	CA	ES			
Do	Program Executive Officer	Vacant		ES			
Do	Confidential Assistant to the Under Secretary of Defense Personnel and Readiness.	Mary E. Woodward	SC	GS	14		
Do	Special Assistant to the Deputy Under Secretary of Defense for Transition Policy and Care Coordination.	Arturo R. Murguia	SC	GS	14		
	Office of Assistant Secretary of Defense (Reserve Affairs)						
Do	Assistant Secretary	Jessica L. Wright	PAS	EX	IV		
Do	Principal Deputy Assistant Secretary	Dennis L. McGinnis	NA	ES			
Do	Deputy Assistant Secretary of Defense (Resources).	Career Incumbent	CA	ES			
Do	Deputy Assistant Secretary of Defense (Manpower and Personnel).	Vacant		ES			
Washington, DC	Deputy Assistant Secretary of Defense (Readiness, Training and Mobilization).	Career Incumbent	CA	ES			
Arlington, VA	Deputy Assistant Secretary of Defense (Materiel and Facilities).	......do	CA	ES			
Do	Principal Director (Readiness, Training and Mobilization).	......do	CA	ES			
Do	Special Assistant to the Assistant Secretary of Defense for Reserve Affairs.	Jacqueline Garrick	SC	GS	15		
	Office of Assistant Secretary of Defense (Public Affairs)						
Do	Assistant Secretary	Vacant	PAS	EX	IV		
Do	Principal Deputy Assistant Secretary	Career Incumbent	CA	ES			
Do	Deputy Assistant Secretary	George E. Little	NA	ES			
Do	Deputy Assistant Secretary of Defense for Community and Public Outreach.	Rene Carbone Bardorf	NA	ES			
Do	Speechwriter	Christopher M. Kirchhoff	SC	GS	15		

DEPARTMENT OF DEFENSE—Continued

OFFICE OF THE SECRETARY OF DEFENSE—Continued

Location	Position	Name of Incumbent	Type of Appt.	Pay Plan	Level, Grade, or Pay	Tenure	Expires
Arlington, VA	Deputy Director for Communication Plans and Integration.	James L. Swartout	SC	GS	15		
Do	Speechwriter	Jacob M. Freedman	SC	GS	14		
Do	......do	Justin D. Mikolay	SC	GS	13		
Do	......do	Gregory M. Grant	SC	GS	13		
Do	Assistant Press Secretary	Carlin R. Woog	SC	GS	13		
Do	Research Assistant	Lucas F. Schleusener	SC	GS	9		
	Office of the Director (Cost Assessment and Program Evaluation)						
Do	Director	Christine H. Fox	PAS	EX	IV		
Do	Deputy Director, Program Evaluation	Career Incumbent	CA	ES			
Do	Deputy Director, Cost Assessment	......do	CA	ES			
Do	Deputy Director, Analysis and Integration	......do	CA	ES			
Do	Deputy Director, Program, Data and Enterprise Services.	......do	CA	ES			
Do	Director, Land Forces Division	......do	CA	ES			
Do	Director, Program Resources and Information Systems Management Division.	......do	CA	ES			
Do	Director, Irregular Warfare Division	......do	CA	ES			
Do	Director, Advanced Systems Cost Analysis Division.	......do	CA	ES			
Do	Director, Intelligence, Surveillance, and Reconnaissance Programs Division.	......do	CA	ES			
Do	Director, Command, Control, Communications and Intelligence (C4) and Information Programs Division.	......do	CA	ES			
Do	Director, Naval Forces Division	......do	CA	ES			
Do	Director, Tactical Air Division	......do	CA	ES			
Do	Director, Projection Forces Division	......do	CA	ES			
Do	Director, Weapon Systems Cost Analysis Division.	......do	CA	ES			
Do	Director, Economic and Manpower Analysis Division.	......do	CA	ES			
Do	Director, Strategic, Defensive, and Space Programs Division.	......do	CA	ES			
Do	Director, Program Analysis Division	Vacant		ES			
Do	Director, Force Structure Risk Assessments	Career Incumbent	CA	ES			
Do	Director, Force and Infrastructure Analysis Division.	......do	CA	ES			
Do	Director, Operating and Support Cost Analysis Division.	Vacant		ES			
Do	Special Assistant for Special Projects	Tanisha R. Dozier	SC	GS	13		
	Office of the Under Secretary of Defense (Comptroller)						
Do	Under Secretary	Robert F. Hale	PAS	EX	III		
Do	Principal Deputy Under Secretary	Michael J. McCord	PAS	EX	IV		
Do	Deputy Comptroller Program/Budget	Career Incumbent	CA	ES			
Do	Deputy Comptroller for Budget and Appropriations Affairs.	Blaine F. Aaron	NA	ES			
Do	Assistant Deputy Comptroller (Program Budget) Program, Budget, and Execution.	Career Incumbent	CA	ES			
Do	Director, Resource Issues	Sandra Veronica Richardson.	NA	ES			
Do	Director for Investment	Career Incumbent	CA	ES			
Do	Director for Revolving Funds	......do	CA	ES			
Do	Director for Operations	......do	CA	ES			
Do	Director for Military Personnel and Construction.	......do	CA	ES			
Do	Associate Director for Military Construction	......do	CA	ES			
Do	Special Assistant to Under Secretary of Defense/Principal Deputy Under Secretary of Defense (Comptroller).	......do	CA	ES			
Do	Associate Director for Air, Space, and Intelligence Programs.	......do	CA	ES			
Do	Director for Financial Improvement and Audit Readiness.	......do	CA	ES			
Do	Director for Accounting and Finance Policy	......do	CA	ES			
Do	Associate Director for Military Operations	......do	CA	ES			
Do	Associate Director for Ground, Sea, and Other Programs.	Vacant		ES			
Do	Associate Director for Personnel and Health Care.	Career Incumbent	CA	ES			

DEPARTMENT OF DEFENSE—Continued

OFFICE OF THE SECRETARY OF DEFENSE—Continued

Location	Position	Name of Incumbent	Type of Appt.	Pay Plan	Level, Grade, or Pay	Tenure	Expires
Arlington, VA	Associate Director, International and Interagency Programs.	Vacant		ES			
Do	Associate Director, Defense-Wide Programs	......do		ES			
Do	Director, Business Integration Office	Career Incumbent	CA	ES			
Do	Associate Director for Contingency and Interagency Programs.	......do	CA	ES			
Do	Associate Director, External Affairs	......do	CA	ES			
Do	Director, Human Capital and Resource Management.	Vacant		ES			
Do	Deputy Director for Program and Financial Control.	Career Incumbent	CA	ES			
Do	Director, Program and Financial Control	......do	CA	ES			
Do	Personal and Confidential Assistant to the Under Secretary of Defense (Comptroller).	Lucia Y. Cho	SC	GS	12		
Do	Special Assistant to the Deputy Under Secretary of Defense (Budget and Appropriations Affairs).	Kyong H. Nam	SC	GS	12		
	Office of Assistant Secretary of Defense (Legislative Affairs)						
Do	Assistant Secretary	Elizabeth Lee King	PAS	EX	IV		
Do	Principal Deputy Assistant Secretary	Eric A. Pierce	NA	ES			
Do	Deputy Assistant Secretary of Defense for Senate Affairs.	Michael John Stella	NA	ES			
Do	Deputy Assistant Secretary of Defense for House Affairs.	Brian S. Morrison	NA	ES			
Do	Director of Operations	Career Incumbent	CA	ES			
Do	Special Assistant for Networks and Information Integration.	Christopher T. Finan	SC	GS	15		
Do	Special Assistant for Acquisition Technology and Logistics.	Jody Bennett	SC	GS	15		
Do	Special Assistant	Iram Ali	SC	GS	15		
Do	Special Assistant for Communications	Loren L. Dealy	SC	GS	14		
Do	Special Assistant	Courtney Ann Littig	SC	GS	14		
Do	......do	Bethany M. Bassett	SC	GS	13		
Do	......do	Joseph F. Hicken	SC	GS	13		
Do	......do	Anna E. Morey	SC	GS	12		
Do	......do	Jorie M. Feldman	SC	GS	12		
Do	......do	Brian Andrew Greer	SC	GS	12		
Do	......do	Mary McVeigh	SC	GS	11		
	Office of Director of Administration and Management						
Do	Director	Career Incumbent	CA	ES			
Do	Director, Washington Headquarters Services/ Deputy Director, Administration and Management.	......do	CA	ES			
Do	Director for Organizational and Management Planning.	......do	CA	ES			
Do	Office of the Secretary of Defense Networks Chief Information Officer.	......do	CA	ES			
Do	Chief Historian	......do	CA	ES			
Do	Director for Department of Defense Privacy and Civil Liberties.	Michael E. Reheuser	TA	ES			11/11/12
	Washington Headquarters Services						
Do	Deputy Director	Career Incumbent	CA	ES			
Do	Director, Financial Management Directorate	......do	CA	ES			
Do	General Counsel	......do	CA	ES			
Do	Director, Executive Services Directorate	......do	CA	ES			
Do	Director, Enterprise Information Technology Services Directorate.	......do	CA	ES			
	White House Military Office						
Washington, DC	Director	......do	CA	ES			
Do	Deputy Director	......do	CA	ES			
Do	Director Presidential Contingency Programs	......do	CA	ES			
Do	Staff Assistant	Grace E. Butler	SC	GS	11		
Do	......do	Jamie E. Eckert	SC	GS	11		
	Defense Fellows						
Arlington, VA	Defense Fellow	Farooq Mitha	SC	GS	12		
Do	......do	Justo Robles III	SC	GS	11		
Do	......do	Matthew M. Gula	SC	GS	11		
Do	......do	Mela L. Norman	SC	GS	9		

DEPARTMENT OF DEFENSE—Continued

OFFICE OF THE SECRETARY OF DEFENSE—Continued

Location	Position	Name of Incumbent	Type of Appt.	Pay Plan	Level, Grade, or Pay	Tenure	Expires
Arlington, VA	Defense Fellow	Katherine L. Corogenes	SC	GS	9		
	Office of the General Counsel						
Do	General Counsel	Jeh C. Johnson	PAS	EX	IV		
Do	Principal Deputy General Counsel	Robert S. Taylor	NA	ES			
Do	Deputy General Counsel (Fiscal)	Career Incumbent	CA	ES			
Do	Deputy General Counsel (International Affairs).	......do	CA	ES			
Do	Deputy General Council (Acquisition and Logistics).	......do	CA	ES			
Do	Deputy General Counsel (Personnel and Health Policy).	......do	CA	ES			
Do	Deputy General Counsel (Legal Counsel)	Robin E. Jacobsohn	NA	ES			
Do	Deputy General Counsel (Environment and Installations).	Monique Rowtham-Kennedy.	NA	ES			
Do	Director, Standards of Conduct Office	Career Incumbent	CA	ES			
Do	Deputy General Counsel (Legislation)	Alissa M. Starzak	NA	ES			
Do	Attorney-Advisor (General)	Brodi Kemp	SC	GS	15		
	Office of the Department of Defense Chief Information Officer						
Do	Chief Information Officer	Teresa Takai	NA	ES			
Do	Principal Deputy	Career Incumbent	CA	ES			
Do	Deputy Chief Information Officer (Cybersecurity).	......do	CA	ES			
Do	Director, Planning and Analysis	......do	CA	ES			
Do	Director, Spectrum Programs and Policy	Vacant		ES			
Do	Principal Director to the Deputy Assistant Secretary of Defense (Information, Management, Integration and Technology).	Career Incumbent	CA	ES			
Do	Deputy Chief Information Officer (Resources and Analysis).	......do	CA	ES			
Do	Principal Director (Information Enterprise)	Vacant		ES			
Do	Principal Director (Cybersecurity)	......do		ES			
Do	Director, C4 and Information Infrastructure	......do		ES			
Do	Director, Planning, Policy and Integration Information Technology Management.	Career Incumbent	CA	ES			
Do	Deputy to the Information Sharing Executive	......do	CA	ES			
Do	Deputy to the Assistant Secretary of Defense (Networks and Information Integration)/ DoD Chief Information Officer, International Affairs.	......do	CA	ES			
Do	Director, Portfolio Management and Enterprise Infrastructure.	......do	CA	ES			
Do	Principal Director (C4 and Information Infrastructure Capabilities).	Vacant		ES			
Do	Principal Director (Resources and Analysis)	Career Incumbent	CA	ES			
Do	Director, Information Technology Investment	......do	CA	ES			
	Office of Under Secretary of Defense (Intelligence)						
Do	Under Secretary	Michael G. Vickers	PAS	EX	III		
Do	Principal Deputy Under Secretary	Thomas A. Ferguson	PAS	EX	IV		
	Office of the Under Secretary of Defense (Acquisition, Technology, and Logistics)						
Do	Under Secretary	Frank Kendall	PAS	EX	II		
Do	Principal Deputy Under Secretary	Vacant	PAS	EX	III		
Do	Assistant Secretary of Defense for Research and Engineering.	Zachary J. Lemnios	PAS	EX	IV		
Do	Assistant Secretary of Defense for Operational Energy Plans and Programs.	Sharon E. Burke	PAS	EX	IV		
Do	Assistant Secretary of Defense (Logistics and Materiel Readiness).	Alan F. Estevez	PAS	EX	IV		
Do	Assistant Secretary of Defense (Acquisition)	Katharina G. McFarland	PAS	EX	IV		
Do	Assistant Secretary of Defense (Nuclear, Chemical and Biological Defense).	Andrew C. Weber	PAS	EX	IV		
Do	Director, Small Business Programs	Andre J. Gudger	NA	ES			
Do	Director, International Cooperation	Career Incumbent	CA	ES			
Do	Deputy Under Secretary of Defense (Installations and Environment).	Dorothy Robyn	NA	ES			
Do	Principal Director, Research	Career Incumbent	CA	ES			
Do	Principal Deputy Assistant Secretary of Defense (Logistics and Materiel Readiness).	Vacant		ES			

DEPARTMENT OF DEFENSE—Continued

OFFICE OF THE SECRETARY OF DEFENSE—Continued

Location	Position	Name of Incumbent	Type of Appt.	Pay Plan	Level, Grade, or Pay	Tenure	Expires
Arlington, VA	Deputy Assistant Secretary of Defense (Command, Control, Communications, Space and Cyber).	Career Incumbent	CA	ES			
Do	Deputy Assistant Secretary of Defense (Strategic and Tactical Systems).	......do	CA	ES			
Do	Director, Systems and Software Engineering	......do	CA	ES			
Do	Principal Deputy to the Assistant to the Secretary of Defense for Nuclear and Chemical and Biological Defense Programs.	John R. Harvey	NA	ES			
Do	Deputy Assistant Secretary of Defense (Rapid Fielding).	Earl C. Wyatt	NA	ES			
Do	Deputy Assistant Secretary of Defense (Systems Engineering).	Stephen P. Welby	NA	ES			
Do	Director, Program Assessment and Root Cause Analysis.	Career Incumbent	CA	ES			
Do	Deputy Assistant Secretary of Defense (Developmental Test and Evaluation)/Director, Test Resource Management Center.	Edward R. Greer	NA	ES			
Do	Deputy Assistant Secretary of Defense (Research).	Louis R. Brothers, Jr.	NA	ES			
Alexandria, VA	President, Defense Acquisition University	Vacant		ES			
Arlington, VA	Director, Office of Economic Adjustment	Career Incumbent	CA	ES			
Do	Deputy Assistant Secretary of Defense (Transportation Policy).	Donald C. Stanton	NA	ES			
Do	Principal Assistant Deputy Under Secretary of Defense (Full Spectrum Dominance).	Career Incumbent	CA	ES			
Do	Director, Basing	......do	CA	ES			
Do	Director, Facilities Energy and Privatization	......do	CA	ES			
Do	Director, Facilities Investment and Management.	......do	CA	ES			
Do	Director, Environmental Management	......do	CA	ES			
Do	Principal Deputy Director, Test Resource Management Center/Deputy Director, Joint Investment Programs and Policy.	......do	CA	ES			
Do	Assistant Deputy Under Secretary of Defense (Installations).	John C. Conger	NA	ES			
Do	Vice President, Defense Acquisition University.	Career Incumbent	CA	ES			
Do	Director, Joint Rapid Acquisition Cell	......do	CA	ES			
Do	Director, Installations and Environment Science and Technology.	Vacant		ES			
Do	Deputy Assistant Secretary of Defense (Program Support).	Career Incumbent	CA	ES			
Do	Director, Counter-Terrorism Technology	......do	CA	ES			
Do	Deputy Assistant Secretary of Defense (Maintenance Policy and Programs).	......do	CA	ES			
Do	Deputy Assistant Secretary of Defense (Materiel Readiness).	......do	CA	ES			
Do	Deputy Assistant Secretary of Defense (Threat Reduction and Arms Control).	......do	CA	ES			
Do	Principal Deputy Director for Systems Engineering.	......do	CA	ES			
Do	Deputy Assistant Secretary of Defense (Supply Chain Integration).	......do	CA	ES			
Do	Director, Human Capital Initiatives	Vacant		ES			
Do	Principal Deputy Assistant Secretary of Defense, Operations Energy Plans and Program.	Edward T. Morehouse, Jr.	NA	ES			
Do	Principal Director, Strategic and Tactical Systems and Director, Acquisition and Program Management.	Career Incumbent	CA	ES			
Do	Director, Test Resources	......do	CA	ES			
Alexandria, VA	Administrator, Defense Technical Information Center.	......do	CA	ES			
Arlington, VA	Director for Basic Research	......do	CA	ES			
Do	Deputy Director, Small and Disadvantaged Business Utilization Policy.	......do	CA	ES			
Do	Director, Command and Control (C2) Programs.	......do	CA	ES			
Do	Deputy Director, Joint Force Integration	......do	CA	ES			
Do	Deputy Director, Systems and Software Engineering (Enterprise Development).	......do	CA	ES			
Do	Director, Defense Laboratory Programs	......do	CA	ES			
Do	Director, Satellite Operations	Vacant		ES			

DEPARTMENT OF DEFENSE—Continued

Office of the Secretary of Defense—Continued

Location	Position	Name of Incumbent	Type of Appt.	Pay Plan	Level, Grade, or Pay	Tenure	Expires
Arlington, VA	Director, Joint Operations Support	Career Incumbent	CA	ES			
Do	Director of Strategy and Operations Integration.	......do	CA	ES			
Do	Deputy Director, Systems Engineering (Developmental Test and Evaluation).	Vacant		ES			
Do	Deputy Director, International Negotiations	Career Incumbent	CA	ES			
Do	Deputy Director, Program Operations	......do	CA	ES			
Do	Deputy Director, Unmanned Warfare	......do	CA	ES			
Do	Deputy Assistant Secretary of Defense (Chemical and Biological Defense).	......do	CA	ES			
Do	Deputy Director, Communications and Networks Programs and Policy.	......do	CA	ES			
Do	Principal Director, Space and Intelligence	Vacant		ES			
Do	Deputy Director, Industrial Policy	......do		ES			
Do	Strategic Coordinator	Career Incumbent	CA	ES			
Do	Assistant Deputy Director, Ground Systems	......do	CA	ES			
Do	Special Assistant to the Under Secretary of Defense (Acquisition, Technology and Logistics).	Andrew P. Hunter	NA	ES			
Do	Special Assistant for Science and Technology Communities of Interest.	Career Incumbent	CA	ES			
Do	Deputy Assistant Secretary of Defense (Manufacturing and Industrial Base Policy).	Brett B. Lambert	NA	ES			
Boston, MA	Director, Defense Pricing	Career Incumbent	CA	ES			
Arlington, VA	Deputy Director, Air Warfare	......do	CA	ES			
Do	Strategic Advisor, Space and Intelligence	Charles L. Beames	TA	ES			
Do	Special Assistant to the Deputy Assistant Secretary of Defense (Manufacturing and Industrial Base Policy).	Neal J. Orringer	SC	GS	15		
Do	Special Assistant to the Deputy Assistant Secretary of Defense, Manufacturing and Industrial Base Policy.	Ellen Y. Chou	SC	GS	15		
Do	Confidential Assistant	Gail J. Henderson-Wishnefsky.	SC	GS	14		
Do	Special Assistant to the Assistant Secretary of Defense for Operational Energy Plans and Programs.	Tarak N. Shah	SC	GS	13		
Do	Special Assistant to the Principal Deputy Under Secretary of Defense (Acquisition, Technology and Logistics).	Vishal D. Doshi	SC	GS	12		
Do	Special Assistant to the Assistant to the Secretary of Defense (Nuclear, Chemical and Biological Defense Programs).	Ian W. Grant	SC	GS	12		
	Defense Advanced Research Projects Agency						
Do	Director	Arati Prabhakar	NA	ES			
Do	Comptroller	Career Incumbent	CA	ES			
Do	General Counsel	......do	CA	ES			
Do	Special Assistant for Strategy and Planning	......do	CA	ES			
Do	Special Assistant, Operations Liaison	......do	CA	ES			
Do	Special Assistant, Tactical Analysis	......do	CA	ES			
	Office of the Joint Chiefs of Staff						
Do	Director for Joint History	......do	CA	ES			
Do	Joint Staff Comptroller	......do	CA	ES			
Do	Deputy Director for Strategic Logistics	......do	CA	ES			
Do	Vice Director for Force Structure, Resources and Assessment.	......do	CA	ES			
Do	Deputy Director for Force Management	......do	CA	ES			
Do	Principal Deputy Director for Strategic Plans and Policy.	......do	CA	ES			
Do	Deputy Director for Strategic Stability	......do	CA	ES			
Do	Civilian Executive Assistant	Kristen Cicio	SC	GS	14		
Do	Staff Assistant	Mary Turner	SC	GS	14		
	Missile Defense Agency						
Do	Executive Director	Career Incumbent	CA	ES			
Washington, DC	Deputy for International Affairs	......do	CA	ES			
Huntsville, AL	Program Director, Ballistic Missile Defense Sensors.	......do	CA	ES			
Arlington, VA	Deputy Program Director, Aegis Ballistic Missile Defense.	Vacant		ES			
Do	General Counsel, Missile Defense Agency	......do		ES			
Huntsville, AL	Deputy Director for Test	Career Incumbent	CA	ES			
Fort Belvoir, VA	Comptroller/Chief Financial Officer	......do	CA	ES			

DEPARTMENT OF DEFENSE—Continued

OFFICE OF THE SECRETARY OF DEFENSE—Continued

Location	Position	Name of Incumbent	Type of Appt.	Pay Plan	Level, Grade, or Pay	Tenure	Expires
Arlington, VA	Director, Security/Intelligence Operations	Vacant		ES			
Auburn, AL	Director, Contracting	......do		ES			
Defense Contract Audit Agency							
Alexandria, VA	General Counsel	Career Incumbent	CA	ES			
Defense Human Resources Activity							
Arlington, VA	Director	......do	CA	ES			
Rosslyn, VA	Director, Interagency Program Office, Department of Defense/Veteran Affairs.	......do	CA	ES			
Arlington, VA	Executive Director, Employer Support of the Guard and Reserve.	......do	CA	ES			
Do	Director, Federal Voting Assistance Program	......do	CA	ES			
Do	Executive Director, Enterprise HR Information Systems.	Vacant		ES			
Do	Deputy Director, Transition to Veterans Program Office.	Career Incumbent	CA	ES			
Defense Contract Management Agency							
Fort Lee, VA	Executive Director, Engineering and Analysis	......do	CA	ES			
Arlington, VA	Defense Acquisition Regulations Counsel	......do	CA	ES			
Defense Information Systems Agency							
Do	General Counsel	......do	CA	ES			
Defense Threat Reduction Agency							
Fort Belvoir, VA	Director	Kenneth A. Myers III	NA	ES			
Do	General Counsel	Career Incumbent	CA	ES			
Defense Security Cooperation Agency							
Arlington, VA	Deputy Director	......do	CA	ES			
Do	Principal Director for Operations	......do	CA	ES			
Do	Principal Director, Business Operations	......do	CA	ES			
Do	Principal Director for Programs	Vacant		ES			
Do	Foreign Relations Defense Policy Manager (Principal Director for Strategy).	Career Incumbent	CA	ES			
Defense Finance and Accounting Service							
Alexandria, VA	Director	......do	CA	ES			
Do	Principal Deputy Director	......do	CA	ES			
Whitehall, OH	Deputy Director for Operations	......do	CA	ES			
Do	Deputy Director, Strategy and Support	......do	CA	ES			
Fort Ben Harrison, IN.	Director, Audit Readiness Office	......do	CA	ES			
Do	Site Director - Indianapolis	......do	CA	ES			
Cleveland, OH	Site Director - Cleveland	......do	CA	ES			
Whitehall, OH	Site Director - Columbus	......do	CA	ES			
Alexandria, VA	Director, Information and Technology	......do	CA	ES			
Do	Director for Internal Review	......do	CA	ES			
Do	General Counsel	......do	CA	ES			
Whitehall, OH	Director for Enterprise Solutions and Standards.	......do	CA	ES			
Fort Ben Harrison, IN.	Director, Enterprise Management Services	Vacant		ES			
Do	Director, Strategy, Policy, and Requirements	Career Incumbent	CA	ES			
Do	Deputy Site Director - Indianapolis	Vacant		ES			
Whitehall, OH	Deputy Site Director - Cleveland	......do		ES			
Do	Deputy Site Director - Columbus	Career Incumbent	CA	ES			
Rome, NY	Site Director - Rome	......do	CA	ES			
Fort Ben Harrison, IN.	Deputy Director for Compliance	Vacant		ES			
Alexandria, VA	Deputy Director for Information and Technology.	Career Incumbent	CA	ES			
Fort Ben Harrison, IN.	Deputy Director for Standards	......do	CA	ES			
Whitehall, OH	Director, Systems	......do	CA	ES			
Fort Ben Harrison, IN.	Chief Financial Officer	......do	CA	ES			
Defense Commissary Agency							
Arlington, VA	Deputy Director/Chief Operating Officer	Vacant		ES			
Fort Lee, VA	Executive Director, Store Operations Group	Career Incumbent	CA	ES			
Do	Executive Director, Sales, Marketing and Policy Group.	......do	CA	ES			
Germany	Executive Director, Infrastructure Support Group.	......do	CA	ES			

DEPARTMENT OF DEFENSE—Continued

OFFICE OF THE SECRETARY OF DEFENSE—Continued

Location	Position	Name of Incumbent	Type of Appt.	Pay Plan	Level, Grade, or Pay	Tenure	Expires
	OFFICE OF THE DEPUTY CHIEF MANAGEMENT OFFICER						
Arlington, VA	Deputy Chief Management Officer	Elizabeth A. McGrath	PAS	EX	III	....	
Do	Assistant Deputy Chief Management Officer	Career Incumbent	CA	ES	....	....	
Do	Director, Technology, Innovation and Engineering.	......do	CA	ES	....	....	
Do	Director, Strategic Management and Performance.	Vacant	....	ES	....	....	
Do	Director, Investment and Acquisition Management.	Career Incumbent	CA	ES	....	....	
Do	Director, Business Integration	......do	CA	ES	....	....	

OFFICE OF THE SECRETARY OF DEFENSE OFFICE OF THE INSPECTOR GENERAL

Location	Position	Name of Incumbent	Type of Appt.	Pay Plan	Level, Grade, or Pay	Tenure	Expires
Alexandria, VA	Inspector General	Vacant	PAS	EX	IV	....	
	OFFICE OF THE INSPECTOR GENERAL						
Do	Chief of Staff	Career Incumbent	CA	ES	....	....	
Philadelphia, PA	Special Deputy Inspector General Southwest Asia.	Joseph T. McDermott	TA	ES	....	....	10/11/12

DEPARTMENT OF DEFENSE—Continued

DEPARTMENT OF THE AIR FORCE

Location	Position	Name of Incumbent	Type of Appt.	Pay Plan	Level, Grade, or Pay	Tenure	Expires
	OFFICE OF THE SECRETARY						
Arlington, VA	Secretary of the Air Force	Michael B. Donley	PAS	EX	II	....	
Do	Special Assistant	Nicholas D. Wilson	SC	GS	13	....	
Do	Executive Speechwriter	Lara M. Battles	SC	GS	15	....	
	Office of the Under Secretary						
Do	Under Secretary of the Air Force	Vacant	PAS	EX	IV	....	
Do	Special Assistant	Rudolph C. Barnes III	NA	ES	....	....	
Do	......do	Averyl E. H Bailey	SC	GS	15	....	
	OFFICE OF THE GENERAL COUNSEL						
Do	General Counsel	Charles A. Blanchard	PAS	EX	IV	....	
Do	Deputy General Counsel (Fiscal Ethics and Civilian Personnel).	Career Incumbent	CA	ES	....	....	
Do	Deputy General Counsel (National Security and Military Affairs).	......do	CA	ES	....	....	
Do	Deputy General Counsel (Contractor Responsibility).	Vacant		ES	....	....	
Washington, DC	Special Assistant	James A. Cadogan	SC	GS	14	....	
Do	Deputy General Counsel (International Affairs).	Career Incumbent	CA	ES	....	....	
Do	Principal Deputy General Counsel	......do	CA	ES	....	....	
Do	Deputy General Counsel (Installations and Environmental Law).	......do	CA	ES	....	....	
Do	Deputy General Counsel (Acquisition)	......do	CA	ES	....	....	
	OFFICE OF ASSISTANT SECRETARY AIR FORCE FOR FINANCIAL MANAGEMENT AND COMPTROLLER						
Arlington, VA	Assistant Secretary (Financial Management and Comptroller).	Jamie M. Morin	PAS	EX	IV	....	
Do	Principal Deputy Assistant Secretary (Financial Management).	Career Incumbent	CA	ES	....	....	
	OFFICE OF ASSISTANT SECRETARY AIR FORCE FOR ACQUISITION						
Do	Assistant Secretary of the Air Force (Acquisition).	Vacant	PAS	EX	IV	....	
Do	Principal Deputy Assistant Secretary (Acquisition and Management).	......do		ES	....	....	
	OFFICE OF ASSISTANT SECRETARY OF THE AIR FORCE FOR MANPOWER AND RESERVE AFFAIRS						
Do	Assistant Secretary of the Air Force	Daniel R. Ginsberg	PAS	EX	IV	....	
Do	Special Assistant	Edmundo A. Gonzales	NA	ES	....	....	
Washington, DC	Principal Deputy Assistant Secretary	Career Incumbent	CA	ES	....	....	
Arlington, VA	Deputy Assistant Secretary for Strategic Diversity Integration.	Jarris L. Taylor, Jr.	NA	ES	....	....	
Washington, DC	Deputy Assistant Secretary for Force Management and Integration.	Career Incumbent	CA	ES	....	....	
	Office Deputy Assistant Secretary Reserve Affairs						
Arlington, VA	Deputy Assistant Secretary	......do	CA	ES	....	....	
	OFFICE OF ASSISTANT SECRETARY AIR FORCE, INSTALLATIONS, ENVIRONMENT, AND LOGISTICS						
Do	Assistant Secretary	Terry A. Yonkers	PAS	EX	IV	....	
Do	Principal Deputy Assistant Secretary	Career Incumbent	CA	ES	....	....	
Do	Deputy Assistant Secretary (Energy, Environment, Safety and Occupational Health).	......do	CA	ES	....	....	
Do	Special Assistant	Camron Gorguinpour	SC	GS	14	....	
Do	......do	Lach R. Litwer	SC	GS	14	....	

DEPARTMENT OF DEFENSE—Continued

DEPARTMENT OF THE ARMY

Location	Position	Name of Incumbent	Type of Appt.	Pay Plan	Level, Grade, or Pay	Tenure	Expires
	OFFICE OF THE SECRETARY OF THE ARMY						
Arlington, VA	Secretary	John M. McHugh	PAS	EX	II		
Do	Special Assistant	Anne R. LeMay	NA	ES			
Washington, DC	Director, District of Columbia National Guard	Errol R. Schwartz	NA	ES			
Do	Deputy Director, District of Columbia National Guard.	Renwick L. Payne	NA	ES			
Arlington, VA	Personal and Confidential Assistant	Kathleen M. Cox	SC	GS	14		
	OFFICE OF THE UNDER SECRETARY OF THE ARMY						
Do	Under Secretary of the Army	Joseph W. Westphal	PAS	EX	III		
Do	Special Assistant to the Chief Management Officer.	James D. Mowrer	SC	GS	14		
	Office of Small Business Programs						
Do	Director	Career Incumbent	CA	ES			
	OFFICE OF THE DEPUTY UNDER SECRETARY OF THE ARMY						
Do	Deputy Under Secretary of the Army	Thomas E. Hawley	NA	ES			
Do	Director, Institutional Army Transformation Commission.	Leonard W. Braverman	TA	ES			02/11/15
Do	Special Assistant	Justin S. Rubin	SC	GS	15		
	OFFICE OF THE ASSISTANT SECRETARY OF THE ARMY (ACQUISITION, LOGISTICS AND TECHNOLOGY)						
Do	Assistant Secretary of the Army	Heidi Shyu	PAS	EX	IV		
Do	Principal Deputy Assistant Secretary of the Army.	Vacant		ES			
Do	Special Assistant	Gabriel O. Camarillo	SC	GS	15		
Do	......do	Amanda Renae Simpson	SC	GS	15		
	OFFICE OF THE ASSISTANT SECRETARY OF THE ARMY (CIVIL WORKS)						
Do	Assistant Secretary of the Army	Jo-Ellen Darcy	PAS	EX	IV		
Do	Principal Deputy Assistant Secretary of the Army (Civil Works) / Deputy Assistant Secretary of the Army (Legislation).	Terrence C. Salt	NA	ES			
Do	Deputy Assistant Secretary of the Army (Project Planning and Review).	Career Incumbent	CA	ES			
Do	Special Assistant to the Assistant Secretary of the Army (Civil Works).	Moira L. Kelley	SC	GS	13		
Do	Special Assistant to the Principal Deputy Assistant Secretary of the Army (Civil Works).	Arnab Raychaudhuri	SC	GS	12		
	OFFICE OF THE ASSISTANT SECRETARY OF THE ARMY (FINANCIAL MANAGEMENT AND COMPTROLLER)						
Do	Assistant Secretary of the Army	Mary Sally Matiella	PAS	EX	IV		
Do	Principal Deputy Assistant Secretary of the Army (Financial Management and Comptroller)/(Controls).	Robert M. Speer	NA	ES			
Do	Special Assistant to the Assistant Secretary of the Army (Financial Management and Comptroller).	Ryan P. McDermott	SC	GS	14		
	OFFICE OF THE ASSISTANT SECRETARY OF THE ARMY (INSTALLATIONS, ENERGY AND ENVIRONMENT)						
Do	Assistant Secretary of the Army	Katherine G. Hammack	PAS	EX	IV		
Do	Principal Deputy Assistant Secretary of the Army.	Career Incumbent	CA	ES			
Do	Deputy Assistant Secretary of the Army (Installations, Housing and Partnership).	Vacant		ES			
Do	Deputy Assistant Secretary of the Army (Energy and Sustainability).	Career Incumbent	CA	ES			
Do	Special Advisor to the Assistant Secretary of the Army (Installations, Energy and Environment).	Lauren R. Bregman	SC	GS	14		

DEPARTMENT OF DEFENSE—Continued

DEPARTMENT OF THE ARMY—Continued

Location	Position	Name of Incumbent	Type of Appt.	Pay Plan	Level, Grade, or Pay	Tenure	Expires
	OFFICE OF THE ASSISTANT SECRETARY OF THE ARMY (MANPOWER AND RESERVE AFFAIRS)						
Arlington, VA	Assistant Secretary of the Army	Thomas R. Lamont	PAS	EX	IV	....	
Do	Principal Deputy Assistant Secretary of the Army.	Career Incumbent	CA	ES	....	....	
Washington, DC	Special Assistant to the Assistant Secretary of the Army.	Jason W. Forrester	SC	GS	15	....	
	OFFICE OF THE GENERAL COUNSEL						
Arlington, VA	General Counsel	Brad R. Carson	PAS	EX	IV	....	
Do	Principal Deputy General Counsel/Chief of Legal Services.	Vacant	....	ES	....	....	
Do	Deputy General Counsel (Acquisition)	Career Incumbent	CA	ES	....	....	
Do	Deputy General Counsel (Operations and Personnel).	......do	CA	ES	....	....	
Do	Deputy General Counsel (Civil Works and Environment).	......do	CA	ES	....	....	
Do	Deputy General Counsel (Ethics and Fiscal) ..	......do	CA	ES	....	....	
Do	Special Assistant to the General Counsel	Yvette K. W. Bourcicot	SC	GS	15	....	
	OFFICE OF THE LEGISLATIVE LIAISON						
Do	Principal Deputy Chief of Legislative Liaison	Career Incumbent	CA	ES	....	....	
	OFFICE OF THE CHIEF OF STAFF						
Do	Director of Management/Vice Director of the Army Staff.	......do	CA	ES	....	....	
	U.S. Army Test and Evaluation Command						
Falls Church, VA ...	Executive Technical Director/Deputy to the Commander.	......do	CA	ES	....	....	
	U.S. Army Installation Management Command						
Fort Sam Houston, TX.	Advisor, Public Works and Logistics (IMCOM).	Gregory S. Kuhr	TA	ES	....	....	09/10/14
	OFFICE OF THE DEPUTY CHIEF OF STAFF, G-1						
Aberdeen Proving Ground, MD.	Director, Civilian Human Resource Agency	Career Incumbent	CA	ES	....	....	
	OFFICE OF THE DEPUTY CHIEF OF STAFF, G-4						
Arlington, VA	Director of Program Development	Vacant	....	ES	....	....	
	OFFICE OF THE DEPUTY CHIEF OF STAFF, G-8						
Do	Deputy Director, Program Analysis and Evaluation Directorate.	Career Incumbent	CA	ES	....	....	
	Center for Army Analysis						
Fort Belvoir, VA	Director	......do	CA	ES	....	....	
Do	Technical Director	Vacant	....	ES	....	....	
	OFFICE OF THE JUDGE ADVOCATE GENERAL						
Arlington, VA	Director, Civilian Personnel, Labor and Employment Law.	Career Incumbent	CA	ES	....	....	
	UNITED STATES ARMY MATERIEL COMMAND						
	Office of the Command Counsel						
Redstone Arsenal, AL.	Command Counsel	Career Incumbent	CA	ES	....	....	
Do	Deputy Command Counsel	......do	CA	ES	....	....	
	United States Army Sustainment Command						
Rock Island, IL	Chief Counsel	......do	CA	ES	....	....	
	United States Army Communications Electronic Command						
Ft. Monmouth, NJ	Chief Counsel	......do	CA	ES	....	....	

DEPARTMENT OF DEFENSE—Continued

DEPARTMENT OF THE ARMY—Continued

Location	Position	Name of Incumbent	Type of Appt.	Pay Plan	Level, Grade, or Pay	Tenure	Expires
	United States Army Aviation and Missile Command						
Redstone Arsenal, AL.	Chief Counsel	Career Incumbent	CA	ES			
	Tank-Automotive and Armaments Command						
Warren, MI	Chief Counsel	......do	CA	ES			
	UNITED STATES ARMY CORPS OF ENGINEERS						
Washington, DC	Chief Counsel	......do	CA	ES			
Do	Deputy Chief Counsel	Vacant		ES			
Winchester, VA	Contingency Regional Business Director	Donn L. Booker	TA	ES			04/21/15
	U.S. ARMY TRAINING AND DOCTRINE COMMAND						
Fort Leonard Wood, MO.	Deputy to the Commanding General Maneuver Support/Director, Capabilities Development and Integration.	Career Incumbent	CA	ES			
	NORTH ATLANTIC TREATY ORGANIZATION						
Brussels, Belgium	Director, Defense Operations and Plans	......do	CA	ES			
Do	Administrative Advisor to the United States Ambassador to North Atlantic Treaty Organization (NATO).	......do	CA	ES			
Do	Director, Infrastructure Logistics and Civil Emergency Planning Division.	......do	CA	ES			
Do	Managing Director, Defense Armaments, Communications Electronics and Investments Division.	......do	CA	ES			
Rome, Italy	Special Advisor to NATO Defense College	Richard D. Hooker, Jr.	TA	ES			08/29/13
	UNITED STATES EUROPEAN COMMAND						
Stuttgart, Germany	J8/Deputy Director for Capabilities and Assessments.	Vacant		ES			

DEPARTMENT OF DEFENSE—Continued

DEPARTMENT OF THE NAVY

Location	Position	Name of Incumbent	Type of Appt.	Pay Plan	Level, Grade, or Pay	Tenure	Expires
	OFFICE OF THE SECRETARY						
Arlington, VA	Secretary	Raymond E. Mabus	PAS	EX	II		
Do	Principal Deputy Chief Information Officer	Career Incumbent	CA	ES			
Do	Special Assistant	Thomas P. Oppel	TA	ES			06/19/13
Do	......do	Jennifer L. Scarbrough	SC	GS	13		
Do	Special Advisor	Kate E. Brandt	SC	GS	13		
	Office of the Under Secretary of the Navy						
Do	Under Secretary	Robert O. Work	PAS	EX	III		
Washington, DC	Director, Small Business Programs	Career Incumbent	CA	ES			
Do	Deputy Under Secretary of the Navy	Robert C. Martinage	NA	ES			
Arlington, VA	Deputy Under Secretary of the Navy/Deputy Chief Management Officer.	Eric Fanning	NA	ES			
Washington, DC	Residential Manager and Social Secretary of the Vice President.	Carlos E. Elizondo	SC	GS	14		
Do	Director, Strategic Communications	Susan P. Lagana	SC	GS	15		
Arlington, VA	Special Assistant	Reema S. Shocair Ali	SC	GS	13		
Do	......do	Seamus P. Ahern	SC	GS	12		
	Office of the Assistant Secretary of Navy (Manpower and Reserve Affairs)						
Do	Assistant Secretary	Juan M. Garcia	PAS	EX	IV		
Do	Deputy Assistant Secretary (Military Manpower and Personnel).	Career Incumbent	CA	ES			
Do	Special Assistant	Veronica M. Valdez	SC	GS	13		
Do	Deputy Assistant Secretary (Reserve Affairs and Total Force Integration).	Career Incumbent	CA	ES			
	Office of the Assistant Secretary of Navy (Energy, Installations and Environment)						
Do	Assistant Secretary	Vacant	PAS	EX	IV		
Do	Deputy Assistant Secretary (Environment)	Career Incumbent	CA	ES			
Washington, DC	Deputy Assistant Secretary (Safety)	......do	CA	ES			
Arlington, VA	Principal Deputy Assistant Secretary	Roger Natsuhara	NA	ES			
Do	Special Assistant	Ryan P. Hilley	SC	GS	14		
	Office Assistant Secretary of the Navy (Research, Development and Acquisition)						
Do	Assistant Secretary of the Navy	Sean J. Stackley	PAS	EX	IV		
Do	Director, Technology Security and Cooperative Programs Directorate.	Career Incumbent	CA	ES			
Washington, DC	Deputy Assistant Secretary, Research Development and Acquisition (Expeditionary Warfare).	Brian R. Detter	NA	ES			
Arlington, VA	Deputy Assistant Secretary (Air Programs)	Career Incumbent	CA	ES			
Do	Special Assistant	David P. Gearey	SC	GS	15		
	Office of the Assistant Secretary of Navy (Financial Management and Comptroller)						
Do	Assistant Secretary	Gladys L. Commons	PAS	EX	IV		
	Office of the General Counsel						
Do	General Counsel	Paul L. Oostburg Sanz	PAS	EX	IV		
Washington, DC	Principal Deputy General Counsel	Career Incumbent	CA	ES			
Do	Associate General Counsel (Litigation) and Director, Navy Litigation Office.	......do	CA	ES			
Do	Deputy General Counsel	......do	CA	ES			
Arlington, VA	Special Assistant	Taylor N. Ferrell	SC	GS	15		
	CHIEF OF NAVAL OPERATIONS						
Do	Director, Training and Education Division	......do	CA	ES			
Arlington, VA	Deputy Director, Warfare Integration	......do	CA	ES			
Washington, DC	Director, Shore Readiness Division	Vacant		ES			
	Naval Observatory						
Do	Scientific Director	Career Incumbent	CA	ES			
	Office of the Commander, United States Pacific Command						
Camp H.M. Smith M Corp B, HI.	Director, Center of Excellence	Vacant		ES			
Do	Director, Pacific Outreach	Career Incumbent	CA	ES			
	U.S. Fleet Cyber Command / U.S. Tenth Fleet						
Fort Meade, MD	Chief Information Officer	......do	CA	ES			

DEPARTMENT OF DEFENSE—Continued

DEPARTMENT OF THE NAVY—Continued

Location	Position	Name of Incumbent	Type of Appt.	Pay Plan	Level, Grade, or Pay	Tenure	Expires
	UNITED STATES MARINE CORPS HEADQUARTERS OFFICE						
Washington, DC	Director, Plans, Policies and Operations	Career Incumbent	CA	ES	....	....	
Do	Deputy Director, Command, Control, Communication, and Computers/Deputy Chief Information Officer-Marine Corps.	Vacant	....	ES	....	....	
Quantico, VA	Assistant Deputy Commandant for Aviation (Sustainment).	......do	....	ES	....	....	
Norfolk, VA	Executive Director, Marine Forces Command	Career Incumbent	CA	ES	....	....	
	Marine Forces Pacific, Hawaii						
Hawaii, HI	Executive Director	......do	CA	ES	....	....	
	MARINE CORPS SYSTEMS COMMAND						
	Marine Corps Combat Development Command; Quantico, Virginia						
Quantico, VA	Executive Deputy, Training and Education Command.	Career Incumbent	CA	ES	....	....	
	Marine Forces Reserve, New Orleans, La						
New Orleans, LA ...	Executive Director	Vacant	....	ES	....	....	

DEPARTMENT OF EDUCATION

Location	Position	Name of Incumbent	Type of Appt.	Pay Plan	Level, Grade, or Pay	Tenure	Expires
	OFFICE OF THE SECRETARY						
Washington, DC	Secretary	Arne Duncan	PAS	EX	I		
Do	Director, International Affairs and Senior Advisor.	Career Incumbent	CA	ES			
Do	Director, Executive Secretariat	.....do	CA	ES			
Do	Senior Advisor	Jo Anderson, Jr.	NA	ES			
Do	Director, Educational Technology	Karen Elise Cator	NA	ES			
Do	Chief of Staff	Joanne S. Weiss	NA	ES			
Do	Director, Executive Management Staff	Career Incumbent	CA	ES			
Do	Special Assistant	Rayna M. Aylward	SC	GS	15		
Do	Special Assistant for College Access	Gregory M. Darnieder	SC	GS	15		
Do	Deputy Chief of Staff	Eric W. Waldo	SC	GS	15		
Do	Special Assistant	Tia D. Borders	SC	GS	14		
Do	.....do	Steven Richard Hicks	SC	GS	13		
Do	.....do	Donald Yoon Yu	SC	GS	15		
Do	Confidential Assistant	Tyler Rodgers	SC	GS	9		
Do	Executive Assistant	Maribel Duran	SC	GS	14		
Do	Deputy Chief of Staff for Operations and Strategy.	Tyra M. Newell	SC	GS	15		
Do	Confidential Assistant	Frankie A. Martinez	SC	GS	12		
Do	Confidential Assistant (Protocol)	Cathy I. Del Duca	SC	GS	11		
Do	Special Assistant	Stephen M. Midgley	SC	GS	15		
Do	Deputy White House Liaison	Margaret C. Olmos	SC	GS	14		
Do	Confidential Assistant	Samuel Salk	SC	GS	12		
Do	Special Assistant	Jon Carl O'Bergh	SC	GS	14		
Do	.....do	Hillary Anne Liepa	SC	GS	13		
Do	.....do	William O. Jawando	SC	GS	14		
Do	Confidential Assistant	Isabel L. Shelton	SC	GS	11		
Do	Director, White House Liaison	Samuel H. Myers	SC	GS	15		
Do	Special Advisor	Mary Susan Andersen	SC	GS	15		
Do	Confidential Assistant	Hannah S. Hawley	SC	GS	11		
Do	.....do	Angelica Z. Annino	SC	GS	11		
Do	Director, Strategic Partnerships	Suzanne C. Immerman	SC	GS	15		
Do	Special Assistant	Richard Culatta	SC	SL			
	Office of the Deputy Secretary						
Do	Deputy Secretary	Anthony Miller	PAS	EX	II		
Do	Director, Technical Assistance and Support	Matthew D. Gandal	NA	ES			
Do	Chief Administrative Officer	Vacant		ES			
Do	Senior Advisor for Policy and Programs	Career Incumbent	CA	ES			
Do	Senior Advisor	.....do	CA	ES			
Do	Director, Policy and Program Implementation, ISU.	Antonia Whalen	NA	ES			
Do	Confidential Assistant	Courtney Taylor Weisman	SC	GS	11		
Do	Risk Management Service	Career Incumbent	CA	ES			
Do	Special Assistant	Ajita R. Talwalker	SC	GS	14		
Do	.....do	Marisa White Bold	SC	GS	15		
Do	Confidential Assistant	Aalok Kanani	SC	GS	9		
Do	.....do	Shannon Kane Winters	SC	GS	12		
Do	Senior Advisor, Risk Management Service	Career Incumbent	CA	ES			
Do	Confidential Assistant	Joshua William Pollack	SC	GS	11		
	Office of the Under Secretary						
Do	Under Secretary	Martha Kanter	PAS	EX	III		
Do	Deputy Under Secretary	Georgia Yuan	NA	ES			
Do	Special Assistant	Michael William Robbins	SC	GS	14		
Do	.....do	Kenneth B. Bedell	SC	GS	14		
Do	Deputy Director, White House Initiative on Educational Excellence for Hispanic Americans.	Marco Antonio Davis	SC	GS	15		
Do	Executive Director, White House Initiative on Asian Americans and Pacific Islanders.	Kiran A. Ahuja	SC	GS	15		
Do	Director, White House Initiative on American Indian and Alaskan Native Education.	William Martin Mendoza	SC	GS	15		
Do	Special Assistant	John Poole Brown, Jr.	SC	GS	15		
Do	Director, White House Initiative on Educational Excellence for Hispanic Americans.	Jose A. Rico	SC	GS	15		
Do	Director, White House Initiative on Historically Black Colleges and Universities.	John Silvanus Wilson, Jr.	SC	GS	15		
Do	Director, Faith-Based and Neighborhood Partnerships.	Brenda M. Girton-Mitchell	SC	GS	15		
Do	Confidential Assistant	Tenicka Boyd	SC	GS	12		
Do	Special Assistant	Audrey Ying Buehring	SC	GS	13		
Do	.....do	Hal W. Plotkin	SC	GS	15		
Do	Confidential Assistant	Alexander David Sanchez	SC	GS	9		
Do	Chief of Staff	Alejandra O. Ceja	SC	GS	15		

DEPARTMENT OF EDUCATION—Continued

Location	Position	Name of Incumbent	Type of Appt.	Pay Plan	Level, Grade, or Pay	Tenure	Expires
	Office of the Chief Financial Officer						
Washington, DC	Chief Financial Officer	Vacant	PAS	EX	IV	....	
Do	Director, Financial Management Operations ..	Career Incumbent	CA	ES	....	....	
	Office of the Chief Information Officer						
Do	Deputy Chief Information Officer	......do	CA	ES	....	....	
Do	Director, Information Technology Services	......do	CA	ES	....	....	
Do	Director, Financial Systems Operations	......do	CA	ES	....	....	
Do	Director, Information Assurance and Chief Information Security Officer.	Vacant	....	ES	....	....	
Do	Director, Information Technology and Program Services.	Career Incumbent	CA	ES	....	....	
	Office of Management						
Do	Assistant Secretary	Vacant	PAS	EX	IV	....	
Do	Principal Deputy Assistant Secretary	Career Incumbent	CA	ES	....	....	
Do	Chief Privacy Officer	......do	CA	ES	....	....	
Do	Director, Security Services	Vacant	....	ES	....	....	
	Office of the General Counsel						
Do	General Counsel	......do	PAS	EX	IV	....	
Do	Deputy General Counsel for Ethics, Regulatory and Legislative Services.	Career Incumbent	CA	ES	....	....	
Do	Deputy General Counsel for Program Service	......do	CA	ES	....	....	
Do	Deputy General Counsel for Postsecondary and Regulatory Service.	Vacant	....	ES	....	....	
Do	Assistant General Counsel for Legislative Counsel Division.	Career Incumbent	CA	ES	....	....	
Do	Assistant General Counsel, Ethics	......do	CA	ES	....	....	
Do	Assistant General Counsel	......do	CA	ES	....	....	
Do	Special Assistant	Jay D. Chen	SC	GS	13	....	
Do	Confidential Assistant	Kyle C. Flood	SC	GS	9	....	
Do	Chief of Staff	Lauren Nicole Thompson ...	SC	GS	15	....	
Do	Special Counsel	Laura Kate Ginns	SC	GS	15	....	
Do	......do	Louis Luke Glisan	SC	GS	15	....	
Do	Senior Counsel	Julie Miceli	SC	GS	15	....	
Do	Deputy General Counsel for Accountability	Etson Franklyn Duporte	SC	GS	15	....	
	Office of Legislation and Congressional Affairs						
Do	Assistant Secretary	Gabriella Gomez	PAS	EX	IV	....	
Do	Confidential Assistant	Aketa Simmons	SC	GS	12	....	
Do	Deputy Assistant Secretary	Julius L. Horwich	SC	GS	15	....	
Do	Confidential Assistant	Kristen Liguori Adams	SC	GS	12	....	
Do	Chief of Staff	Ruthanne Louise Buck	SC	GS	15	....	
Do	Confidential Assistant	Lorenzo Antonio Rodriguez-Olvera.	SC	GS	9	....	
Do	Director, Strategic Outreach	William C. Ragland	SC	GS	13	....	
Do	Deputy Assistant Secretary	Jodie M. Fingland	SC	GS	15	....	
	Office for Civil Rights						
Do	Assistant Secretary	Russlynn Ali	PAS	EX	IV	....	
Do	Enforcement Director	Vacant	....	ES	....	....	
Do	......do	Career Incumbent	CA	ES	....	....	
Do	Deputy Assistant Secretary for Enforcement	......do	CA	ES	....	....	
Do	Principal Deputy Assistant Secretary	Vacant	....	ES	....	....	
Do	Deputy Assistant Secretary for Policy	Seth M. Galanter	NA	ES	....	....	
Do	Special Assistant	Michael G. Lamb	SC	GS	13	....	
Do	Senior Counsel	Robert Kim	SC	GS	15	....	
Do	Confidential Assistant	Andrew James Amore	SC	GS	12	....	
Do	Senior Counsel	Gabriel A. Sandoval	SC	GS	15	....	
Do	Enforcement Director	Vacant	....	ES	....	....	
Do	Senior Counsel	John K. Dipaolo	SC	GS	15	....	
	Office of Elementary and Secondary Education						
Do	Assistant Secretary	Deborah S. Delisle	PAS	EX	IV	....	
Do	Director, Student Achievement and School Accountability.	Vacant	....	ES	....	....	
Do	Deputy Assistant Secretary for Management and Planning.	Career Incumbent	CA	ES	....	....	
Do	Special Assistant	Elizabeth Grant	SC	GS	14	....	
Do	Confidential Assistant	Alexis S. Barrett	SC	GS	12	....	
Do	Special Assistant	Steven Russell Means	SC	GS	15	....	
Do	Deputy Assistant Secretary for Policy and Early Learning.	Jacqueline Jones	SC	GS	15	....	
Do	Confidential Assistant	Margarita Rivas	SC	GS	11	....	

DEPARTMENT OF EDUCATION—Continued

Location	Position	Name of Incumbent	Type of Appt.	Pay Plan	Level, Grade, or Pay	Tenure	Expires
Washington, DC	Deputy Assistant Secretary for Policy and School Turnaround.	Jason T. Snyder	SC	GS	15	....	
Do	Confidential Assistant	Michael E. Itzkowitz	SC	GS	12	....	
Do	......do	Kristen C. Harper	SC	GS	12	....	
Do	Special Assistant	Steven J. Robinson	SC	GS	14	....	
Do	Deputy Assistant Secretary for Policy and Program Coordination.	Michael Keith Yudin	SC	GS	15	....	
Do	Special Assistant	Laura Magali Jimenez	SC	GS	13	....	
	Office of English Language Acquisition, Language Enhancement, and Academic Achievement for Limited English Proficient Students						
Do	Assistant Deputy Secretary and Director, Office of English Language Acquisition.	Rosalinda B. Barrera	NA	ES	....	....	
Do	Deputy Director	Joanne H. Urrutia	SC	GS	15	....	
	Office of Postsecondary Education						
Do	Assistant Secretary	Eduardo M. Ochoa	PAS	EX	IV	....	
Do	Deputy Assistant Secretary, Policy Planning and Innovation.	Career Incumbent	CA	ES	....	....	
Do	Deputy Assistant Secretary, Higher Education Programs.	Debra Saunders-White	NA	ES	....	....	
Do	Director, State Service	Career Incumbent	CA	ES	....	....	
Do	Director, Institutional Service	......do	CA	ES	....	....	
Do	Confidential Assistant	Julie A. Heinz	SC	GS	12	....	
Do	......do	Carmine Perrotti, Jr.	SC	GS	9	....	
	Office of Special Education and Rehabilitative Services						
Do	Assistant Secretary	Alexa E. Posny	PAS	EX	IV	....	
Do	Commissioner, Rehabilitation Services Administration.	Vacant	PAS	EX	V	....	
Do	Director, Special Education Programs	Melody Musgrove	NA	ES	....	....	
Do	Deputy Director, National Institute on Disability and Rehabilitative Research.	Vacant	....	ES	....	....	
Do	Executive Administrator	Career Incumbent	CA	ES	....	....	
Do	Deputy Director, Office of Special Education Programs.	......do	CA	ES	....	....	
Do	Director, National Institute Disability Rehabilitative Research.	K. Charles Lakin	NA	ES	....	....	
Do	Deputy Commissioner, Rehabilitation Services Administration.	Career Incumbent	CA	ES	....	....	
Do	Deputy Assistant Secretary, Special Education and Rehabilitative Services.	Sue Ellen Swenson	NA	ES	....	....	
Do	Confidential Assistant	Alexis M. Perlmutter	SC	GS	11	....	
Do	Special Assistant	Vicki L. Myers	SC	GS	14	....	
	Office of Vocational and Adult Education						
Do	Assistant Secretary	Brenda Dann-Messier	PAS	EX	IV	....	
Do	Senior Advisor for Special Initiatives	Career Incumbent	CA	ES	....	....	
Do	Confidential Assistant	W. Cyrus Garrett	SC	GS	11	....	
Do	Special Assistant	Sue Yee Liu	SC	GS	14	....	
Do	Deputy Assistant Secretary, Policy and Strategic Initiatives.	Johan E. Uvin	SC	GS	15	....	
Do	Confidential Assistant	Russella L. Davis	SC	GS	9	....	
Do	Special Assistant	Adrienne E. Will	SC	GS	13	....	
	Institute of Education Sciences						
Do	Commissioner of Education Statistics	Sean P. Buckley	PAS	EX	II	....	
Do	Director	John Q. Easton	PA	EX	II	....	
Do	Associate Commissioner for Evaluation	Career Incumbent	CA	ES	....	....	
Do	Deputy Director, Administration and Policy ...	......do	CA	ES	....	....	
Do	Commissioner for Education Evaluation and Regional Assistance.	Vacant	XS	AD	....	....	
Do	Commissioner for Education Research	......do	XS	AD	....	....	
	Federal Student Aid						
Do	Chief of Staff	Career Incumbent	CA	ES	....	....	
Do	Deputy Chief Information Officer	......do	CA	ES	....	....	
Do	Director, Budget Group	......do	CA	ES	....	....	
Do	Director, Internal Review	Vacant	....	ES	....	....	
Do	Director, Policy Liaison and Implementation Staff.	Career Incumbent	CA	ES	....	....	
Do	Director, Financial Management Systems Group.	......do	CA	ES	....	....	
Do	Director, Financial Management Group	......do	CA	ES	....	....	

DEPARTMENT OF EDUCATION—Continued

Location	Position	Name of Incumbent	Type of Appt.	Pay Plan	Level, Grade, or Pay	Tenure	Expires
Washington, DC	Director, Strategic Planning and Reporting Group.	Career Incumbent	CA	ES	....	....	
Do	Deputy Chief Operating Officer	Vacant	....	ES	....	....	
	Office of Innovation and Improvement						
Do	Assistant Deputy Secretary	James H. Shelton	NA	ES	....	....	
Do	Associate Assistant Deputy Secretary for Programs.	Career Incumbent	CA	ES	....	....	
Do	Special Assistant	Nancy Poon Lue	SC	GS	15	....	
Do	Chief of Staff	Nia A. Phillips	SC	GS	15	....	
Do	Confidential Assistant	Kathleen E. Herbek	SC	GS	12	....	
Do	Associate Assistant Deputy Secretary	Nadya Chinoy Dabby	SC	GS	15	....	
Do	Director for Special Initiatives	Shivam M. Shah	SC	GS	15	....	
Do	Confidential Assistant	Alise D. Marshall	SC	GS	11	....	
Do	Special Assistant	Jefferson D. Pestronk	SC	GS	15	....	
	Office of Planning, Evaluation and Policy Development						
Do	Assistant Secretary	Carmel Martin	PAS	EX	IV	....	
Do	Deputy Assistant Secretary	Denise Michelle Forte	NA	ES	....	....	
Do	Director, Budget Service	Career Incumbent	CA	ES	....	....	
Do	Director, Cost Estimation and Analysis Division.	......do	CA	ES	....	....	
Do	Director, Special Education, Rehabilitation, and Research Analysis Division.	......do	CA	ES	....	....	
Do	Director, Policy and Program Studies Service	Vacant	....	ES	....	....	
Do	Director, Elementary, Secondary, and Vocational Analysis Division.	Career Incumbent	CA	ES	....	....	
Do	Director, Budget Execution and Administration Analysis Division.	......do	CA	ES	....	....	
Do	Director, Performance Information Management Service.	......do	CA	ES	....	....	
Do	Special Assistant	Charles Jeffrey Appel	SC	GS	15	....	
Do	......do	Heather A. Rieman	SC	GS	14	....	
Do	Confidential Assistant	Manuel Buenrostro	SC	GS	12	....	
Do	......do	Benjamin L. Miller	SC	GS	12	....	
Do	......do	Chad Michael Aldeman	SC	GS	12	....	
Do	Chief of Staff	Melanie M. Muenzer	SC	GS	15	....	
Do	Special Assistant	Sherry Orbach	SC	GS	14	....	
Do	Deputy Assistant Secretary for Planning and Policy Development.	Melanie Lyn Anderson	SC	GS	15	....	
	Office of Communications and Outreach						
Do	Assistant Secretary	Peter Cunningham	PAS	EX	IV	....	
Do	Deputy Assistant Secretary for Communication Services.	Career Incumbent	CA	ES	....	....	
Do	Confidential Assistant	Elizabeth E. Utrup	SC	GS	12	....	
Do	......do	Jacqueline Cortez Wang	SC	GS	12	....	
Do	......do	Stephanie R. Sprow	SC	GS	11	....	
Do	Press Secretary for Strategic Communications	Justin Hamilton	SC	GS	15	....	
Do	Deputy Assistant Secretary for External Affairs and Outreach Services.	Massie E. Ritsch	SC	GS	15	....	
Do	Deputy Assistant Secretary for Communication Development.	David J. Hoff	SC	GS	15	....	
Do	Special Assistant	Timothy J. Tuten	SC	GS	14	....	
Do	Deputy Press Secretary	Daren Kent Briscoe	SC	GS	15	....	
Do	Special Assistant	Cameron H. Brenchley	SC	GS	13	....	
Do	Deputy Assistant Secretary for Rural Outreach.	John L. White	SC	GS	15	....	
Do	Deputy Assistant Secretary for Intergovernmental Affairs.	Stacey E. Jordan	SC	GS	15	....	
Do	Confidential Assistant	Philip M. Martin	SC	GS	12	....	
Do	Special Assistant	Betsy A. Shelton	SC	GS	14	....	
Do	......do	Kimberly R. Morton	SC	GS	13	....	
Do	......do	David Whitman	SC	GS	15	....	
Do	Confidential Assistant	Edward L. Lee	SC	GS	11	....	

DEPARTMENT OF EDUCATION OFFICE OF THE INSPECTOR GENERAL

Location	Position	Name of Incumbent	Type of Appt.	Pay Plan	Level, Grade, or Pay	Tenure	Expires
Washington, DC	Inspector General	Kathleen S. Tighe	PAS	EX	IV	....	

DEPARTMENT OF ENERGY

Location	Position	Name of Incumbent	Type of Appt.	Pay Plan	Level, Grade, or Pay	Tenure	Expires
	OFFICE OF THE SECRETARY						
Washington, DC	Secretary	Steven Chu	PAS	EX	I		
Do	Chief of Staff	Brandon Hurlbut	NA	ES			
Do	Deputy Chief of Staff	Michael Jeff Navin	NA	ES			
Do	Senior Advisor	Lauren L. Azar	NA	ES			
Do	.....do	Richard L. Kauffman	NA	ES			
Do	Director of Public Engagement	Heidi VanGenderen	NA	ES			
Do	Advisor to the Secretary	Adam Robsohn Cohn	SC	GS	15		
Do	White House Liaison	Damian M. Bednarz	SC	GS	15		
Do	Deputy Director for Outreach and Public Engagement.	Colin S. Bishopp	SC	GS	15		
Do	.....do	Amy Bodette Demagistris ..	SC	GS	14		
Do	Special Advisor	Peter M. Ambler	SC	GS	14		
Do	Deputy White House Liaison	Rhonda Marie Carter	SC	GS	12		
Do	Special Assistant	Anthony J. Augustine III ..	SC	GS	12		
Do	Special Assistant to the Secretary	Ian H. Adams	SC	GS	11		
Do	Special Assistant	Teryn Norris-Hale	SC	GS	10		
Do	Special Assistant to the Secretary	Mark C. Appleton	SC	GS	9		
Do	Special Assistant	Christiana Q. James	SC	GS	8		
	OFFICE OF THE DEPUTY SECRETARY						
Do	Deputy Secretary of Energy	Daniel B. Poneman	PAS	EX	II		
Do	Associate Deputy Secretary	Melvin G. Williams, Jr.	NA	ES			
Do	Senior Performance Advisor	David Sterling Brown	TA	ES			07/06/13
Do	Capital Asset Program Manager	Career Incumbent	CA	ES			
Do	Senior Advisor	Jonathan M. Levy	SC	GS	15		
Do	Special Assistant	Natalie Mathews Randolph	SC	GS	12		
Do	.....do	Elizabeth N. Emanuel	SC	GS	9		
	OFFICE OF THE UNDER SECRETARY						
Do	Under Secretary	Vacant	PAS	EX	III		
Do	Senior Advisor	Udai Rohatgi	SC	GS	13		
Do	Special Assistant	Emily A. Fritze	SC	GS	7		
	OFFICE OF THE UNDER SECRETARY FOR NUCLEAR SECURITY						
Do	Under Secretary, Nuclear Security/Administrator for Nuclear Security.	Thomas P. D'Agostino	PAS	EX	IV		
	OFFICE OF THE UNDER SECRETARY FOR SCIENCE						
Do	Under Secretary	Vacant	PAS	EX	IV		
Do	Associate Under Secretary	.....do		ES			
	NATIONAL NUCLEAR SECURITY ADMINISTRATION						
Do	Under Secretary for Nuclear Security/Administrator for Nuclear Security.	Thomas P. D'Agostino	PAS	EX	IV		
	Immediate Office of the Administrator						
Do	Principal Deputy Administrator for National Nuclear Security.	Neile Miller Lutze	PAS	EX	IV		
Do	Associate Principal Deputy Administrator/Associate Administrator for Infrastructure and Operations.	Career Incumbent	CA	ES			
Do	Chief of Staff	Vacant		ES			
Do	Chief Scientist	Career Incumbent	CA	ES			
Do	Senior Policy Advisor	.....do	CA	ES			
Do	Senior Advisor	.....do	CA	ES			
Do	Senior Advisor (National Security Council)	.....do	CA	ES			
Arlington, VA	Senior Advisor	.....do	CA	ES			
Washington, DC	.....do	.....do	CA	ES			
Do	.....do	.....do	CA	ES			
Do	Program Executive Officer for Asset Revitalization.	Vacant		ES			
Livermore, CA	Advisor to the Associate Principal Deputy Administrator Program/Field Integration.	.....do		ES			
Washington, DC	Senior Policy Advisor	.....do		ES			
Do	Special Assistant	Paul J. Frey	SC	GS	11		
	Office of Defense Programs						
Do	Deputy Administrator for Defense Programs	Donald L. Cook	PAS	EX	IV		
Do	Director of Interagency Work Programs	Career Incumbent	CA	ES			
Do	Sites Chief Performance Officer	.....do	CA	ES			
Do	Assistant Deputy Administrator for Stockpile Stewardship.	.....do	CA	ES			
Do	Assistant Deputy Administrator for Stockpile Management.	.....do	CA	ES			

DEPARTMENT OF ENERGY—Continued

Location	Position	Name of Incumbent	Type of Appt.	Pay Plan	Level, Grade, or Pay	Tenure	Expires
Washington, DC	Deputy Assistant Deputy Administrator for Stockpile Management.	Career Incumbent	CA	ES	....	....	
Do	Deputy Administrator for Military Applications and Stockpile Operations.	Vacant		ES	....	....	
Albuquerque, NM ..	Deputy Assistant Deputy Administrator for Stockpile Management.	Career Incumbent	CA	ES	....	....	
Washington, DC	Director, Office of Nuclear Weapons Stockpile	......do	CA	ES	....	....	
Do	Deputy Assistant Deputy Administrator for Program Integration.	......do	CA	ES	....	....	
Albuquerque, NM ..	Assistant Deputy Administrator for Secure Transportation.	......do	CA	ES	....	....	
Washington, DC	Principal Deputy Assistant Deputy Administrator for Secure Transportation.	Vacant		ES	....	....	
Do	Assistant Deputy Administrator for Infrastructure and Construction.	Career Incumbent	CA	ES	....	....	
Do	Deputy Assistant Deputy Administrator for Infrastructure and Construction.	......do	CA	ES	....	....	
Albuquerque, NM ..	Senior Technical Advisor	......do	CA	ES	....	....	
Washington, DC	Assistant Deputy Administrator for Nuclear Safety, Nuclear Operations and Governance Reform.	......do	CA	ES	....	....	
Germantown, MD ..	Director of Environmental Operations	......do	CA	ES	....	....	
Kansas City, MO ...	Manager, Kansas City Site Office	......do	CA	ES	....	....	
Los Alamos, NM	Manager, Los Alamos Site Office	......do	CA	ES	....	....	
Do	Deputy Manager, Los Alamos Site Office	......do	CA	ES	....	....	
Las Vegas, NV	Deputy Manager, Nevada Site Office	......do	CA	ES	....	....	
Albuquerque, NM ..	Los Alamos Site Office Revitalization Manager.	Vacant		ES	....	....	
Amarillo, TX	Manager, Pantex Site Office	Career Incumbent	CA	ES	....	....	
Do	Deputy Manager, Pantex Site Office	Vacant		ES	....	....	
Oak Ridge, TN	Manager, Y-12 Site Office	......do		ES	....	....	
Do	Deputy Manager, Y-12 Site Office	Career Incumbent	CA	ES	....	....	
Albuquerque, NM ..	Deputy Manager, Sandia Site Office	Vacant		ES	....	....	
Do	Deputy Manager, Base Operations	Career Incumbent	CA	ES	....	....	
Aiken, SC	Deputy Manager, Savannah River Site Office	......do	CA	ES	....	....	
	Office of Defense Nuclear Nonproliferation						
Washington, DC	Deputy Administrator	Anne Harrington	PAS	EX	IV	....	
Do	Principal Assistant Deputy Administrator	Career Incumbent	CA	ES	....	....	
Do	Chief Operations Officer	......do	CA	ES	....	....	
Do	Assistant Deputy Administrator for Global Threat Reduction.	......do	CA	ES	....	....	
Do	Associate Assistant Deputy Administrator for Global Threat Reduction.	......do	CA	ES	....	....	
Do	Assistant Deputy Administrator for Nonproliferation Research and Development.	......do	CA	ES	....	....	
Do	Associate Assistant Administrator for Nonproliferation Research and Development.	Vacant		ES	....	....	
Do	Assistant Deputy Administrator for Nonproliferation and International Security.	Career Incumbent	CA	ES	....	....	
Do	Associate Assistant Deputy Administrator for Nonproliferation and International Security.	......do	CA	ES	....	....	
Do	Associate Assistant Deputy Administrator for International Materials Protection and Cooperation.	......do	CA	ES	....	....	
Do	Director, Office of the Second Line of Defense	......do	CA	ES	....	....	
Do	Assistant Deputy Administrator for Fissile Material Disposition.	......do	CA	ES	....	....	
Do	Associate Assistant Deputy Administrator for Fissile Materials Disposition.	......do	CA	ES	....	....	
Aiken, SC	Senior Program Advisor	......do	CA	ES	....	....	
Washington, DC	Executive Director (Beijing)	......do	CA	ES	....	....	
Do	Chief Science and Technology Officer	......do	CA	ES	....	....	
Do	Assistant Deputy Administrator for International Materials Protection and Cooperation.	Vacant		ES	....	....	
	Office of Naval Reactors						
Do	Director, Management and Administration	Career Incumbent	CA	ES	....	....	
Do	Program Manager for Future Carrier Nuclear Propulsion.	Vacant		ES	....	....	
Do	Director, Nuclear Technology Division	Career Incumbent	CA	ES	....	....	
Do	Program Manager, Shipyard Matters	......do	CA	ES	....	....	
Do	Director, Reactor Engineering Division	......do	CA	ES	....	....	
West Mifflin, PA	Assistant Manager for Operations	......do	CA	ES	....	....	

DEPARTMENT OF ENERGY—Continued

Location	Position	Name of Incumbent	Type of Appt.	Pay Plan	Level, Grade, or Pay	Tenure	Expires
Washington, DC	Program Manager, Prototype and Moored Training Ship Operations and Inactivation Program.	Career Incumbent	CA	ES	....	....	
Newport News, VA	Senior Naval Reactors Representative (Newport News, VA).	......do	CA	ES	....	....	
Washington, DC	Program Manager, Advanced Submarines and Facilities.	Vacant		ES	....	....	
Do	Deputy Director, Instrumentation and Control Division.	Career Incumbent	CA	ES	....	....	
Do	Deputy Director, Advanced Submarine Systems Division.	......do	CA	ES	....	....	
United Kingdom	Senior Naval Reactors Representative (United Kingdom).	......do	CA	ES	....	....	
Pittsburgh, PA	Deputy Manager, Naval Reactors Laboratory Field Office.	......do	CA	ES	....	....	
Washington, DC	Program Manager, New Ship Design	......do	CA	ES	....	....	
Do	Director, Information Technology Management.	......do	CA	ES	....	....	
Schenectady, NY ...	Assistant Manager for Operations	......do	CA	ES	....	....	
Washington, DC	Director, Finance and Budget	......do	CA	ES	....	....	
Do	Director, Acquisition Division	Vacant		ES	....	....	
Do	Deputy Program Manager, Virginia Class Submarines.	Career Incumbent	CA	ES	....	....	
Do	Director, Commissioned Submarine Systems Division.	......do	CA	ES	....	....	
	Office of Emergency Operations						
Do	Associate Administrator	......do	CA	ES	....	....	
Do	Deputy Administrator	......do	CA	ES	....	....	
Do	Director, Office of Emergency Response	......do	CA	ES	....	....	
Albuquerque, NM ..	Director, Render Safe Program	......do	CA	ES	....	....	
	Office of Defense Nuclear Security						
Washington, DC	Chief and Associate Administrator	......do	CA	ES	....	....	
Do	Deputy Associate Administrator	......do	CA	ES	....	....	
Do	Director, Office of Field Support	......do	CA	ES	....	....	
Do	Director, Office of Security Operations and Performance Assurance.	......do	CA	ES	....	....	
	Office of Counterterrorism and Counterproliferation						
Do	Deputy Under Secretary	......do	CA	ES	....	....	
Do	Senior Advisor	......do	CA	ES	....	....	
Do	Assistant Deputy Under Secretary	Vacant		ES	....	....	
Do	Deputy Associate Administrator	......do		ES	....	....	
	Management and Budget						
Do	Associate Administrator	Career Incumbent	CA	ES	....	....	
Do	Director, Office of Financial Management	......do	CA	ES	....	....	
Germantown, MD ..	Deputy Director, Office of Financial Management.	......do	CA	ES	....	....	
Washington, DC	Deputy Director of Planning, Programming, Budgeting and Evaluation.	Vacant		ES	....	....	
Do	Director, Office of Human Capital Management.	Career Incumbent	CA	ES	....	....	
Do	Director, Office of Business Operations	......do	CA	ES	....	....	
Do	Director, Office of Performance and Analysis	......do	CA	ES	....	....	
Do	Director, Office of Management	Vacant		ES	....	....	
Do	Diversity and Outreach Manager	Career Incumbent	CA	ES	....	....	
	External Affairs						
Do	Associate Administrator	Clarence T. Bishop	NA	ES	....	....	
Do	Deputy Associate Administrator	Career Incumbent	CA	ES	....	....	
Do	Director of Congressional Affairs	Jed D. D' Ercole	SC	GS	15	....	
Do	Director of Public Affairs	Joshua T. McConaha	SC	GS	14	....	
Do	Congressional Affairs Specialist	Katherine A. Croft	SC	GS	13	....	
Do	Senior Advisor	Matthew T. Bowen	SC	GS	13	....	
Do	Congressional Affairs Specialist	Derrick D. Ramos	SC	GS	12	....	
Do	Deputy Press Secretary	Courtney L. Greenwald	SC	GS	11	....	
Do	Communications Coordinator	Robert D. Middaugh	SC	GS	9	....	
	General Counsel						
Do	General Counsel	Career Incumbent	CA	ES	....	....	
Do	Deputy General Counsel for Procurement	......do	CA	ES	....	....	
Albuquerque, NM ..	Chief Counsel	......do	CA	ES	....	....	
	Acquisition and Project Management						
Washington, DC	Associate Administrator	......do	CA	ES	....	....	
Do	Deputy Associate Administrator	......do	CA	ES	....	....	

DEPARTMENT OF ENERGY—Continued

Location	Position	Name of Incumbent	Type of Appt.	Pay Plan	Level, Grade, or Pay	Tenure	Expires
Washington, DC	Deputy Director, Office of Acquisition and Supply Management.	Career Incumbent	CA	ES	....	....	
Albuquerque, NM ..	Associate Director for Business Services	......do	CA	ES	....	....	
Washington, DC	Director, Office of Enterprise Project Management.	......do	CA	ES	....	....	
Do	Federal Project Director	......do	CA	ES	....	....	
Do	Mox Federal Project Director	......do	CA	ES	....	....	
	Information Management and Chief Information Officer						
Do	Associate Administrator	......do	CA	ES	....	....	
Do	Deputy Associate Administrator	......do	CA	ES	....	....	
	Safety and Health						
Do	Associate Administrator for Safety and Health.	......do	CA	ES	....	....	
Do	Chief, Defense Nuclear Safety	Vacant		ES	....	....	
	OFFICE OF SCIENCE						
Do	Director	William F. Brinkman	PAS	EX	IV	....	
Do	Principal Deputy Director	Vacant		ES	....	....	
Upton, NY	Site Office Manager, Brookhaven	Career Incumbent	CA	ES	....	....	
Argonne, IL	Site Office Manager, Argonne	......do	CA	ES	....	....	
Germantown, MD ..	Associate Director for Biological and Environmental Research.	......do	CA	ES	....	....	
Do	Director Office of Scientific and Technology Information.	......do	CA	ES	....	....	
Do	Associate Director, Office of High Energy Physics.	Vacant		ES	....	....	
Do	Associate Director, Office of Nuclear Physics	Career Incumbent	CA	ES	....	....	
Do	Director, Scientific User Facilities Division	Vacant		ES	....	....	
Berkeley, CA	Site Office Manager, Berkeley	Career Incumbent	CA	ES	....	....	
Stanford, CA	Site Office Manager, Stanford	Vacant		ES	....	....	
Plainsboro, NJ	Site Office Manager, Princeton	Career Incumbent	CA	ES	....	....	
Germantown, MD ..	Associate Director, Office of Advanced Scientific Computing Research.	......do	CA	ES	....	....	
Do	Director, Facilities and Project Management Division.	......do	CA	ES	....	....	
Do	Director, Physics Research Division	Vacant		ES	....	....	
Do	Director, Chemical Sciences, Geosciences, and Biosciences Division.	Career Incumbent	CA	ES	....	....	
Do	Director, Office of Project Assessment	......do	CA	ES	....	....	
Washington, DC	Associate Director, Office of Laboratory Policy and Evaluation.	......do	CA	ES	....	....	
Do	Director, Office of Workforce Development for Teachers and Scientists.	Vacant		ES	....	....	
Germantown, MD ..	Associate Director, Office of Safety, Security and Infrastructure.	Career Incumbent	CA	ES	....	....	
Do	Director, High Energy Research and Technology Division.	......do	CA	ES	....	....	
Do	Director, Office of Budget	Vacant		ES	....	....	
Washington, DC	Deputy Director for Science Programs	Career Incumbent	CA	ES	....	....	
Do	Deputy Director for Resource Management	......do	CA	ES	....	....	
Germantown, MD ..	Associate Director, Office of Basic Energy Sciences.	......do	CA	ES	....	....	
Do	Director, Biological Systems Science Division	......do	CA	ES	....	....	
Do	Director, Facilities Division	......do	CA	ES	....	....	
Do	Director, Research Division	......do	CA	ES	....	....	
Do	Associate Director, Office of Fusion Energy Sciences.	......do	CA	ES	....	....	
Do	Director, Material Sciences and Engineering Division.	......do	CA	ES	....	....	
Do	Director, Climate and Environmental Sciences Division.	......do	CA	ES	....	....	
Do	Associate Deputy Director for Field Operations.	......do	CA	ES	....	....	
Argonne, IL	Deputy Manager Chicago Office	......do	CA	ES	....	....	
Do	Assistant Manager, Office of Acquisition and Assistance.	......do	CA	ES	....	....	
Oak Ridge, TN	Chief Financial Officer	......do	CA	ES	....	....	
Warrenville, IL	Site Manager Fermi	......do	CA	ES	....	....	
Washington, DC	Special Assistant	Marcos Huerta	SC	GS	12	....	
	Chicago Office						
Argonne, IL	Manager	Career Incumbent	CA	ES	....	....	
Do	Chief Financial Officer	Vacant		ES	....	....	
Do	Chief Counsel	Career Incumbent	CA	ES	....	....	
Chicago, IL	Chief Operations Officer	Vacant		ES	....	....	

DEPARTMENT OF ENERGY—Continued

Location	Position	Name of Incumbent	Type of Appt.	Pay Plan	Level, Grade, or Pay	Tenure	Expires
	Oak Ridge Office						
Oak Ridge, TN	Manager	Vacant	....	ES	....	....	
Do	Deputy Manager	......do	....	ES	....	....	
Do	Assistant Manager for Environment Safety and Health.	Career Incumbent	CA	ES	....	....	
Do	Assistant Manager for Environmental Management.	Vacant	....	ES	....	....	
Do	Assistant Manager for Nuclear Fuel Supply ..	......do	....	ES	....	....	
Newport News, VA	Site Manager, Thomas Jefferson National Accelerator Facility.	Career Incumbent	CA	ES	....	....	
Oak Ridge, TN	Assistant Manager for Science	......do	CA	ES	....	....	
	ASSISTANT SECRETARY FOR CONGRESSIONAL AND INTERGOVERNMENTAL AFFAIRS						
Washington, DC ...	Assistant Secretary	Jeffrey A. Lane	PAS	EX	IV	....	
Do	Principal Deputy Assistant Secretary	Bradley R. Crowell	NA	ES	....	....	
Do	Deputy Assistant Secretary for Intergovernmental and External Affairs.	Clyde H. Henderson III	NA	ES	....	....	
Do	Chief Operations Officer	Career Incumbent	CA	ES	....	....	
Do	Legislative Policy Advisor	Hannah C. Irsfeld	SC	GS	15	....	
Do	Director for Tribal and Intergovernmental Affairs.	David F. Conrad	SC	GS	15	....	
Do	Deputy Assistant Secretary for Congressional Affairs.	Christopher E. Davis	SC	GS	15	....	
Do	Intergovernmental Affairs Advisor	Esther F. Morales	SC	GS	14	....	
Do	Legislative Affairs Specialist	James V. Secreto	SC	GS	13	....	
Do	.....do	Clarence K. Tong	SC	GS	13	....	
Do	Special Assistant	Ali A. Zaidi	SC	GS	11	....	
	ASSISTANT SECRETARY FOR ELECTRICITY DELIVERY AND ENERGY RELIABILITY						
Do	Assistant Secretary	Patricia Hoffman	PAS	EX	IV	....	
Do	Deputy Assistant Secretary for Research and Development.	Career Incumbent	CA	ES	....	....	
Do	Deputy Assistant Secretary for Permitting Siting and Analysis.	......do	CA	ES	....	....	
Do	Deputy Assistant Secretary	......do	CA	ES	....	....	
Do	Chief Operating Officer	......do	CA	ES	....	....	
Do	Deputy Director	Vacant	....	ES	....	....	
Do	Senior Technical Advisor	Career Incumbent	CA	ES	....	....	
Do	Senior Advisor	Michelle Dallafior	SC	GS	15	....	
Do	Special Assistant	Titilayo Ogunyale	SC	GS	13	....	
	ASSISTANT SECRETARY FOR ENERGY EFFICIENCY AND RENEWABLE ENERGY						
Do	Assistant Secretary	David T. Danielson	PAS	EX	IV	....	
Do	Principal Deputy Assistant Secretary	Michael S. Carr	NA	ES	....	....	
Do	Senior Advisor	Henry C. Kelly	NA	ES	....	....	
Do	Program Manager Office of Geothermal Technologies.	Career Incumbent	CA	ES	....	....	
Do	Director, Office of Information and Business Management Systems.	......do	CA	ES	....	....	
Do	Director, Office of Program Execution Support.	Vacant	....	ES	....	....	
Do	Program Manager, Office of Solar Energy Technology.	......do	....	ES	....	....	
Do	Program Manager Office of Building Technologies Program.	......do	....	ES	....	....	
Do	Program Manager Office of Vehicle Technology Program.	Career Incumbent	CA	ES	....	....	
Do	Deputy Assistant Secretary for Renewable Energy.	......do	CA	ES	....	....	
Do	Deputy Assistant Secretary for Energy Efficiency.	......do	CA	ES	....	....	
Do	Director, Field Performance Management	......do	CA	ES	....	....	
Do	Program Manager	......do	CA	ES	....	....	
Do	Deputy Assistant Secretary for Business Administration.	......do	CA	ES	....	....	
Do	Senior Advisor	......do	CA	ES	....	....	
Do	Senior Advisor for Research Policy	......do	CA	ES	....	....	
Do	Program Manager for Biomass	Vacant	....	ES	....	....	
Do	Program Manager for the Fuel Cell Technologies.	......do	....	ES	....	....	

DEPARTMENT OF ENERGY—Continued

Location	Position	Name of Incumbent	Type of Appt.	Pay Plan	Level, Grade, or Pay	Tenure	Expires
Washington, DC	Program Manager for Fuel Cell Technologies Program.	Career Incumbent	CA	ES	....	....	
Do	Senior Advisor	......do	CA	ES	....	....	
Do	Program Manager Office of Federal Energy Management Programs.	......do	CA	ES	....	....	
Do	Deputy Program Manager, Office of Solar Energy Technologies.	......do	CA	ES	....	....	
Golden, CO	Manager, Golden Field Office	......do	CA	ES	....	....	
Do	Deputy Manager, Golden Field Office	Vacant		ES	....	....	
Washington, DC	Director, Office of Planning, Budget and Analysis.	Career Incumbent	CA	ES	....	....	
Do	Senior Advisor	Jason Walsh	SC	GS	15	....	
Do	Special Projects Director	Rachel Tronstein	SC	GS	14	....	
Do	Senior Advisor	Peter Gage	SC	GS	14	....	
Do	Special Assistant	Adriana K. Costello-Dougherty.	SC	GS	9	....	
	ASSISTANT SECRETARY FOR ENVIRONMENTAL MANAGEMENT						
Do	Assistant Secretary	Vacant	PAS	EX	IV	....	
Do	Principal Deputy Assistant Secretary	Career Incumbent	CA	ES	....	....	
Do	Director of External Affairs	Paul E. Seidler	NA	ES	....	....	
Do	Associate Principal Deputy Assistant Secretary.	Career Incumbent	CA	ES	....	....	
Do	Director, Office of Procurement Planning	Vacant		ES	....	....	
Do	Director, Office of Budget	......do		ES	....	....	
Do	Deputy Assistant Secretary, Acquisition and Project Management.	Career Incumbent	CA	ES	....	....	
Germantown, MD ..	Director, Office of Strategic Planning and Analysis.	......do	CA	ES	....	....	
Washington, DC	Director, Office of Ground Water and Soil Remediation.	......do	CA	ES	....	....	
Germantown, MD ..	Director, Office of Operations Oversight	......do	CA	ES	....	....	
Washington, DC	Deputy Assistant Secretary, Program Planning and Budget.	......do	CA	ES	....	....	
Do	Director, Office of Safeguards and Security/ Emergency Preparedness.	......do	CA	ES	....	....	
Germantown, MD ..	Director, Office of Packaging and Transportation.	......do	CA	ES	....	....	
Washington, DC	Director, Office of Corporate Information and Services.	......do	CA	ES	....	....	
Germantown, MD ..	Deputy Assistant Secretary, Tank Waste Nuclear Material.	......do	CA	ES	....	....	
Washington, DC	Deputy Assistant Secretary for Human Capital and Corporation Services.	......do	CA	ES	....	....	
Do	Senior Advisor	......do	CA	ES	....	....	
Do	Associate Deputy Assistant Secretary, Human Capital and Corporate Services.	......do	CA	ES	....	....	
Germantown, MD ..	Associate Deputy Assistant Secretary, Waste Management.	......do	CA	ES	....	....	
Washington, DC	Director, Office of Human Capital	......do	CA	ES	....	....	
Do	Senior Advisor	......do	CA	ES	....	....	
Do	Director, Office of Procurement Planning	......do	CA	ES	....	....	
Do	Deputy Assistant Secretary, Site Restoration	......do	CA	ES	....	....	
Germantown, MD ..	Associate Deputy Assistant Secretary, Site Restoration.	......do	CA	ES	....	....	
Washington, DC	Deputy Assistant Secretary, Waste Management.	......do	CA	ES	....	....	
Germantown, MD ..	Director, Office of Environmental Compliance	......do	CA	ES	....	....	
Aiken, SC	Assistant Manager, Waste Disposition Project	......do	CA	ES	....	....	
Washington, DC	Director, Management Systems and Analysis	......do	CA	ES	....	....	
Do	Communications Specialist	Mekell T. Mikell	SC	GS	12	....	
	Environmental Management Consolidated Business Center						
Cincinnati, OH	Director	Career Incumbent	CA	ES	....	....	
Do	Deputy Director	......do	CA	ES	....	....	
Do	Chief Counsel	......do	CA	ES	....	....	
Do	Program Manager	......do	CA	ES	....	....	
	Portsmouth/Paducah Project Office						
Lexington, KY	Manager	......do	CA	ES	....	....	
Do	Deputy Manager	......do	CA	ES	....	....	
	Richland Operations Office						
Richland, WA	Manager	......do	CA	ES	....	....	
Do	Deputy Manager	......do	CA	ES	....	....	
Seattle, WA	Assistant Manager, Mission Support	......do	CA	ES	....		

DEPARTMENT OF ENERGY—Continued

Location	Position	Name of Incumbent	Type of Appt.	Pay Plan	Level, Grade, or Pay	Tenure	Expires
Richland, WA	Assistant Manager, Tank Farms	Career Incumbent	CA	ES			
Do	Chief Counsel	......do	CA	ES			
Do	Assistant Manager, Waste Treatment and Immobilization Plant, ORP.	Vacant		ES			
Do	Assistant Manager, Safety and Environment	Career Incumbent	CA	ES			
Do	Deputy Manager, Office of River Protection	......do	CA	ES			
Do	Manager Office of River Protection	......do	CA	ES			
Do	Manager, WTP Start-Up and Commissioning Integration.	......do	CA	ES			
Do	Assistant Manager, Business and Financial Operations (Chief Financial Officer).	......do	CA	ES			
Do	Assistant Manager, River and Plateau	......do	CA	ES			
Do	Assistant Manager, Technical and Regulatory Support.	......do	CA	ES			
	Savannah River Operations Office						
Aiken, SC	Manager	Vacant		ES			
Do	Deputy Manager	Career Incumbent	CA	ES			
Do	Chief Counsel	Vacant		ES			
Do	Assistant Manager, Nuclear Material Stabilization Project.	Career Incumbent	CA	ES			
Do	Assistant Manager, Infrastructure and Environmental Stewardship.	......do	CA	ES			
Do	Director, Salt Waste Processing Facility Project Office.	Vacant		ES			
Do	Assistant Manager, Integration and Planning	......do		ES			
Do	Assistant Manager, Mission Support	Career Incumbent	CA	ES			
	ASSISTANT SECRETARY FOR FOSSIL ENERGY						
Washington, DC	Assistant Secretary	Charles D. McConnell	PAS	EX	IV		
Pittsburgh, PA	Principal Deputy Assistant Secretary	Career Incumbent	CA	ES			
Washington, DC	Deputy Assistant Secretary, Clean Coal	James F. Wood	NA	ES			
Do	Deputy Assistant Secretary, Oil and Natural Gas.	Christopher A. Smith	NA	ES			
New Orleans, LA	Project Manager, Strategic Petroleum Reserve.	Career Incumbent	CA	ES			
Germantown, MD	Senior Financial and Procurement Director	......do	CA	ES			
Morgantown, WV	Director, Institutional and Business Operations.	......do	CA	ES			
Albany, OR	Director, Research and Development	......do	CA	ES			
Washington, DC	Senior Policy Advisor	Vacant		ES			
Bruceton, PA	Deputy Director	......do		ES			
Washington, DC	Deputy Assistant Secretary, Petroleum Reserves.	Career Incumbent	CA	ES			
Do	Deputy Assistant Secretary, International Affairs.	......do	CA	ES			
Bruceton, PA	Director National Energy Technology Laboratory.	......do	CA	ES			
Morgantown, WV	Chief Operating Officer	......do	CA	ES			
Do	Director, Project Management Center	......do	CA	ES			
Washington, DC	Director, Oil and Gas Global Security and Supply.	......do	CA	ES			
Bruceton, PA	Chief Counsel	......do	CA	ES			
Washington, DC	Director, Clean Energy Systems	......do	CA	ES			
Do	Product-Line Director for Natural Gas and Petroleum-Upstream Technology.	......do	CA	ES			
Do	Senior Advisor	John E. Richards	SC	GS	15		
Do	Advisor	Robert Fee	SC	GS	10		
	ASSISTANT SECRETARY FOR NUCLEAR ENERGY						
Do	Assistant Secretary	Peter B. Lyons	PAS	EX	IV		
Do	Deputy Assistant Secretary	Career Incumbent	CA	ES			
Do	Senior Policy Advisor	Vacant		ES			
Germantown, MD	Associate Director, Isotope Production and Distribution.	......do		ES			
Washington, DC	Associate Director	......do		ES			
Do	Deputy Assistant Secretary for Corporate Business Operations.	......do		ES			
Do	Director, Office of Corporate and Global Partnership Development.	......do		ES			
Do	Chief Operating Officer	Career Incumbent	CA	ES			
Germantown, MD	Director, Office of Facilities Management	......do	CA	ES			
Do	Deputy Director, Office of Advanced Reactor Concepts.	......do	CA	ES			

DEPARTMENT OF ENERGY—Continued

Location	Position	Name of Incumbent	Type of Appt.	Pay Plan	Level, Grade, or Pay	Tenure	Expires
Germantown, MD ..	Director, Office of Space and Defense Power Systems.	Career Incumbent	CA	ES	....	....	
Washington, DC	Director Off of Used Nuclear Fuel Disposition Research and Development.	......do	CA	ES	....	....	
Germantown, MD ..	Director, Integrated Safety and Program Assurance.	......do	CA	ES	....	....	
Do	Director, Office of Light Water Reactor Deployment.	......do	CA	ES	....	....	
Do	Associate Deputy Assistant Secretary, Nuclear Reactor Technology.	......do	CA	ES	....	....	
Do	Director, Office of Gas Cooled Reactor Technologies.	......do	CA	ES	....	....	
Do	Deputy Assistant Secretary, Nuclear Facility Operations.	......do	CA	ES	....	....	
Washington, DC	Deputy Assistant Secretary, International Nuclear Energy Policy and Coop.	......do	CA	ES	....	....	
Germantown, MD ..	Associate Deputy Assistant Secretary, Fuel Cycle Technology.	......do	CA	ES	....	....	
Washington, DC	Associate Deputy Assistant Secretary, International Nuclear Energy Policy and Co-operation.	......do	CA	ES	....	....	
Do	Deputy Assistant Secretary, Nuclear Reactor Technologies.	Vacant	....	ES	....	....	
Do	Special Assistant	Elizabeth F. Ramsay	SC	GS	12	....	
	Idaho Operations Office						
Idaho Falls, ID	Manager	Career Incumbent	CA	ES	....	....	
Do	Deputy Manager	Vacant	....	ES	....	....	
Do	Deputy Manager, Nuclear Energy	Career Incumbent	CA	ES	....	....	
Do	Deputy Assistant Manager, Operations	......do	CA	ES	....	....	
Do	Deputy Manager, Idaho Cleanup Project	......do	CA	ES	....	....	
Do	Assistant Manager, Chief Financial and Administrative Office.	......do	CA	ES	....	....	
Do	Assistant Manager, Technical Support	......do	CA	ES	....	....	
Do	Assistant Manager, Research and Development.	Vacant	....	ES	....	....	
Do	......do	......do		ES	....	....	
Do	Chief Counsel	......do	....	ES	....	....	
Do	......do	......do	....	ES	....	....	
	ASSISTANT SECRETARY FOR POLICY AND INTERNATIONAL AFFAIRS						
Washington, DC	Assistant Secretary	David Sandalow	PAS	EX	IV	....	
Do	Principal Deputy Assistant Secretary	Jonathan Harold Elkind	NA	ES	....	....	
Do	Deputy Assistant Secretary, Office of Climate Change Policy and Technology.	Richard D. Duke, Jr.	NA	ES	....	....	
Do	Director, Office of African and Middle Eastern Affairs.	Career Incumbent	CA	ES	....	....	
Do	Deputy Assistant Secretary for Policy Analysis.	......do	CA	ES	....	....	
Do	Director, Office of European and Asian Affairs.	Vacant	....	ES	....	....	
Do	Director, Office of American Affairs	Career Incumbent	CA	ES	....	....	
Do	Deputy Director, Office of Climate Change Policy and Technology.	......do	CA	ES	....	....	
Do	Deputy Assistant Secretary for Asia, Europe and the Americas.	......do	CA	ES	....	....	
Do	Director Office of European and Asian Pacific Affairs.	......do	CA	ES	....	....	
Do	Director, Office of East Asian Affairs	......do	CA	ES	....	....	
Do	Deputy Assistant Secretary for Middle East, Africa and Eurasia.	......do	CA	ES	....	....	
Do	Senior Policy Advisor	Leslie Holmes Hummel	SC	GS	14	....	
Do	Special Assistant	Udoaku C. Ihenetu	SC	GS	11	....	
Do	......do	Desiree E. Pipkins	SC	GS	11	....	
Do	......do	James R. Covey	SC	GS	9	....	
	OFFICE OF ECONOMIC IMPACT AND DIVERSITY						
Do	Director, Office of Minority Economic Impact	Ladoris G. Harris	PAS	EX	IV	....	
Do	Principal Deputy Director	Career Incumbent	CA	ES	....	....	
Do	Director, Office of the Ombudsman	......do	CA	ES	....	....	
Do	Deputy Director	......do	CA	ES	....	....	
Do	Special Assistant	Saba D. Abebe	SC	GS	11	....	
	OFFICE OF GENERAL COUNSEL						
Do	General Counsel	Gregory H. Woods	PAS	EX	IV	....	
Do	Deputy General Counsel	Career Incumbent	CA	ES	....	....	

DEPARTMENT OF ENERGY—Continued

Location	Position	Name of Incumbent	Type of Appt.	Pay Plan	Level, Grade, or Pay	Tenure	Expires
Washington, DC	Deputy General Counsel for Environment and Nuclear Programs.	Priya R. Aiyar	NA	ES	....	....	
Do	Deputy General Counsel for Litigation	Timothy G. Lynch	NA	ES	....	....	
Do	Deputy General Counsel, Technology Transfer and Procurement.	Career Incumbent	CA	ES	....	....	
Do	Assistant General Counsel, Federal Litigation	......do	CA	ES	....	....	
Do	Assistant General Counsel, Regulatory Interventions.	Vacant	....	ES	....	....	
Do	Assistant General Counsel, Energy Efficiency	......do	....	ES	....	....	
Do	Assistant General Counsel, Civilian Nuclear Program.	Career Incumbent	CA	ES	....	....	
Do	Assistant General Counsel, International and National Security Programs.	Vacant	....	ES	....	....	
Do	Director, Office of National Environmental Policy Act (NEPA) Policy and Compliance.	Career Incumbent	CA	ES	....	....	
Do	Deputy General Counsel, Energy Policy	Vacant	....	ES	....	....	
Do	Assistant General Counsel, Legislation and Regulatory Law.	Career Incumbent	CA	ES	....	....	
Do	Assistant General Counsel, Procurement and Financial Assistance.	Vacant	....	ES	....	....	
Do	Assistant General Counsel, International and National Security Programs.	Career Incumbent	CA	ES	....	....	
Do	Assistant General Counsel, Legislation and Regulatory Law.	......do	CA	ES	....	....	
Do	Assistant General Counsel, Electricity and Power Marketing.	......do	CA	ES	....	....	
Do	Deputy General Counsel, Technology Transfer and Procurement.	......do	CA	ES	....	....	
Do	Director, Office of Standard Contract Management.	......do	CA	ES	....	....	
Do	Assistant General Counsel, Technology Transfer and Intellectual Property.	......do	CA	ES	....	....	
Do	Assistant General Counsel, Labor and Pension Law.	......do	CA	ES	....	....	
Do	Director, Legal Strategy and Analysis	......do	CA	ES	....	....	
Do	Assistant General Counsel, Environment	......do	CA	ES	....	....	
Do	Assistant General Counsel, Enforcement	......do	CA	ES	....	....	
Do	Senior Legal Advisor	Noah C. Shaw	SC	GS	15	....	
Do	Staff Assistant	Paul Moon	SC	GS	5	....	
	OFFICE OF HEALTH, SAFETY AND SECURITY						
Germantown, MD ..	Chief Health, Safety and Security Officer	Career Incumbent	CA	ES	....	....	
Do	Principal Deputy Chief, Corporate Functions	......do	CA	ES	....	....	
Washington, DC	Principal Deputy Chief, Mission Support Operations.	......do	CA	ES	....	....	
Do	Principal Deputy Chief, Nuclear Safety and Technical Matters.	......do	CA	ES	....	....	
Germantown, MD ..	Director, Office of Security	......do	CA	ES	....	....	
Do	Congressional and Public Affairs Manager	......do	CA	ES	....	....	
Do	Director, Office of Security and Cyber Evaluations.	......do	CA	ES	....	....	
Do	Director, Office of Nuclear Safety	......do	CA	ES	....	....	
Do	Director, Office of Classification	......do	CA	ES	....	....	
Do	Director, Office of Corporate Safety Programs	......do	CA	ES	....	....	
Do	Director, Office of Enforcement	......do	CA	ES	....	....	
Washington, DC	Director, Office of Environmental Protection, Sustainability Support, and Corporate Safety Analysis.	......do	CA	ES	....	....	
Germantown, MD ..	Director, Office of Field Assistance	......do	CA	ES	....	....	
Washington, DC	Director, Office of Headquarters Security Operations.	......do	CA	ES	....	....	
Germantown, MD ..	Director, Office of Health and Safety	......do	CA	ES	....	....	
Washington, DC	Director, Office Resource Management	......do	CA	ES	....	....	
Do	Director, Office of Security Operations	......do	CA	ES	....	....	
Albuquerque, NM ..	Director, Office of the National Training Center.	......do	CA	ES	....	....	
Germantown, MD ..	Director, Office of Work Safety and Health Policy.	......do	CA	ES	....	....	
Do	Deputy Director, Enforcement	......do	CA	ES	....	....	
Do	Deputy Director, Nuclear Safety	......do	CA	ES	....	....	
Do	Deputy Director, Oversight	......do	CA	ES	....	....	
Do	Deputy Director, Office of Security	......do	CA	ES	....	....	
Do	Departmental Representative to the Defense Nuclear Facility Safety Board.	......do	CA	ES	....	....	
Washington, DC	Senior Advisor	......do	CA	ES	....	....	

DEPARTMENT OF ENERGY—Continued

Location	Position	Name of Incumbent	Type of Appt.	Pay Plan	Level, Grade, or Pay	Tenure	Expires
Washington, DC	Associate Deputy Chief	Career Incumbent	CA	ES	....	....	
	OFFICE OF HEARINGS AND APPEALS						
Do	Director	......do	CA	ES	....	....	
Do	Deputy Director	......do	CA	ES	....	....	
	OFFICE OF INTELLIGENCE AND COUNTERINTELLIGENCE						
Do	Director	......do	CA	ES	....	....	
Do	Principal Deputy Director	......do	CA	ES	....	....	
Do	Deputy Director for Intelligence Analysis	......do	CA	ES	....	....	
Do	Deputy Director for Counterintelligence	......do	CA	ES	....	....	
	OFFICE OF LEGACY MANAGEMENT						
Do	Director	......do	CA	ES	....	....	
	OFFICE OF MANAGEMENT						
Do	Director, Office of Executive Secretariat	Alison J. Markovitz	NA	ES	....	....	
Do	Director, Office of Management	Career Incumbent	CA	ES	....	....	
Do	Director, Office of Acquisition and Project Management.	......do	CA	ES	....	....	
Do	Director, Office of Contract Management	......do	CA	ES	....	....	
Do	Director, Office of Administration	......do	CA	ES	....	....	
Do	Director, Office of Procurement and Assistance Policy.	Vacant	....	ES	....	....	
Do	Director, Office of Policy	Career Incumbent	CA	ES	....	....	
Do	Director, Project Management	......do	CA	ES	....	....	
Do	Deputy Director, Office of Acquisition and Project Management.	......do	CA	ES	....	....	
Do	Director, Office of Facilities Management and Professional Development.	......do	CA	ES	....	....	
Do	Director, Systems and Professional Development.	Vacant	....	ES	....	....	
Do	Director, Office of Scheduling and Advance	Anthony Rediger	SC	GS	12	....	
Do	Trip Director for the Deputy Secretary	Devin Hampton	SC	GS	11	....	
Do	Lead Advance Representative	Ronald A. Carson	SC	GS	11	....	
Do	Deputy Director of Scheduling and Advance ..	Brian R. Levey	SC	GS	10	....	
Do	Scheduler	Haley S. Smith	SC	GS	10	....	
Do	Special Assistant	Mackenzie L. Huffman	SC	GS	9	....	
Do	......do	Alexander C. Sewell	SC	GS	7	....	
Do	Deputy Scheduler	Kirsten E. Lance	SC	GS	6	....	
	OFFICE OF PUBLIC AFFAIRS						
Do	Director	Daniel Leistikow	NA	ES	....	....	
Do	Deputy Director	Damien J. Lavera	SC	GS	15	....	
Do	Senior Advisor and Director of New Media	Cammie L. Croft	SC	GS	14	....	
Do	Director, User Experience and Digital Technologies.	Robert F. Roberts	SC	GS	14	....	
Do	Press Secretary	Jennifer A. Stutsman	SC	GS	14	....	
Do	Deputy Press Secretary	Keri Danielle Fulton	SC	GS	12	....	
Do	......do	William B. Gibbons	SC	GS	11	....	
Do	Speechwriter	Evelyn Z. Hsieh	SC	GS	11	....	
Do	Senior Digital Communications Strategist	Amanda Scott	SC	GS	10	....	
Do	Deputy Press Secretary for Regional and Online Outreach.	Judith A. Kargbo	SC	GS	10	....	
Do	Press Assistant	Steven Robert Thai	SC	GS	8	....	
Do	New Media Specialist	Benjamin Dotson	SC	GS	7	....	
	OFFICE OF THE CHIEF FINANCIAL OFFICER						
Do	Chief Financial Officer	Vacant	PAS	EX	IV	....	
Do	Director, Office of Finance and Oversight	Career Incumbent	CA	ES	....	....	
Germantown, MD ..	Director, Office of Finance and Accounting	......do	CA	ES	....	....	
Washington, DC ...	Director, Budget Operations	......do	CA	ES	....	....	
Do	Director, Office of Risk Management	......do	CA	ES	....	....	
Germantown, MD ..	Director, Office of Corporate Information Systems.	......do	CA	ES	....	....	
Washington, DC ...	Director, Office of Energy Finance and Accounting Service Center.	......do	CA	ES	....	....	
Do	Deputy Director, Budget Operations	......do	CA	ES	....	....	
Do	Deputy Director for Analysis and Coordination.	......do	CA	ES	....	....	
Do	Program Manager (Office of District Energy Programs).	Vacant	....	ES	....	....	
Do	Special Assistant	Derrick K. Nayo	SC	GS	8	....	
	OFFICE OF THE CHIEF HUMAN CAPITAL OFFICER						
Do	Chief Human Capital Officer	Vacant	....	ES	....		

DEPARTMENT OF ENERGY—Continued

Location	Position	Name of Incumbent	Type of Appt.	Pay Plan	Level, Grade, or Pay	Tenure	Expires
Washington, DC	Deputy Chief Human Capital Officer	Career Incumbent	CA	ES	....	....	
Do	Director, Human Capital Management	......do	CA	ES	....	....	
Do	Director, Office of Human Resources Services	......do	CA	ES	....	....	
Do	Director, Office of Strategic Planning and Policy.	......do	CA	ES	....	....	
	OFFICE OF THE CHIEF INFORMATION OFFICER						
Do	Chief Information Officer	Vacant	....	ES	....	....	
Do	Deputy Chief Information Officer	Career Incumbent	CA	ES	....	....	
Do	Associate CIO for IT Planning, Architecture, and E-Government.	......do	CA	ES	....	....	
Do	Associate CIO, Energy IT Services	......do	CA	ES	....	....	
Do	Associate CIO, IT Corporate Management	......do	CA	ES	....	....	
Do	Associate CIO, Cyber Security	......do	CA	ES	....	....	
	OFFICE OF THE SECRETARY OF ENERGY ADVISORY BOARD						
Do	Executive Director	Vacant	....	ES	....	....	
Do	Executive Director	......do	....	ES	....	....	
	ADVANCED RESEARCH PROJECTS AGENCY - ENERGY						
Do	Director	......do	PAS	EX	III	....	
Do	Chief Counsel	Career Incumbent	CA	ES	....	....	
	CARLSBAD FIELD OFFICE						
Carlsbad, NM	Manager	......do	CA	ES	....	....	
Do	Deputy Manager	......do	CA	ES	....	....	
	INDIAN ENERGY POLICY AND PROGRAMS						
Washington, DC	Director	Tracey LeBeau	XS	AD	....	....	
	LOAN PROGRAMS OFFICE						
Do	Executive Director	Vacant	....	ES	....	....	
Do	Senior Advisor	David Y. Yeh	NA	ES	....	....	
Do	Director, Loan Guarantee Origination Division.	Career Incumbent	CA	ES	....	....	
Do	Chief Operating Officer/Deputy Loan Programs Office.	Vacant	....	ES	....	....	
Do	Director, Technical and Project Management Division.	Career Incumbent	CA	ES	....	....	
Do	Director for Portfolio Management	......do	CA	ES	....	....	
Do	Director, Risk Management Division	Vacant	....	ES	....	....	
Do	Director, Management Operations Division	......do	....	ES	....	....	
Do	Chief Counsel, LPO	Career Incumbent	CA	ES	....	....	
	BONNEVILLE POWER ADMINISTRATION						
Portland, OR	Administrator and Chief Executive Officer	......do	CA	ES	....	....	
Do	Deputy Administrator	......do	CA	ES	....	....	
Do	Chief Information Officer	......do	CA	ES	....	....	
Do	Senior Vice President and General Counsel ...	......do	CA	ES	....	....	
Do	Senior Vice President, Transmission Services	......do	CA	ES	....	....	
Do	Chief Operating Officer	......do	CA	ES	....	....	
Do	Vice President, Environment, Fish and Wildlife.	......do	CA	ES	....	....	
Do	Vice President, Requirements Marketing	......do	CA	ES	....	....	
Vancouver, WA	Vice President, Transmission Field Services Bus Line.	......do	CA	ES	....	....	
Portland, OR	Executive Vice President, Corporate Strategy	......do	CA	ES	....	....	
Vancouver, WA	Vice President, Planning and Asset Management.	......do	CA	ES	....	....	
Portland, OR	Vice President, Engineering and Technical Services.	......do	CA	ES	....	....	
Do	Senior Vice President, Power Services	......do	CA	ES	....	....	
Do	Executive Vice President, Internal Business Services.	......do	CA	ES	....	....	
Washington, DC	Vice President, Energy Efficiency	Vacant	....	ES	....	....	
Do	Vice President, Marketing and Sales	Career Incumbent	CA	ES	....	....	
Portland, OR	Executive Vice President, Industry Restructuring.	Vacant	....	ES	....	....	
Do	Vice President and Chief Financial Officer	Career Incumbent	CA	ES	....	....	
Do	Vice President, Generation Asset Management.	......do	CA	ES	....	....	
Do	Vice President, Bulk Marketing	......do	CA	ES	....	....	

DEPARTMENT OF ENERGY—Continued

Location	Position	Name of Incumbent	Type of Appt.	Pay Plan	Level, Grade, or Pay	Tenure	Expires
	SOUTHEASTERN POWER ADMINISTRATION						
Elberton, GA	Administrator	Career Incumbent	CA	ES	....	....	
	SOUTHWESTERN POWER ADMINISTRATION						
Tulsa, OK	Administrator	Vacant	....	ES	....	....	
	WESTERN AREA POWER ADMINISTRATION						
Lakewood, CO	Administrator	......do	....	ES	....	....	
Do	General Counsel	Career Incumbent	CA	ES	....	....	
Billings, MT	Regional Manager, Upper Great Plains Region.	......do	CA	ES	....	....	
Phoenix, AZ	Regional Manager, Desert Southwest Region	......do	CA	ES	....	....	
Loveland, CO	Regional Manager, Rocky Mountain Region ...	......do	CA	ES	....	....	
Folsom, CA	Regional Manager, Sierra Nevada Region	......do	CA	ES	....	....	
Lakewood, CO	Chief Information Officer	......do	CA	ES	....	....	
Do	Chief Financial Officer	......do	CA	ES	....	....	
Lakewood, CA	Transmission Infrastructure Program Manager.	......do	CA	ES	....	....	
Lakewood, CO	Chief Operating Officer	......do	CA	ES	....	....	
	U.S. ENERGY INFORMATION ADMINISTRATION						
Washington, DC	Administrator	Adam E. Sieminski	PAS	EX	IV	....	
Do	Deputy Administrator	Career Incumbent	CA	ES	....	....	
Do	Assistant Administrator for Communications	......do	CA	ES	....	....	
Do	Assistant Administrator for Energy Analysis	......do	CA	ES	....	....	
Do	Assistant Administrator for Energy Statistics	......do	CA	ES	....	....	
Do	Director, Office of Electricity, Renewables and Uranium Statistics.	......do	CA	ES	....	....	
Do	Director, Office of Energy Consumption and Efficiency Statistics.	......do	CA	ES	....	....	
Do	Director, Office of Petroleum, Natural Gas and Biofuels Analysis.	......do	CA	ES	....	....	
Do	Director, Office of Electricity, Coal, Nuclear and Renewables Analysis.	......do	CA	ES	....	....	
Do	Director, Office of Oil, Gas and Coal Supply Statistics.	......do	CA	ES	....	....	
Do	Director, Office of Integrated and International Energy Analysis.	......do	CA	ES	....	....	
Do	Deputy Assistant Secretary for Safety and Security.	......do	CA	ES	....	....	
Do	Director, Office of Petroleum and Biofuels Statistics.	......do	CA	ES	....	....	
Do	Director, Office of Survey Development and Statistical Integration.	......do	CA	ES	....	....	

DEPARTMENT OF ENERGY OFFICE OF THE INSPECTOR GENERAL

Location	Position	Name of Incumbent	Type of Appt.	Pay Plan	Level, Grade, or Pay	Tenure	Expires
Washington, DC	Inspector General	Gregory H. Friedman	PAS	OT	$170,259	....	

DEPARTMENT OF HEALTH AND HUMAN SERVICES

Location	Position	Name of Incumbent	Type of Appt.	Pay Plan	Level, Grade, or Pay	Tenure	Expires
	OFFICE OF THE SECRETARY						
Washington, DC	Secretary	Kathleen Sebelius	PAS	EX	I		
Do	Confidential Assistant	Georgette T. Lewis	SC	GS	12		
Do	Counselor	John T. Monahan	NA	ES			
Do	Counselor for Health Policy	Rima J. Cohen	NA	ES			
Do	Counselor for Public Health and Science	Caya B. Lewis	NA	ES			
Do	......do	Andrea J. Palm	NA	ES			
Do	Counselor for Human Services Policy	Sharon Elaine Parrott	NA	ES			
Do	Special Assistant to the Counselors	Noelle C. Lee	SC	GS	13		
Do	Chief of Staff	Sally Howard	NA	ES			
Do	Deputy Chief of Staff	Dawn M. O'Connell	NA	ES			
Do	Confidential Assistant to the Chief of Staff	Subhan Nasrullah Cheema	SC	GS	9		
Do	Executive Secretary to the Department	Jennifer M. Cannistra	NA	ES			
Do	Senior Advisor to the Executive Secretary	C'Reda J. Weeden	SC	GS	15		
Do	Deputy Executive Secretary	Career Incumbent	CA	ES			
Do	White House Liaison for Political Personnel, Boards and Commissions.	Michael W. McCauley	NA	ES			
Do	Deputy White House Liaison for Political Personnel, Boards and Commissions.	Rebecca M. Adelman	SC	GS	14		
Do	Director, Office of Disability	Henry David Claypool	NA	ES			
Do	Senior Executive Advisor	Vacant		ES			
Do	Director, Scheduling and Advance	Kathryn Lea Wolff	SC	GS	14		
Do	Deputy Director, Scheduling and Advance	Keri Ann Kohler	SC	GS	14		
Do	Advance Lead	Rebecca H. Chappell	SC	GS	9		
Do	......do	Eli Fleet	SC	GS	12		
	OFFICE OF THE DEPUTY SECRETARY						
Do	Deputy Secretary	William V. Corr	PAS	EX	II		
Do	Chief of Staff to the Deputy Secretary	Jarel Lapan Hill	SC	GS	15		
Do	Chair, Departmental Appeals Board	Career Incumbent	CA	ES			
Do	Associate Deputy Secretary	......do	CA	ES			
	Office of Intergovernmental and External Affairs						
Do	Director	Paul Dioguardi	NA	ES			
Do	Director, Office of External Affairs	Anton Jelaine Gunn	NA	ES			
Do	Senior Advisor	Jay Bernard Angoff	NA	ES			
Do	Deputy Director for Regional Outreach	Emily Alyssa Barson	SC	GS	15		
Do	Special Assistant	Kasia Leigh Witkowski	SC	GS	13		
Do	Confidential Assistant	Tori L. Scarborough	SC	GS	12		
Do	Special Assistant	Seth Hanon Wainer	SC	GS	13		
Do	Confidential Assistant	Benidicto Feliciano Belton	SC	GS	11		
Do	Director of Business Outreach	Sol Joshua Ross	SC	GS	15		
Boston, MA	Regional Director, Boston, Massachusetts, Region I.	Christie Lynn Hager	SC	GS	15		
New York, NY	Regional Director, New York, New York, Region II.	Jaime Rafael Torres	SC	GS	15		
Philadelphia, PA	Regional Director, Philadelphia, Pennsylvania, Region III.	Joanne Grossi	SC	GS	15		
Atlanta, GA	Regional Director, Atlanta, Georgia, Region IV.	Career Incumbent	SC	GS	15		
Chicago, IL	Regional Director, Chicago, Illinois-Region V	Kenneth Munson	SC	GS	15		
Dallas, TX	Regional Director, Dallas, Texas, Region VI ...	Marjorie McColl Petty	SC	GS	15		
Kansas City, MO ...	Regional Director, Kansas City, Missouri, Region VII.	Career Incumbent	SC	GS	15		
Denver, CO	Regional Director, Denver, Colorado, Region VIII.	Marguerite Salazar	SC	GS	15		
San Francisco, CA	Regional Director, San Francisco, California, Region IX.	Herb Kenneth Schultz	SC	GS	15		
Seattle, WA	Regional Director, Seattle, Washington, Region X.	Susan M. Johnson	SC	GS	15		
	Office of the National Coordinator for Health Information Technology						
Washington, DC	National Health Information Technology Coordinator.	Farzad Mostashari, M.D. ...	NA	ES			
Do	Principal Deputy National Coordinator	David S. Muntz	NA	ES			
Do	Special Assistant	Wilbur Wei-Pen Yu	SC	GS	15		
Do	......do	Damon L. Davis	SC	GS	15		
Do	Chief Privacy Officer	Joy L. Pritts	NA	ES			
Do	Director, Office of Health Information Technology Adoption.	Vacant		ES			
Do	Health Care Reform Coordinator	Career Incumbent	CA	ES			
Do	Senior Advisor	Vacant		ES			
Do	Director, Office of Policy and Research	Career Incumbent	CA	ES			
Do	Deputy National Coordinator for Programs and Policy.	......do	CA	ES			

DEPARTMENT OF HEALTH AND HUMAN SERVICES—Continued

Location	Position	Name of Incumbent	Type of Appt.	Pay Plan	Level, Grade, or Pay	Tenure	Expires
Washington, DC	Deputy National Coordinator for Operations ..	Career Incumbent	CA	ES	....	....	
Do	Director, Office of Standards and Interoperability.	......do	CA	ES	....	....	
	Office of the Assistant Secretary for Financial Resources						
Do	Assistant Secretary	Ellen G. Murray	PAS	EX	IV	....	
Do	Deputy Assistant Secretary, Budget	Career Incumbent	CA	ES	....	....	
Do	Principal Deputy Assistant Secretary, Resources and Technology.	......do	CA	ES	....	....	
Do	Director, Division of Health Benefits and Income Security.	......do	CA	ES	....	....	
Do	Director, Division of Discretionary Programs	......do	CA	ES	....	....	
Do	Deputy Associate Secretary, Office of Grants and Acquisitions.	......do	CA	ES	....	....	
Do	Director, Division of the Office of the Secretary Budget.	......do	CA	ES	....	....	
Do	Director, Division of Budget Policy, Execution, and Review.	......do	CA	ES	....	....	
Do	Director, Office of Program Management and Systems Policy.	......do	CA	ES	....	....	
Do	Associate Deputy Assistant Secretary, Budget	......do	CA	ES	....	....	
Do	Director, Office of Program Integrity Coordination.	......do	CA	ES	....	....	
Do	Deputy Assistant Secretary, Recovery Act Coordination.	......do	CA	ES	....	....	
	Office of the Assistant Secretary for Preparedness and Response						
Do	Assistant Secretary	Nicole Lurie, M.D.	PAS	EX	IV	....	
Do	Special Assistant to the Assistant Secretary ..	Stacy Louise Elmer	SC	GS	13	....	
Do	Principal Deputy Director, Office of Public Health Emergency Medical Countermeasures.	Career Incumbent	CA	ES	....	....	
Do	Director, Office of Medicine, Science and Public Health.	......do	CA	ES	....	....	
Do	Director, Resource Planning and Evaluation ..	......do	CA	ES	....	....	
Do	Director, Influenza and Emerging Diseases	......do	CA	ES	....	....	
Do	Director, Office of Preparedness and Emergency Operations.	......do	CA	ES	....	....	
Do	Principal Deputy Director, Office of Preparedness and Emergency Operations.	......do	CA	ES	....	....	
Do	Deputy Assistant Secretary and Director, Biomedical Advanced Development and Research Authority.	......do	CA	ES	....	....	
Do	Principal Deputy Assistant Secretary for Preparedness and Response.	......do	CA	ES	....	....	
Do	Chief Operating Officer	......do	CA	ES	....	....	
	Office of Medicare Hearings and Appeals						
Do	Director, Office of Operations	......do	CA	ES	....	....	
Do	Director, Office of Programs	......do	CA	ES	....	....	
	OFFICE OF THE ASSISTANT SECRETARY FOR LEGISLATION						
Do	Assistant Secretary	Jim Esquea	PAS	EX	IV	....	
Do	Deputy Assistant Secretary (Discretionary Health Programs).	Jeremy Beck Sharp	NA	ES	....	....	
Do	Deputy Assistant Secretary (Human Services)	Douglas Lee Steiger	NA	ES	....	....	
Do	Deputy Assistant Secretary (Congressional Liaison).	Fatima Annalie Cuevas	NA	ES	....	....	
Do	Deputy Assistant Secretary (Mandatory Health Programs).	Bridgett Elaine Taylor	NA	ES	....	....	
Do	Confidential Assistant	Lisa Marie Thimjon	SC	GS	12	....	
Do	......do	Lisa J. Strumwasser	SC	GS	9	....	
Do	Special Assistant	Russell M. Anello	SC	GS	13	....	
Do	Confidential Assistant (Mandatory Health Programs).	Rose M. Hacking	SC	GS	11	....	
Do	Special Assistant (Discretionary Health Programs).	Averi E. Pakulis	SC	GS	14	....	
	OFFICE OF THE ASSISTANT SECRETARY FOR ADMINISTRATION						
Do	Assistant Secretary	Edward J. Holland, Jr.	NA	ES	....	....	
Do	Deputy Assistant Secretary, Human Resources.	Career Incumbent	CA	ES	....	....	
Do	Deputy Assistant Secretary, Business Transformation.	......do	CA	ES	....	....	

DEPARTMENT OF HEALTH AND HUMAN SERVICES—Continued

Location	Position	Name of Incumbent	Type of Appt.	Pay Plan	Level, Grade, or Pay	Tenure	Expires
Washington, DC	Deputy Assistant Secretary, Security	Career Incumbent	CA	ES	....	....	
Do	Deputy Assistant Secretary, Information Technology/Chief Information Officer.	......do	CA	ES	....	....	
Do	Deputy Assistant Secretary, Program Support	......do	CA	ES	....	....	
Do	Deputy Assistant Secretary, Facilities Management and Policy.	......do	CA	ES	....	....	
Do	Associate Deputy Assistant Secretary, Human Resources.	......do	CA	ES	....	....	
Do	Director, Client Services Center, National Capital Region.	......do	CA	ES	....	....	
Do	Director, Strategic Programs Division	......do	CA	ES	....	....	
	OFFICE OF THE ASSISTANT SECRETARY FOR PUBLIC AFFAIRS						
Do	Assistant Secretary	Vacant	PAS	EX	IV	....	
Do	Principal Deputy Assistant Secretary	Dorinda A. Salcido	NA	ES	....	....	
Do	Deputy Assistant Secretary (Public Health) ...	Tait Sye	NA	ES	....	....	
Do	Communications Director (Public Health)	John P. Bray	SC	GS	14	....	
Do	Deputy Assistant Secretary (Health Care)	Jason Michael Young	NA	ES	....	....	
Do	Director for Health Care Initiatives	Jaime Erin Mulligan	SC	GS	14	....	
Do	Communications Director for Health Care	Erin E. Shields	SC	GS	14	....	
Do	Director, News Division	Career Incumbent	CA	ES	....	....	
Do	Director, Web and Media Communications Division.	......do	CA	ES	....	....	
Do	Deputy Assistant Secretary (Human Services)	......do	CA	ES	....	....	
Do	Press Secretary	Keith Richard Maley	SC	GS	13	....	
Do	Speechwriter	Robert Lott	SC	GS	13	....	
Do	Press Secretary	Fabien Moshe Levy	SC	GS	12	....	
Do	Confidential Assistant to the Deputy Assistant Secretary for Public Affairs.	Julia Parker Eisman	SC	GS	12	....	
Do	Confidential Assistant to the Assistant Secretary for Public Affairs.	Alyson C. Jordan	SC	GS	9	....	
Do	Special Assistant	Sherice Dillard	SC	GS	13	....	
Do	Senior Advisor	Nathaniel W. Jackson	SC	GS	15	....	
	OFFICE OF THE ASSISTANT SECRETARY FOR PLANNING AND EVALUATION						
Do	Assistant Secretary	Vacant	PAS	EX	IV	....	
Do	Principal Deputy Assistant Secretary	Donald B. Moulds	NA	ES	....	....	
Do	Deputy Assistant Secretary (Human Services Policy).	Ajay Chaudry	NA	ES	....	....	
Do	Deputy Assistant Secretary (Health Policy)	Richard Gray Kronick	NA	ES	....	....	
Do	Deputy Assistant Secretary (Disability, Aging, and Long-Term Care Policy).	Peter Kemper	NA	ES	....	....	
Do	Associate Deputy Assistant Secretary (Disability, Aging, and Long-Term Care Policy).	Career Incumbent	CA	ES	....	....	
Do	Deputy Assistant Secretary for Planning and Evaluation (Science and Data Policy).	......do	CA	ES	....	....	
Do	Director, Center for Faith Based and Community Initiatives.	Alexia Kathryn Kelley	NA	ES	....	....	
Do	Deputy Director	Acacia Tyler Bremberg Salatti.	SC	GS	14	....	
Do	Senior Advisor, Center for Faith-Based and Neighborhood Partnerships.	Mara L. Vanderslice	SC	GS	15	....	
Do	Director, Office of Health Reform	Michael M. Hash	NA	ES	....	....	
Do	Deputy Director, Office of Health Reform	Yvette Emad Fontenot	NA	ES	....	....	
Do	Director of Public Health Policy (Office of Health Reform).	Mayra Erika Alvarez	SC	GS	14	....	
Do	Director of Policy Coverage (Office of Health Reform).	Chiquita White Brooks-Lasure.	SC	GS	15	....	
Do	Director of Delivery System Reform (Office of Health Reform).	Christopher J. Dawe	SC	GS	15	....	
Do	Senior Policy Analyst (Office of Health Reform).	Catherine Rose Oakar	SC	GS	14	....	
Do	Associate Deputy Assistant Secretary (Health Policy).	Career Incumbent	CA	ES	....	....	
	OFFICE OF THE ASSISTANT SECRETARY FOR HEALTH						
Do	Assistant Secretary	Howard K. Koh, M.D.	PAS	EX	IV	....	
Do	Surgeon General	Regina M. Benjamin, M.D. ...	PAS	OT	....	4 Years	11/02/13
Do	Senior Advisor	Vacant	....	ES	....	....	
New York, NY	Regional Health Administrator, Region II, New York.	Career Incumbent	CA	ES	....	....	
Philadelphia, PA	Regional Health Administrator, Region III, Philadelphia.	......do	CA	ES	....	....	

DEPARTMENT OF HEALTH AND HUMAN SERVICES—Continued

Location	Position	Name of Incumbent	Type of Appt.	Pay Plan	Level, Grade, or Pay	Tenure	Expires
Kansas City, MO ...	Regional Health Administrator, Region VII, Kansas City.	Career Incumbent	CA	ES	....	....	
Washington, DC	Principal Deputy Assistant Secretary	......do	CA	ES	....	....	
Do	Deputy Assistant Secretary (Healthcare Quality).	......do	CA	ES	....	....	
Do	Director, Office of HIV/AIDS Policy	......do	CA	ES	....	....	
Do	Director, Office of Research Integrity	......do	CA	ES	....	....	
Do	Deputy Assistant Secretary for Population Affairs.	Marilyn Keefe	NA	ES	....	....	
Do	Deputy Assistant Secretary (Science and Medicine).	Career Incumbent	CA	ES	....	....	
Do	Director of Communications	Jenny Thalheimer Rosenberg.	SC	GS	15	....	
Do	Executive Director, President's Council on Fitness, Sports and Nutrition.	Shellie Yvonne Pfohl	SC	GS	15	....	
Do	Special Assistant	Bradley Edward Wolters ...	SC	GS	13	....	
Do	Confidential Assistant	Kirby L. K. Bumpus	SC	GS	11	....	
	OFFICE OF GLOBAL HEALTH AFFAIRS						
Do	Director	Nils Daulaire, M.D.	NA	ES	....	....	
Do	Deputy Director	Career Incumbent	CA	ES	....	....	
Do	Senior Advisor	Vacant	....	ES	....	....	
Do	Associate Director, Strategy and Policy Division.	Holly Wong	NA	ES	....	....	
Do	Special Assistant to the Director	Maeve McKean	SC	GS	14	....	
	OFFICE OF THE GENERAL COUNSEL						
Do	General Counsel	Vacant	PAS	EX	IV	....	
Do	Principal Deputy General Counsel	William B. Schultz	NA	ES	....	....	
Do	Deputy General Counsel and Counselor to the Office of Health Reform.	Kenneth Young Choe	NA	ES	....	....	
Do	Deputy General Counsel	Gia Lee	NA	ES	....	....	
Do	......do	Career Incumbent	CA	ES	....	....	
Do	Senior Advisor	......do	CA	ES	....	....	
Do	Associate General Counsel	......do	CA	ES	....	....	
Do	Deputy Associate General Counsel, Public Health (National Institutes of Health).	......do	CA	ES	....	....	
Do	Deputy Associate General Counsel, Program Integrity.	......do	CA	ES	....	....	
Do	Special Assistant to the Deputy General Counsel.	......do	CA	ES	....	....	
Do	Confidential Assistant	Daniel R. Suvor	SC	GS	12	....	
	Chief Counsels						
New York, NY	Chief Counsel Region II	Career Incumbent	CA	ES	....	....	
Atlanta, GA	Chief Counsel, Region IV	......do	CA	ES	....	....	
Chicago, IL	Chief Counsel, Region V	......do	CA	ES	....	....	
Dallas, TX	Chief Counsel, Region VI	......do	CA	ES	....	....	
San Francisco, CA	Chief Counsel, Region IX	......do	CA	ES	....	....	
Seattle, WA	Chief Counsel, Region X	Vacant	....	ES	....	....	
	Associate General Counsel Divisions						
Washington, DC	Associate General Counsel, Legislation Division.	Career Incumbent	CA	ES	....	....	
Rockville, MD	Associate General Counsel, Public Health	......do	CA	ES	....	....	
Do	Deputy Associate General Counsel, Public Health and Science.	......do	CA	ES	....	....	
Do	Associate General Counsel, Food and Drug Division.	......do	CA	ES	....	....	
Washington, DC	Associate General Counsel, Civil Rights Division.	......do	CA	ES	....	....	
Do	Associate General Counsel, Centers for Medicaid and Medicare Services.	......do	CA	ES	....	....	
Do	Deputy Associate General Counsel, Procurement, Fiscal, and Information Law.	......do	CA	ES	....	....	
Do	Deputy Associate General Counsel, Centers for Medicare and Medicaid Services Division.	......do	CA	ES	....	....	
Woodlawn, MD	Deputy Associate General Counsel, Litigation	......do	CA	ES	....	....	
Washington, DC	Associate General Counsel Children, Family and Aging Division.	......do	CA	ES	....	....	
Do	Deputy Associate General Counsel	Vacant	....	ES	....	....	
Atlanta, GA	Deputy Associate General Counsel for Public Health (Disease Control).	Career Incumbent	CA	ES	....	....	
	OFFICE FOR CIVIL RIGHTS						
Washington, DC	Director	Leon Rodriguez	NA	ES	....	....	
Do	Deputy Director	Career Incumbent	CA	ES	....	....	

DEPARTMENT OF HEALTH AND HUMAN SERVICES—Continued

Location	Position	Name of Incumbent	Type of Appt.	Pay Plan	Level, Grade, or Pay	Tenure	Expires
Washington, DC	Deputy Director for Management Operations	Vacant	....	ES	....	....	
Do	Deputy Director for Programs and Policy	Karen V. Walker Bryce	NA	ES	....	....	
Do	Senior Advisor	Juliet Kwon Choi	NA	ES	....	....	
Do	Deputy Director for Health Information Privacy.	Career Incumbent	CA	ES	....	....	
Do	Senior Advisor	......do	CA	ES	....	....	
Do	Deputy Director, Enforcement and Regional Operations.	......do	CA	ES	....	....	
	ADMINISTRATION ON AGING						
Do	Assistant Secretary	Kathy J. Greenlee	PAS	EX	IV	....	
Do	Deputy Assistant Secretary for Policy and Management.	Career Incumbent	CA	ES	....	....	
Do	Deputy Assistant Secretary for Policy and Programs.	......do	CA	ES	....	....	
Do	Director, Office of Actuarial Integrity	......do	CA	ES	....	....	
Do	Special Assistant	Erin Bailey Fitzgerald	SC	GS	13	....	
	OFFICE OF THE ASSISTANT SECRETARY FOR CHILDREN AND FAMILIES						
Do	Assistant Secretary	Vacant	PAS	EX	IV	....	
Do	Principal Deputy Assistant Secretary	George Henry Sheldon	NA	ES	....	....	
Do	Director, Office of Planning, Research and Evaluation.	Career Incumbent	CA	ES	....	....	
Do	Deputy Assistant Secretary and Inter-Departmental Liaison for Early Childhood Development.	Linda Kay Smith	NA	ES	....	....	
Do	Deputy Assistant Secretary for Policy	Mark H. Greenberg	NA	ES	....	....	
Do	Senior Advisor	Career Incumbent	CA	ES	....	....	
Do	Chief Medical Officer	George Lamonte Askew, M.D..	NA	ES	....	....	
Do	Director, Office of Child Care	Shannon L. Rudisill	NA	ES	....	....	
Do	Senior Advisor	Melissa Jaacks	TA	ES	....	....	09/09/14
Do	.....do	Miriam Elena Calderon	SC	GS	15	....	
Do	Confidential Assistant	Miya Nicole Cain	SC	GS	11	....	
Do	Confidential Assistant to the Deputy Assistant Secretary and Inter-Departmental Liaison for Early Childhood Development.	Shantel Elizabeth Meek	SC	GS	12	....	
Do	Confidential Assistant to the Deputy Assistant Secretary for Policy, Administration for Children and Families.	Alicia Lynn Sutton	SC	GS	12	....	
Do	Special Assistant to the Principal Deputy Assistant Secretary.	Mariestella Fischer	SC	GS	13	....	
	Office of Information Systems Management						
Boston, MA	Regional Hub Director	Career Incumbent	CA	ES	....	....	
Atlanta, GA	......do	......do	CA	ES	....	....	
New York, NY	......do	......do	CA	ES	....	....	
San Francisco, CA	......do	......do	CA	ES	....	....	
Washington, DC	Director Regional Operations and State Systems.	......do	CA	ES	....	....	
Dallas, TX	Regional Hub Director	......do	CA	ES	....	....	
	Administrator for Children, Youth and Families / Office of Commissioner						
Washington, DC	Commissioner	Bryan H. Samuels	PAS	EX	V	....	
Do	Special Assistant	Sarah Elizabeth Hunter	SC	GS	13	....	
Do	Project Manager	Vacant		ES	....	....	
Do	Senior Advisor	......do		ES	....	....	
Do	Director, Office of Head Start	Yvette L. Sanchez-Fuentes	NA	ES	....	....	
Do	Deputy Director, Office of Head Start	Career Incumbent	CA	ES	....	....	
Do	Project Manager, Office of Head Start	Vacant		ES	....	....	
Do	Director, Office of Information Services and Deputy Chief Information Officer.	Career Incumbent	CA	ES	....	....	
	Office of Family Assistance / Office of the Director						
Do	Director	Earl Stephen Johnson III ..	NA	ES	....	....	
	Office of Child Support Enforcement / Office of the Director						
Do	Deputy Director	Vicki Anne Turetsky	NA	ES	....	....	
	Office of Refugee Resettlement / Office of the Director						
Do	Director	Eskinder Negash	NA	ES	....	....	

DEPARTMENT OF HEALTH AND HUMAN SERVICES—Continued

Location	Position	Name of Incumbent	Type of Appt.	Pay Plan	Level, Grade, or Pay	Tenure	Expires
	Administration on Developmental Disability/ Office of Commissioner						
Washington, DC	Commissioner	Sharon B. Lewis	NA	ES	....	....	
	Administration for Native Americans/Office of Commissioner						
Do	Commissioner	Lillian A. Sparks	PAS	EX	V	....	
	Office of Legislative Affairs and Budget						
Do	Director	Career Incumbent	CA	ES	....	....	
	Office of Public Affairs						
Do	Director	Marrianne McMullen	SC	GS	15	....	
Do	Special Assistant	Jesus Gonzalo Garcia	SC	GS	13	....	
	Office of Community Services/Office of the Director						
Do	Director	Eugenia Lynn Chaffin	NA	ES	....	....	
	CENTERS FOR MEDICARE AND MEDICAID SERVICES						
Do	Administrator	Vacant	PAS	EX	IV	....	
Woodlawn, MD	Principal Deputy Administrator	Marilyn B. Tavenner	NA	ES	....	....	
Do	Deputy Chief Operating Officer	Career Incumbent	CA	ES	....	....	
Baltimore, MD	Chief of Staff	Aryana C. Khalid	NA	ES	....	....	
Do	Senior Advisor	Ajay Gupta	SC	GS	15	....	
Do	Confidential Assistant to the Chief of Staff	Nicole Michelle Dickelson ..	SC	GS	9	....	
Washington, DC	Special Assistant to the Administrator	Charles Joseph McCannon	SC	GS	15	....	
	Center for Consumer Information and Insurance Oversight						
Do	Deputy Administrator and Director	Vacant	....	ES	....	....	
Woodlawn, MD	Deputy Center Director	......do	CA	ES	....	....	
Washington, DC	Senior Advisor	Teresa Diane Miller	NA	ES	....	....	
Do	Director, Oversight Group	Career Incumbent	CA	ES	....	....	
Do	Director, Insurance Programs Group	Richard Arthur Popper	NA	ES	....	....	
Do	Director, Consumer Support Group	Career Incumbent	CA	ES	....	....	
	Center for Medicare and Medicaid Innovation						
Woodlawn, MD	Director	Richard J. Gilfillan	NA	ES	....	....	
Baltimore, MD	Deputy Director	Vacant	....	ES	....	....	
Woodlawn, MD	Deputy Director for Operations	Career Incumbent	CA	ES	....	....	
Do	Senior Advisor	Rahul Rajkumar	NA	ES	....	....	
Do	Associate Director for Campaign Leadership and Co-Director, Partnership for Patients Initiative.	Career Incumbent	CA	ES	....	....	
	Office of Public Engagement						
Washington, DC	Director	Maria Teresa Nino	NA	ES	....	....	
Do	Director, Office of Communications, Centers for Medicare and Medicaid Services.	Julia Green Bataille	NA	ES	....	....	
Woodlawn, MD	Director, Medicare Ombudsman Group	Career Incumbent	CA	ES	....	....	
Washington, DC	Director, Emergency Preparedness and Response Operations.	......do	CA	ES	....	....	
	Office of Legislation						
Do	Director	Lauren E. Aronson	NA	ES	....	....	
Do	Deputy Director	Career Incumbent	CA	ES	....	....	
	Office of Strategic Operations and Regulatory Affairs						
Do	Director	Vacant	....	ES	....	....	
	Office of Clinical Standards and Quality						
Woodlawn, MD	Director	Career Incumbent	CA	ES	....	....	
Do	Deputy Director	......do	CA	ES	....	....	
Do	Director, Information System Group	......do	CA	ES	....	....	
Do	Director, Quality Improvement Group	......do	CA	ES	....	....	
	Center for Strategic Planning						
Baltimore, MD	Deputy Administrator	Anthony D. Rodgers	NA	ES	....	....	
Woodlawn, MD	Director, Federal Coordinated Health Care Office.	Melanie Marie Bella	NA	ES	....	....	
	Center for Medicare						
Baltimore, MD	Director, Center for Medicare Management ...	Jonathan D. Blum	NA	ES	....	....	
Woodlawn, MD	Director, Chronic Care Policy Group	Career Incumbent	CA	ES	....	....	
Do	Director Provider Billing Group	......do	CA	ES	....	....	
Do	Deputy Center Director	......do	CA	ES	....	....	
Baltimore, MD	Director, Hospital and Ambulatory Policy Group.	......do	CA	ES	....	....	

DEPARTMENT OF HEALTH AND HUMAN SERVICES—Continued

Location	Position	Name of Incumbent	Type of Appt.	Pay Plan	Level, Grade, or Pay	Tenure	Expires
Woodlawn, MD	Director, Medicare Drug and Health Plan Contract Administration Group.	Career Incumbent	CA	ES	....	....	
Do	Director, Medicare Drug Benefit Group	......do	CA	ES	....	....	
Do	Director, Medicare Enrollment and Appeals Group.	Vacant	....	ES	....	....	
Do	Director, Medicare Plan Payment Group	Career Incumbent	CA	ES	....	....	
Do	Deputy Center Director, Center for Medicare	......do	CA	ES	....	....	
Do	Director, Program Compliance and Oversight Group.	Vacant	....	ES	....	....	
	Center for Program Integrity						
Baltimore, MD	Deputy Administrator	Peter Paul Budetti	NA	ES	....	....	
Woodlawn, MD	Deputy Director for Policy	Career Incumbent	CA	ES	....	....	
Do	Deputy Director for Operations	......do	CA	ES	....	....	
	Center for Medicaid, Chip and Survey and Certification						
Do	Director, Center for Medicaid State Operations.	Cynthia R. Mann	NA	ES	....	....	
Do	Deputy Center Director	Career Incumbent	CA	ES	....	....	
Do	Director, Family and Children's Health Programs Group.	......do	CA	ES	....	....	
Do	Director, Disabled and Elderly Health Programs Group.	......do	CA	ES	....	....	
Do	Director, Survey and Certification Group	......do	CA	ES	....	....	
Do	Deputy Center Director	......do	CA	ES	....	....	
Do	Director, Data and Systems Group	......do	CA	ES	....	....	
Do	Director, Financial Management Group	......do	CA	ES	....	....	
	Chief Operating Officer						
Do	Director Budget and Analysis Group	......do	CA	ES	....	....	
Do	Director, Office of Operations Management	......do	CA	ES	....	....	
Do	Deputy Director, Office of Operations Management.	......do	CA	ES	....	....	
Do	Director, Enterprise Databases Group	......do	CA	ES	....	....	
Do	Director, Financial Management Systems Group.	......do	CA	ES	....	....	
Do	Director, Enterprise Architecture and Strategy Group.	......do	CA	ES	....	....	
Do	Director, Enterprise Data Center Group	......do	CA	ES	....	....	
Do	Director, Business Applications Management Group.	......do	CA	ES	....	....	
Do	Director, Information Services Design and Development Group.	Vacant	....	ES	....	....	
Chicago, IL	Chicago Consortium Administrator	Career Incumbent	CA	ES	....	....	
New York, NY	New York Consortium Administrator	......do	CA	ES	....	....	
Kansas City, MO ...	Kansas City Consortium Administrator	......do	CA	ES	....	....	
Dallas, TX	Dallas Consortium Administrator	......do	CA	ES	....	....	
Atlanta, GA	Atlanta Regional Administrator	......do	CA	ES	....	....	
Philadelphia, PA	Philadelphia Regional Administrator	......do	CA	ES	....	....	
Boston, MA	Boston Regional Administrator	Vacant	....	ES	....	....	
Seattle, WA	Seattle Regional Administrator	Career Incumbent	CA	ES	....	....	
San Francisco, CA	San Francisco Regional Administrator	......do	CA	ES	....	....	
Denver, CO	Denver Regional Administrator	......do	CA	ES	....	....	
Woodlawn, MD	Director, Provider Compliance Group	......do	CA	ES	....	....	
	OFFICE OF THE ASSISTANT SECRETARY FOR HEALTH						
Washington, DC	Deputy Assistant Secretary	......do	CA	ES	....	....	
	SUBSTANCE ABUSE AND MENTAL HEALTH SERVICES ADMINISTRATION						
Rockville, MD	Administrator	Pamela S. Hyde	PAS	EX	IV	....	
Do	Deputy Administrator	Vacant	....	ES	....	....	
Do	Deputy for Operations	Career Incumbent	CA	ES	....	....	
Do	Principal Deputy Administrator	......do	CA	ES	....	....	
Do	Director, Office of Policy, Planning and Innovation.	......do	CA	ES	....	....	
Do	Executive Director President's New Freedom Commission.	Vacant	....	ES	....	....	
Do	Senior Associate for Medical Affairs	......do	....	ES	....	....	
Do	Senior Advisor to the Administrator	......do	....	ES	....	....	
Do	Executive Officer/Director, Office of Program Services.	Career Incumbent	CA	ES	....	....	
Do	Deputy Director, Office of Program Services ..	Vacant	....	ES	....	....	
Do	Director, Office of Applied Studies	......do	....	ES	....	....	
Do	Associate Administrator, Extramural Affairs	......do	....	ES	....	....	
Do	Associate Administrator, Communications	......do	....	ES	....	....	

DEPARTMENT OF HEALTH AND HUMAN SERVICES—Continued

Location	Position	Name of Incumbent	Type of Appt.	Pay Plan	Level, Grade, or Pay	Tenure	Expires
Rockville, MD	Senior Advisor to the Administrator	Miriam E. Delphin-Rittmon.	NA	ES	....	....	
Do	Director of Special Initiatives	Vacant	....	ES	....	....	
Washington, DC	Senior Associate for Behavioral Health and Interagency Coordination.	......do	....	ES	....	....	
	Center for Substance Abuse Prevention						
Rockville, MD	Director	Career Incumbent	CA	ES	....	....	
Do	Deputy Director	......do	CA	ES	....	....	
Do	......do	Vacant	....	ES	....	....	
Do	Director, Division of Systems Development	......do	....	ES	....	....	
	Center for Mental Health Services						
Do	Deputy Director	Career Incumbent	CA	ES	....	....	
	Center for Substance Abuse Treatment						
Do	Director	......do	CA	ES	....	....	
Do	Deputy Director	......do	CA	ES	....	....	
	CENTERS FOR DISEASE CONTROL AND PREVENTION						
Atlanta, GA	Director	Thomas R. Frieden	NA	ES	....	....	
Washington, DC	Associate Director	Career Incumbent	CA	ES	....	....	
Atlanta, GA	Director, Human Capital and Resources Management Office.	Vacant	....	ES	....	....	
Do	Chief Information Officer	Career Incumbent	CA	ES	....	....	
Do	Chief Security Officer	Vacant	....	ES	....	....	
Do	Senior Advisor to the Director of the Chief Human Capital and Resources Office.	Career Incumbent	CA	ES	....	....	
Do	Deputy Chief Operating Officer	Vacant	....	ES	....	....	
Do	Chief Information Security Officer	Career Incumbent	CA	ES	....	....	
Do	Supervisory Public Health Advisor	......do	CA	ES	....	....	
Do	Senior Advisor to the Director for Global Health Affairs.	Vacant	....	ES	....	....	
Do	Budget Officer	Career Incumbent	CA	ES	....	....	
Do	Deputy Chief Financial Officer	Vacant	....	ES	....	....	
Do	Associate Director, Policy	Career Incumbent	CA	ES	....	....	
Do	Associate Director, Communications	Vacant	....	ES	....	....	
Do	Chief Operating Officer	......do	....	ES	....	....	
Do	Deputy Director, State, Tribal, Local, and Territorial Support.	Career Incumbent	CA	ES	....	....	
Do	Special Advisor to the Center for Disease Control Director.	......do	CA	ES	....	....	
Do	Director, Office of Diversity Management and Equal Employment Opportunity.	......do	CA	ES	....	....	
Do	Deputy Director, Global Health Policy and Communications.	......do	CA	ES	....	....	
Do	Associate Director, Global Health Development.	......do	CA	ES	....	....	
Do	Deputy Director, Management and Overseas Operations.	......do	CA	ES	....	....	
Do	Financial Manager	......do	CA	ES	....	....	
Do	Special Projects Advisor	......do	CA	ES	....	....	
Do	Business Services Performance Officer	......do	CA	ES	....	....	
Do	Program Management Officer	......do	CA	ES	....	....	
	National Center for Chronic Disease Prevention and Health Promotion						
Do	Deputy Director	......do	CA	ES	....	....	
	Office of Terrorism Preparedness and Emergency Response						
Do	Director, Strategic National Stockpile	......do	CA	ES	....	....	
Do	Deputy Director, Office of Public Health Preparedness and Response.	......do	CA	ES	....	....	
	Coordinating Center for Infectious Diseases						
Do	Deputy Director, National Center for HIV/AIDS, Viral Hepatitis, Sexually Transmitted Diseases, and Tuberculosis Prevention.	......do	CA	ES	....	....	
	FOOD AND DRUG ADMINISTRATION						
	Office of the Commissioner						
Rockville, MD	Commissioner of Food and Drugs	Margaret A. Hamburg, M.D..	PAS	EX	IV	....	
Do	Assistant Commissioner for Science Coordination.	Vacant	....	ES	....	....	
Do	Chief of Staff	Lisa L. Barclay	NA	ES	....	....	

DEPARTMENT OF HEALTH AND HUMAN SERVICES—Continued

Location	Position	Name of Incumbent	Type of Appt.	Pay Plan	Level, Grade, or Pay	Tenure	Expires
Silver Spring, MD	Senior Advisor	Meghan Scott	SC	GS	15		
Rockville, MD	Deputy Commissioner for Operations (Chief Operating Officer).	Vacant		ES			
Do	Assistant Commissioner for International Programs.	Career Incumbent	CA	ES			
Do	Deputy Commissioner for Policy	Vacant		ES			
Do	Senior Advisor for International Policy and Communications.	......do		ES			
Do	Director, Office of Budget Formulation and Presentation.	Career Incumbent	CA	ES			
Do	Associate Commissioner for Legislation	......do	CA	ES			
Do	Deputy Chief of Staff, Food and Drug Administration.	Vacant		ES			
Do	Assistant Commissioner for Legislation	......do		ES			
Do	Assistant Commissioner for Management (Operations).	......do		ES			
Do	Director, Resource Planning and Strategic Management Staff, Office of Foods.	......do		ES			
Do	Deputy Chief Information Officer	Career Incumbent	CA	ES			
Do	Associate Commissioner for Operations	Vacant		ES			
Do	Assistant Commissioner for Policy	Career Incumbent	CA	ES			
Do	Executive Officer, Office of the Commissioner	......do	CA	ES			
Do	Associate Director for Management	......do	CA	ES			
White Oak, MD	Director of Policy, Center for Tobacco Products.	......do	CA	ES			
Rockville, MD	Associate Director, Office of Regulations	......do	CA	ES			
Do	Senior Advisor, Office of Scientific Integrity	......do	CA	ES			
Do	Senior Economic Advisor, Office of Policy, Planning and Budget.	Vacant		ES			
Do	Director, Office of Financial Operations	Career Incumbent	CA	ES			
White Oak, MD	Deputy Commissioner for Administration	Vacant		ES			
Rockville, MD	Deputy Commissioner for Foods	Career Incumbent	CA	ES			
Do	Counselor to the Commissioner	......do	CA	ES			
Do	Associate Commissioner for Administration	Vacant		ES			
White Oak, MD	Director, Office of Health Communication and Education.	Career Incumbent	CA	ES			
Silver Spring, MD	Deputy Commissioner for Global Regulatory Operations and Policy.	......do	CA	ES			
	Office of External Relations						
Rockville, MD	Associate Commissioner for External Affairs	Virginia A. Cox	NA	ES			
Silver Spring, MD	Assistant Commissioner for Public Affairs	Steven T. Immergut	NA	ES			
Rockville, MD	Assistant Commissioner for External Relations.	Career Incumbent	CA	ES			
	Office of Policy and Planning						
Do	Assistant Commissioner for Planning	......do	CA	ES			
Do	Associate Commissioner for Policy and Planning.	Vacant		ES			
	Office of Chief Counsel						
Do	Deputy Associate General Counsel for Litigation Food and Drug Division.	Career Incumbent	CA	ES			
Do	Associate General Counsel Food and Drug Division.	Vacant		ES			
Do	Deputy Associate General Counsel/Deputy Chief Counsel.	......do		ES			
Do	Associate Deputy Chief Counsel for Litigation	......do		ES			
	Office of Management						
Do	Associate Commissioner	......do		ES			
Do	Chief Information Officer	......do		ES			
Do	Chief of Shared Services	......do		ES			
Do	Director, Office of Real Property Services	......do		ES			
Do	Director, Office of Information Technology Shared Services, Office of Management.	......do		ES			
Do	Director White Oak Consolidation Program	Career Incumbent	CA	ES			
Do	Assistant Commissioner for Management	Vacant		ES			
Do	Associate Director for Management	Career Incumbent	CA	ES			
Do	Director, Information Technology Systems	Vacant		ES			
Do	Director, Information Technology Infrastructure.	......do		ES			
Silver Spring, MD	Director, Office of Facilities	......do		ES			
	Office of Regulatory Affairs						
United States	Deputy Associate Commissioner for Regulatory Affairs.	......do	CA	ES			
Rockville, MD	Director, Office of Regional Operations	......do		ES			

DEPARTMENT OF HEALTH AND HUMAN SERVICES—Continued

Location	Position	Name of Incumbent	Type of Appt.	Pay Plan	Level, Grade, or Pay	Tenure	Expires
Rockville, MD	Director, Office of Resource Management	Vacant	....	ES	....	....	
Philadelphia, PA	Regional Food and Drug Director, Central Region.	Career Incumbent	CA	ES	....	....	
Rockville, MD	Regional Food and Drug Director, Pacific Region.	......do	CA	ES	....	....	
	Center for Biologics Evaluation and Research						
Bethesda, MD	Associate Center Director for Policy	......do	CA	ES	....	....	
	Center for Drug Evaluation and Research						
Rockville, MD	Director, Office of Pharmaceutical Science	Career Incumbent	CA	ES	....	....	
Do	Associate Director for Planning and Business	Career Incumbent	CA	ES	....	....	
Do	Associate Director for Policy	......do	CA	ES	....	....	
Do	Senior Advisor	Vacant	....	ES	....	....	
	Center for Devices and Radiological Health						
Silver Spring, MD	Deputy Director for Policy, Center for Devices and Radiological Health.	Career Incumbent	CA	ES	....	....	
Rockville, MD	Deputy Director, Office of Compliance	Vacant	....	ES	....	....	
Do	Deputy Director, Center for Devices and Radiological Health.	......do	....	ES	....	....	
Do	Senior Associate Director, Center for Devices and Radiological Health.	......do	....	ES	....	....	
Do	Executive Officer	Career Incumbent	CA	ES	....	....	
Do	Director, Office of Surveillance and Biometrics.	Vacant	....	ES	....	....	
Do	Director, Office of Communications, Education and Radiation Programs.	Career Incumbent	CA	ES	....	....	
	Center for Food Safety and Applied Nutrition						
Washington, DC	Director	......do	CA	ES	....	....	
Do	Associate Director of Regulations	Vacant	....	ES	....	....	
Rockville, MD	Executive Officer	Career Incumbent	CA	ES	....	....	
	Center for Veterinary Medicine						
Rockville, MD	Director, Office of New Animal and Drug Evaluation.	......do	CA	ES	....	....	
Do	Deputy Director	......do	CA	ES	....	....	
Do	Associate Director for Policy and Regulations	Vacant	....	ES	....	....	
Do	Associate Director for Policy and Executive Programs.	Career Incumbent	CA	ES	....	....	
Do	**HEALTH RESOURCES AND SERVICES ADMINISTRATION OFFICE OF THE ADMINISTRATOR** Administrator	Mary K. Wakefield, Ph.D.	NA	ES	....	....	
Do	Director, Office of Financial Policy and Controls and Chief Financial Officer.	Career Incumbent	CA	ES	....	....	
Do	Deputy Administrator	......do	CA	ES	....	....	
Do	Director, Office of Budget	......do	CA	ES	....	....	
Do	Director, Office of Legislation	Vacant	....	ES	....	....	
Do	Associate Administrator	Career Incumbent	CA	ES	....	....	
Do	Associate Administrator for Operations	......do	CA	ES	....	....	
Do	Director, Office of Acquisitions Management and Policy.	......do	CA	ES	....	....	
Do	Director, Office of Planning and Evaluation ...	......do	CA	ES	....	....	
Do	Associate Administrator, Chief Financial Officer.	......do	CA	ES	....	....	
Do	Director, Office of Equal Opportunity and Civil Rights.	......do	CA	ES	....	....	
Do	Associate Administrator, Office of Rural Health Policy.	......do	CA	ES	....	....	
Do	Associate Administrator, Office of Regional Operations.	......do	CA	ES	....	....	
Do	Director, Office of Information Technology and Chief Information Officer.	......do	CA	ES	....	....	
Do	Associate Administrator, Healthcare Systems Bureau.	......do	CA	ES	....	....	
Do	Special Assistant to the Administrator	......do	CA	ES	....	....	
Do	Deputy Associate Administrator, Healthcare Systems Bureau.	......do	CA	ES	....	....	
Do	Director, Office of Communications	......do	CA	ES	....	....	
Do	Associate Administrator, Office of Federal Assistance Management.	......do	CA	ES	....	....	
Do	Special Assistant	Elizabeth Shipman Lee	SC	GS	13	....	
	Office of Performance Review						
Do	Deputy Associate Administrator	Career Incumbent	CA	ES	....	....	

DEPARTMENT OF HEALTH AND HUMAN SERVICES—Continued

Location	Position	Name of Incumbent	Type of Appt.	Pay Plan	Level, Grade, or Pay	Tenure	Expires
	Office of Healthcare Systems Bureau						
Rockville, MD	Deputy Associate Administrator	Career Incumbent	CA	ES	....	....	
Do	Senior Advisor for Special Initiatives, Healthcare Systems Bureau.	......do	CA	ES	....	....	
Do	Deputy Associate Administrator	......do	CA	ES	....	....	
	HIV/AIDS Bureau						
Do	Deputy Associate Administrator	......do	CA	ES	....	....	
	Bureau of Clinician Recruitment and Services						
Do	Associate Administrator	......do	CA	ES	....	....	
Do	Deputy Associate Administrator	......do	CA	ES	....	....	
	Maternal and Child Health Bureau						
Do	Associate Administrator	......do	CA	ES	....	....	
Do	Deputy Associate Administrator	......do	CA	ES	....	....	
Do	Director, Division of Services for Children With Special Health Needs.	......do	CA	ES	....	....	
	Bureau of Health Professions						
Do	Associate Administrator	Vacant	....	ES	....	....	
Do	Deputy Associate Administrator	Career Incumbent	CA	ES	....	....	
	Bureau of Primary Health Care						
Do	Associate Administrator	......do	CA	ES	....	....	
Do	Deputy Associate Administrator	Vacant	....	ES	....	....	
Do	Executive Associate Administrator for Programs.	Career Incumbent	CA	ES	....	....	
	INDIAN HEALTH SERVICE						
Do	Director	Yvette D. Roubideaux, M.D..	PAS	EX	V	....	
Do	Deputy Director for Management Operations	Career Incumbent	CA	ES	....	....	
Do	Director, Office of Information Technology	......do	CA	ES	....	....	
Do	Director, Office of Resource Access and Partnerships.	......do	CA	ES	....	....	
Do	Deputy Director for Indian Health Policy	......do	CA	ES	....	....	
Do	Senior Advisor to the Director	Geoffrey Scott Roth	NA	ES	....	....	
Phoenix, AZ	Chief Executive Officer, Phoenix Indian Medical Center.	Vacant	....	ES	....	....	
Rockville, MD	Deputy Director	Career Incumbent	CA	ES	....	....	
Do	Director, Office of Direct Service and Contracting Tribes.	Vacant	....	ES	....	....	
Anchorage, AK	Director, Alaska Area	Career Incumbent	CA	ES	....	....	
Window Rock, AZ ..	Director, Navajo Area	......do	CA	ES	....	....	
Phoenix, AZ	Director, Phoenix Area Office	......do	CA	ES	....	....	
Sacramento, CA	Director, California Area	......do	CA	ES	....	....	
Rockville, MD	Associate Director for Planning, Evaluation, and Legislation.	Vacant	....	ES	....	....	
Bemidji, MN	Director, Bemidji Area	Career Incumbent	CA	ES	....	....	
Rockville, MD	Director, Office of Information Technology	Vacant	....	ES	....	....	
Billings, MT	Director, Billings Area	Career Incumbent	CA	ES	....	....	
Aberdeen, SD	Director, Aberdeen Area Indian Health Service.	......do	CA	ES	....	....	
Rockville, MD	Director, Office of Tribal Self-Governance	......do	CA	ES	....	....	
Nashville, TN	Director Nashville Area	Vacant	....	ES	....	....	
Albuquerque, NM ..	Director, Albuquerque Area	Career Incumbent	CA	ES	....	....	
Rockville, MD	Director, Office of Urban Indian Health Policy.	......do	CA	ES	....	....	
Oklahoma City, OK	Director, Oklahoma City Area	......do	CA	ES	....	....	
Rockville, MD	Director Office of Public Health Support	Vacant	....	ES	....	....	
Do	Director, Office of Clinical and Preventive Services.	......do	....	ES	....	....	
Phoenix, AZ	Executive Advisor to the Director	Career Incumbent	CA	ES	....	....	
Portland, OR	Director, Portland Area	Vacant	....	ES	....	....	
Rockville, MD	Deputy Director, Office of Management Services.	Career Incumbent	CA	ES	....	....	
Billings, MT	Director, Billings Area	Vacant	....	ES	....	....	
Tucson, AZ	Director, Tucson Area	Career Incumbent	CA	ES	....	....	
Rockville, MD	Director, Office of Tribal Self-Governance	Vacant	....	ES	....	....	
Portland, OR	Director, Portland Area	Career Incumbent	CA	ES	....	....	
Rockville, MD	Director, Office of Management Services	Vacant	....	ES	....	....	
	NATIONAL INSTITUTES OF HEALTH						
	Office of the Director						
Bethesda, MD	Director	Francis S. Collins, M.D., Ph.D..	PAS	EX	IV	....	
Do	Director, Office of Management Assessment ..	Career Incumbent	CA	ES	....	....	

DEPARTMENT OF HEALTH AND HUMAN SERVICES—Continued

Location	Position	Name of Incumbent	Type of Appt.	Pay Plan	Level, Grade, or Pay	Tenure	Expires
Bethesda, MD	Associate Director for Management	Career Incumbent	CA	ES			
Do	Associate Director for Communications and Public Liaison.	......do	CA	ES			
Do	Associate Director for Budget	......do	CA	ES			
Durham, NC	Associate Director of Management	......do	CA	ES			
Bethesda, MD	Director, Human Resources	Vacant		ES			
Do	Director, Office of Research Services	Career Incumbent	CA	ES			
Do	Associate Director, Legislative Policy Analysis	......do	CA	ES			
Do	Associate Director, Research on Women's Health.	Vacant		ES			
Do	Director, Office of Equal Opportunity	Career Incumbent	CA	ES			
Do	Deputy Director, Management	......do	CA	ES			
Do	Senior Advisor to Deputy Director	Vacant		ES			
Do	Deputy Director, Division of Program Coordination, Planning, and Strategic Initiatives.	Career Incumbent	CA	ES			
	National Heart, Lung and Blood Institute						
Do	Associate Director for Administrative Management.	......do	CA	ES			
	National Cancer Institute						
Do	Director	Harold E. Varmus	PA	OT			
Do	Deputy Director	Career Incumbent	CA	ES			
Rockville, MD	Director, Office of Communications and Education.	......do	CA	ES			
	National Institutes of Allergy and Infectious Diseases						
Bethesda, MD	Director, Office of Strategic Planning and Financial Management.	Vacant		ES			
Do	Chief, Laboratory of Molecular Microbiology	Malcolm A. Martin	XS	OT	$194,017		
	National Institutes of Child Health and Human Development						
Do	Associate Director, Office of Science Policy, Analysis and Communication.	Career Incumbent	CA	ES			
	National Institutes of Neurological Disorders and Stroke						
Do	Associate Director for Management	......do	CA	ES			
Do	Senior Advisor to the Director	Vacant		ES			
	Center for Information Technology						
Do	Deputy Director	Career Incumbent	CA	ES			
	National Human Genome Research Institute						
Do	Assistant Director for Policy and Public Affairs.	Vacant		ES			
	National Institute on Drug Abuse						
Rockville, MD	Director, Office of Science Policy and Communications.	......do		ES			
	National Institute of Mental Health						
Do	Associate Director for Management	Career Incumbent	CA	ES			
	AGENCY FOR HEALTHCARE RESEARCH AND QUALITY						
Do	Director	......do	CA	ES			
Do	Deputy Director	......do	CA	ES			
Do	Director, Center for Outcomes and Evidence	......do	CA	ES			
Do	Senior Science Advisor for Information Technology.	......do	CA	ES			
Do	Director, Policy Coordination, Executive Secretary and Department Liaison.	......do	CA	ES			
Do	Director, Information Technology	......do	CA	ES			

DEPARTMENT OF HEALTH AND HUMAN SERVICES OFFICE OF THE INSPECTOR GENERAL

Location	Position	Name of Incumbent	Type of Appt.	Pay Plan	Level, Grade, or Pay	Tenure	Expires
Washington, DC	Inspector General	Daniel R. Levinson	PAS	OT	$170,259		

DEPARTMENT OF HOMELAND SECURITY

Location	Position	Name of Incumbent	Type of Appt.	Pay Plan	Level, Grade, or Pay	Tenure	Expires
	OFFICE OF THE SECRETARY						
Washington, DC	Secretary	Janet A. Napolitano	PAS	EX	I		
Do	Senior Counselor	Alice C. Hill	NA	ES			
Do	Counselor	Subhasri Ramanathan	NA	ES			
Do	....do	John Sandweg	NA	ES			
Do	Confidential Assistant	Jacquenetta Wright	SC	GS	15		
	Office of the Chief of Staff						
Do	Chief of Staff	Noah Kroloff	NA	ES			
Do	Deputy Chief of Staff	Amy L. Shlossman	NA	ES			
Do	White House Liaison	Alison K. Schwartz	SC	GS	15		
Do	Deputy White House Liaison	Jacklyn Dao	SC	GS	13		
Do	Special Assistant to the Deputy Chief of Staff	Neema S. Guliani	SC	GS	14		
Do	......do	Matthew Angelo	SC	GS	12		
Do	......do	Daniel Grant	SC	GS	12		
Do	......do	Stephanie K Y Speirs	SC	GS	9		
Do	Deputy Director of Scheduling	Abigail A. Page	SC	GS	12		
Do	Deputy Director of Scheduling and Protocol Coordination.	Mary Ellen Brown	SC	GS	14		
Do	Confidential Assistant to the Chief of Staff	Brianna McCullough	SC	GS	7		
Do	Advance Representative	Dina Hadziselimovic	SC	GS	11		
	Office of the Executive Secretary for Operations and Administration						
Do	Executive Secretary	Philip A. McNamara	NA	ES			
Do	Senior Liaison Officer	Diane Saunders	SC	GS	15		
Do	Secretary Briefing Book Coordinator	Andrew C. Ledbetter	SC	GS	9		
Do	Deputy Secretary Briefing Book Coordinator	Jordan Acker	SC	GS	11		
	OFFICE OF THE DEPUTY SECRETARY						
Do	Deputy Secretary	Jane Holl Lute	PAS	EX	II		
Do	Chief of Staff and Counselor	Brian deVallance	NA	ES			
Do	Counselor	Career Incumbent	CA	ES			
Do	Executive Assistant	Erin A. O'Connor	SC	GS	15		
Do	Special Assistant	Philip M. Stupak	SC	GS	12		
Do	Advisor to the Chief of Staff	Jacob N. Heller	SC	GS	12		
	Office of the Chief Privacy Officer						
Do	Chief Privacy Officer	Mary Ellen Callahan	NA	ES			
Do	Deputy Chief Privacy Officer	Vacant		ES			
Do	Deputy Chief Freedom of Information Act Officer.	Career Incumbent	CA	ES			
Do	Special Assistant	Jennifer M. Lee	SC	GS	13		
	Office for Civil Rights and Civil Liberties						
Do	Officer for Civil Rights and Civil Liberties	Vacant		ES			
	Office of Counternarcotics Enforcement						
Do	Director	......do	PAS	EX			
	Ombudsman, Citizenship and Immigration Services						
Do	Ombudsman	......do		ES			
	Office of the Assistant Secretary for Public Affairs						
Do	Assistant Secretary	......do		ES			
Do	Principal Deputy Assistant Secretary	Career Incumbent	CA	ES			
Do	Deputy Assistant Secretary for Strategic Communications.	Heather Wendy Wong	NA	ES			
Do	Director of Speechwriting	Gregory Michaelidis	SC	GS	15		
Do	Speechwriter to the Secretary	Harry Julius Kruglik	SC	GS	14		
Do	Press Secretary	Matthew M. Chandler	SC	GS	13		
Do	Deputy Press Secretary	Marsha L. Catron	SC	GS	13		
Do	......do	Peter C. Boogaard	SC	GS	12		
Do	Director of Strategic Communications	Sara A. Kuban	SC	GS	13		
Do	Assistant Press Secretary	Nicole Theresa Stickel	SC	GS	11		
Do	Director of Special Projects	Colin D. Walsh	SC	GS	11		
Do	Press Assistant	Sze-Yian Lee	SC	GS	7		
	Office of the Assistant Secretary for Intergovernmental Affairs						
Do	Assistant Secretary	Elizabeth H. Markey	NA	ES			
Do	Principal Deputy Assistant Secretary	Jarrod N. Bernstein	NA	ES			
Do	State and Local Coordinator	Jennifer Hoelzle	SC	GS	14		
Do	Local Affairs Coordinator	Danielle Kimberly Decker	SC	GS	9		
Do	Confidential Assistant	Katelyn Anna Horne	SC	GS	7		

DEPARTMENT OF HOMELAND SECURITY—Continued

Location	Position	Name of Incumbent	Type of Appt.	Pay Plan	Level, Grade, or Pay	Tenure	Expires
	Office of Assistant Secretary for Legislative Affairs						
Washington, DC	Assistant Secretary	Nelson Peacock	NA	ES	....	....	
Do	Deputy Assistant Secretary	Leslie M. Gross-Davis	NA	ES	....	....	
Do	......do	Dennis Michael Stroud, Jr.	NA	ES	....	....	
Do	Director of Legislative Affairs for Intelligence and Analysis.	Connie LaRossa	SC	GS	15	....	
Do	Senior Advisor to the Assistant Secretary	Kimonia L. Alfred	SC	GS	14	....	
Do	Legislative Affairs Specialist	Chloe I. Himmel	SC	GS	11	....	
Do	......do	Alfonso Lopez	SC	GS	11	....	
	Office of Operations Coordination and Planning Directorate						
Do	Director	Career Incumbent	CA	ES	....	....	
Do	Deputy Director	......do	CA	ES	....	....	
Do	Chief of Staff	......do	CA	ES	....	....	
Do	Senior Advisor to the Chief of Staff	Barbara A. Saliunas	TA	ES	....	....	12/04/13
Do	Director, National Operations Center	Career Incumbent	CA	ES	....	....	
Do	Director, Resources Division	......do	CA	ES	....	....	
Do	Director, Incident Management and Interagency Planning Division.	......do	CA	ES	....	....	
Do	Director, Operations Coordination Division	......do	CA	ES	....	....	
Do	Director, Doctrine and Concept Development ...	......do	CA	ES	....	....	
Do	Department of Homeland Security Advisor to the Department of Defense.	......do	CA	ES	....	....	
	Domestic Nuclear Detection Office						
Do	Director	Vacant	....	ES	....	....	
	OFFICE OF THE ASSISTANT SECRETARY FOR HEALTH AFFAIRS AND CHIEF MEDICAL OFFICER						
Do	Assistant Secretary	Alexander G. Garza	PAS	EX	IV	....	
Do	Deputy Assistant Secretary, Health Threats Resilience.	Career Incumbent	CA	ES	....	....	
Do	Deputy Director, Health Threats Resilience ...	Vacant	....	ES	....	....	
	OFFICE OF THE ASSISTANT SECRETARY FOR POLICY						
Do	Assistant Secretary	David F. Heyman	PAS	EX	IV	....	
Do	Principal Deputy Assistant Secretary	Leonard P. Joseph	NA	ES	....	....	
Do	Senior Director, Immigration and Border Security.	Vacant	....	ES	....	....	
Do	Senior Advisor, Immigration	Esther Olavarria	TA	ES	....	....	09/11/13
Do	Executive Director for Analysis	Career Incumbent	CA	ES	....	....	
Do	Executive Director for Strategy and Planning ...	......do	CA	ES	....	....	
Do	Deputy Assistant Secretary of Chemical, Biological, Radiological, and Nuclear Office.	......do	CA	ES	....	....	
Do	Deputy Assistant Secretary for Transborder ..	......do	CA	ES	....	....	
Do	Assistant Secretary for Strategy, Planning, Analysis and Risk.	......do	CA	ES	....	....	
Do	Assistant Secretary for State and Local Law Enforcement.	Louis F. Quijas, Jr.	NA	ES	....	....	
Do	Assistant Secretary for Private Sector	Douglas A. Smith	NA	ES	....	....	
Do	Assistant Secretary for Policy Development ...	David Pressman	NA	ES	....	....	
Do	Deputy Assistant Secretary for Counterterrorism Policy.	Career Incumbent	CA	ES	....	....	
Do	Assistant Secretary for International Affairs and Chief Diplomatic Officer.	Alan D. Bersin	NA	ES	....	....	
Do	Deputy Assistant Secretary for International Affairs.	Career Incumbent	CA	ES	....	....	
Do	Deputy Assistant Secretary for International (Policy).	Vacant	....	ES	....	....	
London, United Kingdom.	Department of Homeland Security Attaché to London.	Career Incumbent	CA	ES	....	....	
Kabul, Afghanistan	Department of Homeland Security Attaché to Kabul, Afghanistan.	Vacant	....	ES	....	....	
Washington, DC	Deputy Assistant Secretary for Screening Coordination.	Career Incumbent	CA	ES	....	....	
Do	Executive Director, Homeland Security Advisory Council.	Rebecca L. Sharp	SC	GS	15	....	
Do	Senior Advisor to the Assistant Secretary for Policy.	Holly E. Canevari	SC	GS	15	....	
Do	Special Assistant	Meagen L. Manning	SC	GS	14	....	
Do	Chief of Staff, Office of International Affairs ..	Katrina R. Hartman	SC	GS	14	....	
Do	Deputy Executive Director, Homeland Security Advisory Council.	Patrick D. McQuillan III ...	SC	GS	13	....	

DEPARTMENT OF HOMELAND SECURITY—Continued

Location	Position	Name of Incumbent	Type of Appt.	Pay Plan	Level, Grade, or Pay	Tenure	Expires
Washington, DC	Executive Assistant	Karen Kay Heinrich	SC	GS	13		
Do	Policy Analyst	Matthew J. Wein	SC	GS	12		
Do	Advisor to the Assistant Secretary for International Affairs and Chief Diplomatic Officer.	Brian Albert	SC	GS	12		
Do	Director, Homeland Security Advisory Council.	William C. Smith, Jr.	SC	GS	11		
Do	Special Assistant	Rebecca Wexler	SC	GS	9		
	OFFICE OF THE GENERAL COUNSEL						
Do	General Counsel	Ivan K. Fong	PAS	EX	IV		
Do	Counselor to the General Counsel	Jonathan E. Meyer	NA	ES			
Do	Principal Deputy General Counsel	Career Incumbent	CA	ES			
Do	Chief of Staff	Vacant		ES			
Do	Deputy General Counsel	Seth Grossman	NA	ES			
Do	.....do	Audrey J. Anderson	NA	ES			
Do	.....do	Theodore Chuang	NA	ES			
Do	Associate General Counsel for General Law	Career Incumbent	CA	ES			
Do	Associate General Counsel for Immigration	......do	CA	ES			
Do	Associate General Counsel for Technology Programs.	Vacant		ES			
Do	Associate General Counsel for Intelligence	Career Incumbent	CA	ES			
Do	Associate General Counsel for Regulatory Affairs.	......do	CA	ES			
Do	Associate General Counsel for Legal Counsel	Vacant		ES			
Do	Deputy Associate General Counsel for Legal Counsel.	Career Incumbent	CA	ES			
Do	Associate General Counsel for Operations and Enforcement.	......do	CA	ES			
Do	Associate General Counsel for National Protection and Programs Directorate.	......do	CA	ES			
Do	Deputy Associate General Counsel for National Protection and Programs Directorate.	......do	CA	ES			
Do	Managing Counsel	Vacant		ES			
Do	Special Advisor to the General Counsel	Jennifer E. Johnston	SC	GS	14		
Do	Counselor to the Principal Deputy General Counsel.	Gena Chieco	SC	GS	13		
Do	Special Assistant to the General Counsel and Attorney Advisor.	J. Lynn Parker	SC	GS	13		
	OFFICE OF THE UNDER SECRETARY FOR NATIONAL PROTECTION AND PROGRAMS DIRECTORATE						
Do	Under Secretary	R. Rand Beers	PAS	EX	III		
Do	Deputy Under Secretary	Suzanne E. Spaulding	NA	ES			
Do	Counselor to the Deputy Under Secretary	Bruce W. McConnell	NA	ES			
Do	Chief of Staff	Vacant		ES			
Do	Director of Communications	Robert M. Davis	TA	ES			08/13/14
Do	Director, Risk Analysis and Modeling	John F. Murphy	TA	ES			11/06/14
Do	Director, National Protection and Programs Directorate (NPPD) Transition	Randolph Kruger	TA	ES			07/02/14
Do	Associate Director, National Protection and Programs Directorate (NPPD) Transition Program Management Office.	Patrice L. Ward	TA	ES			06/04/13
Do	Assistant Secretary for Infrastructure Protection.	Caitlin A. Durkovich	PA	ES			
Do	Assistant Secretary for Cybersecurity and Telecommunications.	Michael W. Locatis III	NA	ES			
Do	Deputy Under Secretary, Cybersecurity	Mark Weatherford	NA	ES			
Do	Director, United States Visitor and Immigrant Status Indicator Technology (US-VISIT) Program.	Career Incumbent	CA	ES			
Do	Chief Technology Officer	......do	CA	ES			
Do	Chief of Staff, Office of Infrastructure Protection.	Michael A. Beland	SC	GS	15		
Do	Special Advisor	Bridger E. McGaw	SC	GS	15		
Do	Program Analyst - Cybersecurity Strategist	Thomas M. Finan	SC	GS	15		
Do	Senior Advisor for Public Affairs	Gina Flores	SC	GS	15		
Do	Special Counselor to the Under Secretary	Robert K. Knake	SC	GS	15		
Do	Cybersecurity Strategist	Davis A. Hake	SC	GS	12		
Do	Program Coordinator	Caroline B. Simmons	SC	GS	11		
Do	Special Assistant to the Under Secretary, National Protection and Programs.	Patrick Barry	SC	GS	9		
Do	Confidential Assistant	Kindall Johnson	SC	GS	7		

DEPARTMENT OF HOMELAND SECURITY—Continued

Location	Position	Name of Incumbent	Type of Appt.	Pay Plan	Level, Grade, or Pay	Tenure	Expires
	OFFICE OF THE UNDER SECRETARY FOR INTELLIGENCE AND ANALYSIS						
Washington, DC	Under Secretary	Caryn A. Wagner	PAS	EX	III	....	
Do	Principal Deputy Under Secretary	Career Incumbent	CA	ES	....	....	
Do	Deputy Under Secretary for State and Local Program Office.	......do	CA	ES	....	....	
Do	Deputy Under Secretary for Enterprise and Mission Support.	......do	CA	ES	....	....	
Do	Director, Knowledge Management Division	......do	CA	ES	....	....	
Do	Director, Counterintelligence Programs Division.	......do	CA	ES	....	....	
Do	Deputy Under Secretary for Plans, Policy and Performance Management.	......do	CA	ES	....	....	
Do	Director, Information Sharing and Intelligence Enterprise Management Division.	Vacant	....	ES	....	....	
Do	Director, Air Domain Intelligence Integration Element.	Career Incumbent	CA	ES	....	....	
Do	Deputy Under Secretary for Analysis	Vacant	....	ES	....	....	
Do	Associate Deputy Under Secretary for Analysis.	Career Incumbent	CA	ES	....	....	
Do	Director, Border Security Division	......do	CA	ES	....	....	
Do	Director, Homeland Counterterrorism Division.	......do	CA	ES	....	....	
Do	Director, Current Intelligence Division	......do	CA	ES	....	....	
Do	Liaison	Jason P. Houser	SC	GS	15	....	
Do	Liaison for Community Partnership and Strategic Engagement.	Nathaniel L. Snyder	SC	GS	14	....	
	OFFICE OF THE UNDER SECRETARY FOR SCIENCE AND TECHNOLOGY						
Do	Under Secretary	Tara J. O'Toole	PAS	EX	III	....	
Do	Deputy Under Secretary	Career Incumbent	CA	ES	....	....	
Do	Chief of Staff	Vacant	....	ES	....	....	
Do	Special Assistant to the Under Secretary	......do	CA	ES	....	....	
Do	......do	......do	CA	ES	....	....	
Do	Director, Administration and Support Division.	Career Incumbent	CA	ES	....	....	
Do	Chief Systems Engineer	......do	CA	ES	....	....	
Do	Director of Support to the Homeland Security Enterprise and First Responders.	......do	CA	ES	....	....	
Do	Director, Homeland Security Advanced Research Projects Agency.	......do	CA	ES	....	....	
Do	Director, Research and Development Partnerships.	......do	CA	ES	....	....	
Do	Director, Plum Island Animal Disease Center	......do	CA	ES	....	....	
Do	Special Assistant to the Under Secretary	Austin-William R. Rackets	SC	GS	9	....	
	OFFICE OF THE UNDER SECRETARY FOR MANAGEMENT						
Do	Under Secretary	Rafael Borras	PAS	EX	II	....	
Do	Deputy Under Secretary	Chris Cummiskey	NA	ES	....	....	
Do	Chief of Staff	Career Incumbent	CA	ES	....	....	
Do	Senior Advisor to the Under Secretary	......do	CA	ES	....	....	
Do	Senior Counselor	......do	CA	ES	....	....	
Do	Executive Director, Management Integration	Kenneth J. Buck	TA	ES	....	....	08/01/13
Do	Director, Headquarters Consolidation Outreach.	Carol J. Mitten	TA	ES	....	....	02/26/14
Do	Executive Director, Academic Engagement ...	Lauren Kielsmeier	NA	ES	....	....	
Do	Senior Advisor	Lavita Zanette Legrys	SC	GS	15	....	
Do	Advisor	Daniel J. Harper	SC	GS	14	....	
	Office of the Chief Financial Officer						
Do	Chief Financial Officer	Peggy Sherry	PAS	EX	IV	....	
Do	Deputy Chief Financial Officer	Stacey A. Marcott	TA	ES	....	....	05/19/15
Do	Deputy Director, Office of Budget	Career Incumbent	CA	ES	....	....	
Do	Director, Headquarters Operations	......do	CA	ES	....	....	
Do	Director, Grants Policy and Oversight	......do	CA	ES	....	....	
Do	Director, Program Analysis and Evaluation ...	Morgan B. Geiger	TA	ES	....	....	01/14/15
	Office of the Chief Procurement Officer						
Do	Director, Office of Small and Disadvantaged Business Utilization.	Career Incumbent	CA	ES	....	....	
Do	Director, Office of Selective Acquisitions	David R. Dasher	TA	ES	....	....	05/05/15
	Office of the Chief Human Capital Officer						
Do	Chief Human Capital Officer	Career Incumbent	CA	ES	....	....	
Do	Chief Learning Officer	......do	CA	ES	....	....	

DEPARTMENT OF HOMELAND SECURITY—Continued

Location	Position	Name of Incumbent	Type of Appt.	Pay Plan	Level, Grade, or Pay	Tenure	Expires
Washington, DC	Executive Director, Enterprise Leader Development Programs.	Career Incumbent	CA	ES	....	....	
Do	Executive Director, Policy and Programs	Jeanarta C. McEachron	TA	ES	....	....	05/05/13
Do	Executive Director, Balanced Workforce Program Management Office.	Career Incumbent	CA	ES	....	....	
	Office of the Chief Information Officer						
Do	Chief Information Officer	Richard A. Spires	PA	ES	....	....	
	Office of the Chief Administrative Services						
Do	Chief, Administrative Services Officer	Career Incumbent	CA	ES	....	....	
Do	Deputy Director for Real Estate	Richard R. Espinoza	TA	ES	....	....	07/30/14
Do	Deputy Director for Capital Planning	Gregory C. Ewing	TA	ES	....	....	08/27/14
	FEDERAL LAW ENFORCEMENT TRAINING CENTER						
Do	Assistant Director	Kevin S. Livingston	TA	ES	....	....	12/19/12
	UNITED STATES COAST GUARD						
Do	Director for Civil Rights	Career Incumbent	CA	ES	....	....	
Do	Deputy Assistant Commandant for Engineering and Logistics.	Albert Curry, Jr.	TA	ES	....	....	10/20/12
Do	Deputy Judge Advocate General and Deputy Chief Counsel.	Career Incumbent	CA	ES	....	....	
Do	Director of Commercial Regulations and Standards.	......do	CA	ES	....	....	
Do	Director, International Affairs and Foreign Policy Advisor.	......do	CA	ES	....	....	
Do	Director of Personnel Management	......do	CA	ES	....	....	
Do	Deputy Director of Governmental and Public Affairs.	......do	CA	ES	....	....	
Norfolk, VA	Deputy, Force Readiness Command	......do	CA	ES	....	....	
	U.S. CUSTOMS AND BORDER PROTECTION						
Washington, DC	Commissioner	Vacant	PAS	EX	III	....	
Do	Chief of Staff	Kimberly Ann O'Connor	NA	ES	....	....	
Do	Assistant Commissioner for Congressional Affairs.	Michael J. Yeager	NA	ES	....	....	
Do	Senior Advisor for Trade	Maria Luisa O'Connell	NA	ES	....	....	
Do	Chief Counsel	Career Incumbent	CA	ES	....	....	
Do	Director, Policy and Planning	David J. Danelo	NA	ES	....	....	
Do	Assistant Commissioner for Public Affairs	Melanie N. Roe	SC	GS	15	....	
Do	Senior Advisor to the Commissioner	Grady J. Harn	SC	GS	14	....	
Do	Policy Advisor	Ben Rohrbaugh	SC	GS	14	....	
Do	Counselor to the Commissioner	Nathan A. Bruggeman	SC	GS	14	....	
Do	Advisor to the Chief of Staff	Brett Laduzinsky	SC	GS	11	....	
	U.S. IMMIGRATION AND CUSTOMS ENFORCEMENT						
Do	Assistant Secretary	John T. Morton	PAS	EX	IV	....	
Do	Chief of Staff	Suzanne Barr	NA	ES	....	....	
Do	Executive Director, Balanced Workforce Strategy.	Robert L. Parsons	TA	ES	....	....	03/12/13
Do	Principal Legal Advisor	Peter S. Vincent	NA	ES	....	....	
Do	Director, Office of Policy	Career Incumbent	CA	ES	....	....	
Do	Director, Office of Detention Policy and Planning.	Kevin J. Landy	NA	ES	....	....	
Do	Director of Congressional Relations	Elliot C. F. Williams	SC	GS	15	....	
Do	Director of Communications	Brian Patrick Hale	SC	GS	15	....	
Do	Special Assistant	Lacy E. Ettehad	SC	GS	9	....	
Do	......do	Sherrod J. Smith	SC	GS	7	....	
	U.S. CITIZENSHIP AND IMMIGRATION SERVICES						
Do	Director	Alejandro Mayorkas	PAS	EX	III	....	
Do	Deputy Director	Career Incumbent	CA	ES	....	....	
Do	Chief of Staff	Rebecca S. Carson	NA	ES	....	....	
Do	Chief, Policy and Strategy	Denise A. Vanison	NA	ES	....	....	
Do	Chief, Office of Communications	Edna Z. Ruano	NA	ES	....	....	
Do	Chief Counsel	Stephen H. Legomsky	NA	ES	....	....	
Do	Senior Counselor to the Director	Robert P. Silvers	SC	GS	15	....	
Do	Counselor to the Director	Elizabeth Elkiss	SC	GS	15	....	
Do	......do	Victoria Wenshan Lai	SC	GS	15	....	
Do	Special Assistant	Andrea R. Flores	SC	GS	7	....	

DEPARTMENT OF HOMELAND SECURITY—Continued

Location	Position	Name of Incumbent	Type of Appt.	Pay Plan	Level, Grade, or Pay	Tenure	Expires
	FEDERAL EMERGENCY MANAGEMENT AGENCY						
	Office of the Administrator						
Washington, DC	Administrator	W. Craig Fugate	PAS	EX	II	....	
Do	Deputy Administrator	Richard Serino	PAS	EX	III	....	
Do	Chief of Staff	Jason R. McNamara	NA	ES	....	....	
Do	Director, Center for Faith Based and Community Initiatives.	David L. Myers	NA	ES	....	....	
Do	Senior Law Enforcement Liaison	Career Incumbent	CA	ES	....	....	
Do	Deputy Director of the Center for Faith Based and Community Initiatives.	Jannah Gina Scott	SC	GS	15	....	
Do	Counselor to the Administrator	Michael A. Coen, Jr.	SC	GS	15	....	
Do	Senior Advisor to the Deputy Administrator ..	Patrick J. Hart, Jr.	SC	GS	15	....	
Do	Confidential Assistant to the Administrator ...	Michael George	SC	GS	13	....	
	Office of External Affairs						
Do	Director of External Affairs and Communications.	Jessica Smith	NA	ES	....	....	
Do	Director of Intergovernmental Affairs	Gwen Camp	SC	GS	15	....	
Do	Director of Public Affairs	Lars D. Anderson	SC	GS	15	....	
Do	Associate Director of Public Affairs/Press Secretary.	Daniel M. Watson	SC	GS	12	....	
	Office of Policy and Program Analysis						
Do	Director	David J. Kaufman	NA	ES	....	....	
	Office of General Counsel						
Do	Chief Counsel	Career Incumbent	CA	ES	....	....	
	Office of the Chief Financial Officer						
Do	Budget Director	......do	CA	ES	....	....	
	Office of the Mission Support Bureau						
Do	Associate Administrator	Vacant	....	ES	....	....	
Do	Chief Component Human Capital Officer	Career Incumbent	CA	ES	....	....	
Do	Chief Information Officer	......do	CA	ES	....	....	
Do	Deputy Chief Information Officer	......do	CA	ES	....	....	
	Office of Response and Recovery						
Do	Associate Administrator	William L. Carwile III	NA	ES	....	....	
Do	Deputy Associate Administrator	Elizabeth A. Zimmerman ..	NA	ES	....	....	
Do	Assistant Administrator for Recovery	Career Incumbent	CA	ES	....	....	
Do	Deputy Assistant Administrator for Recovery	......do	CA	ES	....	....	
Do	Assistant Administrator for Response	......do	CA	ES	....	....	
Do	National Incident Management Assistance Team Leader.	Vacant	....	ES	....	....	
Do	National Incident Management Assistance Team Leader, East.	Career Incumbent	CA	ES	....	....	
Sacramento, CA	National Incident Management Assistance Team Leader, West.	......do	CA	ES	....	....	
Washington, DC ...	Director, Individual Assistance Division	......do	CA	ES	....	....	
Do	Director, Public Assistance Division	......do	CA	ES	....	....	
Do	Director, Operations Division	......do	CA	ES	....	....	
Do	Assistant Administrator, Logistics	......do	CA	ES	....	....	
Do	Deputy Assistant Administrator, Logistics	......do	CA	ES	....	....	
	Office of Protection and National Preparedness						
Do	Deputy Administrator	Timothy W. Manning	PAS	EX	III	....	
Do	Assistant Administrator, Grants Programs	Elizabeth M. Harman	PAS	EX	IV	....	
Do	Assistant Administrator, National Continuity Programs.	Damon C. Penn	NA	ES	....	....	
Do	Deputy Assistant Administrator, National Continuity Programs.	Career Incumbent	CA	ES	....	....	
Bluemont, VA	Executive Administrator, Mount Weather Emergency Operations Center.	......do	CA	ES	....	....	
Washington, DC ...	Director, Office of National Capital Region Coordination.	Steward D. Beckham	NA	ES	....	....	
Do	Assistant Administrator, National Preparedness.	Career Incumbent	CA	ES	....	....	
Emmitsburg, MD ...	Superintendent, Emergency Management Institute.	......do	CA	ES	....	....	
Washington, DC	Director, National Integration Center	......do	CA	ES	....	....	
Do	Director, Individual and Community Preparedness.	Paulette Aniskoff	SC	GS	15	....	
	Office of Federal Insurance and Mitigation						
Do	Associate Administrator	David L. Miller	NA	ES	....	....	

DEPARTMENT OF HOMELAND SECURITY—Continued

Location	Position	Name of Incumbent	Type of Appt.	Pay Plan	Level, Grade, or Pay	Tenure	Expires
Washington, DC	Director, Business Management Division	Career Incumbent	CA	ES	....	....	
Do	Senior Advisor to the Associate Administrator	Kristin E. Robinson	SC	GS	15	....	
	Office of the Fire Administration						
Do	Administrator	Ernest Mitchell, Jr.	PAS	EX	IV	....	
Emmitsburg, MD ...	Deputy Assistant Administrator	Career Incumbent	CA	ES	....	....	
Do	Superintendent, National Fire Academy	......do	CA	ES	....	....	
	Regional Administrators						
Boston, MA	Regional Administrator, Region I (Boston)	Donald R. Boyce	NA	ES	....	....	
New York, NY	Regional Administrator, Region II (New York)	Lynn G. Canton	NA	ES	....	....	
Philadelphia, PA	Regional Director, Region III (Philadelphia) ..	Career Incumbent	CA	ES	....	....	
Atlanta, GA	Regional Director, Region IV (Atlanta)	......do	CA	ES	....	....	
Chicago, IL	Regional Administrator, Region V (Chicago) ..	Andrew Velasquez III	NA	ES	....	....	
Dallas, TX	Regional Administrator, Region VI (Dallas) ...	Vacant		ES	....	....	
Kansas City, MO ...	Regional Administrator, Region VII (Kansas City).	Beth A. Freeman	NA	ES	....	....	
Denver, CO	Regional Administrator, Region VIII (Denver)	Robin A. Fudge Finegan	NA	ES	....	....	
San Francisco, CA	Regional Director, Region IX (San Francisco)	Career Incumbent	CA	ES	....	....	
Seattle, WA	Regional Administrator, Region X (Seattle)	Kenneth D. Murphy	NA	ES	....	....	
	TRANSPORTATION SECURITY ADMINISTRATION						
Arlington, VA	Assistant Secretary	John S. Pistole	PAS	EX	IV	....	
Do	Chief of Staff	Vacant	XS	OT	....	....	
Do	Special Advisor to the Assistant Secretary	......do	XS	OT	....	....	
Do	Assistant Administrator of Legislative Affairs	Sarah M. Dietch	XS	OT	....	....	
Do	Assistant Administrator for Public Relations and External Communications.	Vacant	XS	OT	....	....	

DEPARTMENT OF HOMELAND SECURITY OFFICE OF THE INSPECTOR GENERAL

Location	Position	Name of Incumbent	Type of Appt.	Pay Plan	Level, Grade, or Pay	Tenure	Expires
Washington, DC	Inspector General	Vacant	PAS	EX	II	....	

DEPARTMENT OF HOUSING AND URBAN DEVELOPMENT

Location	Position	Name of Incumbent	Type of Appt.	Pay Plan	Level, Grade, or Pay	Tenure	Expires
	OFFICE OF THE SECRETARY						
Washington, DC	Secretary	Shaun Donovan	PAS	EX	I	....	
Do	Chief of Staff	Laurel A. Blatchford	NA	ES	....	....	
Do	Senior Advisor	Estelle B. Richman	NA	ES	....	....	
Do	Senior Advisor for Housing Finance	Robert C. Ryan	NA	ES	....	....	
Do	Senior Advisor for Disaster Programs	Frederick Tombar III	NA	ES	....	....	
Do	Executive Operations Officer	Vacant	....	ES	....	....	
Do	Deputy Chief of Staff for Policy and Programs	Jonathan M. Harwitz	SC	GS	15	....	
Do	Deputy Chief of Staff	Lopa P. Kolluri	SC	GS	15	....	
Do	White House Liaison	William N. Jenkins III	SC	GS	15	....	
Do	Special Assistant	Patience R. Singleton	SC	GS	15	....	
Do	Special Policy Advisor	Rodin A. Mehrbani	SC	GS	15	....	
Do	Financial Analyst for Housing Finance	Sterling A. Cross	SC	GS	13	....	
Do	Special Assistant	Marianna B. Leavy-Sperounis.	SC	GS	13	....	
Do	......do	Ioanna T. Kefalas	SC	GS	12	....	
	Office of the Deputy Secretary						
Do	Deputy Secretary	Maurice A. Jones	PAS	EX	II	....	
Do	Senior Advisor	Michael A. Anderson	NA	ES	....	....	
	Office of Strategic Planning and Management						
Do	Director	Vacant	....	ES	....	....	
Do	Deputy Director	Lisa E. Danzig	SC	GS	15	....	
Do	Senior Policy Advisor	Beatrice M. Hidalgo	SC	GS	15	....	
	Office of Sustainable Housing and Communities						
Do	Director	Shelley R. Poticha	NA	ES	....	....	
Do	Senior Advisor	Salin G. Geevarghese	SC	GS	15	....	
	Office of the Chief Human Capital Officer						
Do	General Deputy Assistant Secretary for Administration/Chief Human Capital Officer.	Vacant	....	ES	....	....	
Do	Chief Performance Officer	Career Incumbent	CA	ES	....	....	
Do	Director, Executive Secretariat	......do	CA	ES	....	....	
Do	Associate, General Deputy Assistant Secretary/Deputy Chief Human Capital Officer.	Vacant	....	ES	....	....	
Do	Deputy Assistant Secretary for Budget and Management Support.	......do	....	ES	....	....	
Do	Deputy Assistant Secretary for Operations	......do	....	ES	....	....	
Do	Deputy Assistant Secretary for Technical Services.	......do	....	ES	....	....	
Do	Director, Office of Executive Scheduling and Operations.	Anthony D. McLarty	SC	GS	15	....	
Do	Director of Scheduling	Melissa S. Bruns	SC	GS	12	....	
Do	Director of Advance	Candace R. Wint	SC	GS	12	....	
Do	Scheduling Assistant	Christina M. Cue	SC	GS	9	....	
	OFFICE OF THE ADMINISTRATION						
Do	Assistant Secretary	Vacant	PAS	EX	IV	....	
Do	Senior Advisor	......do	....	ES	....	....	
Do	Deputy Assistant Secretary	......do	....	ES	....	....	
	Office of the Chief Financial Officer						
Do	Chief Financial Officer	......do	PAS	EX	IV	....	
	OFFICE OF THE CHIEF INFORMATION OFFICER						
Do	Chief Information Officer	Career Incumbent	CA	ES	....	....	
Do	Deputy Chief Information Officer	......do	CA	ES	....	....	
Do	Deputy Chief Information Officer for Information Technology Operations.	......do	CA	ES	....	....	
Do	Deputy Chief Information Officer for Cyber Security and Privacy Information.	......do	CA	ES	....	....	
Do	Chief Information Technology Transformation Officer.	Patsy A. Garnett	TA	ES	....	....	08/27/13
Do	Chief Architect for Information Technology	Vacant	....	ES	....	....	
	Office of the Chief Procurement Officer						
Do	Chief Procurement Officer	Career Incumbent	CA	ES	....	....	
Do	Deputy Chief Procurement Officer for Policy, Risk Management and Administration.	Vacant	....	ES	....	....	
Do	Associate Chief Procurement Officer, Acquisition Workload, Planning, Management Oversight.	......do	....	ES	....	....	

DEPARTMENT OF HOUSING AND URBAN DEVELOPMENT—Continued

Location	Position	Name of Incumbent	Type of Appt.	Pay Plan	Level, Grade, or Pay	Tenure	Expires
	OFFICE OF COMMUNITY PLANNING AND DEVELOPMENT						
Washington, DC	Assistant Secretary	Vacant	PAS	EX	IV	....	
Do	General Deputy Assistant Secretary	Career Incumbent	CA	ES	....	....	
Do	Director, Office of Block Grant Assistance	......do	CA	ES	....	....	
Do	Director, Office of Technical Assistance and Management.	......do	CA	ES	....	....	
Do	Deputy Assistant Secretary for Operations	Vacant	....	ES	....	....	
Do	Deputy Assistant Secretary for Grant Programs.	Yolanda Chavez	NA	ES	....	....	
Do	Deputy Assistant Secretary for Economic Development.	Valerie G. Piper	NA	ES	....	....	
Do	Director, Office of Affordable Housing Programs.	Vacant	....	ES	....	....	
Do	Director, Office of Field Management	......do	....	ES	....	....	
Do	Director, Environment and Energy	......do	....	ES	....	....	
	OFFICE OF CONGRESSIONAL AND INTERGOVERNMENTAL RELATIONS						
Do	Assistant Secretary	Peter Kovar	PAS	EX	IV	....	
Do	General Deputy Assistant Secretary	Vacant	....	ES	....	....	
Do	Deputy Assistant Secretary	......do	....	ES	....	....	
Do	Deputy Assistant Secretary for Legislation	......do	....	ES	....	....	
Do	Deputy Assistant Secretary for Intergovernmental Relations.	......do	....	ES	....	....	
Do	Deputy Assistant Secretary for Congressional Relations.	Bernard B. Fulton	SC	GS	15	....	
Do	Deputy Assistant Secretary for Intergovernmental Affairs.	Jennifer L. Szubrowski	SC	GS	15	....	
Do	Senior Legislative Advisor	Thomas E. Heinemann	SC	GS	15	....	
Do	Congressional Relations Officer	Erica L. Jacquez	SC	GS	15	....	
Do	Congressional Relations and Legislative Specialist.	Adria F. Crutchfield	SC	GS	13	....	
Do	Congressional Relations Officer	LeLaine V. Bigelow	SC	GS	13	....	
Do	Congressional Relations Specialist	Alejandro Aviles	SC	GS	12	....	
Do	Deputy Director of Intergovernmental Relations.	Michael A. Brown	SC	GS	12	....	
	OFFICE OF FAITH-BASED AND COMMUNITY INITIATIVES						
Do	Director	Career Incumbent	CA	ES	....	....	
	OFFICE OF DEPARTMENTAL OPERATIONS AND COORDINATION						
Do	Director	......do	CA	ES	....	....	
Do	Deputy Director	Vacant	....	ES	....	....	
Do	Senior Advisor	Career Incumbent	CA	ES	....	....	
	OFFICE OF FAIR HOUSING AND EQUAL OPPORTUNITY						
Do	Assistant Secretary	John D. Trasvina	PAS	EX	IV	....	
Do	General Deputy Assistant Secretary	Career Incumbent	CA	ES	....	....	
Do	Deputy Assistant Secretary for Operations and Management.	......do	CA	ES	....	....	
Do	Deputy Assistant Secretary for Enforcement and Programs.	......do	CA	ES	....	....	
Do	Director, Office of Policy, Legislative Initiatives and Outreach.	Vacant	....	ES	....	....	
Do	Senior Advisor	Janet M. Hostetler	SC	GS	15	....	
	Office of the General Counsel						
Do	General Counsel	Helen R. Kanovsky	PAS	EX	IV	....	
Do	Principal Deputy General Counsel	Kevin M. Simpson	NA	ES	....	....	
Do	Deputy General Counsel for Operations	Career Incumbent	CA	ES	....	....	
Do	Deputy General Counsel for Enforcement	Michelle M. Aronowitz	NA	ES	....	....	
Do	Deputy General Counsel for Housing Programs.	Career Incumbent	CA	ES	....	....	
Do	Associate General Counsel for Insured Housing.	......do	CA	ES	....	....	
Do	Associate General Counsel for Assisted Housing and Community Development.	......do	CA	ES	....	....	
Do	Associate General Counsel for Fair Housing ..	......do	CA	ES	....	....	
Do	Associate General Counsel for Legislation and Regulations.	......do	CA	ES	....	....	
Do	Associate General Counsel for Litigation	......do	CA	ES	....	....	
Do	Associate General Counsel for Ethics and Personnel Law.	......do	CA	ES	....	....	

DEPARTMENT OF HOUSING AND URBAN DEVELOPMENT—Continued

Location	Position	Name of Incumbent	Type of Appt.	Pay Plan	Level, Grade, or Pay	Tenure	Expires
Washington, DC	Associate General Counsel for Finance and Regulatory Compliance.	Career Incumbent	CA	ES	....	....	
Do	Deputy Assistant Secretary for Enforcement	Vacant	....	ES	....	....	
Do	General Deputy General Counsel	......do	....	ES	....	....	
Do	Senior Counsel	Damon Y. Smith	SC	GS	15	....	
Do	......do	Elliot M. Mincberg	SC	GS	15	....	
Do	Special Assistant to the General Counsel	Kathie A. Soroka	SC	GS	15	....	
	GOVERNMENT NATIONAL MORTGAGE ASSOCIATION						
Do	President	Theodore W. Tozer	PAS	EX	IV	....	
Do	Executive Vice President	Career Incumbent	CA	ES	....	....	
	Office of Healthy Homes Initiatives and Lead Hazard Control						
Do	Director	......do	CA	ES	....	....	
Do	Deputy Director	Vacant	....	ES	....	....	
Do	Director, Office of Lead-Based Paint Abatement and Poisoning.	......do	....	ES	....	....	
	OFFICE OF HOUSING						
Do	Assistant Secretary for Housing, Federal Housing Commissioner.	......do	PAS	EX	IV	....	
Do	General Deputy Assistant Secretary	Carol J. Galante	NA	ES	....	....	
Do	Associate General Deputy Assistant Secretary	Vacant	....	ES	....	....	
Do	Deputy Assistant Secretary for Multifamily Housing.	Marie D. Head	NA	ES	....	....	
Do	Associate Deputy Assistant Secretary for Multifamily Housing.	Vacant	....	ES	....	....	
Do	Associate Deputy Assistant Secretary for Multifamily Housing Programs (Programs and Policy).	Career Incumbent	CA	ES	....	....	
Do	Director, Office of Multifamily Development ..	Vacant	....	ES	....	....	
Do	Deputy Assistant Secretary for Single Family Housing.	Charles S. Coulter	NA	ES	....	....	
Do	Associate Deputy Assistant Secretary for Single Family Housing.	Vacant	....	ES	....	....	
Do	Deputy Assistant Secretary for Operations	Career Incumbent	CA	ES	....	....	
Do	Deputy Assistant Secretary for Risk Management and Regulatory Affairs.	Vacant	....	ES	....	....	
Do	Associate Deputy Assistant Secretary for Risk Management and Regulatory Affairs.	Career Incumbent	CA	ES	....	....	
Do	Director, Office of Asset Management	......do	CA	ES	....	....	
Do	Special Advisor for Project Management	......do	CA	ES	....	....	
Do	Senior Financial Advisor	......do	CA	ES	....	....	
Do	Senior Advisor	......do	CA	ES	....	....	
Do	......do	......do	CA	ES	....	....	
Do	Special Assistant	James M. Parrott	SC	GS	15	....	
Do	Senior Policy Advisor	Genger Charles	SC	GS	15	....	
Do	Program Analyst	Catherine S. Neale	SC	GS	12	....	
	OFFICE OF POLICY DEVELOPMENT AND RESEARCH						
Do	Assistant Secretary	Vacant	PAS	EX	IV	....	
Do	General Deputy Assistant Secretary	Career Incumbent	CA	ES	....	....	
Do	Deputy Assistant Secretary for Policy Development.	Erika C. Poethig	NA	ES	....	....	
Do	Associate Deputy Assistant Secretary for Policy Development.	Career Incumbent	CA	ES	....	....	
Do	Deputy Assistant Secretary for Economic Affairs.	......do	CA	ES	....	....	
Do	Associate Deputy Assistant Secretary for Economic Affairs.	Vacant	....	ES	....	....	
Do	Executive Director for Strong Cities and Strong Communities.	Mark A. Linton	NA	ES	....	....	
Do	Deputy Assistant Secretary for International and Philanthropic Innovation.	Vacant	....	ES	....	....	
Do	Senior Advisor for Research Development	......do	....	ES	....	....	
Do	Director, Policy Development Division	......do	....	ES	....	....	
Do	Senior Advisor for Research Management	......do	....	ES	....	....	
Do	Deputy Assistant Secretary for International and Philanthropic Affairs.	Ana M. Argilagos	SC	GS	15	....	
Do	Special Assistant	Patrick J. Pontius	SC	GS	14	....	
Do	Special Policy Advisor	Lucas L. Tate	SC	GS	14	....	
	OFFICE OF PUBLIC AFFAIRS						
Do	Assistant Secretary	Vacant	PAS	EX	IV	....	

DEPARTMENT OF HOUSING AND URBAN DEVELOPMENT—Continued

Location	Position	Name of Incumbent	Type of Appt.	Pay Plan	Level, Grade, or Pay	Tenure	Expires
Washington, DC	Chief External Affairs Officer/General Deputy Assistant Secretary.	Neill M. Coleman	NA	ES	....	....	
Do	Deputy Assistant Secretary	Career Incumbent	CA	ES	....	....	
Do	Deputy Assistant Secretary for Public Engagement.	Francey L. Youngberg	SC	GS	15	....	
Do	Senior Advisor for Public Engagement	Raul Alvillar	SC	GS	14	....	
Do	Senior Speechwriter	Matthew J. Weiner	SC	GS	14	....	
Do	Press Secretary	Derrick L. Plummer	SC	GS	13	....	
Do	Deputy Press Secretary	George I. Gonzalez	SC	GS	13	....	
Do	Assistant Press Secretary	Charmion N. Kinder	SC	GS	12	....	
Do	Internal Communications Specialist	Larkin E. Barker	SC	GS	11	....	
	OFFICE OF PUBLIC AND INDIAN HOUSING						
Do	Assistant Secretary	Sandra B. Henriquez	PAS	EX	IV	....	
Do	General Deputy Assistant Secretary	Career Incumbent	CA	ES	....	....	
Do	Deputy Assistant Secretary for Public Housing and Voucher Programs.	......do	CA	ES	....	....	
Do	Deputy Assistant Secretary for Field Operations.	......do	CA	ES	....	....	
Do	Deputy Assistant Secretary for the Real Estate Assessment Center.	......do	CA	ES	....	....	
Do	Deputy Assistant Secretary for Native American Programs.	......do	CA	ES	....	....	
Do	Deputy Assistant Secretary for Public Housing Investments.	......do	CA	ES	....	....	
Do	Director, Office of Receivership Oversight	......do	CA	ES	....	....	
Do	Senior Advisor to the Assistant Secretary for Public and Indian Housing.	Vacant	....	ES	....	....	
Do	Senior Advisor for Project Management	......do	....	ES	....	....	
Do	Director, Office of Troubled Agency Recovery ...	......do	....	ES	....	....	
Do	Special Assistant	Jennifer C. Jones	SC	GS	15	....	
Do	Special Policy Advisor	David A. Lipsetz	SC	GS	15	....	
	OFFICE OF FIELD POLICY AND MANAGEMENT						
Do	Assistant Deputy Secretary	Vacant	....	ES	....	....	
Do	Director	Career Incumbent	CA	ES	....	....	
Do	Deputy Director	......do	CA	ES	....	....	
Do	Senior Advisor (Associate Assistant Deputy Secretary).	......do	CA	ES	....	....	
Do	Senior Advisor	......do	CA	ES	....	....	
Do	Senior Advisor to the Assistant Deputy Secretary.	Vacant	....	ES	....	....	
	New England (Boston)						
Boston, MA	Regional Administrator	Barbara G. Fields	SC	GS	15	....	
	New York/New Jersey (New York)						
New York, NY	Regional Administrator	Vacant	....	ES	....	....	
	Mid-Atlantic (Philadelphia)						
Philadelphia, PA	Regional Administrator	Jane C.W. Vincent	SC	GS	15	....	
	Southeast (Atlanta)						
Atlanta, GA	Regional Administrator	Edwards L. Jennings, Jr. ..	NA	ES	....	....	
	Midwest (Chicago)						
Chicago, IL	Regional Administrator	Antonio R. Riley	NA	ES	....	....	
Do	Deputy Regional Director	Career Incumbent	CA	ES	....	....	
	Southwest (Fort Worth)						
Fort Worth, TX	Regional Administrator	Vacant	....	ES	....	....	
Do	Senior Advisor	Career Incumbent	CA	ES	....	....	
	Great Plains (Kansas City)						
Kansas City, MO ...	Regional Administrator	Derrith R. Watchman-Moore.	SC	GS	15	....	
	Rocky Mountain (Denver)						
Denver, CO	Regional Administrator	Rick M. Garcia	SC	GS	15	....	
	Pacific/Hawaii (San Francisco)						
San Francisco, CA ..	Regional Administrator	Ophelia B. Basgal	NA	ES	....	....	
Do	Deputy Regional Administrator	Vacant	....	ES	....	....	
	Northwest/Alaska (Seattle)						
Seattle, WA	Regional Administrator	Mary E. McBride	SC	GS	15	....	

DEPARTMENT OF HOUSING AND URBAN DEVELOPMENT OFFICE OF THE INSPECTOR GENERAL

Location	Position	Name of Incumbent	Type of Appt.	Pay Plan	Level, Grade, or Pay	Tenure	Expires
Washington, DC	Inspector General	David A. Montoya	PAS	EX	III	....	

DEPARTMENT OF THE INTERIOR

Location	Position	Name of Incumbent	Type of Appt.	Pay Plan	Level, Grade, or Pay	Tenure	Expires
Washington, DC	Secretary	Kenneth Salazar	PAS	EX	I	....	
	SECRETARY'S IMMEDIATE OFFICE						
Do	Chief Information Officer	Career Incumbent	CA	ES	....	....	
Do	Director of Executive Secretariat and Office of Regulatory Affairs.	......do	CA	ES	....	....	
Do	Chief of Staff	Laura Daniel Davis	NA	ES	....	....	
Do	Communications Director	Katherine P. Kelly	NA	ES	....	....	
Do	Deputy Chief of Staff	Matthew Lee-Ashley	NA	ES	....	....	
Do	Counselor to the Secretary	Steven W. Black	NA	ES	....	....	
Do	Senior Advisor to the Secretary	Kenneth L. Lane	NA	ES	....	....	
Do	......do	Robert G. Stanton	NA	ES	....	....	
Sacramento, CA	Senior Advisor for California and Nevada	David Nawi	NA	ES	....	....	
Washington, DC	Director, Intergovernmental Affairs	Gail A. Adams	NA	ES	....	....	
Do	Counselor for America's Great Outdoors	William G. Shafroth	NA	ES	....	....	
Do	Senior Advisor to the Secretary	Rebecca R. Wodder	NA	ES	....	....	
Do	Special Assistant to the Secretary	Joan Padilla	SC	GS	15	....	
Do	Senior Advisor for Alaskan Affairs	Kim Steven Elton	SC	GS	15	....	
Do	Special Assistant	Nealesh A. Kemkar	SC	GS	15	....	
Do	......do	Janea A. Scott	SC	GS	14	....	
Anchorage, AK	Deputy Alaska Director	Patrick J. Pourchot	SC	GS	14	....	
Missoula, MT	Senior Advisor for Northwest Region	Stephen A. Doherty	SC	GS	15	....	
Denver, CO	Senior Advisor for Southwest and Rocky Mountain Regions.	Alan J. Gilbert	SC	GS	15	....	
Washington, DC	Director of New Media	Timothy A. Fullerton	SC	GS	14	....	
Do	Staff Assistant	Jennifer R. Sisk	SC	GS	9	....	
Do	Deputy Director, Intergovernmental Affairs ...	Francisco Carrillo	SC	GS	13	....	
Do	Special Assistant for Advance	Jenny E. Sarabia	SC	GS	13	....	
Do	Press Secretary	Adam K. Fetcher	SC	GS	13	....	
Do	Senior Advisor to the Secretary	Sarah Devins Greenberger	SC	GS	15	....	
Do	White House Liaison	Benjamin E. Milakofsky	SC	GS	13	....	
Do	Program Coordinator	Christopher Danny Hosein	SC	GS	11	....	
Do	Trip Director	Jonathan E. Adler	SC	GS	13	....	
Do	Special Assistant	Nana Efua E. Embil	SC	GS	11	....	
Do	......do	Kristina T. Broadie	SC	GS	9	....	
Do	Deputy Director, External Affairs	Teresa L. Johnson	SC	GS	14	....	
Do	Special Assistant	Israporn Pananon	SC	GS	9	....	
Do	......do	Marc C. Littlejohn	SC	GS	13	....	
Do	Deputy Director of Scheduling	Jason M. Fink	SC	GS	12	....	
Do	Special Assistant to Scheduling in the Office of Scheduling and Advance.	Francis Iacobucci	SC	GS	11	....	
Do	Deputy Communications Director	Blake J. Androff	SC	GS	14	....	
Do	Press Assistant	Queen C. Muse	SC	GS	8	....	
	OFFICE OF THE DEPUTY SECRETARY						
Do	Deputy Secretary	David J. Hayes	PAS	EX	II	....	
Do	Associate Deputy Secretary	Elizabeth Anne Klein	NA	ES	....	....	
Do	Counselor	Alletta Belin	NA	ES	....	....	
Do	Special Assistant	James E. Anderson	SC	GS	7	....	
Do	Chief of Staff	Elizabeth S. Marsters	SC	GS	12	....	
Do	Counselor	Raya V. Bakalov	SC	GS	14	....	
	OFFICE OF CONGRESSIONAL AND LEGISLATIVE AFFAIRS						
Do	Legislative Counsel	Career Incumbent	CA	ES	....	....	
Do	Director	Christopher J. Mansour	NA	ES	....	....	
Do	Deputy Director	Heather M. Urban	SC	GS	15	....	
Do	......do	Jason L. Buckner	SC	GS	15	....	
Do	Special Assistant	Lauren Bogard	SC	GS	11	....	
	OFFICE OF SPECIAL TRUSTEE FOR AMERICAN INDIANS						
Do	Special Trustee	Vacant	PAS	EX	II	....	
Albuquerque, NM ..	Director, Office of Trust Records	Career Incumbent	CA	ES	....	....	
Do	Deputy Special Trustee - Trust Accountability	......do	CA	ES	....	....	
Do	Principal Deputy Special Trustee	Vacant		ES	....	....	
Do	Deputy Special Trustee - Trust Services	......do		ES	....	....	
Do	Deputy Special Trustee - Field Operations	Career Incumbent	CA	ES	....	....	
Do	Director, Trust Review and Audit	Vacant		ES	....	....	
Do	Regional Fiduciary Trust Administrator	Career Incumbent	CA	ES	....	....	
Do	......do	......do	CA	ES	....	....	
Do	......do	Vacant		ES	....	....	
Do	......do	Career Incumbent	CA	ES	....	....	
Do	......do	......do	CA	ES	....	....	
Do	......do	......do	CA	ES	....	....	
Do	Associate Principal Deputy Special Trustee ...	......do	CA	ES	....	....	
Washington, DC	Senior Advisor	......do	CA	ES	....	....	

DEPARTMENT OF THE INTERIOR—Continued

Location	Position	Name of Incumbent	Type of Appt.	Pay Plan	Level, Grade, or Pay	Tenure	Expires
	NATIONAL INDIAN GAMING COMMISSION						
Washington, DC	Chairman	Tracie Lee Stevens	PAS	EX	IV	....	
Do	Associate Member	Steffani A. Cochran	XS	AD	$145,700	....	
Do	.....do	Daniel J. Little	XS	AD	$145,700	....	
Do	General Counsel	Lawrence Scott Roberts	XS	AD	$155,500	....	
	OFFICE OF THE SOLICITOR						
Do	Solicitor	Hilary C. Tompkins	PAS	EX	IV	....	
Do	Associate Solicitor (Indian Affairs)	Career Incumbent	CA	ES		....	
Do	Associate Solicitor (Land and Water Resources).	.....do	CA	ES		....	
Do	Associate Solicitor (General Law)	Vacant	....	ES		....	
Do	Associate Solicitor (Division of Parks and Wildlife).	Career Incumbent	CA	ES		....	
Do	Deputy Solicitor	.....do	CA	ES		....	
Do	Associate Solicitor (Division of Mineral Resources).	.....do	CA	ES		....	
Do	Deputy Solicitor	Rachel Jacobson	NA	ES		....	
Do	Deputy Solicitor (Parks and Wildlife)	Martha Macgill Colhoun Williams.	NA	ES		....	
Do	Deputy Solicitor (Indian Affairs)	Partice H. Kunesh	NA	ES		....	
Do	Deputy Solicitor	Career Incumbent	CA	ES		....	
Do	Deputy Solicitor (Land Resources)	Edward A. Boling	NA	ES		....	
Do	Deputy Solicitor (Water Resources)	Paul F. Holleman	NA	ES		....	
Do	Counselor to the Solicitor	Robert Scott Nuzum	SC	GS	12	....	
	Field Offices						
Portland, OR	Regional Solicitor, Pacific Northwest Region ..	Career Incumbent	CA	ES		....	
Anchorage, AK	Regional Solicitor, Alaska Region	Vacant	....	ES		....	
Lakewood, CO	Regional Solicitor, Rocky Mountain Region	Career Incumbent	CA	ES		....	
Newton, MA	Regional Solicitor, Northeast Region	.....do	CA	ES		....	
Albuquerque, NM ..	Regional Solicitor, Southwest Region	.....do	CA	ES		....	
Atlanta, GA	Regional Solicitor, Southeast Region	.....do	CA	ES		....	
Salt Lake City, UT	Regional Solicitor, Intermountain Region	.....do	CA	ES		....	
Los Angeles, CA	Regional Solicitor, Pacific Southwest Region ..	.....do	CA	ES		....	
	ASSISTANT SECRETARY - POLICY, MANAGEMENT AND BUDGET						
Washington, DC	Assistant Secretary	Rhea S. Suh	PAS	EX	IV	....	
Do	Director, Office of Civil Rights	Career Incumbent	CA	ES		....	
Do	Director, Office of Environmental Policy and Compliance.	.....do	CA	ES		....	
Do	Director, Office of Budget	.....do	CA	ES		....	
Do	Director, Office of Policy Analysis	.....do	CA	ES		....	
Do	Deputy Director, Office of Budget	.....do	CA	ES		....	
Do	Deputy Assistant Secretary, Policy and International Affairs.	Lorraine V. Faeth	NA	ES		....	
Do	Deputy Director, Office of Policy Analysis	Career Incumbent	CA	ES		....	
Do	Deputy Director, Office of Environmental Policy and Compliance.	.....do	CA	ES		....	
Do	Director, Office of Wildland Fire Coordination	Vacant	....	ES		....	
Do	Director, Office of Planning and Performance Management.	Career Incumbent	CA	ES		....	
Do	Associate Director, Facility and Property Management.	.....do	CA	ES		....	
Do	Deputy Chief Information Officer	.....do	CA	ES		....	
Do	Director, Office of Acquisition and Property Management.	.....do	CA	ES		....	
Do	Director, Strategic Employee Development	.....do	CA	ES		....	
Do	Director, Office of Restoration and Damage Assessment.	.....do	CA	ES		....	
Do	Interagency Borderland Coordinator	.....do	CA	ES		....	
Do	Director, Office of Emergency Management ...	.....do	CA	ES		....	
Do	Director, Office of Valuation Services	.....do	CA	ES		....	
Do	Senior Advisor to the Deputy Assistant Secretary - Budget, Finance, Performance and Acquisition.	.....do	CA	ES		....	
Do	Deputy Assistant Secretary - Technology, Information and Business Services.	Joseph Andrew Jackson	NA	ES		....	
Do	FBMS Program Coordinator	Hope Y. Mentore-Smith	TA	ES		....	02/14/13
Do	Chief Diversity Officer	Career Incumbent	CA	ES		....	
Do	Senior Advisor to the Deputy Assistant Secretary, Law Enforcement, Security and Emergency Management.	.....do	CA	ES		....	
Do	Deputy Assistant Secretary, Natural Resources Revenue Management.	Paul A. Mussenden	NA	ES		....	

DEPARTMENT OF THE INTERIOR—Continued

Location	Position	Name of Incumbent	Type of Appt.	Pay Plan	Level, Grade, or Pay	Tenure	Expires
Washington, DC	Deputy Director, Office of Strategic Employee and Organizational Development.	Career Incumbent	CA	ES	....	....	
Do	Associate Deputy Chief Information Officer ...	......do	CA	ES	....	....	
Do	Senior Advisor	......do	CA	ES	....	....	
Do	Deputy Chief Information Officer - Shared Services.	......do	CA	ES	....	....	
Herndon, VA	FBMS Program Director	......do	CA	ES	....	....	
Washington, DC	Special Assistant	Sarah E. Peterson	SC	GS	14	....	
Do	......do	Nahal Hamidi	SC	GS	11	....	
	National Business Center						
Washington, DC	Director	Career Incumbent	CA	ES	....	....	
Boise, ID	Associate Director, Aviation Management Directorate.	......do	CA	ES	....	....	
Washington, DC	Associate Director, Human Resources Directorate.	......do	CA	ES	....	....	
Herndon, VA	Associate Director, Acquisition Services Directorate.	Vacant	....	ES	....	....	
Washington, DC	Deputy Director	Career Incumbent	CA	ES	....	....	
Do	Chief Financial Officer	......do	CA	ES	....	....	
Do	Assistant Director, Information Resources	Edmund Crump	TA	ES	....	....	12/31/13
	Office of Natural Resources Revenue Management						
Do	Director	Career Incumbent	CA	ES	....	....	
	Office of Hearings and Appeals						
Do	Principal Deputy Director	......do	CA	ES	....	....	
	ASSISTANT SECRETARY - INSULAR AFFAIRS						
Do	Assistant Secretary	Anthony M. Babauta	PAS	EX	IV	....	
Do	Director	Career Incumbent	CA	ES	....	....	
	ASSISTANT SECRETARY - FISH AND WILDLIFE AND PARKS						
Do	Assistant Secretary	Vacant	PAS	EX	IV	....	
Do	Counselor	Michael J. Bean	NA	ES	....	....	
Miami, FL	Director Everglades Restoration Initiatives	Career Incumbent	CA	ES	....	....	
Washington, DC	Deputy Assistant Secretary	......do	CA	ES	....	....	
Do	Principal Deputy Assistant Secretary	Vacant	....	ES	....	....	
Do	Chief of Staff	Melissa B. Koenigsberg	NA	ES	....	....	
Do	Special Assistant	Fatima M. Ahmad	SC	GS	15	....	
Do	......do	Jorge G. Silva-Banuelos	SC	GS	14	....	
	United States Fish and Wildlife Service						
Do	Director	Daniel M. Ashe	PAS	EX	V	....	
Atlanta, GA	Regional Director - Atlanta	Career Incumbent	CA	ES	....	....	
Hadley, MA	Regional Director - Hadley	......do	CA	ES	....	....	
Denver, CO	Regional Director - Denver	......do	CA	ES	....	....	
Albuquerque, NM ..	Regional Director - Albuquerque	......do	CA	ES	....	....	
Sacramento, CA	Regional Director - Sacramento	......do	CA	ES	....	....	
Anchorage, AK	Regional Director - Anchorage	......do	CA	ES	....	....	
Minneapolis, MN ...	Regional Director - Twin Cities	......do	CA	ES	....	....	
Portland, OR	Regional Director - Portland	......do	CA	ES	....	....	
Washington, DC	Director, National Conservation Training Center.	......do	CA	ES	....	....	
Do	Assistant Director - Wildlife and Sportfish Restoration Programs.	......do	CA	ES	....	....	
Do	Assistant Director - Fisheries and Habitat Conservation.	......do	CA	ES	....	....	
Do	Assistant Director - International Affairs	Vacant	....	ES	....	....	
Do	Assistant Director - External Affairs	Career Incumbent	CA	ES	....	....	
Do	Assistant Director - Budget, Planning and Human Capital.	......do	CA	ES	....	....	
Do	Assistant Director - Business Management and Operations.	......do	CA	ES	....	....	
Do	Assistant Director - Migratory Bird Programs ..	......do	CA	ES	....	....	
Do	Assistant Director - Endangered Species	......do	CA	ES	....	....	
Do	Deputy Director - Operations	......do	CA	ES	....	....	
Do	Deputy Director - Program Management and Policy.	Vacant	....	ES	....	....	
Do	Chief of Staff	Betsy Hildebrandt	NA	ES	....	....	
Do	Assistant Director - Information Resources	Kenneth Taylor	TA	ES	....	....	06/18/13
Do	Chief, National Wildlife Refuge System	Career Incumbent	CA	ES	....	....	
	National Park Service						
Do	Director	Jonathan B. Jarvis	PAS	EX	V	....	
Do	Regional Director, National Capital Region	Career Incumbent	CA	ES	....	....	

DEPARTMENT OF THE INTERIOR—Continued

Location	Position	Name of Incumbent	Type of Appt.	Pay Plan	Level, Grade, or Pay	Tenure	Expires
Atlanta, GA	Regional Director, Southeast Region (Atlanta)	Career Incumbent	CA	ES	....	....	
Omaha, NE	Regional Director, Midwest Region (Omaha) ..	......do	CA	ES	....	....	
San Francisco, CA	Regional Director, Pacific West Region (San Francisco).	......do	CA	ES	....	....	
Denver, CO	Regional Director, Intermountain Region (Denver).	......do	CA	ES	....	....	
Washington, DC	Associate Director, Parks Planning, Facilities and Lands.	......do	CA	ES	....	....	
Do	Assistant Director, Workforce Management ...	......do	CA	ES	....	....	
Oak Ridge, TN	Superintendent, Great Smoky Mountain National Park.	......do	CA	ES	....	....	
Denver, CO	Manager, Denver Service Center	......do	CA	ES	....	....	
San Francisco, CA	Park Manager (Superintendent)	......do	CA	ES	....	....	
Washington, DC	Deputy Director for Communications and Community Assistance.	Milton Lewis Fearn	NA	ES	....	....	
Do	Associate Director, Visitor Resource and Protection.	Vacant	....	ES	....	....	
Boulder City, NV ...	Park Manager (Superintendent), Lake Mead National Recreation Area.	Career Incumbent	CA	ES	....	....	
Anchorage, AK	Regional Director, Alaska Area (Anchorage) ..	......do	CA	ES	....	....	
Washington, DC	Associate Director, Business Services	......do	CA	ES	....	....	
New York, NY	Executive Director, National Parks of New York Harbor.	......do	CA	ES	....	....	
Philadelphia, PA	Regional Director, Northeast Region	......do	CA	ES	....	....	
Washington, DC	Deputy Director, Operations	......do	CA	ES	....	....	
Do	Superintendent, National Mall and Memorial Parks.	......do	CA	ES	....	....	
Moose, WY	Park Manager (Superintendent), Grand Teton National Park.	......do	CA	ES	....	....	
Washington, DC	Associate Director, Cultural Resources	......do	CA	ES	....	....	
Do	Assistant Director, Information Resources	Jeffrey Shane Compton	TA	ES	....	....	06/03/13
Do	Associate Director, Natural Resource Stewardship and Science.	Career Incumbent	CA	ES	....	....	
Do	Assistant Director, Communications	Celinda Marie Pena	SC	GS	14	....	
Do	Special Assistant to the Director	Ali C. Kelley	SC	GS	7	....	
	ASSISTANT SECRETARY - WATER AND SCIENCE						
Do	Assistant Secretary	Anne J. Castle	PAS	EX	IV	....	
Do	Deputy Assistant Secretary	Lori L. Caramanian	NA	ES	....	....	
Do	......do	John E. Tubbs	NA	ES	....	....	
Do	Counselor to the Assistant Secretary	Tanya M. Trujillo	SC	GS	15	....	
	Bureau of Reclamation						
Do	Commissioner	Michael L. Connor	PAS	EX	V	....	
Do	Deputy Commissioner (Program, Administration and Budget).	Career Incumbent	CA	ES	....	....	
Do	Deputy Commissioner (Director, Operations)	......do	CA	ES	....	....	
Do	Deputy Commissioner (External and Intergovernmental Affairs).	Kira Finkler	NA	ES	....	....	
Boulder City, NV ...	Regional Director, Lower Colorado	Vacant	....	ES	....	....	
Sacramento, CA	Regional Director, Mid-Pacific	Career Incumbent	CA	ES	....	....	
Salt Lake City, UT	Regional Director, Upper Colorado	......do	CA	ES	....	....	
Billings, MT	Regional Director, Great Plains Region	......do	CA	ES	....	....	
Boise, ID	Regional Director, Pacific Northwest Region ..	......do	CA	ES	....	....	
Lakewood, CO	Director, Safety, Security, and Law Enforcement.	......do	CA	ES	....	....	
Washington, DC	Director, Program and Budget	......do	CA	ES	....	....	
Denver, CO	Director, Technical Resources	......do	CA	ES	....	....	
Do	Director, Policy and Administration	......do	CA	ES	....	....	
Do	Senior Advisor	Career Incumbent	CA	ES	....	....	
Denver, CO	Assistant Director, Information Resources	Bruce C. Muller, Jr.	TA	ES	....	....	07/16/13
Washington, DC	Chief, Congressional and Legislative Affairs Office.	Dionne E. Thompson	SC	GS	15	....	
	United States Geological Survey						
Reston, VA	Director	Marcia K. McNutt	PAS	EX	V	....	
	ASSISTANT SECRETARY - LAND AND MINERALS MANAGEMENT						
Washington, DC	Assistant Secretary	Vacant	PAS	EX	IV	....	
Do	Deputy Assistant Secretary	Edward P. Farquhar	NA	ES	....	....	
Do	......do	Sylvia V. Baca	NA	ES	....	....	
Do	Senior Advisor to the Assistant Secretary	Mary Katherine Ishee	NA	ES	....	....	
	Bureau of Land Management						
Do	Director	Vacant	PAS	EX	V	....	
Salt Lake City, UT	State Director, Utah	Career Incumbent	CA	ES	....	....	

DEPARTMENT OF THE INTERIOR—Continued

Location	Position	Name of Incumbent	Type of Appt.	Pay Plan	Level, Grade, or Pay	Tenure	Expires
Cheyenne, WY	State Director, Wyoming	Career Incumbent	CA	ES			
Billings, MT	State Director, Montana	......do	CA	ES			
Sacramento, CA	State Director, California	......do	CA	ES			
Anchorage, AK	State Director, Alaska	......do	CA	ES			
Portland, OR	State Director, Oregon	Vacant		ES			
Phoenix, AZ	State Director, Arizona	Career Incumbent	CA	ES			
Santa Fe, NM	State Director, New Mexico	......do	CA	ES			
Boise, ID	State Director, Idaho	......do	CA	ES			
Reno, NV	State Director, Nevada	......do	CA	ES			
Denver, CO	State Director, Colorado	......do	CA	ES			
Washington, DC	State Director, Eastern States	......do	CA	ES			
Do	Deputy Director, Operations	......do	CA	ES			
Do	Director, National Operations Center	Career Incumbent	CA	ES			
Do	Director, Office of the National Landscape Conservation System.	......do	CA	ES			
Do	Director Law Enforcement, Security and Protection.	......do	CA	ES			
Do	Assistant Director, Renewable Resources and Planning.	......do	CA	ES			
Do	Assistant Director, Business and Fiscal Resources.	......do	CA	ES			
Do	Assistant Director, Human Capital Management.	......do	CA	ES			
Do	Assistant Director, Minerals, Realty and Resource Protection.	......do	CA	ES			
Denver, CO	Assistant Director, Office of Information Resources Management.	Vacant		ES			
Washington, DC	Deputy Director, Programs and Policy	Marcilynn A. Burke	NA	ES			
Do	Senior Advisor	Neil Kornze	NA	ES			
Do	Assistant Director, Fire and Aviation	Vacant		ES			
	Office of Surface Mining						
Do	Director, Office of Surface Mining Reclamation and Enforcement.	Joseph G. Pizarchik	PAS	EX	V		
Do	Assistant Director, Program Support	Career Incumbent	CA	ES			
Do	Deputy Director	......do	CA	ES			
Do	Assistant Director for Finance and Administration.	......do	CA	ES			
St. Louis, MO	Regional Director, Mid Continent Regional Coordinating Center.	......do	CA	ES			
Washington, DC	Chief of Staff	Michele Jan Altemus	NA	ES			
	Bureau of Ocean Energy Management						
Do	Director	Tommy Beaudreau	NA	ES			
Do	Science Advisor	Career Incumbent	CA	ES			
Do	Deputy Director	......do	CA	ES			
New Orleans, LA	Gulf of Mexico Regional Director	......do	CA	ES			
Anchorage, AK	Alaska Regional Director	......do	CA	ES			
Washington, DC	Chief Environmental Officer	......do	CA	ES			
Do	Senior Advisor	Shoshana M. Lew	SC	GS	15		
Do	Special Assistant	Jordan N. Finegan	SC	GS	9		
	Bureau of Safety and Environmental Enforcement						
Do	Director	James Watson	NA	ES			
Do	Associate Director for Administration	Vacant		ES			
Do	Regulatory Programs Chief	Career Incumbent	CA	ES			
Jefferson, LA	Gulf of Mexico Regional Director	......do	CA	ES			
Washington, DC	Senior Advisor	Michael D. Farber	NA	ES			
Do	Deputy Director	Career Incumbent	CA	ES			
Do	Senior Advisor	Allyson K. Anderson	NA	ES			
Do	......do	Steven H. Feldgus	SC	GS	15		
Do	Special Assistant to the Director	Kirk M. Sander	SC	GS	13		
	ASSISTANT SECRETARY - INDIAN AFFAIRS						
Do	Assistant Secretary	Vacant	PAS	EX	IV		
Do	Principal Deputy Assistant Secretary	Donald E. Laverdure	NA	ES			
Do	Deputy Assistant Secretary - Management	Vacant		ES			
Do	Deputy Assistant Secretary - Policy and Economic Development.	Vacant		ES			
Do	Deputy Assistant Secretary - Indian Affairs	......do		ES			
Do	......do	......do		ES			
Do	Chief Financial Officer	Career Incumbent	CA	ES			
Do	Director, Office of Indian Gaming Management.	......do	CA	ES			
Do	Budget Officer	......do	CA	ES			

DEPARTMENT OF THE INTERIOR—Continued

Location	Position	Name of Incumbent	Type of Appt.	Pay Plan	Level, Grade, or Pay	Tenure	Expires
Washington, DC	Director, Facilities, Environmental, Safety and Cultural Resources Management.	Vacant	....	ES	....	....	
Do	Director, Indian Energy and Economic Development.	Career Incumbent	CA	ES	....	....	
Do	Director, Office of Self-Governance	......do	CA	ES	....	....	
Albuquerque, NM ..	Director, Office of Regulatory Affairs and Collaborative Action.	Career Incumbent	CA	ES	....	....	
Washington, DC	Chief of Staff	Vacant	....	ES	....	....	
Do	Assistant Director - Information Resources	Alvin Foster	TA	ES	....	....	06/18/13
Do	Special Assistant to the Assistant Secretary ..	Career Incumbent	CA	ES	....	....	
Do	Senior Advisor to the Assistant Secretary - Indian Affairs.	Bryan T. Newland	SC	GS	14	....	
Do	......do	Jacquelynn K. Hanley	SC	GS	13	....	
	Bureau of Indian Affairs						
Muskogee, OK	Regional Director, Eastern Oklahoma Region	Vacant	....	ES	....	....	
Anadarko, OK	Regional Director, Southern Plains Region	Career Incumbent	CA	ES	....	....	
Portland, OR	Regional Director, Northwest Region	......do	CA	ES	....	....	
Juneau, AK	Regional Director, Alaska Region	......do	CA	ES	....	....	
Sacramento, CA	Regional Director, Pacific Region	......do	CA	ES	....	....	
Minneapolis, MN ...	Regional Director, Midwest Region	......do	CA	ES	....	....	
Washington, DC	Regional Director, Eastern Region	......do	CA	ES	....	....	
Aberdeen, SD	Regional Director, Great Plains Region	......do	CA	ES	....	....	
Billings, MT	Regional Director, Rocky Mountain Region	......do	CA	ES	....	....	
Gallup, NM	Regional Director, Navajo Region	......do	CA	ES	....	....	
Albuquerque, NM ..	Regional Director, Southwest	......do	CA	ES	....	....	
Phoenix, AZ	Regional Director, Western Region	......do	CA	ES	....	....	
Washington, DC	Deputy Director, Indian Services	......do	CA	ES	....	....	
Do	Deputy Director Justice Services	......do	CA	ES	....	....	
Do	Director, Bureau of Indian Affairs	......do	CA	ES	....	....	
Ashland, WI	Director, Indian Land Consolidation Center ..	Vacant	....	ES	....	....	
Washington, DC	Deputy Director, Trust Services	Career Incumbent	CA	ES	....	....	
	Bureau of Indian Education						
Washington, DC	Director	......do	CA	ES	....	....	
Albuquerque, NM ..	Deputy Director, School Operations	Vacant	....	ES	....	....	
Washington, DC	Deputy Director, Policy, Evaluation and Post Secondary Education.	Vacant	....	ES	....	....	
Minnesota, MN	Associate Deputy Director - East	Career Incumbent	CA	ES	....	....	
Window Rock, AZ ..	Associate Deputy Director - Navajo	......do	CA	ES	....	....	
Albuquerque, NM ..	Associate Deputy Director - West	......do	CA	ES	....	....	
Do	Assistant Deputy Director, Administration	......do	CA	ES	....	....	
Do	Associate Deputy Director, Compliance, Monitoring and Accountability.	Career Incumbent	CA	ES	....	....	

DEPARTMENT OF THE INTERIOR OFFICE OF THE INSPECTOR GENERAL

Location	Position	Name of Incumbent	Type of Appt.	Pay Plan	Level, Grade, or Pay	Tenure	Expires
	OFFICE OF THE INSPECTOR GENERAL						
Washington, DC	Inspector General	Vacant	PAS	EX	....	....	

DEPARTMENT OF JUSTICE

Location	Position	Name of Incumbent	Type of Appt.	Pay Plan	Level, Grade, or Pay	Tenure	Expires
	OFFICE OF THE ATTORNEY GENERAL						
Washington, DC	Attorney General	Eric H. Holder, Jr.	PAS	EX	I		
Do	Chief of Staff	Gary G. Grindler	NA	ES			
Do	Deputy Chief of Staff and Counselor to the Attorney General.	Margaret Richardson	NA	ES			
Do	Counselor to the Attorney General	Channing Phillips	TA	ES			05/20/15
Do	.....do	Helaine Ann Greenfeld	NA	ES			
Do	.....do	Molly J. Moran	NA	ES			
Do	.....do	Stuart Delery	NA	ES			
Do	Counsel	Jenny Rachelle Mosier	SC	GS	15		
Do	White House Liaison	Sharon Werner	SC	GS	15		
Do	Confidential Assistant	Paula A. Bradley	SC	GS	14		
Do	Special Assistant	Patrick J. Shearns	SC	GS	12		
Do	.....do	Sarah Moss	SC	GS	11		
	OFFICE OF THE DEPUTY ATTORNEY GENERAL						
Do	Deputy Attorney General	James Michael Cole	PAS	EX	II		
Do	Principal Associate Deputy Attorney General	Career Incumbent	CA	ES			
Do	Chief of Staff and Counselor	Vacant		ES			
Do	Associate Deputy Attorney General	Career Incumbent	CA	ES			
Do	.....do	.....do	CA	ES			
Do	.....do	Vacant		ES			
Do	.....do	.....do		ES			
Do	.....do	Steven Reich	NA	ES			
Do	.....do	Charlotte A. Burrows	NA	ES			
Do	.....do	Vacant		ES			
Do	National Criminal Discovery Coordinator	Career Incumbent	CA	ES			
Do	Chief Privacy and Civil Liberties Officer	Vacant		ES			
Do	Deputy Chief of Staff and Senior Counsel	Monica Marie Ramirez	SC	GS	15		
Do	Senior Counsel	Eric Randal Columbus	SC	GS	15		
Do	.....do	Crystal Lynne Brown	SC	GS	15		
Do	.....do	Trisha Anderson	SC	GS	15		
Do	.....do	Miriam Barnett Vogel	SC	GS	15		
Do	Counsel	Jessica R. Hertz	SC	GS	14		
Do	Confidential Assistant	Melanie L. Dix	SC	GS	13		
	Criminal Division						
Do	Assistant Attorney General	Lanny A. Breuer	PAS	EX	IV		
Do	Principal Deputy Assistant Attorney General and Chief of Staff.	Mythili Raman	NA	ES			
Do	Deputy Assistant Attorney General	Vacant		ES			
Do	.....do	Jason Marc Weinstein	NA	ES			
Do	.....do	Career Incumbent	CA	ES			
Do	.....do	.....do	CA	ES			
Do	.....do	.....do	CA	ES			
Do	Director, Office of Enforcement Operations	.....do	CA	ES			
Do	Deputy Director, Office of Enforcement Operations.	.....do	CA	ES			
Do	Director, Office of International Affairs	.....do	CA	ES			
Do	Deputy Director, Office of International Affairs.	.....do	CA	ES			
Do	Director, Office of Policy and Legislation	.....do	CA	ES			
Do	Chief, Capital Case Unit	.....do	CA	ES			
Do	Director, Human Rights Enforcement Strategy and Policy.	.....do	CA	ES			
Do	Counselor to the Assistant Attorney General	Amy Pope	NA	ES			
Do	Senior Counsel	Vacant		ES			
Do	Counsel to the Assistant Attorney General	Paul Michael Rosen	SC	GS	15		
	National Security Division						
Do	Assistant Attorney General	Lisa Monaco	PAS	EX	IV		
Do	Principal Deputy Assistant Attorney General and Chief of Staff.	Career Incumbent	CA	ES			
Do	Deputy Assistant Attorney General	.....do	CA	ES			
Do	.....do	.....do	CA	ES			
Do	Director, FOIA and Declassification Program	.....do	CA	ES			
Do	Chief, Counterespionage Section	.....do	CA	ES			
Do	Chief, Counterterrorism Section	.....do	CA	ES			
Do	Chief, Policy-Office of Law and Policy	Vacant		ES			
Do	Counsel	Kate Heinzelman	SC	GS	14		
	Office of Legislative Affairs						
Do	Assistant Attorney General	Vacant	PAS	EX	IV		
Do	Deputy Assistant Attorney General	Mark David Agrast	NA	ES			
Do	.....do	Judith Carol Appelbaum	NA	ES			
Do	.....do	Vacant		ES			

DEPARTMENT OF JUSTICE—Continued

Location	Position	Name of Incumbent	Type of Appt.	Pay Plan	Level, Grade, or Pay	Tenure	Expires
Washington, DC	Special Counsel	Career Incumbent	CA	ES	....	....	
Do	Director, Office of Intergovernmental and Public Liaison.	Portia Lucille Roberson	NA	ES	....	....	
Do	Attorney Advisor	Rita Christine Aguilar	SC	GS	15	....	
Do	......do	Molly Gulland Gaston	SC	GS	13	....	
Do	Associate Director, Office of Intergovernmental and Public Liaison.	Alexa K. Chappell	SC	GS	13	....	
Do	Legislative Assistant	Peter James Kralovec	SC	GS	11	....	
	Office of Legal Counsel						
Do	Assistant Attorney General	Virginia Seitz	PAS	EX	IV	....	
Do	Principal Deputy Assistant Attorney General	Caroline D. Krass	NA	ES	....	....	
Do	Deputy Assistant Attorney General	Career Incumbent	CA	ES	....	....	
Do	......do	Karl Remon Thompson	NA	ES	....	....	
Do	......do	Cristina Maria Rodriguez ..	NA	ES	....	....	
Do	......do	John Edward Bies	NA	ES	....	....	
Do	......do	Benjamin Mizer	NA	ES	....	....	
Do	Special Counsel	Vacant	....	ES	....	....	
	Office of Legal Policy						
Do	Assistant Attorney General	Christopher Schroeder	PAS	EX	IV	....	
Do	Principal Deputy Assistant Attorney General	Elana Joy Tyrangiel	NA	ES	....	....	
Do	Deputy Assistant Attorney General	Vacant	....	ES	....	....	
Do	......do	Michael Arthur Zubrensky ..	NA	ES	....	....	
Do	......do	Career Incumbent	CA	ES	....	....	
Do	......do	......do	CA	ES	....	....	
Do	Senior Advisor	Kenneth E. Melson	NA	ES	....	....	
Do	Senior Counsel	Lisa Michelle Ellman	SC	GS	15	....	
Do	Counsel	Julian En-Jun Yap	SC	GS	14	....	
Do	Researcher	Daysi Alonzo	SC	GS	9	....	
	United States Parole Commission						
Do	Chairman	Isaac Fulwood, Jr.	PAS	EX	IV	....	
Do	Parole Commissioner	Cranston J. Mitchell	PAS	EX	V	....	
Do	......do	Charles T. Massarone	PAS	EX	V	....	
Do	......do	Patricia K. Cushwa	PAS	EX	V	....	
Do	......do	Jerrolyn Patricia Smoot	PAS	EX	V	....	
	Executive Office for United States Attorneys						
Do	Director	Career Incumbent	CA	ES	....	....	
Do	Principal Deputy and Chief of Staff	......do	CA	ES	....	....	
Do	Deputy Director and Counsel to the Director	......do	CA	ES	....	....	
Do	Project Manager, Palmetto Project	......do	CA	ES	....	....	
Do	Chief of Planning, Evaluation and Performance.	......do	CA	ES	....	....	
Montgomery, AL	United States Attorney, Alabama, Middle District.	George L. Beck, Jr.	PAS	AD	$155,500	....	
Huntsville, AL	United States Attorney, Alabama, Northern District.	Joyce Vance	PAS	AD	$155,500	....	
Mobile, AL	United States Attorney, Alabama, Southern District.	Kenyen R. Brown	PAS	AD	$155,500	....	
Anchorage, AK	United States Attorney, Alaska	Karen L. Loeffler	PAS	AD	$155,500	....	
Phoenix, AZ	United States Attorney, Arizona	John S. Leonardo	PAS	AD	$155,500	....	
Little Rock, AR	United States Attorney, Arkansas, Eastern District.	Christopher R. Thyer	PAS	AD	$155,500	....	
Fort Smith, AR	United States Attorney, Arkansas, Western District.	William Conner Eldridge, Jr..	PAS	AD	$155,500	....	
Los Angeles, CA	United States Attorney, California, Central District.	Andre Birotte, Jr.	PAS	AD	$155,500	....	
Sacramento, CA	United States Attorney, California, Eastern District.	Benjamin B. Wagner	PAS	AD	$155,500	....	
San Francisco, CA	United States Attorney, California, Northern District.	Melinda L. Haag	PAS	AD	$155,500	....	
San Diego, CA	United States Attorney, California, Southern District.	Laura Elizabeth Duffy	PAS	AD	$155,500	....	
Denver, CO	United States Attorney, Colorado	John F. Walsh III	PAS	AD	$155,500	....	
New Haven, CT	United States Attorney, Connecticut	David B. Fein	PAS	AD	$155,500	....	
Wilmington, DE	United States Attorney, Delaware	Charles M. Oberly III	PAS	AD	$155,500	....	
Washington, DC	United States Attorney, District of Columbia	Ronald C. Machen	PAS	AD	$155,500	....	
Tampa, FL	United States Attorney, Florida, Middle District.	Robert E. O Neill	PAS	AD	$155,500	....	
Tallahassee, FL	United States Attorney, Florida, Northern District.	Pamela Cothran Marsh	PAS	AD	$155,500	....	
Miami, FL	United States Attorney, Florida, Southern District.	Wifredo A. Ferrer	PAS	AD	$155,500	....	
Macon, GA	United States Attorney, Georgia, Middle District.	Michael J. Moore	PAS	AD	$155,500	....	

DEPARTMENT OF JUSTICE—Continued

Location	Position	Name of Incumbent	Type of Appt.	Pay Plan	Level, Grade, or Pay	Tenure	Expires
Atlanta, GA	United States Attorney, Georgia, Northern District.	Sally Quillian Yates	PAS	AD	$155,500	....	
Savannah, GA	United States Attorney, Georgia, Southern District.	Edward J. Tarver	PAS	AD	$155,500	....	
Agana, Guam	United States Attorney, Guam	Alicia Limtiaco	PAS	AD	$155,500	....	
Honolulu, HI	United States Attorney, Hawaii	Florence T. Nakakuni	PAS	AD	$155,500	....	
Boise, ID	United States Attorney, Idaho	Wendy J. Olson	PAS	AD	$155,500	....	
Springfield, IL	United States Attorney, Illinois, Central District.	James Andrew Lewis	PAS	AD	$155,500	....	
Chicago, IL	United States Attorney, Illinois, Northern District.	Vacant	PAS	AD		....	
Fairview Heights, IL.	United States Attorney, Illinois, Southern District.	Stephen R. Wigginton	PAS	AD	$155,500	....	
Dyer, IN	United States Attorney, Indiana, Northern District.	David A. Capp	PAS	AD	$155,500	....	
Indianapolis, IN	United States Attorney, Indiana, Southern District.	Joseph H. Hogsett	PAS	AD	$155,500	....	
Cedar Rapids, IA ...	United States Attorney, Iowa, Northern District.	Stephanie Marie Rose	PAS	AD	$155,500	....	
Des Moines, IA	United States Attorney, Iowa, Southern District.	Nicholas A. Klinefeldt	PAS	AD	$155,500	....	
Wichita, KS	United States Attorney, Kansas	Barry R. Grissom	PAS	AD	$155,500	....	
Lexington, KY	United States Attorney, Kentucky, Eastern District.	Kerry B. Harvey	PAS	AD	$155,500	....	
Louisville, KY	United States Attorney, Kentucky, Western District.	David J. Hale	PAS	AD	$155,500	....	
New Orleans, LA ...	United States Attorney, Louisiana, Eastern District.	James B. Letten	PAS	AD	$155,500	....	
Baton Rouge, LA ...	United States Attorney, Louisiana, Middle District.	Donald J. Cazayoux, Jr.	PAS	AD	$155,500	....	
Shreveport, LA	United States Attorney, Louisiana, Western District.	Stephanie A. Finley	PAS	AD	$155,500	....	
Portland, ME	United States Attorney, Maine	Thomas E. Delahanty II	PAS	AD	$155,500	....	
Baltimore, MD	United States Attorney, Maryland	Rod J. Rosenstein	PAS	AD	$155,500	....	
Boston, MA	United States Attorney, Massachusetts	Carmen M. Ortiz	PAS	AD	$155,500	....	
Detroit, MI	United States Attorney, Michigan, Eastern District.	Barbara L. McQuade	PAS	AD	$155,500	....	
Grand Rapids, MI ..	United States Attorney, Michigan, Western District.	Patrick A. Miles, Jr.	PAS	AD	$155,500	....	
Minneapolis, MN ...	United States Attorney, Minnesota	Byron T. Jones	PAS	AD	$155,500	....	
Oxford, MS	United States Attorney, Mississippi, Northern District.	Felicia Colette Adams	PAS	AD	$155,500	....	
Jackson, MS	United States Attorney, Mississippi, Southern District.	Gregory K. Davis	PAS	AD	$155,500	....	
St. Louis, MO	United States Attorney, Missouri, Eastern District.	Richard Callahan	PAS	AD	$155,500	....	
Kansas City, MO ...	United States Attorney, Missouri, Western District.	Vacant	PAS	AD		....	
Billings, MT	United States Attorney, Montana	Michael Cotter	PAS	AD	$155,500	....	
Omaha, NE	United States Attorney, Nebraska	Deborah R. Gilg	PAS	AD	$155,500	....	
Las Vegas, NV	United States Attorney, Nevada	Daniel G. Bogden	PAS	AD	$155,500	....	
Concord, NH	United States Attorney, New Hampshire	John Paul Kacavas	PAS	AD	$155,500	....	
Newark, NJ	United States Attorney, New Jersey	Paul Joseph Fishman	PAS	AD	$155,500	....	
Albuquerque, NM ..	United States Attorney, New Mexico	Kenneth J. Gonzales	PAS	AD	$155,500	....	
New York-Kings, NY.	United States Attorney, New York, Eastern District.	Loretta Lynch	PAS	AD	$155,500	....	
Syracuse, NY	United States Attorney, New York, Northern District.	Richard S. Hartunian	PAS	AD	$155,500	....	
New York, NY	United States Attorney, New York, Southern District.	Preetinder Singh Bharara	PAS	AD	$155,500	....	
Buffalo, NY	United States Attorney, New York, Western District.	William J. Hochul	PAS	AD	$155,500	....	
Raleigh, NC	United States Attorney, North Carolina, Eastern District.	Thomas G. Walker	PAS	AD	$155,500	....	
Greensboro, NC	United States Attorney, North Carolina, Middle District.	Ripley E. Rand	PAS	AD	$155,500	....	
Charlotte, NC	United States Attorney, North Carolina, Western District.	Anne Magee Tompkins	PAS	AD	$155,500	....	
Fargo, ND	United States Attorney, North Dakota	Timothy Q. Purdon	PAS	AD	$155,500	....	
Cleveland, OH	United States Attorney, Ohio, Northern District.	Steven Dettelbach	PAS	AD	$155,500	....	
Dayton, OH	United States Attorney, Ohio, Southern District.	Carter M. Stewart	PAS	AD	$155,500	....	
Muskogee, OK	United States Attorney, Oklahoma, Eastern District.	Mark F. Green	PAS	AD	$155,500	....	

DEPARTMENT OF JUSTICE—Continued

Location	Position	Name of Incumbent	Type of Appt.	Pay Plan	Level, Grade, or Pay	Tenure	Expires
Tulsa, OK	United States Attorney, Oklahoma, Northern District.	Danny C. Williams, Sr.	PAS	AD	$155,500	....	
Oklahoma City, OK	United States Attorney, Oklahoma, Western District.	Sanford C. Coats	PAS	AD	$155,500	....	
Portland, OR	United States Attorney, Oregon	S. Amanda Marshall	PAS	AD	$155,500	....	
Philadelphia, PA	United States Attorney, Pennsylvania, Eastern District.	Zane D. Memeger	PAS	AD	$155,500	....	
Williamsport, PA ...	United States Attorney, Pennsylvania, Middle District.	Peter J. Smith	PAS	AD	$155,500	....	
Pittsburgh, PA	United States Attorney, Pennsylvania, Western District.	David J. Hickton	PAS	AD	$155,500	....	
Hato Rey, Puerto Rico.	United States Attorney, Puerto Rico	Rosa Rodriguez-Velez	PAS	AD	$155,500	....	
Providence, RI	United States Attorney, Rhode Island	Peter F. Neronha	PAS	AD	$155,500	....	
Columbia, SC	United States Attorney, South Carolina	William N. Nettles	PAS	AD	$155,500	....	
Sioux Falls, SD	United States Attorney, South Dakota	Brendan Johnson	PAS	AD	$155,500	....	
Chattanooga, TN ...	United States Attorney, Tennessee, Eastern District.	William C. Killian	PAS	AD	$155,500	....	
Nashville, TN	United States Attorney, Tennessee, Middle District.	Gerald E. Martin	PAS	AD	$155,500	....	
Memphis, TN	United States Attorney, Tennessee, Western District.	Edward L. Stanton III	PAS	AD	$155,500	....	
Plano, TX	United States Attorney, Texas, Eastern District.	John Malcolm Bales	PAS	AD	$155,500	....	
Fort Worth, TX	United States Attorney, Texas, Northern District.	Sarah Ruth Saldana	PAS	AD	$155,500	....	
Houston, TX	United States Attorney, Texas, Southern District.	Kenneth Magidson	PAS	AD	$155,500	....	
San Antonio, TX	United States Attorney, Texas, Western District.	Robert L. Pitman	PAS	AD	$155,500	....	
Salt Lake City, UT	United States Attorney, Utah	David B. Barlow	PAS	AD	$155,500	....	
Burlington, VT	United States Attorney, Vermont	Tristram Joseph Coffin	PAS	AD	$155,500	....	
St. Croix, Virgin Islands.	United States Attorney, Virgin Islands	Ronald W. Sharpe	PAS	AD	$155,500	....	
Alexandria, VA	United States Attorney, Virginia, Eastern District.	Neil H. MacBride	PAS	AD	$155,500	....	
Roanoke, VA	United States Attorney, Virginia, Western District.	Timothy J. Heaphy	PAS	AD	$155,500	....	
Spokane, WA	United States Attorney, Washington, Eastern District.	Michael C. Ormsby	PAS	AD	$155,500	....	
Seattle, WA	United States Attorney, Washington, Western District.	Jenny A. Durkan	PAS	AD	$155,500	....	
Wheeling, WV	United States Attorney, West Virginia, Northern District.	William J. Ihlenfeld II	PAS	AD	$155,500	....	
Charleston, WV	United States Attorney, West Virginia, Southern District.	Robert Booth Goodwin II ...	PAS	AD	$155,500	....	
Milwaukee, WI	United States Attorney, Wisconsin, Eastern District.	James Lewis Santelle	PAS	AD	$155,500	....	
Madison, WI	United States Attorney, Wisconsin, Western District.	John W. Vaudreuil	PAS	AD	$155,500	....	
Cheyenne, WY	United States Attorney, Wyoming	Christopher A. Crofts	PAS	AD	$155,500	....	
Washington, DC	Counsel	Elizabeth Alexander	SC	GS	15	....	
Do	......do	Aaron M. Lewis	SC	GS	15	....	
Do	......do	Jason F. Cunningham	SC	GS	11	....	
	Executive Office for Immigration Review						
Falls Church, VA ...	Director	Career Incumbent	CA	ES	....		
Do	Deputy Director	Vacant	....	ES	....		
	Office of the Pardon Attorney						
Washington, DC	Pardon Attorney	Career Incumbent	CA	ES			
	Office of Public Affairs						
Do	Director	Tracy Alice Schmaler	NA	ES	....		
Do	Deputy Director	Nanda Chitre	SC	GS	15	....	
Do	Senior Public Affairs Specialist	Allison Price	SC	GS	15	....	
Do	Speechwriter	Brianne Holloran Frazier ..	SC	GS	15	....	
Do	Press Secretary	Adora Michelle Andy	SC	GS	15	....	
Do	Public Affairs Specialist	Beverley Lumpkin	SC	GS	14	....	
Do	New Media Specialist	Tracy Russo	SC	GS	14	....	
Do	Deputy Speechwriter	Riley Land Roberts	SC	GS	9	....	
Do	Confidential Assistant	Katherine Elizabeth Dixon	SC	GS	7	....	
Do	Press Assistant	Mitchell Ryan Rivard	SC	GS	7	....	
Do	......do	Michael R. Passman	SC	GS	7	....	
	Rule of Law Office						
Baghdad, Iraq	Justice Attaché	James Clayton Joyner	TA	ES	....	....	11/20/12
Kabul, Afghanistan	Justice Attaché Afghanistan	David J. Schwendiman	TA	ES	....	....	07/01/13

DEPARTMENT OF JUSTICE—Continued

Location	Position	Name of Incumbent	Type of Appt.	Pay Plan	Level, Grade, or Pay	Tenure	Expires
	Executive Office for Organized Crime Drug Enforcement Task Forces						
Washington, DC	Director, Organized Crime Drug Enforcement Task Forces, Fusion Center.	Vacant	....	ES	....	....	
Do	Deputy Director, OCDETF	Career Incumbent	CA	ES	....	....	
	OFFICE OF THE ASSOCIATE ATTORNEY GENERAL						
Do	Associate Attorney General	Vacant	PAS	EX	III	....	
Do	Principal Deputy Associate Attorney General	Elizabeth Gordon Taylor ...	NA	ES	....	....	
Do	Deputy Associate Attorney General	A. Marisa Chun	NA	ES	....	....	
Do	......do	Vacant	....	ES	....	....	
Do	......do	Samuel Hirsch	NA	ES	....	....	
Do	......do	Julia Elizabeth McEvoy	NA	ES	....	....	
Do	Senior Counsel	Daniel Benjamin Olmos	SC	GS	15	....	
Do	......do	Melanca Durham Clark	SC	GS	15	....	
Do	......do	Karen Ann Lash	SC	GS	15	....	
Do	Counsel	Mala Adiga	SC	GS	14	....	
Do	Attorney Advisor	Cindy Chang	SC	GS	14	....	
	Antitrust Division						
Do	Assistant Attorney General	Vacant	PAS	EX	IV	....	
Do	Principal Deputy Assistant Attorney General	Joseph F. Wayland	NA	ES	....	....	
Do	Deputy Assistant Attorney General	Renatta B. Hesse	NA	ES	....	....	
Do	......do	Career Incumbent	CA	ES	....	....	
Do	......do	Leslie Suzanne Overton	NA	ES	....	....	
Do	......do	Vacant	....	ES	....	....	
Do	......do	......do	....	ES	....	....	
Do	Director of Operations	Career Incumbent	CA	ES	....	....	
San Francisco, CA	Director, Criminal Enforcement	......do	CA	ES	....	....	
Washington, DC	Chief, Litigation I Section	......do	CA	ES	....	....	
Do	Chief, Appellate Section	......do	CA	ES	....	....	
Do	Chief, Foreign Commerce Section	......do	CA	ES	....	....	
Do	Chief, Transportation/Energy/Agriculture Section.	Vacant	....	ES	....	....	
Cleveland, OH	Chief, Cleveland Field Office	Career Incumbent	CA	ES	....	....	
Chicago, IL	Chief, Chicago Field Office	......do	CA	ES	....	....	
San Francisco, CA	Chief, San Francisco Field Office	......do	CA	ES	....	....	
Philadelphia, PA	Chief, Philadelphia Field Office	......do	CA	ES	....	....	
Atlanta, GA	Chief, Atlanta Field Office	......do	CA	ES	....	....	
New York, NY	Chief, New York Field Office	......do	CA	ES	....	....	
Dallas, TX	Chief, Dallas Field Office	......do	CA	ES	....	....	
Washington, DC	Chief, Legal Policy Section	......do	CA	ES	....	....	
Do	Chief, Economic Litigation Section	......do	CA	ES	....	....	
Do	Chief, Litigation II Section	......do	CA	ES	....	....	
Do	Chief, National Criminal Enforcement Section.	......do	CA	ES	....	....	
Do	Chief, Networks and Technology Enforcement Section.	......do	CA	ES	....	....	
Do	Chief, Litigation III Section	......do	CA	ES	....	....	
Do	Chief, Competition Policy Section	Vacant	....	ES	....	....	
Do	Deputy Chief, Legal Policy Section	......do	....	ES	....	....	
Do	Senior Counsel (Competition Policy)	Terrell McSweeny	NA	ES	....	....	
Do	Chief of Staff and Counsel to the Assistant Attorney General.	Jamillia Magdalena Padua Ferris.	SC	GS	15	....	
Do	Counsel	Courtney Lauren Weiner ...	SC	GS	14	....	
Do	Confidential Assistant	Jean Claire Meikle	SC	GS	12	....	
	Civil Division						
Do	Assistant Attorney General	Tony West	PAS	EX	IV	....	
Do	Principal Deputy Assistant Attorney General	Vacant	....	ES	....	....	
Do	Deputy Assistant Attorney General	......do	....	ES	....	....	
Do	......do	Brian Philip Hauck	NA	ES	....	....	
Do	......do	Vacant	....	ES	....	....	
Do	......do	Maame Ewusi-Mensah Frimpong.	NA	ES	....	....	
Do	......do	Ian H. Gershengorn	NA	ES	....	....	
Do	......do	Beth Susan Brinkmann	NA	ES	....	....	
Do	Director, Appellate Staff	Career Incumbent	CA	ES	....	....	
Do	Director, Commercial Litigation Branch, Civil Fraud Section.	......do	CA	ES	....	....	
Do	Director, Commercial Litigation Branch, National Courts Section.	......do	CA	ES	....	....	
Do	Branch Director, Federal Programs Branch I	......do	CA	ES	....	....	
Do	Branch Director, Federal Programs Branch II	......do	CA	ES	....	....	
Do	Director, Commercial Litigation Branch, Corporate/Financial Section.	......do	CA	ES	....	....	

DEPARTMENT OF JUSTICE—Continued

Location	Position	Name of Incumbent	Type of Appt.	Pay Plan	Level, Grade, or Pay	Tenure	Expires
Washington, DC	Director, Federal Tort Claims Act Section	Career Incumbent	CA	ES	....	....	
Do	Director, Intellectual Property Section	......do	CA	ES	....	....	
Do	Director, Constitutional and Specialized Tort Litigation Section.	......do	CA	ES	....	....	
Do	Director, Aviation and Admiralty Section	......do	CA	ES	....	....	
Do	Branch Director, Federal Programs Branch III.	......do	CA	ES	....	....	
Do	Director, Office of Immigration Litigation, Appellate Section.	......do	CA	ES	....	....	
Do	Director, Environmental Tort Litigation Section.	......do	CA	ES	....	....	
Do	Deputy Director, Commercial Litigation Branch, National Courts Section.	......do	CA	ES	....	....	
Do	Director, Office of Immigration Litigation, Federal District Court Section.	......do	CA	ES	....	....	
Do	Counselor to the Assistant Attorney General	Vacant	....	ES	....	....	
Do	Special Litigation Counsel, Federal Programs	Career Incumbent	CA	ES	....	....	
Do	Appellate Litigation Counsel	Vacant	....	ES	....	....	
Do	Senior Counsel	Natalia Tania Sorgente	SC	GS	15	....	
Do	Counsel and Chief of Staff	Jonathan Foster Olin	SC	GS	15	....	
Do	Counsel	Geoffrey Graber	SC	GS	15	....	
Do	......do	Brian Jeffrey Martinez	SC	GS	15	....	
Do	......do	Melanie Therese Singh	SC	GS	15	....	
	Civil Rights Division						
Do	Assistant Attorney General	Thomas E. Perez	PAS	EX	IV	....	
Do	Principal Deputy Assistant Attorney General	Jocelyn Samuels	NA	ES	....	....	
Do	Deputy Assistant Attorney General	Career Incumbent	CA	ES	....	....	
Do	......do	Roy Austin, Jr.	NA	ES	....	....	
Do	......do	Matthew Byron Colangelo	NA	ES	....	....	
Do	......do	Victoria Helen Schultz	NA	ES	....	....	
Do	Counselor to the Assistant Attorney General	Vacant	....	ES	....	....	
Do	Counsel to the Assistant Attorney General	Career Incumbent	CA	ES	....	....	
Do	Chief, Employment Litigation Section	......do	CA	ES	....	....	
Do	Chief, Appellate Section	......do	CA	ES	....	....	
Do	Chief, Criminal Section	......do	CA	ES	....	....	
Do	Chief, Housing and Civil Enforcement Section	......do	CA	ES	....	....	
Do	Chief, Voting Section	......do	CA	ES	....	....	
Do	Chief, Educational Opportunities Section	......do	CA	ES	....	....	
Do	Chief, Special Litigation Section	......do	CA	ES	....	....	
Do	Chief, Coordination and Review Section	......do	CA	ES	....	....	
Do	Chief, Disability Rights Section	......do	CA	ES	....	....	
Do	Principal Deputy Chief, Criminal Section	......do	CA	ES	....	....	
Do	Principal Deputy Chief, Voting Section	......do	CA	ES	....	....	
Do	Deputy Special Counsel for Immigration-Related Unfair Employment Practices.	......do	CA	ES	....	....	
Do	Counsel to the Special Litigation Section Chief.	......do	CA	ES	....	....	
Do	Special Counsel for Immigration-Related Unfair Employment Practices.	Vacant	PAS	SL	....	....	
Do	Senior Counsel	Eve Lynne Hill	SC	GS	15	....	
Do	Counsel	Mazen Mohammed Basrawi.	SC	GS	15	....	
Do	......do	Emily Martha Loeb	SC	GS	13	....	
	Environment and Natural Resources Division						
Do	Assistant Attorney General	Ignacia S. Moreno	PAS	EX	IV	....	
Do	Principal Deputy Assistant Attorney General	Robert G. Dreher	NA	ES	....	....	
Do	Deputy Assistant Attorney General	Career Incumbent	CA	ES	....	....	
Do	......do	Steven C. Silverman	NA	ES	....	....	
Do	......do	Ethan Gregory Shenkman	NA	ES	....	....	
Do	......do	Career Incumbent	CA	ES	....	....	
Do	Chief, Law and Policy Section	......do	CA	ES	....	....	
Do	Deputy Chief, Appellate Section	......do	CA	ES	....	....	
Do	Special Assistant	Paulo Custodio Palugod	SC	GS	11	....	
	Tax Division						
Do	Assistant Attorney General	Kathryn Keneally	PAS	EX	IV	....	
Do	Deputy Assistant Attorney General	Tamara W. Ashford	NA	ES	....	....	
Do	......do	Career Incumbent	CA	ES	....	....	
Do	......do	......do	CA	ES	....	....	
Do	......do	Vacant	....	ES	....	....	
Do	Counsel	Dean Paik	SC	GS	15	....	
	Office of Justice Programs						
Do	Assistant Attorney General	Vacant	PAS	EX	IV	....	
Do	Principal Deputy Assistant Attorney General	Mary Lou Leary	NA	ES	....	....	

DEPARTMENT OF JUSTICE—Continued

Location	Position	Name of Incumbent	Type of Appt.	Pay Plan	Level, Grade, or Pay	Tenure	Expires
Washington, DC	Deputy Assistant Attorney General, Operations and Management.	Career Incumbent	CA	ES	....	....	
Do	Chief Information Officer	......do	CA	ES	....	....	
Do	General Counsel	......do	CA	ES	....	....	
Do	Director, Bureau of Justice Statistics	James Patrick Lynch	PAS	EX	IV	....	
Do	Director, National Institute of Justice	John Henry Laub	PAS	EX	IV	....	
Do	Director, Bureau of Justice Assistance	Denise O'Donnell	PAS	EX	IV	....	
Do	Director, Office for Victims of Crime	Vacant	PAS	EX	IV	....	
Do	Director, Community Capacity Development Office.	......do	....	ES	....	....	
Do	Deputy Director for Programs, Bureau of Justice Assistance.	Career Incumbent	CA	ES	....	....	
Do	Deputy Director, Policy and Management, Bureau of Justice Assistance.	......do	CA	ES	....	....	
Do	Deputy Director for Planning, Bureau of Justice Assistance.	......do	CA	ES	....	....	
Do	Deputy Director, National Institute of Justice	......do	CA	ES	....	....	
Do	Deputy Director, Bureau of Justice Statistics	......do	CA	ES	....	....	
Do	Deputy Director, Office for Victims of Crime ..	......do	CA	ES	....	....	
Do	Administrator, Office of Juvenile Justice and Delinquency Prevention.	Vacant	PAS	EX	IV	....	
Do	Principal Deputy Administrator, Office of Juvenile Justice and Delinquency Prevention.	Melodee Hanes	NA	ES	....	....	
Do	Deputy Administrator for Programs, Office of Juvenile Justice and Delinquency Prevention.	Career Incumbent	CA	ES	....	....	
Do	SMART Program Coordinator	Linda M. Baldwin	NA	ES	....	....	
Do	Deputy Administrator for Policy	Career Incumbent	CA	ES	....	....	
Do	Executive Science Advisor, National Institute of Justice.	......do	CA	ES	....	....	
Do	Senior Advisor to the Assistant Attorney General.	Lynn Dudley Overmann	SC	GS	15	....	
Do	......do	Amy Solomon	SC	GS	15	....	
Do	Chief of Staff	Thomas Peter Abt	SC	GS	15	....	
Do	......do	Anna Dolores Martinez	SC	GS	15	....	
Do	Senior Advisor	Ellen Claire Williams	SC	GS	15	....	
Do	Director, Faith-Based and Neighborhood Partnerships.	Eugene Lawrence Schneeberg Sr..	SC	GS	14	....	
Do	Special Assistant	Jacqueline L. Rivers	SC	GS	12	....	
Do	Policy Advisor	Theron Phillip Pride, Jr. ...	SC	GS	12	....	
	Community Relations Service						
Do	Director	Grande H. Lum	PAS	EX	IV	....	
Do	Senior Counsel	Becky Lyn Monroe	SC	GS	15	....	
	Foreign Claims Settlement Commission						
Do	Chairman	Timothy J. Feighery	PAS	EX	V	....	
Do	Member	Rafael E. Martinez	PAS	EX	V	....	
Do	......do	Anuj Desai	PAS	EX	V	....	
Do	Special Assistant to the Chairman	Avin Pravind Sharma	SC	GS	14	....	
	Office on Violence Against Women						
Do	Director	Vacant	PAS	EX	V	....	
Do	Principal Deputy Director	Beatrice Hanson	NA	ES	....	....	
Do	Deputy Director for Policy Development	Virginia Davis	SC	GS	15	....	
Do	Confidential Assistant	Elisabeth Walker Evans	SC	GS	9	....	
Do	Special Assistant	Brenda Auterman	SC	GS	9	....	
	Executive Office for United States Trustees						
Do	Director	Career Incumbent	CA	ES	....	....	
Do	Deputy Director, Field Operations	Vacant	....	ES	....	....	
Do	Deputy Director, Management	Career Incumbent	CA	ES	....	....	
Do	Deputy Director General Counsel	......do	CA	ES	....	....	
Do	Counsel to the Director	......do	CA	ES	....	....	
	Community Oriented Policing Services						
Do	Director	Bernard Keith Melekian	NA	ES	....	....	
Do	Principal Deputy Director	Career Incumbent	CA	ES	....	....	
	OFFICE OF THE SOLICITOR GENERAL						
Do	Solicitor General	Donald Beaton Verrilli, Jr.	PAS	EX	III	....	
	Office of Information Policy						
Do	Director, Policy and Litigation	Career Incumbent	CA	ES	....	....	
	OFFICE OF THE SOLICITOR GENERAL						
Do	Principal Deputy Solicitor General	Srikanth Srinivasan	NA	ES	....	....	
Do	Deputy Solicitor General	Career Incumbent	CA	ES	....	....	
Do	......do	......do	CA	ES	....	....	

DEPARTMENT OF JUSTICE—Continued

Location	Position	Name of Incumbent	Type of Appt.	Pay Plan	Level, Grade, or Pay	Tenure	Expires
Washington, DC	Deputy Solicitor General	Career Incumbent	CA	ES	....	....	
	FEDERAL BUREAU OF INVESTIGATION						
Do	Director	Robert S. Mueller III	PAS	EX	II	....	
	DRUG ENFORCEMENT ADMINISTRATION						
Do	Administrator	Michele M. Leonhart	PAS	EX	III	....	
Do	Deputy Administrator	Thomas M. Harrigan	PAS	EX	V	....	
	BUREAU OF ALCOHOL, TOBACCO, FIREARMS AND EXPLOSIVES						
Do	Director	Vacant	PAS	EX	III	....	
Do	Deputy Chief Counsel	Career Incumbent	CA	ES	....	....	
Do	Chief Counsel	Vacant	....	ES	....	....	
	UNITED STATES MARSHALS SERVICE						
Arlington, VA	Director	Stacia A. Hylton	PAS	EX	IV	....	
Do	General Counsel	Career Incumbent	CA	ES	....	....	
Do	Director, United States National Central Bureau of Interpol.	Timothy A. Williams	TA	ES	....	....	10/12/12
Do	Special Assistant for Financial Systems	Career Incumbent	CA	ES	....	....	
Montgomery, AL	United States Marshal, Alabama, Middle District.	Arthur D. Baylor	PAS	GS	15	....	
Birmingham, AL	United States Marshal, Alabama, Northern District.	Chester M. Keely	PAS	GS	15	....	
Mobile, AL	United States Marshal, Alabama, Southern District.	Charles E. Andrews	PAS	GS	15	....	
Anchorage, AK	United States Marshal, Alaska	Robert W. Heun	PAS	GS	15	....	
Phoenix, AZ	United States Marshal, Arizona	David P. Gonzales	PAS	SL	$155,500	....	
Little Rock, AR	United States Marshal, Arkansas, Eastern District.	Clifton T. Massanelli	PAS	GS	15	....	
Fort Smith, AR	United States Marshal, Arkansas, Western District.	Harold M. Oglesby	PAS	GS	15	....	
Los Angeles, CA	United States Marshal, California, Central District.	David Singer	PAS	SL	$155,500	....	
Sacramento, CA	United States Marshal, California, Eastern District.	Albert Najera	PAS	SL	$155,500	....	
San Francisco, CA ..	United States Marshal, California, Northern District.	Donald M. O'Keefe	PAS	SL	$155,500	....	
San Diego, CA	United States Marshal, California, Southern District.	Steven C. Stafford	PAS	SL	$155,500	....	
Denver, CO	United States Marshal, Colorado	John L. Kammerzell	PAS	SL	$155,500	....	
New Haven, CT	United States Marshal, Connecticut	Joseph P. Faughnan	PAS	GS	15	....	
Wilmington, DE	United States Marshal, Delaware	Joseph A. Papili	PAS	GS	15	....	
Washington, DC	United States Marshal, District of Columbia, District Court.	Edwin D. Sloane	PAS	SL	$155,500	....	
Do	United States Marshal, Superior Court Washington, District of Columbia.	Michael A. Hughes	PAS	SL	$155,500	....	
Tampa, FL	United States Marshal, Florida, Middle District.	William B. Berger, Sr.	PAS	SL	$155,500	....	
Tallahassee, FL	United States Marshal, Florida, Northern District.	Edward M. Spooner	PAS	SL	$155,500	....	
Miami, FL	United States Marshal, Florida, Southern District.	Vacant	PAS	SL	....	....	
Macon, GA	United States Marshal, Georgia, Middle District.	Willie L. Richardson	PAS	GS	15	....	
Atlanta, GA	United States Marshal, Georgia, Northern District.	Beverly J. Harvard	PAS	SL	$155,500	....	
Savannah, GA	United States Marshal, Georgia, Southern District.	Stephen J. Smith	PAS	GS	15	....	
Honolulu, HI	United States Marshal, Hawaii	Gervin K. Miyamoto	PAS	GS	15	....	
Boise, ID	United States Marshal, Idaho	Brian T. Underwood	PAS	GS	15	....	
Springfield, IL	United States Marshal, Illinois, Central District.	Kenneth F. Bohac	PAS	GS	15	....	
Chicago, IL	United States Marshal, Illinois, Northern District.	Darryl Keith McPherson ...	PAS	SL	$155,500	....	
East St. Louis, IL ..	United States Marshal, Illinois, Southern District.	Don Slazinik	PAS	GS	15	....	
South Bend, IN	United States Marshal, Indiana, Northern District.	Myron M. Sutton	PAS	GS	15	....	
Indianapolis, IN	United States Marshal, Indiana, Southern District.	Kerry J. Forestal	PAS	GS	15	....	
Cedar Rapids, IA ...	United States Marshal, Iowa, Northern District.	Kenneth J. Runde	PAS	GS	15	....	
Des Moines, IA	United States Marshal, Iowa, Southern District.	Michael R. Bladel	PAS	GS	15	....	

DEPARTMENT OF JUSTICE—Continued

Location	Position	Name of Incumbent	Type of Appt.	Pay Plan	Level, Grade, or Pay	Tenure	Expires
Topeka, KS	United States Marshal, Kansas	Walter R. Bradley	PAS	GS	15		
Lexington, KY	United States Marshal, Kentucky, Eastern District.	Parker L. Carl	PAS	GS	15		
Louisville, KY	United States Marshal, Kentucky, Western District.	James E. Clark	PAS	GS	15		
New Orleans, LA	United States Marshal, Louisiana, Eastern District.	Genevieve L. May	PAS	GS	15		
Baton Rouge, LA	United States Marshal, Louisiana, Middle District.	Kevin C. Harrison	PAS	GS	15		
Shreveport, LA	United States Marshal, Louisiana, Western District.	Henry L. Whitehorn	PAS	GS	15		
Portland, ME	United States Marshal, Maine	Noel C. March	PAS	GS	15		
Baltimore, MD	United States Marshal, Maryland	Johnny L. Hughes	PAS	SL	$155,500		
Boston, MA	United States Marshal, Massachusetts	John Gibbons	PAS	SL	$155,500		
Detroit, MI	United States Marshal, Michigan, Eastern District.	Robert M. Grubbs	PAS	SL	$155,500		
Grand Rapids, MI	United States Marshal, Michigan, Western District.	Peter C. Munoz	PAS	GS	15		
Minneapolis, MN	United States Marshal, Minnesota	Sharon Lubinski	PAS	SL	$155,500		
Oxford, MS	United States Marshal, Mississippi, Northern District.	Dennis J. Erby	PAS	GS	15		
Jackson, MS	United States Marshal, Mississippi, Southern District.	George White	PAS	GS	15		
St. Louis, MO	United States Marshal, Missouri, Eastern District.	William C. Sibert	PAS	SL	$155,500		
Kansas City, MO	United States Marshal, Missouri, Western District.	Alfred Lomax	PAS	GS	15		
Billings, MT	United States Marshal, Montana	Darrell J. Bell	PAS	GS	15		
Omaha, NE	United States Marshal, Nebraska	Mark A. Martinez	PAS	GS	15		
Las Vegas, NV	United States Marshal, Nevada	Christopher T. Hoye	PAS	SL	$155,500		
Concord, NH	United States Marshal, New Hampshire	David L. Cargill, Jr.	PAS	GS	15		
Newark, NJ	United States Marshal, New Jersey	Juan Mattos, Jr.	PAS	SL	$155,500		
Albuquerque, NM	United States Marshal, New Mexico	Conrad E. Candelaria	PAS	SL	$155,500		
New York-Kings, NY.	United States Marshal, New York, Eastern District.	Charles G. Dunne	PAS	SL	$155,500		
Syracuse, NY	United States Marshal, New York, Northern District.	David L. McNulty	PAS	GS	15		
New York, NY	United States Marshal, New York, Southern District.	Joseph R. Guccione	PAS	SL	$155,500		
Buffalo, NY	United States Marshal, New York, Western District.	Charles F. Salina	PAS	GS	15		
Raleigh, NC	United States Marshal, North Carolina, Eastern District.	Scott J. Parker	PAS	GS	15		
Greensboro, NC	United States Marshal, North Carolina, Middle District.	Willie R. Stafford III	PAS	GS	15		
Charlotte, NC	United States Marshal, North Carolina, Western District.	Kelly M. Nesbit	PAS	GS	15		
Bismarck, ND	United States Marshal, North Dakota	Paul Ward	PAS	GS	15		
Cleveland, OH	United States Marshal, Ohio, Northern District.	Peter J. Elliott	PAS	SL	$155,500		
Cincinnati, OH	United States Marshal, Ohio, Southern District.	Vacant	PAS	SL			
Muskogee, OK	United States Marshal, Oklahoma, Eastern District.	John W. Loyd	PAS	GS	15		
Tulsa, OK	United States Marshal, Oklahoma, Northern District.	Clayton D. Johnson	PAS	GS	15		
Oklahoma City, OK	United States Marshal, Oklahoma, Western District.	Charles T. Weeks II	PAS	GS	15		
Portland, OR	United States Marshal, Oregon	Russel E. Burger	PAS	SL	$155,500		
Philadelphia, PA	United States Marshal, Pennsylvania, Eastern District.	David Blake Webb	PAS	SL	$155,500		
Lackawanna, PA	United States Marshal, Pennsylvania, Middle District.	Martin J. Pane	PAS	SL	$155,500		
Pittsburgh, PA	United States Marshal, Pennsylvania, Western District.	Steven R. Frank	PAS	GS	15		
San Juan, Puerto Rico.	United States Marshal, Puerto Rico	Vacant	PAS	SL			
Providence, RI	United States Marshal, Rhode Island	Jamie Hainsworth	PAS	GS	15		
Columbia, SC	United States Marshal, South Carolina	Kelvin C. Washington	PAS	SL	$155,500		
Sioux Falls, SD	United States Marshal, South Dakota	Paul C. Thielen	PAS	GS	15		
Knoxville, TN	United States Marshal, Tennessee, Eastern District.	James T. Fowler	PAS	GS	15		
Nashville, TN	United States Marshal, Tennessee, Middle District.	Denny W. King	PAS	GS	15		
Memphis, TN	United States Marshal, Tennessee, Western District.	Jeffrey T. Holt	PAS	GS	15		

DEPARTMENT OF JUSTICE—Continued

Location	Position	Name of Incumbent	Type of Appt.	Pay Plan	Level, Grade, or Pay	Tenure	Expires
Beaumont, TX	United States Marshal, Texas, Eastern District.	Vacant	PAS	SL	....	....	
Dallas, TX	United States Marshal, Texas, Northern District.	Randy P. Ely	PAS	SL	$155,500	....	
Houston, TX	United States Marshal, Texas, Southern District.	Vacant	PAS	SL	....	....	
San Antonio, TX	United States Marshal, Texas, Western District.	Robert R. Almonte	PAS	SL	$155,500	....	
Salt Lake City, UT	United States Marshal, Utah	James A. Thompson	PAS	GS	15	....	
Burlington, VT	United States Marshal, Vermont	David E. Demag	PAS	GS	15	....	
St. Thomas, Virgin Islands.	United States Marshal, Virgin Islands	Vacant	PAS	GS	15	....	
Alexandria, VA	United States Marshal, Virginia, Eastern District.	Robert W. Mathieson	PAS	SL	$155,500	....	
Roanoke, VA	United States Marshal, Virginia, Western District.	Gerald S. Holt	PAS	GS	15	....	
Spokane, WA	United States Marshal, Washington, Eastern District.	Craig E. Thayer	PAS	GS	15	....	
Seattle, WA	United States Marshal, Washington, Western District.	Mark L. Ericks	PAS	SL	$155,500	....	
Clarksburg, WV	United States Marshal, West Virginia, Northern District.	Gary M. Gaskins	PAS	GS	15	....	
Beckley, WV	United States Marshal, West Virginia, Southern District.	John D. Foster	PAS	GS	15	....	
Milwaukee, WI	United States Marshal, Wisconsin, Eastern District.	Kevin A. Carr	PAS	GS	15	....	
Madison, WI	United States Marshal, Wisconsin, Western District.	Dallas S. Neville	PAS	GS	15	....	
Cheyenne, WY	United States Marshal, Wyoming	Joseph C. Moore	PAS	GS	15	....	
Agana, Guam	United States Marshal, Guam/Northern Mariana Islands.	Frank Leon Guerrero	PAS	GS	15	....	
	FEDERAL BUREAU OF PRISONS						
Washington, DC	Director	Career Incumbent	CA	ES	....	....	
Do	Director National Institute of Corrections	Morris L. Thigpen	NA	ES	....	....	

DEPARTMENT OF JUSTICE OFFICE OF THE INSPECTOR GENERAL

Location	Position	Name of Incumbent	Type of Appt.	Pay Plan	Level, Grade, or Pay	Tenure	Expires
Washington, DC	**FRONT OFFICE** Inspector General	Michael E. Horowitz	PAS	OT	$170,259	....	

DEPARTMENT OF LABOR

Location	Position	Name of Incumbent	Type of Appt.	Pay Plan	Level, Grade, or Pay	Tenure	Expires
	OFFICE OF THE SECRETARY						
Washington, DC	Secretary	Hilda Solis	PAS	EX	I	....	
Do	Chief of Staff	Ana Mak Ma	NA	ES	....	....	
Do	Deputy Chief of Staff	Mary Elizabeth Maxwell ...	NA	ES	....	....	
Do	White House Liaison	Maya E. Goines	SC	GS	14	....	
Do	Executive Assistant and Director of Scheduling and Advance.	Cortney Elizabeth Hoover-Bright.	SC	GS	14	....	
Do	Special Assistant	Cindy I. Chen	SC	GS	13	....	
Do	......do	Maria Lucero Ortiz	SC	GS	13	....	
Do	......do	Joseph Henriquez McNearney.	SC	GS	13	....	
Do	Chief Economist	Adriana D. Kugler	SC	SL	....	....	
Do	Senior Counselor	Irasema T. Garza	NA	ES	....	....	
Do	Director of Recovery for Auto Communities and Workers.	Roy Kojo Jawara Williams	NA	ES	....	....	
Do	Deputy Director of Recovery for Auto Communities and Workers.	John T. Metcalf	SC	GS	15	....	
Do	Director, Faith Based and Community Initiatives.	Philip Tom	SC	GS	15	....	
Do	Associate Director, Faith Based and Community Initiatives.	Benjamin Seigel	SC	GS	15	....	
Do	Director, Public Engagement	Gabriela D. Lemus	SC	GS	15	....	
Do	Policy Advisor	Zachary A. Epstein	SC	GS	11	....	
Do	Special Assistant	Roberto Carlos Soberanis ..	SC	GS	13	....	
Do	......do	Harin J. Contractor	SC	GS	13	....	
Do	......do	Meki Bracken	SC	GS	13	....	
Do	Scheduler	Soledad N. Roybal	SC	GS	13	....	
Do	Special Assistant	Tom L. Kelly	SC	GS	12	....	
Do	......do	Jeremy Bishop	SC	GS	12	....	
Do	......do	Joseph J. Martinez	SC	GS	12	....	
Do	......do	Lauren E. Leonard	SC	GS	11	....	
Do	......do	A'Shanti Fayshel Gholar ...	SC	GS	11	....	
Do	Staff Assistant	Jose Alberto Rodriguez	SC	GS	9	....	
	Office of the Deputy Secretary						
Do	Deputy Secretary	Seth Harris	PAS	EX	II	....	
Do	Associate Deputy Secretary	Laura V. McClintock	NA	ES	....	....	
Do	......do	Nancy M. Rooney	TA	ES	....	....	06/19/13
Do	Counselor in the Office of the Deputy Secretary.	Yvette Marie Meftah	NA	ES	....	....	
Do	Executive Secretary	Elizabeth O. Kim	NA	ES	....	....	
Do	Senior Advisor to the Deputy Secretary	Xavier Hughes	SC	GS	15	....	
Do	Special Assistant	Natalie Palugyai	SC	GS	15	....	
Do	......do	Adam Brickman	SC	GS	9	....	
	WOMEN'S BUREAU						
Do	Director	Vacant	PAS	SL	....	....	
Do	Deputy Director	Latifa Lyles	NA	ES	....	....	
Do	Chief of Staff	Sandra Vega	SC	GS	15	....	
Do	Senior Policy Advisor	Nancy Santiago Negron	SC	GS	15	....	
Do	Special Assistant	Kathleen Gaspard	SC	GS	11	....	
	OFFICE OF PUBLIC AFFAIRS						
Do	Assistant Secretary	Vacant	PAS	EX	IV	....	
Do	Senior Advisor for Communications and Public Affairs.	Carl A. Fillichio	NA	ES	....	....	
Do	Senior Managing Director	Elizabeth N. Alexander	NA	ES	....	....	
Do	Speechwriter	Eric Kleiman	SC	GS	15	....	
Do	......do	Emilia Pablo Montano	SC	GS	12	....	
Do	......do	Adrian Solorzano Haro	SC	GS	11	....	
Do	Special Assistant	Joshua R. Lamont	SC	GS	15	....	
Do	......do	Jason Surbey	SC	GS	14	....	
Do	......do	Sonia Melendez	SC	GS	14	....	
Do	......do	David S. Roberts	SC	GS	13	....	
Do	......do	Clarisse A. Young	SC	GS	12	....	
Do	......do	Treci Johnson	SC	GS	11	....	
Do	......do	Jesse W. Lawder	SC	GS	11	....	
Do	......do	Jason Kuruvilla	SC	GS	9	....	
Do	......do	Adriano T. Llosa	SC	GS	7	....	
	OFFICE OF CONGRESSIONAL AND INTERGOVERNMENTAL AFFAIRS						
Do	Assistant Secretary	Brian Vincent Kennedy	PAS	EX	IV	....	
Do	Deputy Assistant Secretary	Adri D. Jayaratne	NA	ES	....	....	
Do	Deputy Assistant Secretary for Operations	Terry Bergman	NA	ES	....	....	
Do	Chief of Staff	Julia McKinney	SC	GS	14	....	
Do	Director, Intergovernmental Affairs	Elmy A. Bermejo	SC	GS	15	....	

DEPARTMENT OF LABOR—Continued

Location	Position	Name of Incumbent	Type of Appt.	Pay Plan	Level, Grade, or Pay	Tenure	Expires
Washington, DC	Deputy Director of Intergovernmental Affairs	Carrianna Suiter	SC	GS	11	....	
Do	Senior Counselor	Patrick Findlay	SC	GS	15	....	
Do	Senior Legislative Officer	Margaret M. Cantrell	SC	GS	15	....	
Chicago, IL	Regional Representative	Kenneth F. Williams-Bennett.	SC	GS	15	....	
New York, NY	......do	Robert Asaro Angelo	SC	GS	15	....	
Miami, FL	......do	Marie Milagros Herrera	SC	GS	15	....	
Los Angeles, CA	......do	Alicia Villarreal	SC	GS	15	....	
Denver, CO	......do	Dusti Gurule	SC	GS	14	....	
Washington, DC	Senior Legislative Officer	Anthony D. Zaffirini	SC	GS	14	....	
Do	......do	Laura MacDonald	SC	GS	14	....	
Do	Legislative Officer	Andria D. Oliver	SC	GS	13	....	
Do	......do	Laura De La Torre	SC	GS	11	....	
Do	......do	Michelle Rose	SC	GS	11	....	
Do	......do	Carmen Torres	SC	GS	11	....	
Do	Legislative Assistant	Rahsheim A. Wright	SC	GS	9	....	
Do	......do	Brittany Diegel	SC	GS	5	....	
	BUREAU OF INTERNATIONAL LABOR AFFAIRS						
Do	Deputy Under Secretary for International Affairs.	Vacant	....	ES	....	....	
Do	Associate Deputy Under Secretary for International Affairs.	Carol Pier	NA	ES	....	....	
Do	Director, Office of Child Labor, Forced Labor Human Trafficking.	Career Incumbent	CA	ES	....	....	
Do	Chief of Staff	Amit Pandya	SC	GS	15	....	
Do	Senior Policy Advisor for International Labor Affairs.	Eric R. Biel	SC	GS	15	....	
Do	Special Assistant	Kathleen Nell Schalch	SC	GS	15	....	
	OFFICE OF THE ASSISTANT SECRETARY FOR POLICY						
Do	Assistant Secretary	Vacant	PAS	EX	IV	....	
Do	Deputy Assistant Secretary	Megan Uzzell	NA	ES	....	....	
Do	Deputy Assistant Secretary (Operations and Analysis).	Vacant	....	ES	....	....	
Do	Director, Office of Regulatory and Programmatic Policy.	......do	....	ES	....	....	
Do	Associate Assistant Secretary for Regulatory Affairs.	......do	....	ES	....	....	
Do	Senior Policy Advisor	Jonathan Njus	SC	GS	14	....	
Do	Special Assistant	Justin N. Allen	SC	GS	11	....	
	OFFICE OF THE SOLICITOR						
Do	Solicitor of Labor	Mary P. Smith	PAS	EX	IV	....	
Do	Deputy Solicitor of Labor	Deborah Greenfield	NA	ES	....	....	
Do	Senior Counselor to the Solicitor	John Sullivan	SC	GS	15	....	
Do	Special Assistant	Rajesh D. Nayak	SC	GS	14	....	
	OFFICE OF CHIEF FINANCIAL OFFICER						
Do	Chief Financial Officer	James Taylor	PAS	EX	IV	....	
	OFFICE OF THE ASSISTANT SECRETARY FOR ADMINISTRATION AND MANAGEMENT						
Do	Assistant Secretary	T. Michael Kerr	PAS	EX	IV	....	
Do	Deputy Assistant Secretary for Policy	Charlotte A. Hayes	NA	ES	....	....	
Do	Senior Advisor	Vacant	....	ES	....	....	
Do	Deputy Chief Information Officer	......do	....	ES	....	....	
Do	Director, Program Management Office	Career Incumbent	CA	ES	....	....	
Do	Director, Division of Enterprise Services	Vacant	....	ES	....	....	
Do	Project Officer	Curtis W. Turner	TA	ES	....	....	05/06/14
Do	Human Resources Program Officer	Kim Sasajima	TA	ES	....	....	06/30/15
Do	Special Assistant	Laura Peralta	SC	GS	11	....	
	OFFICE OF FEDERAL CONTRACT COMPLIANCE PROGRAMS						
Do	Director	Patricia Shiu	NA	ES	....	....	
Do	Deputy Director	Leslie Jin	NA	ES	....	....	
Atlanta, GA	Regional Director, Office of Federal Contracts Compliance Programs.	Career Incumbent	CA	ES	....	....	
Chicago, IL	Regional Director, Office of Federal Contract Compliance Programs.	Vacant	....	ES	....	....	
Dallas, TX	......do	......do	....	ES	....	....	
New York, NY	......do	......do	....	ES	....	....	
Philadelphia, PA ...	......do	......do	....	ES	....	....	

DEPARTMENT OF LABOR—Continued

Location	Position	Name of Incumbent	Type of Appt.	Pay Plan	Level, Grade, or Pay	Tenure	Expires
San Francisco, CA	Regional Director, Office of Federal Contract Compliance Programs.	Career Incumbent	CA	ES	....	....	
Washington, DC	Special Assistant	Claudia L. Gordon	SC	GS	15	....	
Do	......do	Claudia F. Montelongo	SC	GS	11	....	
	WAGE AND HOUR DIVISION						
Do	Administrator	Vacant	PAS	EX	V	....	
Do	Deputy Administrator	Nancy J. Leppink	NA	ES	....	....	
Do	Senior Advisor	Career Incumbent	CA	ES	....	....	
Do	Chief of Staff	Manuel A. I. Martinez III ..	SC	GS	15	....	
Do	Senior Policy Advisor	Melvina C. Ford	SC	GS	15	....	
Do	Special Assistant	Idania Tania Mejia	SC	GS	7	....	
	OFFICE OF WORKERS' COMPENSATION PROGRAMS						
Do	Director	Vacant		ES	....	....	
Do	Deputy Director	Career Incumbent	CA	ES	....	....	
Do	Senior Advisor	Miranda Chiu	TA	ES	....	....	11/05/13
Do	......do	Steven D. Breeskin	TA	ES	....	....	10/10/13
	OFFICE OF LABOR-MANAGEMENT STANDARDS						
Do	Deputy Assistant Secretary	John Lund	NA	ES	....	....	
Chicago, IL	Regional Director (Central)	Career Incumbent	CA	ES	....	....	
Philadelphia, PA	Regional Director (Northeastern)	......do	CA	ES	....	....	
	EMPLOYEE BENEFITS SECURITY ADMINISTRATION						
Washington, DC	Assistant Secretary	Phyllis Borzi	PAS	EX	IV	....	
Do	Deputy Assistant Secretary for Policy	Michael Davis	NA	ES	....	....	
Do	Chief Economist and Director of Policy and Research.	Career Incumbent	CA	ES	....	....	
Do	Senior Advisor	Jane Norman	SC	GS	15	....	
Do	Special Assistant	Meredith E. Regine	SC	GS	12	....	
	BUREAU OF LABOR STATISTICS						
Do	Commissioner	Vacant	PAS	EX	IV	4 Years	
	EMPLOYMENT AND TRAINING ADMINISTRATION						
Do	Assistant Secretary	Jane Oates	PAS	EX	IV	....	
Do	Deputy Assistant Secretary	Roberta Gassman	NA	ES	....	....	
Do	Deputy Assistant Secretary (Operations and Management).	Career Incumbent	CA	ES	....	....	
Do	Administrator, Office of Management and Administration.	......do	CA	ES	....	....	
Do	Administrator, Office of Workforce Investment.	Career Incumbent	CA	ES	....	....	
Do	Administrator, Office of Foreign Labor Certification.	......do	CA	ES	....	....	
Do	Administrator, Office of Contract Management.	......do	CA	ES	....	....	
Do	Administrator, Office of Workforce Security ...	Vacant		ES	....	....	
Do	Administrator, Office of National Response	Career Incumbent	CA	ES	....	....	
Do	Administrator, Apprenticeship and Training, Employee and Labor Services.	......do	CA	ES	....	....	
Do	Administrator, Office of Job Corps	......do	CA	ES	....	....	
Boston, MA	Regional Administrator	......do	CA	ES	....	....	
Philadelphia, PA ...	......do	......do	CA	ES	....	....	
Atlanta, GA	......do	......do	CA	ES	....	....	
Dallas, TX	......do	......do	CA	ES	....	....	
Chicago, IL	......do	......do	CA	ES	....	....	
San Francisco, CA	......do	......do	CA	ES	....	....	
Washington, DC	Chief of Staff	Christopher Sean Cartwright.	SC	GS	15	....	
Do	Senior Policy Advisor	Sang Hyun Samuel Yoon ...	SC	GS	14	....	
	OCCUPATIONAL SAFETY AND HEALTH ADMINISTRATION						
Do	Assistant Secretary	David Michaels	PAS	EX	IV	....	
Do	Deputy Assistant Secretary	Jordan Barab	NA	ES	....	....	
Do	......do	Career Incumbent	CA	ES	....	....	
Do	Director, Office of Whistleblower Protection Program.	Vacant		ES	....	....	
Do	Director of Construction	Career Incumbent	CA	ES	....	....	
Do	Director of Standards and Guidance	......do	CA	ES	....	....	
Des Plaines, IL	Director, Office of Training and Education	......do	CA	ES	....	....	
Washington, DC	Director, Enforcement Programs	......do	CA	ES	....	....	

DEPARTMENT OF LABOR—Continued

Location	Position	Name of Incumbent	Type of Appt.	Pay Plan	Level, Grade, or Pay	Tenure	Expires
Washington, DC	Director, Technical Support and Emergency Management.	Career Incumbent	CA	ES	....	....	
Boston, MA	Regional Administrator - Boston	......do	CA	ES	....	....	
New York, NY	Regional Administrator - New York	......do	CA	ES	....	....	
Atlanta, GA	Regional Administrator - Atlanta	......do	CA	ES	....	....	
Chicago, IL	Safety and Health Administrator - Chicago	......do	CA	ES	....	....	
Dallas, TX	Regional Administrator - Dallas	......do	CA	ES	....	....	
Kansas City, MO ...	Safety and Health Administrator - Kansas City.	......do	CA	ES	....	....	
Denver, CO	Regional Administrator - Denver	......do	CA	ES	....	....	
San Francisco, CA	Regional Administrator - San Francisco	......do	CA	ES	....	....	
Seattle, WA	Regional Administrator - Seattle	......do	CA	ES	....	....	
Philadelphia, PA	Regional Administrator - Philadelphia	Vacant	....	ES	....	....	
Washington, DC	Chief of Staff	Deborah E. Berkowitz	SC	GS	15	....	
Do	Special Assistant	Ernesto Archila	SC	GS	12	....	
	MINE SAFETY AND HEALTH ADMINISTRATION						
Arlington, VA	Assistant Secretary	Joseph A. Main	PAS	EX	IV	....	
Do	Deputy Assistant Secretary (Policy)	Vacant	....	ES	....	....	
Do	Deputy Assistant Secretary (Operations)	Career Incumbent	CA	ES	....	....	
Do	Administrator (Coal Mine Safety and Health)	......do	CA	ES	....	....	
Do	Deputy Administrator (Coal Mine Safety and Health).	......do	CA	ES	....	....	
Do	Administrator for Metal and Nonmetal	......do	CA	ES	....	....	
Do	Director, Assessments	......do	CA	ES	....	....	
Do	Director, Educational Policy and Development	......do	CA	ES	....	....	
Do	Chief of Staff	Julie Aaronson	SC	GS	15	....	
Do	Special Assistant	Douglas Leon Parker	SC	GS	15	....	
	VETERANS EMPLOYMENT AND TRAINING SERVICE						
Washington, DC	Assistant Secretary	Vacant	PAS	EX	IV	....	
Do	Deputy Assistant Secretary	Ismael Ortiz, Jr.	NA	ES	....	....	
Do	Director, Department of Labor Homeless Assistance Programs.	Career Incumbent	CA	ES	....	....	
	OFFICE OF DISABILITY EMPLOYMENT POLICY						
Do	Assistant Secretary	Kathleen Martinez	PAS	EX	IV	....	
Do	Deputy Assistant Secretary	Vacant	....	ES	....	....	
Do	Chief of Staff	Rhonda Basha	SC	GS	15	....	
Do	Advisor	Dylan Orr	SC	GS	12	....	

DEPARTMENT OF LABOR OFFICE OF INSPECTOR GENERAL

Location	Position	Name of Incumbent	Type of Appt.	Pay Plan	Level, Grade, or Pay	Tenure	Expires
Washington, DC	Inspector General	Vacant	PAS	OT	....	....	

DEPARTMENT OF STATE

Location	Position	Name of Incumbent	Type of Appt.	Pay Plan	Level, Grade, or Pay	Tenure	Expires
	OFFICE OF THE SECRETARY						
Washington, DC	Secretary	Hillary Rodham Clinton	PAS	EX	I		
Do	Chief of Staff/Counselor	Cheryl Mills	NA	ES			
Do	Senior Advisor	Jeannemarie E. Smith	NA	ES			
Do	Special Assistant	Lona Valmoro	SC	GS	14		
Do	.....do	Joanne Laszczych	SC	GS	14		
Do	.....do	Monica Hanley	SC	GS	13		
Do	Staff Assistant	Robert V. Russo	SC	GS	11		
Do	.....do	Nora F. Toiv	SC	GS	12		
	Foreign Policy Planning Staff						
Do	Director, Policy Planning Staff and Deputy Chief of Staff.	Jacob J. Sullivan	NA	ES			
Do	Principal Deputy Director	Bathsheba N. Crocker	NA	ES			
Do	Deputy Director	Career Incumbent	CA	ES			
Do	Policy Advisor and Chief Speechwriter	Joshua James Daniel	NA	ES			
Do	Policy Advisor/Speechwriter	Megan Elizabeth Rooney ..	SC	GS	14		
Do	Special Assistant	Michael Hochman Fuchs ..	SC	GS	13		
Do	Staff Assistant/Speechwriter	Daniel B. Schwerin	SC	GS	12		
Do	Staff Assistant	Mira Patel	SC	GS	11		
Do	.....do	William Case Button	SC	GS	11		
Do	.....do	Marisa McAuliffe	SC	GS	11		
Do	.....do	Amira Kulsum Valliani	SC	GS	9		
	Office of the Chief of Protocol						
Do	Chief of Protocol	Capricia Penavic Marshall	PAS	EX	IV		
Do	Deputy Chief of Protocol	Mark Edward Walsh	NA	ES			
Do	.....do	Natalie Rita Jones	SC	GS	15		
Do	Senior Advisor	Grace A. Garcia	SC	GS	15		
Do	Assistant Chief of Protocol (Visits)	Shilpa Pesaru	SC	GS	14		
Do	Assistant Chief of Protocol (Ceremonials)	Jessica D. Zielke	SC	GS	14		
Do	Senior Protocol Officer (Visits)	Nicholas McArthur Schmit IV.	SC	GS	14		
Do	Senior Protocol Officer (Gifts)	Lindsey Katherine Jack	SC	GS	12		
Do	Assistant Chief of Protocol (Diplomatic Partnerships).	Ali M. Rubin	SC	GS	13		
Do	Protocol Officer (Diplomatic Partnerships)	Katherine Forest Michaels	SC	GS	12		
Do	Protocol Officer (Gifts)	Jennifer Claire Paolino	SC	GS	11		
Do	Protocol Officer (Visits)	Jason Michael Rahlan	SC	GS	9		
Do	.....do	James Infanzon	SC	GS	9		
Do	Protocol Assistant	Carl C. Gray II	SC	GS	7		
	Office of Civil Rights						
Do	Director	Career Incumbent	CA	ES			
Do	Deputy Director	.....do	CA	ES			
	Office of the Deputy Secretary						
Do	Deputy Secretary	William J. Burns	PAS	EX	II		
	Office of the Deputy Secretary for Management and Resources						
Do	Deputy Secretary	Thomas Richard Nides	PAS	EX	II		
Do	Senior Advisor	Maya Davidson Seiden	NA	ES			
Do	.....do	David McKean	NA	ES			
Do	.....do	Edward F. Meier	SC	GS	15		
Do	.....do	Krishanti Vignarajah	SC	GS	15		
Do	Staff Assistant	Jared Ehrich Goodman	SC	GS	9		
	Office of the Director of Foreign Assistance						
Do	Deputy Director	Career Incumbent	CA	ES			
Do	Office Director	.....do	CA	ES			
Do	Managing Director	.....do	CA	ES			
	Office of the U.S. Aids Coordinator						
Do	Ambassador and HIV/AIDS Coordinator	Eric P. Goosby	PAS	EX	IV		
Do	Special Assistant	David McKey	SC	GS	13		
	Office of the Global Women's Issues						
Do	Ambassador-At-Large for Global Women's Issues.	Melanne Verveer	PAS	EX	IV		
Do	Senior Advisor	June Shih	SC	GS	15		
Do	.....do	Jennifer L. Klein	SC	GS	15		
Do	Special Assistant	Rachel B. Vogelstein	SC	GS	14		
Do	.....do	Wenchi Yu	SC	GS	13		
Do	Staff Assistant	Ellen Kathleen Connell	SC	GS	12		
	Office of Global Partnership Initiative						
Do	Special Representative	Kris M. Balderston	NA	ES			
Do	Senior Advisor	Gloria B. Cabe	NA	ES			

DEPARTMENT OF STATE—Continued

Location	Position	Name of Incumbent	Type of Appt.	Pay Plan	Level, Grade, or Pay	Tenure	Expires
Washington, DC	Special Assistant	Sarah E. Nolan	SC	GS	14	....	
	Office of the Special Representative for Afghanistan and Pakistan						
Do	Special Representative for Afghanistan and Pakistan.	Marc I. Grossman	TA	ES	....	....	02/24/14
	Office of the Special Representative to the Muslim Communities						
Do	Special Representative to the Muslim Communities.	Farah Anwar Pandith	NA	ES	....	....	
	Office of the Special Envoy for Climate Change						
Do	Special Envoy for Climate Change	Todd D. Stern	NA	ES	....	....	
Do	Deputy Special Envoy for Climate Change	Jonathan Cooper Pershing	NA	ES	....	....	
Do	Senior Advisor	David M. Turk	SC	GS	15	....	
	Office of the Global Health Initiative						
Do	Executive Director for the Global Health Initiative.	Lois E. Quam	NA	ES	....	....	
	Office of the Special Envoy for Closure of the Guantanamo Detention Facility						
Do	Staff Assistant	Brock Johnson	SC	GS	11	....	
	Office of Innovation and Technology						
Do	Senior Advisor to the Secretary on Innovation	Alexander J. Ross	NA	ES	....	....	
Do	Special Assistant	Kathleen W. Dowd	SC	GS	14	....	
Do	......do	Angela C. Baker	SC	GS	13	....	
Do	Staff Assistant	Rebecca P. Wainess	SC	GS	7	....	
	Office of the Special Representative for Global Intergovernmental Affairs						
Do	Senior Advisor	Rhonda S. Binda	SC	GS	15	....	
Do	......do	Steven Lewis Diminuco	SC	GS	15	....	
	Bureau of Legislative Affairs						
Do	Assistant Secretary	David Adams	PAS	EX	IV	....	
Do	Deputy Assistant Secretary	Ur Mendoza Jaddou	SC	GS	15	....	
Do	Legislative Management Officer	Sharyn Magarian	SC	GS	12	....	
Do	......do	Kristin Devine	SC	GS	12	....	
Do	Legislative Management Officer (Director of House Affairs).	Patrick J. Alwine	SC	GS	12	....	
Do	Legislative Management Officer (Director of Senate Affairs).	Rori A. Kramer	SC	GS	12	....	
Do	Legislative Management Officer	Sheila Elizabeth Menz	SC	GS	11	....	
	Office of the Legal Adviser						
Do	Legal Adviser	Harold H. Koh	PAS	EX	IV	....	
Do	Principal Deputy Legal Adviser	Career Incumbent	CA	ES	....	....	
Do	Deputy Legal Adviser	......do	CA	ES	....	....	
Do	......do	......do	CA	ES	....	....	
Do	......do	......do	CA	ES	....	....	
Do	Deputy Assistant Legal Adviser	......do	CA	ES	....	....	
Do	Assistant Legal Adviser	......do	CA	ES	....	....	
Do	......do	......do	CA	ES	....	....	
Do	......do	......do	CA	ES	....	....	
Do	......do	......do	CA	ES	....	....	
Do	......do	......do	CA	ES	....	....	
Do	......do	......do	CA	ES	....	....	
Do	......do	......do	CA	ES	....	....	
Do	......do	......do	CA	ES	....	....	
Do	......do	......do	CA	ES	....	....	
Do	......do	......do	CA	ES	....	....	
Do	......do	......do	CA	ES	....	....	
Do	......do	......do	CA	ES	....	....	
Do	......do	......do	CA	ES	....	....	
Do	......do	......do	CA	ES	....	....	
Do	......do	Maegan L. Conklin	TA	ES	....	....	11/05/12
Do	......do	Career Incumbent	CA	ES	....	....	
Do	......do	......do	CA	ES	....	....	
Do	......do	......do	CA	ES	....	....	
Do	......do	......do	CA	ES	....	....	
Do	......do	......do	CA	ES	....	....	
	Bureau of Intelligence and Research						
Do	Assistant Secretary	Philip S. Goldberg	PAS	EX	IV	....	

DEPARTMENT OF STATE—Continued

Location	Position	Name of Incumbent	Type of Appt.	Pay Plan	Level, Grade, or Pay	Tenure	Expires
Washington, DC	Deputy Assistant Secretary, Policy and Co-ordination.	Career Incumbent	CA	ES	....	....	
Do	Deputy Assistant Secretary	......do	CA	ES	....	....	
Do	Director, Office of Analysis for Terrorism	......do	CA	ES	....	....	
Do	Office Director, Office of Analysis for Russia and Eurasia.	......do	CA	ES	....	....	
Do	Office Director, Office of Analysis for Western Hemisphere Affairs.	......do	CA	ES	....	....	
Do	Office Director, Office of Economic Analysis ...	......do	CA	ES	....	....	
Do	Office Director, Office of Analysis for East Asia and Pacific.	......do	CA	ES	....	....	
Do	Executive Director	......do	CA	ES	....	....	
Do	Geographer	......do	CA	ES	....	....	
	Office of the Under Secretary for Public Diplomacy and Public Affairs						
Do	Under Secretary for Public Diplomacy	Tara D. Sonenshine	PAS	EX	III	....	
Do	Senior Advisor	Aviva Rosenthal	SC	GS	15	....	
Do	Special Assistant for Content Development	Desson P. Thomson	SC	GS	13	....	
Do	Assistant Secretary for Educational and Cultural Affairs.	Judith Ann Stock	PAS	EX	IV	....	
Do	Deputy Assistant Secretary	Meghann A. Curtis	NA	ES	....	....	
Do	......do	Lee A. Satterfield	NA	ES	....	....	
Do	......do	Robin J. Lerner	NA	ES	....	....	
Do	Senior Advisor	Career Incumbent	CA	ES	....	....	
Do	Strategic Advisor	......do	CA	ES	....	....	
Do	Managing Director	Vacant	....	ES	....	....	
Do	Director, International Visitor's Program	Alma R. Candelaria	SC	GS	15	....	
Do	Public Affairs Specialist	Rebekah T. Sergent	SC	GS	13	....	
Do	Staff Assistant	Chelsea Vaofu'A Maughan	SC	GS	12	....	
Do	......do	Kathryn P. Balcerzak	SC	GS	11	....	
Do	......do	Allison Ehrich Bernstein ...	SC	GS	7	....	
Do	......do	David Y. Kim	SC	GS	7	....	
Do	Coordinator, International Information Programs.	Dawn L. McCall	NA	ES	....	....	
Do	Executive Director	Manuela Monika Tantawy	TA	ES	....	....	11/06/12
Do	Assistant Secretary for Public Affairs	Michael A. Hammer	PAS	EX	IV	....	
Do	Deputy Assistant Secretary	Cheryl Ann Benton	NA	ES	....	....	
Do	......do	Philippe Reines	SC	GS	15	....	
Do	Deputy Assistant Secretary for Digital Media	Victoria Esser	SC	GS	15	....	
Do	Senior Advisor	Moira Whelan	SC	GS	15	....	
Do	Director, Office of the Historian	Career Incumbent	CA	ES	....	....	
Do	Public Affairs Officer	Adam K. Bazbaz	SC	GS	13	....	
Do	Special Assistant	Caroline Adler	SC	GS	13	....	
Do	......do	Nicholas Merrill	SC	GS	13	....	
Do	Staff Assistant	Andrew R. Lewis	SC	GS	9	....	
Do	......do	Lauren Ashley Hickey	SC	GS	7	....	
	Office of the Under Secretary for Civilian Security, Democracy, and Human Rights						
Do	Under Secretary	Maria Otero	PAS	EX	III	....	
Do	Senior Advisor	Sharon L. Waxman	NA	ES	....	....	
Do	Special Advisor to the Secretary for Global Youth Issues.	Zeenat Rahman	SC	GS	15	....	
Do	Special Assistant	Laura Pena	SC	GS	13	....	
Do	Staff Assistant	Caroline P. Mauldin	SC	GS	12	....	
Do	Assistant Secretary for Crisis and Stabilization Operations.	Frederick D. Barton	PAS	EX	IV	....	
Do	Deputy Assistant Secretary	Karin L. Vonhippel	NA	ES	....	....	
Do	......do	Gerard Bolton White	NA	ES	....	....	
Do	Director of Overseas Operations	Carter Malkasian	SC	GS	15	....	
Do	Director of Policy and Programs	Cindy Yung-Leh Huang	SC	GS	14	....	
Do	Coordinator for Counter-Terrorism	Daniel S. Benjamin	PAS	EX	IV	....	
Do	Deputy Coordinator for Operations	Career Incumbent	CA	ES	....	....	
Do	Assistant Secretary for Democracy, Human Rights and Labor.	Michael H. Posner	PAS	EX	IV	....	
Do	Ambassador-At-Large for International Religious Freedom.	Suzan D. Johnson Cook	PAS	EX	IV	....	
Do	Deputy Assistant Secretary	Thomas Owen Melia	NA	ES	....	....	
Do	......do	Daniel Brooks Baer	NA	ES	....	....	
Do	Senior Advisor	Career Incumbent	CA	ES	....	....	
Do	......do	......do	CA	ES	....	....	
Do	Special Advisor for International Disability Rights.	Judith E. Heumann	NA	ES	....	....	
Do	Special Representative for International Labor Affairs.	Barbara Shailor-Borosage	NA	ES	....	....	

DEPARTMENT OF STATE—Continued

Location	Position	Name of Incumbent	Type of Appt.	Pay Plan	Level, Grade, or Pay	Tenure	Expires
Washington, DC	Special Envoy for Monitoring and Combating Anti-Semitism.	Hannah S. Rosenthal	NA	ES	....	....	
Do	Executive Director	Vacant	....	ES	....	....	
Do	Special Assistant	Katherine Guernsey	SC	GS	13	....	
Do	Staff Assistant	Emily Stanfield	SC	GS	11	....	
Do	Assistant Secretary for International Narcotics and Law Enforcement.	William R. Brownfield	PAS	EX	IV	....	
Do	Deputy Assistant Secretary	Melanie Brooke Darby	TA	ES	....	....	03/11/13
Do	Office Director, Office of Criminal Justice Asst and Partnership.	Career Incumbent	CA	ES	....	....	
Patrick Air Force Base, FL.	Office Director, Office of Aviation	......do	CA	ES	....	....	
Washington, DC	Controller/Executive Director	......do	CA	ES	....	....	
Do	Special Assistant	Todd A. Levett	SC	GS	14	....	
Do	.....do	De' Ara Balenger	SC	GS	12	....	
Do	Assistant Secretary for Population, Refugees and Migration.	Anne C. Richard	PAS	EX	IV	....	
Do	Deputy Assistant Secretary	Career Incumbent	CA	ES	....	....	
Do	.....do	Catherine A. Wiesner	SC	GS	15	....	
Do	Office Director, Office of Multilateral Coordination and External Relations.	Career Incumbent	CA	ES	....	....	
Do	Office Director, Office of Policy and Resource Planning.	......do	CA	ES	....	....	
Do	Office Director, Office of Refugee Admissions	......do	CA	ES	....	....	
Do	Office Director, Office of Refugee Assistance to Africa.	......do	CA	ES	....	....	
Do	Comptroller	......do	CA	ES	....	....	
Do	Staff Assistant	Caroline Raclin	SC	GS	9	....	
Do	Ambassador-At-Large for Combating and Monitoring Trafficking in Persons.	Luis E. C.deBaca	PAS	EX	IV	....	
Do	Staff Assistant	Timothy R. Mulvey	SC	GS	12	....	
Do	Ambassador-At-Large for Global Criminal Justice.	Stephen J. Rapp	PAS	EX	IV	....	
	Office of the Under Secretary for Political Affairs						
Do	Under Secretary	Wendy Sherman	PAS	EX	III	....	
Do	Staff Assistant	Margaret T. Morris	SC	GS	12	....	
Do	Assistant Secretary for African Affairs	Johnnie Carson	PAS	EX	IV	....	
Do	Special Envoy for Sudan and South Sudan	Princeton Nathan Lyman ..	TA	ES	....	....	10/02/13
Do	Assistant Secretary for European and Eurasian Affairs.	Philip H. Gordon	PAS	EX	IV	....	
Do	Office Director, Office of Policy and Global Issues.	Career Incumbent	CA	ES	....	....	
Do	Coordinator, US Assistance to Europe and Eurasia.	......do	CA	ES	....	....	
Do	Assistant Secretary for East Asian and Pacific Affairs.	Kurt Campbell	PAS	EX	IV	....	
Do	Deputy Assistant Secretary	Nirav Sudhir Patel	SC	GS	15	....	
Do	Special Envoy for North Korea Human Rights Issues.	Robert R. King	PAS	OT	....	....	
Do	Assistant Secretary for Near Eastern Affairs	Vacant	PAS	EX	IV	....	
Do	Legislative Liaison Specialist	Mira Kogen Resnick	SC	GS	11	....	
Do	Assistant Secretary for South Asian Affairs ...	Robert Orris Blake, Jr.	PAS	EX	IV	....	
Do	Assistant Secretary for Western Hemisphere Affairs.	Roberta Ann Jacobson	PAS	EX	IV	....	
Do	Deputy Assistant Secretary	Fabiola E. Rodriguez-Ciampoli.	SC	GS	15	....	
Do	Public Affairs Specialist	Maria Paula Uribe	SC	GS	12	....	
Do	.....do	Barbara Jean Adair	SC	GS	11	....	
Do	Assistant Secretary for International Organization Affairs.	Esther D. Brimmer	PAS	EX	IV	....	
Do	Deputy Assistant Secretary	Career Incumbent	CA	ES	....	....	
Do	.....do	Paula G. Schriefer	NA	ES	....	....	
Do	.....do	Victoria K. Holt	NA	ES	....	....	
Do	Director, United Nations System Administration.	Career Incumbent	CA	ES	....	....	
Do	Executive Director, U.S. National Commission for UNESCO.	Eric W. Woodard	SC	GS	13	....	
New York, NY	United States Representative to the United Nations.	Susan E. Rice	PAS	EX	II	....	
Do	United States Deputy Representative to the United Nations.	Rosemary A. DiCarlo	PAS	AD	....	....	
Do	Alternate Representative to the United Nations for Special Political Affairs.	Jeffrey DeLaurentis	PAS	AD	....	....	

DEPARTMENT OF STATE—Continued

Location	Position	Name of Incumbent	Type of Appt.	Pay Plan	Level, Grade, or Pay	Tenure	Expires
New York, NY	Representative to the Economic and Social Council (ECOSOC) of the United Nations.	Elizabeth M. Cousens	PAS	AD	....	....	
Do	Representative to the United Nations for Management and Reform.	Joseph M. Torsella	PAS	AD	....	....	
Washington, DC	Counselor, International Legal Affairs	Career Incumbent	CA	ES	....	....	
Addis Ababa, Ethiopia.	Representative of the United States to the African Union.	Michael Battle	PAS	FA	....	....	
Washington, DC	Permanent Representative of the United States to the Organization of American States.	Carmen Lomellin	PAS	FA	....	....	
Vienna, Austria	Representative of the United States to the Organization for Security and Cooperation in Europe.	Ian Kelly	PAS	FA	....	....	
Do	Representative of the United States to the Vienna Office of the United Nations and Representative of the United States to the International Atomic Energy Agency.	Vacant	PAS	FA	....	....	
Brussels, Belgium	Permanent Representative of the United States on the Council of the North Atlantic Treaty Organizations.	Ivo Daalder	PAS	FA	....	....	
Paris, France	Representative of the United States to the Organization for Economic Cooperation and Development.	Karen Kornbluh	PAS	FA	....	....	
Geneva, Switzerland.	U.S. Representative to the Office of the United Nations and International Organizations in Geneva.	Betty King	PAS	FA	....	....	
Brussels, Belgium	Representative of the United States to the European Union.	Williams Kennard	PAS	FA	....	....	
Jakarta, Java, Indonesia.	Representative of the United States to the Association of Southeast Asian Nations.	David Carden	PAS	FA	....	....	
Geneva, Switzerland.	Representative of the United States to the Conference on Disarmament.	Laura Kennedy	SC	OT	....	....	
Rome, Italy	Representative of the United States to the UN Agencies for Food and Agriculture.	David Lane	SC	OT	....	....	
The Hague, Netherlands.	Representative of the United States to the Organization for the Prohibition of Chemical Weapons.	Robert Mikulak	SC	OT	....	....	
Paris, France	Permanent Representative of the United States to the United Nations Educational, Scientific, and Cultural Organization.	David Killion	SC	OT	....	....	
Washington, DC	Representative of the United States to the Commission on the Status of Women.	Melanne Verveer	PA	AD	....	....	
Montreal, Quebec, Canada.	Representative of the United States to the International Civil Aviation Organization.	Duane Woerth	PA	EX	IV	....	
Geneva, Switzerland.	Representative of the United States to the UN Human Rights Council.	Eileen Chamberlain Donahoe.	PA	OT	....	....	
Washington, DC	Special Representative and Policy Coordinator for Burma.	Derek Mitchell	PAS	OT	....	....	
New York, NY	Public Delegate, Alternate U.S. Representative to the UN General Assembly.	Mary B. DeRosa	PAS	AD	....	....	09/10/12
Do	......do	Frank E. Loy	PAS	AD	....	....	09/10/12
Do	Public Delegate, U.S. Representative to the UN General Assembly.	Kendrick B. Meek	PAS	AD	....	....	09/10/12
Do	Representative of the United States to the United Nations Children's Fund.	Carmen R. Nazario	PA	GS	15	....	
Do	Alternate Representative of the United States to the United Nations Children's Fund.	Charles J. Lyons	PA	OT	....	....	
Kabul, Afghanistan	Chief of Mission, Islamic Republic of Afghanistan.	Ryan C. Crocker	PAS	FA	....	....	
Tirane, Albania	Chief of Mission, Republic of Albania	Alexander Arvizu	PAS	FA	....	....	
Algiers, Algeria	Chief of Mission, Democratic and Popular Republic of Algeria.	Henry Ensher	PAS	FA	....	....	
Luanda, Angola	Chief of Mission, Republic of Angola	Christopher McMullen	PAS	FA	....	....	
Buenos Aires, Argentina.	Chief of Mission, Argentina	Vilma Martinez	PAS	FA	....	....	
Yerevan, Armenia	Chief of Mission, Republic of Armenia	John Heffren	PAS	FA	....	....	
Canberra, Australia	Chief of Mission, Australia	Jeffrey Bleich	PAS	FA	....	....	
Vienna, Austria	Chief of Mission, Republic of Austria	William C. Eacho III	PAS	FA	....	....	
Baku, Azerbaijan ...	Chief of Mission, Republic of Azerbaijan	Vacant	PAS	FA	....	....	
Nassau, The Bahamas.	Chief of Mission, The Commonwealth of the Bahamas.	......do	PAS	FA	....	....	
Manama, Bahrain	Chief of Mission, Kingdom of Bahrain	Thomas Krajeski	PAS	FA	....	....	
Dhaka, Bangladesh	Chief of Mission, People's Republic of Bangladesh.	Dan Mozena	PAS	FA	....	....	
Bridgetown, Barbados.	Chief of Mission, Barbados	Larry Leon Palmer	PAS	FA	....	....	

DEPARTMENT OF STATE—Continued

Location	Position	Name of Incumbent	Type of Appt.	Pay Plan	Level, Grade, or Pay	Tenure	Expires
Bridgetown, Barbados.	Chief of Mission, Antigua and Barbuda	Larry Leon Palmer	PAS	FA	....	....	
Do	Chief of Mission, Grenada	......do	PAS	FA	....	....	
Do	Chief of Mission, Saint Lucia	......do	PAS	FA	....	....	
Do	Chief of Mission, Saint Vincent and the Grenadines.	......do	PAS	FA	....	....	
Do	Chief of Mission, St. Kitts and Nevis	......do	PAS	FA	....	....	
Do	Chief of Mission, Commonwealth of Dominica	......do	PAS	FA	....	....	
Minsk, Belarus	Chief of Mission, Republic of Belarus	Vacant	PAS	FA	....	....	
Brussels, Belgium	Chief of Mission, Belgium	Howard Gutman	PAS	FA	....	....	
Belmopan, Belize	Chief of Mission, Belize	Vinai Thummalapally	PAS	FA	....	....	
Cotonou, Benin	Chief of Mission, Republic of Benin	James Knight	PAS	FA	....	....	
La Paz, Bolivia	Chief of Mission, Plurinational State of Bolivia.	Vacant	PAS	FA	....	....	
Sarajevo, Bosnia and Herzegovina.	Chief of Mission, Bosnia and Herzegovina	Patrick Moon	PAS	FA	....	....	
Gaborone, Botswana.	Chief of Mission, Republic of Botswana	Michelle D. Gavin	PAS	FA	....	....	
Brasilia, Brazil	Chief of Mission, Federative Republic of Brazil.	Thomas A. Shannon, Jr.	PAS	FA	....	....	
Bandar Seri Begawan Darussalam, Brunei Darussalam.	Chief of Mission, Brunei Darussalam	Daniel Shields	PAS	FA	....	....	
Sofia, Bulgaria	Chief of Mission, Republic of Bulgaria	James Warlick	PAS	FA	....	....	
Ouagadougou, Burkina Faso.	Chief of Mission, Burkina Faso	Thomas J. Dougherty	PAS	FA	....	....	
Rangoon, Burma	Chief of Mission, Union of Burma	Vacant	PAS	FA	....	....	
Bujumbura, Burundi.	Chief of Mission, Republic of Burundi	......do	PAS	FA	....	....	
Phnom Penh, Cambodia.	Chief of Mission, Kingdom of Cambodia	William E. Todd	PAS	FA	....	....	
Yaounde, Cameroon.	Chief of Mission, Republic of Cameroon	Robert Porter Jackson	PAS	FA	....	....	
Kanata, Ottowa, Canada.	Chief of Mission, Canada	David Jacobson	PAS	FA	....	....	
Praia, Cape Verde	Chief of Mission, Republic of Cape Verde	Adrienne O'Neal	PAS	FA	....	....	
Bangui, Central African Republic.	Chief of Mission, Central African Republic	Laurence Wohlers	PAS	FA	....	....	
Ndjamena, Chad	Chief of Mission, Republic of Chad	Mark Boulware	PAS	FA	....	....	
Santiago, Chile	Chief of Mission, Republic of Chile	Alejandro Wolff	PAS	FA	....	....	
Beijing, China	Chief of Mission, People's Republic of China	Gary Locke	PAS	FA	....	....	
Bogota, Colombia	Chief of Mission, Republic of Colombia	Michael P. McKinley	PAS	FA	....	....	
Kinshasa, Congo, Democratic Republic of the.	Chief of Mission, Democratic Republic of the Congo.	James Entwistle	PAS	FA	....	....	
Brazzaville, Congo	Chief of Mission, Republic of the Congo	Christopher Murray	PAS	FA	....	....	
San Jose, Costa Rica.	Chief of Mission, Republic of Costa Rica	Anne Andrew	PAS	FA	....	....	
Abidjan, Cote d'Ivoire.	Chief of Mission, Republic of Cote d'Ivoire	Philip Carter III	PAS	FA	....	....	
Zagreb, Croatia	Chief of Mission, Republic of Croatia	James Foley	PAS	FA	....	....	
Nicosia, Cyprus	Chief of Mission, Republic of Cyprus	Vacant	PAS	FA	....	....	
Prague, Czech Republic.	Chief of Mission, Czech Republic	Norman Eisen	PAS	FA	....	....	
Copenhagen, Denmark.	Chief of Mission, Kingdom of Denmark	Laurie Fulton	PAS	FA	....	....	
Djibouti, Djibouti	Chief of Mission, Republic of Djibouti	Geeta Pasi	PAS	FA	....	....	
Santo Domingo, Dominican Republic.	Chief of Mission, Dominican Republic	Raul Yzaguirre	PAS	FA	....	....	
Dili, East Timor	Chief of Mission, Democratic Republic of East Timor.	Judith Fergin	PAS	FA	....	....	
Quito, Ecuador	Chief of Mission, Republic of Ecuador	Adam Namm	PAS	FA	....	....	
Cairo, Egypt	Chief of Mission, Arab Republic of Egypt	Anne Patterson	PAS	FA	....	....	
San Salvador, El Salvador.	Chief of Mission, Republic of El Salvador	Vacant	PAS	FA	....	....	
Malabo, Equatorial Guinea.	Chief of Mission, Republic of Equatorial Guinea.	......do	PAS	FA	....	....	
Asmara, Eritrea	Chief of Mission, State of Eritrea	......do	PAS	FA	....	....	
Tallinn, Estonia	Chief of Mission, Republic of Estonia	Michael C. Polt	PAS	FA	....	....	
Addis Ababa, Ethiopia.	Chief of Mission, Federal Democratic Republic of Ethiopia.	Donald Booth	PAS	FA	....	....	
Suva, Viti Levu, Fiji.	Chief of Mission, Republic of the Fiji Islands	Frankie Annette Reed	PAS	FA	....	....	
Do	Chief of Mission, Republic of Kiribati	......do	PAS	FA	....		

DEPARTMENT OF STATE—Continued

Location	Position	Name of Incumbent	Type of Appt.	Pay Plan	Level, Grade, or Pay	Tenure	Expires
Suva, Viti Levu, Fiji.	Chief of Mission, Republic of Nauru	Frankie Annette Reed	PAS	FA			
Do	Chief of Mission, Tuvalu	......do	PAS	FA			
Do	Chief of Mission, Kingdom of Tonga	......do	PAS	FA			
Helsinki, Finland	Chief of Mission, Republic of Finland	Bruce Oreck	PAS	FA			
Paris, France	Chief of Mission, France	Charles Rivkin	PAS	FA			
Do	Chief of Mission, Monaco	......do	PAS	FA			
Libreville, Gabon	Chief of Mission, Gabonese Republic	Eric Benjaminson	PAS	FA			
Do	Chief of Mission, Democratic Republic of Sao Tome and Principe.	......do	PAS	FA			
Banjul, Gambia The.	Chief of Mission, Republic of The Gambia	Pamela Ann White	PAS	FA			
Tbilisi, Georgia	Chief of Mission, Georgia	John R. Bass	PAS	FA			
Berlin, Germany	Chief of Mission, Federal Republic of Germany.	Philip D. Murphy	PAS	FA			
Accra, Ghana	Chief of Mission, Republic of Ghana	Donald Teitelbaum	PAS	FA			
Athens, Greece	Chief of Mission, Greece	Daniel Bennett Smith	PAS	FA			
Guatemala, Guatemala.	Chief of Mission, Republic of Guatemala	Arnold Chacon	PAS	FA			
Conakry, Guinea	Chief of Mission, Republic of Guinea	Patricia Newton Moller	PAS	FA			
Georgetown, Guyana.	Chief of Mission, Co-Operative Republic of Guyana.	D. Brent Hardt	PAS	FA			
Port-Au-Prince, Haiti.	Chief of Mission, Republic of Haiti	Kenneth Merten	PAS	FA			
Vatican City, Vatican City.	Chief of Mission, Holy See	Miguel H. Diaz	PAS	FA			
Tegucigalpa, Honduras.	Chief of Mission, Republic of Honduras	Lisa Kubiske	PAS	FA			
Budapest, Hungary	Chief of Mission, Republic of Hungary	Eleni Tsakopoulos-Kounalakis.	PAS	FA			
Reykjavik, Iceland	Chief of Mission, Republic of Iceland	Luis Arreaga-Rodas	PAS	FA			
New Delhi, India	Chief of Mission, India	Nancy J. Powell	PAS	FA			
Jakarta, Java, Indonesia.	Chief of Mission, Republic of Indonesia	Scot Alan Marciel	PAS	FA			
Baghdad, Iraq	Chief of Mission, Republic of Iraq	Vacant	PAS	FA			
Dublin, Ireland	Chief of Mission, Ireland	Daniel M. Rooney	PAS	FA			
Tel Aviv, Israel	Chief of Mission, State of Israel	Daniel Shapiro	PAS	FA			
Rome, Italy	Chief of Mission, Italy	David Thorne	PAS	FA			
Do	Chief of Mission, Most Serene Republic of San Marino.	......do	PAS	FA			
Kingston, Jamaica	Chief of Mission, Jamaica	Pamela E. Bridgewater Awkard.	PAS	FA			
Tokyo, Japan	Chief of Mission, Japan	John Victor Roos	PAS	FA			
Amman, Jordan	Chief of Mission, Hashemite Kingdom of Jordan.	Stuart E. Jones	PAS	FA			
Astana, Kazakhstan.	Chief of Mission, Republic of Kazakhstan	Kenneth Fairfax	PAS	FA			
Nairobi, Kenya	Chief of Mission, Republic of Kenya	Jonathan Scott Gration	PAS	FA			
Seoul, Korea, Republic of.	Chief of Mission, Republic of Korea	Sung Y. Kim	PAS	FA			
Pristina, Kosovo	Chief of Mission, Republic of Kosovo	Christopher Dell	PAS	FA			
Kuwait, Kuwait	Chief of Mission, State of Kuwait	Matthew H. Tueller	PAS	FA			
Bishkek, Kyrgyzstan.	Chief of Mission, Kyrgyz Republic	Pamela Spratlen	PAS	FA			
Vientiane, Laos	Chief of Mission, Lao People's Democratic Republic.	Karen Stewart	PAS	FA			
Riga, Latvia	Chief of Mission, Republic of Latvia	Judith Garber	PAS	FA			
Beirut, Lebanon	Chief of Mission, Republic of Lebanon	Maura Connelly	PAS	FA			
Maseru, Lesotho	Chief of Mission, Kingdom of Lesotho	Michele Thoren Bond	PAS	FA			
Monrovia, Liberia	Chief of Mission, Republic of Liberia	Vacant	PAS	FA			
Tripoli, Libya	Chief of Mission, Great Socialist Libyan Arab Jamahiriya.	John C. Stevens	PAS	FA			
Vilnius, Lithuania	Chief of Mission, Republic of Lithuania	Anne Derse	PAS	FA			
Luxembourg, Luxembourg.	Chief of Mission, Grand Duchy of Luxembourg.	Robert Mandell	PAS	FA			
Skopje, Macedonia	Chief of Mission, Republic of Macedonia	Paul Wohlers	PAS	FA			
Antananarivo, Madagascar.	Chief of Mission, Republic of Madagascar	Vacant	PAS	FA			
Do	Chief of Mission, Union of Comoros	......do	PAS	FA			
Lilongwe, Malawi	Chief of Mission, Republic of Malawi	Jeanine Jackson	PAS	FA			
Kuala Lumpur, Malaysia.	Chief of Mission, Malaysia	Paul Jones	PAS	FA			
Bamako, Mali	Chief of Mission, Republic of Mali	Mary Beth Leonard	PAS	FA			
Valletta, Malta	Chief of Mission, Republic of Malta	Gina Abercrombie-Winstanley.	PAS	FA			

DEPARTMENT OF STATE—Continued

Location	Position	Name of Incumbent	Type of Appt.	Pay Plan	Level, Grade, or Pay	Tenure	Expires
Majuro Atoll, Marshall Islands.	Chief of Mission, Republic of the Marshall Islands.	Martha Larzelere Campbell.	PAS	FA	....	....	
Nouakchott, Mauritania.	Chief of Mission, Islamic Republic of Mauritania.	Jo Ellen Powell	PAS	FA	....	....	
Port Louis, Mauritius.	Chief of Mission, Republic of Mauritius	Vacant	PAS	FA	....	....	
Do	Chief of Mission, Republic of Seychelles	......do	PAS	FA	....	....	
Mexico City, Mexico.	Chief of Mission, Mexico	Earl Anthony Wayne	PAS	FA	....	....	
Kolonia, Micronesia, Federated States of.	Chief of Mission, Federated States of Micronesia.	Peter Alan Prahar	PAS	FA	....	....	
Chisinau, Moldova	Chief of Mission, Republic of Moldova	William H. Moser	PAS	FA	....	....	
Ulaanbaatar, Mongolia.	Chief of Mission, Mongolia	Jonathan S. Addleton	PAS	FA	....	....	
Podgorica, Montenegro.	Chief of Mission, Republic of Montenegro	Sue Katharine Brown	PAS	FA	....	....	
Rabat, Morocco	Chief of Mission, Kingdom of Morocco	Samuel Louis Kaplan	PAS	FA	....	....	
Maputo, Mozambique.	Chief of Mission, Republic of Mozambique	Leslie V. Rowe	PAS	FA	....	....	
Windhoek, Namibia	Chief of Mission, Republic of Namibia	Wanda L. Nesbitt	PAS	FA	....	....	
Katmandu, Nepal ..	Chief of Mission, Kingdom of Nepal	Scott H. Delisi	PAS	FA	....	....	
The Hague, Netherlands.	Chief of Mission, Kingdom of the Netherlands	Vacant	PAS	FA	....	....	
Wellington, New Zealand.	Chief of Mission, New Zealand	David Huebner	PAS	FA	....	....	
Do	Chief of Mission, Samoa	......do	PAS	FA	....	....	
Managua, Nicaragua.	Chief of Mission, Republic of Nicaragua	Phyllis Marie Powers	PAS	FA	....	....	
Niamey, Niger	Chief of Mission, Republic of Niger	Bisa Williams	PAS	FA	....	....	
Abuja, Nigeria	Chief of Mission, Federal Republic of Nigeria	Terence Patrick McCulley	PAS	FA	....	....	
Oslo, Norway	Chief of Mission, Norway	Barry B. White	PAS	FA	....	....	
Muscat, Oman	Chief of Mission, Sultanate of Oman	Richard J. Schmierer	PAS	FA	....	....	
Islamabad, Pakistan.	Chief of Mission, Islamic Republic of Pakistan	Cameron Munter	PAS	FA	....	....	
Koror, Palau	Chief of Mission, Republic of Palau	Helen Patricia Reed-Rowe	PAS	FA	....	....	
Panama, Panama ..	Chief of Mission, Republic of Panama	Jonathan D. Farrar	PAS	FA	....	....	
Port Moresby, Papua New Guinea.	Chief of Mission, Papua New Guinea	Teddy Bernard Taylor	PAS	FA	....	....	
Do	Chief of Mission, Solomon Islands	......do	PAS	FA	....	....	
Do	Chief of Mission, Republic of Vanuatu	......do	PAS	FA	....	....	
Asuncion, Paraguay	Chief of Mission, Republic of Paraguay	James Harold Thessin	PAS	FA	....	....	
Lima, Peru	Chief of Mission, Republic of Peru	Rose M. Likins	PAS	FA	....	....	
Manila, Philippines	Chief of Mission, Republic of the Philippines	Harry K. Thomas, Jr.	PAS	FA	....	....	
Warsaw, Poland	Chief of Mission, Republic of Poland	Lee Andrew Feinstein	PAS	FA	....	....	
Lisbon, Portugal ...	Chief of Mission, Republic of Portugal	Allan J. Katz	PAS	FA	....	....	
Doha, Qatar	Chief of Mission, State of Qatar	Susan Laila Ziadeh	PAS	FA	....	....	
Bucharest, Romania.	Chief of Mission, Romania	Mark Henry Gitenstein	PAS	FA	....	....	
Moscow, Russia	Chief of Mission, Russian Federation	Michael Anthony McFaul ..	PAS	FA	....	....	
Kigali, Rwanda	Chief of Mission, Republic of Rwanda	Donald W. Koran	PAS	FA	....	....	
Riyadh, Saudi Arabia.	Chief of Mission, Kingdom of Saudi Arabia	James B. Smith	PAS	FA	....	....	
Dakar, Senegal	Chief of Mission, Republic of Senegal	Lewis Alan Lukens	PAS	FA	....	....	
Do	Chief of Mission, Republic of Guinea-Bissau ..	......do	PAS	FA	....	....	
Belgrade, Serbia	Chief of Mission, Serbia	Mary Burce Warlick	PAS	FA	....	....	
Freetown, Sierra Leone.	Chief of Mission, Republic of Sierra Leone	Michael S. Owen	PAS	FA	....	....	
Singapore, Singapore.	Chief of Mission, Republic of Singapore	David Adelman	PAS	FA	....	....	
Bratislava, Slovakia.	Chief of Mission, Slovak Republic	Theodore Sedgwick	PAS	FA	....	....	
Ljubljana, Slovenia	Chief of Mission, Republic of Slovenia	Joseph A. Mussomeli	PAS	FA	....	....	
Pretoria, South Africa.	Chief of Mission, Republic of South Africa	Donald Henry Gips	PAS	FA	....	....	
Juba, South Sudan	Chief of Mission, Republic of South Sudan	Susan Denise Page	PAS	FA	....	....	
Madrid, Spain	Chief of Mission, Spain	Alan D. Solomont	PAS	FA	....	....	
Do	Chief of Mission, Andorra	......do	PAS	FA	....	....	
Colombo, Sri Lanka	Chief of Mission, Democratic Republic of Sri Lanka.	Patricia A. Butenis	PAS	FA	....	....	
Do	Chief of Mission, Republic of Maldives	......do	PAS	FA	....	....	
Paramaribo, Suriname.	Chief of Mission, Republic of Suriname	John R. Nay	PAS	FA	....	....	
Mbabane, Swaziland.	Chief of Mission, Kingdom of Swaziland	Earl Michael Irving	PAS	FA	....	....	

DEPARTMENT OF STATE—Continued

Location	Position	Name of Incumbent	Type of Appt.	Pay Plan	Level, Grade, or Pay	Tenure	Expires
Stockholm, Sweden	Chief of Mission, Sweden	Mark Francis Brzezinski	PAS	FA			
Bern, Switzerland	Chief of Mission, Switzerland	Donald Sternoff Beyer, Jr.	PAS	FA			
Do	Chief of Mission, Principality of Liechtenstein	......do	PAS	FA			
Damascus, Syria	Chief of Mission, Syrian Arab Republic	Robert Stephen Ford	PAS	FA			
Dushanbe, Tajikistan.	Chief of Mission, Republic of Tajikistan	Kenneth E. Gross, Jr.	PAS	FA			
Dar es Salaam, Tanzania.	Chief of Mission, United Republic of Tanzania	Alfonso E. Lenhardt	PAS	FA			
Bangkok, Thailand	Chief of Mission, Kingdom of Thailand	Kristie Anne Kenney	PAS	FA			
Lome, Togo	Chief of Mission, Togolese Republic	Robert E. Whitehead	PAS	FA			
Port of Spain, Trinidad and Tobago.	Chief of Mission, Republic of Trinidad and Tobago.	Beatrice Wilkinson Welters	PAS	FA			
Tunis, Tunisia	Chief of Mission, Republic of Tunisia	Gordon Gray	PAS	FA			
Ankara, Turkey	Chief of Mission, Republic of Turkey	Francis Joseph Ricciardone, Jr..	PAS	FA			
Ashgabat, Turkmenistan.	Chief of Mission, Turkmenistan	Robert Patterson	PAS	FA			
Kampala, Uganda	Chief of Mission, Republic of Uganda	Jerry P. Lanier	PAS	FA			
Kyiv, Ukraine	Chief of Mission, Ukraine	John F. Tefft	PAS	FA			
Abu Dhabi, United Arab Emirates.	Chief of Mission, United Arab Emirates	Michael H. Corbin	PAS	FA			
London, United Kingdom.	Chief of Mission, United Kingdom of Great Britain and Northern Ireland.	Louis B. Susman	PAS	FA			
Montevideo, Uruguay.	Chief of Mission, Oriental Republic of Uruguay.	Julissa Reynoso	PAS	FA			
Tashkent, Uzbekistan.	Chief of Mission, Republic of Uzbekistan	George Albert Krol	PAS	FA			
Caracas, Venezuela	Chief of Mission, Bolivarian Republic of Venezuela.	Vacant	PAS	FA			
Hanoi, Vietnam	Chief of Mission, Socialist Republic of Vietnam.	David Bruce Shear	PAS	FA			
San'A, Yemen	Chief of Mission, Republic of Yemen	Gerald M. Feierstein	PAS	FA			
Lusaka, Zambia	Chief of Mission, Republic of Zambia	Mark Charles Storella	PAS	FA			
Harare, Zimbabwe	Chief of Mission, Republic of Zimbabwe	Charles Aaron Ray	PAS	FA			
	Office of the Under Secretary for Management						
Washington, DC	Under Secretary	Patrick F. Kennedy	PAS	EX	III		
Do	Senior Advisor	Shireen L. Dodson	TA	ES			07/17/13
Do	White House Liaison	Heather Faye Samuelson	SC	GS	14		
Do	Staff Assistant	Kelly Mehlenbacher	SC	GS	11		
Do	Managing Director	Vacant		ES			
Do	Assistant Secretary for Administration	Joyce A. Barr	PAS	EX	IV		
Do	Deputy Assistant Secretary for Operations	Vacant		ES			
Do	Deputy Assistant Secretary for Global Information Services.	Career Incumbent	CA	ES			
Do	Senior Advisor for Privacy Policy	Charlene W. Thomas	TA	ES			01/02/13
Do	Office Director, Office of Language Services	Career Incumbent	CA	ES			
Do	Office Director, Office of Logistics Operations	......do	CA	ES			
Do	Office Director, Office of Program Management and Policy.	......do	CA	ES			
Do	Office Director, Office of Information Programs and Services.	......do	CA	ES			
Do	Executive Director	Vacant		ES			
Do	Procurement Executive	Career Incumbent	CA	ES			
Do	Education Program Administrator	......do	CA	ES			
Do	Assistant Secretary for Consular Affairs	Janice Lee Jacobs	PAS	EX	IV		
Do	Deputy Assistant Secretary for Passport Services.	Career Incumbent	CA	ES			
Do	Managing Director, Passport Services	......do	CA	ES			
Do	Managing Director, Passport Support Services.	......do	CA	ES			
Do	Managing Director, Overseas Citizens Services.	......do	CA	ES			
Do	Office Director, Office of Legislation, Regulations, and Advisory Assistance.	......do	CA	ES			
Do	Comptroller	......do	CA	ES			
Do	Staff Assistant	Luz Mendez	SC	GS	12		
Do	Assistant Secretary for Diplomatic Security	Eric J. Boswell	PAS	EX	IV		
Do	Executive Director	Career Incumbent	CA	ES			
Do	Director, Office of Foreign Missions	Eric J. Boswell	PAS	EX	IV		
Do	Office Director	Career Incumbent	CA	ES			
Do	Director, Foreign Service Institute	......do	CA	ES			
Do	Associate Director for Management	......do	CA	ES			
Do	Office Director, Education Programs	......do	CA	ES			
Do	Associate Dean	......do	CA	ES			
Do	......do	......do	CA	ES			

DEPARTMENT OF STATE—Continued

Location	Position	Name of Incumbent	Type of Appt.	Pay Plan	Level, Grade, or Pay	Tenure	Expires
Washington, DC	Associate Dean	Career Incumbent	CA	ES			
Do	......do	......do	CA	ES			
Do	Chief Financial Officer	Patrick F. Kennedy	PAS	EX	IV		
Do	Deputy Chief Financial Officer	Career Incumbent	CA	ES			
Do	Deputy Assistant Secretary for Budget and Planning.	......do	CA	ES			
Charleston, SC	Deputy Assistant Secretary for Global Financial Services.	......do	CA	ES			
Do	Managing Director, Global Financial Operations Directorate.	......do	CA	ES			
Do	Managing Director, Global Compensation	......do	CA	ES			
Washington, DC	Managing Director, Global Financial Management Systems Directorate.	......do	CA	ES			
Do	Executive Director	......do	CA	ES			
Do	Office Director	......do	CA	ES			
Do	Office Director, Office of Budget Operations ...	......do	CA	ES			
Do	Office Director, Office of Resource Planning and Budget Information.	......do	CA	ES			
Do	Director General of the Foreign Service Director of Human Resources.	Linda Thomas-Greenfield ..	PAS	EX	IV		
Do	Office Director, Office of Shared Services	Career Incumbent	CA	ES			
Do	Deputy Assistant Secretary	......do	CA	ES			
Do	......do	......do	CA	ES			
Do	Executive Director	......do	CA	ES			
Do	Director, Grievance Staff	......do	CA	ES			
Do	Deputy Chief Information Officer	Vacant	....	ES			
Do	Senior Advisor	Career Incumbent	CA	ES			
Do	Director, Systems Integration Office	......do	CA	ES			
Do	Office Director, Project Services Office	......do	CA	ES			
Do	Office Director, Enterprise Architecture and Planning.	......do	CA	ES			
Do	Office Director, Messaging Systems Office	......do	CA	ES			
Do	Office Director, Enterprise Network Management.	Vacant	....	ES			
Do	Special Advisor	Bryan M. Pagliano	SC	GS	15		
Do	Director, Overseas Building Operations	Lydia J. Muniz	NA	ES			
Do	Deputy Director, Resource Management	Career Incumbent	CA	ES			
Do	Office Director, Office of Design and Engineering.	......do	CA	ES			
Do	Managing Director, Program Development, Coordination and Support.	......do	CA	ES			
Do	Office Director, Special Projects Coordination Division.	......do	CA	ES			
Do	Director, Art in Embassies Program	Beth Ellen Dozoretz	SC	GS	15		
Chicago, IL	Senior Coordinator for the G8 and NATO Summits.	Carrie S. Devine	TA	ES			06/30/12
	Office of the Under Secretary for Arms Control and International Security Affairs						
Washington, DC	Under Secretary for Arms Control and Security Affairs.	Vacant	PAS	EX	III		
Do	Senior Advisor	Career Incumbent	CA	ES			
Do	Special Assistant	Jonathan E. Kaplan	SC	GS	13		
Do	Staff Assistant	Peter B. Crail	SC	GS	12		
Do	Assistant Secretary for Arms Control, Verification, and Compliance.	Rose E. Gottemoeller	PAS	EX	IV		
Do	Principal Deputy Assistant Secretary	Vacant	....	ES			
Do	Deputy Assistant Secretary	Frank A. Rose	NA	ES			
Do	Managing Director	Career Incumbent	CA	ES			
Do	Office Director, Office of Chemical and Biological Weapons Affairs.	......do	CA	ES			
Do	Office Director, Office of Strategic Affairs	......do	CA	ES			
Do	Office Director, Office of Verification and Transparency Technology.	......do	CA	ES			
Do	Office Director, Office of Multilateral and Nuclear Affairs.	......do	CA	ES			
Do	Director, Office of Euro-Atlantic Security Affairs.	......do	CA	ES			
Do	Public Affairs Specialist	Alexandra F. Bell	SC	GS	12		
Do	......do	Jamie Mannina	SC	GS	11		
Do	Assistant Secretary for International Security and Nonproliferation Affairs.	Thomas More Countryman	PAS	EX	IV		
Do	Principal Deputy Assistant Secretary	Vacant	....	ES			
Do	Special Representative of the President for Nuclear Non-Proliferation With the Rank of Ambassador.	Susan Burk	PAS	EX	IV		

DEPARTMENT OF STATE—Continued

Location	Position	Name of Incumbent	Type of Appt.	Pay Plan	Level, Grade, or Pay	Tenure	Expires
Washington, DC	Coordinator for Threat Reduction Programs, with the Rank of Ambassador.	Bonnie Denise Jenkins	PAS	OT	....	....	
Do	Deputy Assistant Secretary	Simon G. Limage	NA	ES	....	....	
Do	Senior Advisor	Atman M. Trivedi	SC	GS	15	....	
Do	Special Adviser	Robert J. Einhorn	NA	ES	....	....	
Do	Executive Director	Vacant	....	ES	....	....	
Do	Office Director, Office of Nuclear Energy, Safety, and Security.	Career Incumbent	CA	ES	....	....	
Do	Office Director	......do	CA	ES	....	....	
Do	Office Director, Office of Conventional Arms Threat Reduction.	......do	CA	ES	....	....	
Do	Office Director, Office of Counterproliferation Initiatives.	......do	CA	ES	....	....	
Do	Office Director, Office of Regional Affairs	......do	CA	ES	....	....	
Do	Office Director, Office of Missile, Biological and Chemical Nonproliferation.	......do	CA	ES	....	....	
Do	Assistant Secretary for Political-Military Affairs.	Andrew J. Shapiro	PAS	EX	IV	....	
Do	Deputy Assistant Secretary for Plans, Programs, and Operations.	Vacant	....	ES	....	....	
Do	Deputy Assistant Secretary for Defense Trade and Regional Security.	......do	....	ES	....	....	
Do	Political Advisor	Career Incumbent	CA	ES	....	....	
Do	Office Director, Office of Plans, Policy and Analysis.	......do	CA	ES	....	....	
Do	Office Director, Office of Weapons Removal and Abatement.	......do	CA	ES	....	....	
Do	Staff Assistant	Julia Reed	SC	GS	11	....	
	Office of the Under Secretary for Economic Growth, Energy, and the Environment						
Do	Under Secretary	Robert D. Hormats	PAS	EX	III	....	
Do	Special Coordinator	Career Incumbent	CA	ES	....	....	
Do	Chief Economist	Heidi Crebo-Rediker	NA	ES	....	....	
Do	Assistant Secretary for Economic and Business Affairs.	Jose W. Fernandez	PAS	EX	IV	....	
Do	Deputy Assistant Secretary	Career Incumbent	CA	ES	....	....	
Do	Deputy Assistant Secretary of State for International Communications and Information Policy in the Bureau of Economic and Business Affairs and U. S. Coordinator for International Communications and Information Policy.	Phillip L. Verveer	NA	OT	....	....	
Do	Deputy Assistant Secretary	Peter Harrell	SC	GS	15	....	
Do	Special Envoy for Eurasian Energy	Richard L. Morningstar	NA	ES	....	....	
Do	Special Representative for Commercial and Business Affairs.	Lorraine J. Hariton	NA	ES	....	....	
Do	Senior Advisor	Manu Kumar Bhardwaj	SC	GS	15	....	
Do	Foreign Affairs Officer	Career Incumbent	CA	ES	....	....	
Do	Special Assistant	Shraddha K. Patel	SC	GS	14	....	
Do	Special Assistant	Andrew Bergen McCracken	SC	GS	14	....	
Do	......do	Michael L. Szymanski	SC	GS	13	....	
Do	Staff Assistant	Joseph T. Figueiredo	SC	GS	9	....	
Do	Assistant Secretary for International Energy Resources.	Vacant	PAS	EX	IV	....	
Do	Staff Assistant	Ethan M. Gelber	SC	GS	11	....	
Do	Office Director, Office of Electricity and Energy Efficiency.	Vacant	....	ES	....	....	
Do	Assistant Secretary Oceans International Environmental and Scientific Affairs.	Kerri-Ann Jones	PAS	EX	IV	....	
Do	Deputy Assistant Secretary for Oceans	Career Incumbent	CA	ES	....	....	
Do	Deputy Assistant Secretary for Environment and Natural Resources.	......do	CA	ES	....	....	
Do	Senior Advisor	......do	CA	ES	....	....	
Do	Office Director, Office of Marine Conservation	......do	CA	ES	....	....	
Do	Office Director, Office of Oceans and Polar Affairs.	......do	CA	ES	....	....	
Do	Office Director, Office of Ecology and Conservation.	......do	CA	ES	....	....	
Do	Office Director, Office of Global Change	......do	CA	ES	....	....	
Do	Office Director, Office of Space and Advanced Technology.	Vacant	....	ES	....	....	

DEPARTMENT OF STATE OFFICE OF THE INSPECTOR GENERAL

Location	Position	Name of Incumbent	Type of Appt.	Pay Plan	Level, Grade, or Pay	Tenure	Expires
	OFFICE OF THE INSPECTOR GENERAL						
Washington, DC	Inspector General	Vacant	PAS	OT	....	....	
Do	Assistant Inspector General for Inspections ...	Career Incumbent	CA	ES	....	....	

DEPARTMENT OF TRANSPORTATION

Location	Position	Name of Incumbent	Type of Appt.	Pay Plan	Level, Grade, or Pay	Tenure	Expires
	OFFICE OF THE SECRETARY						
	Secretary						
Washington, DC	Secretary	Ray LaHood	PAS	EX	I	....	
Do	Deputy Secretary	John D. Porcari	PAS	EX	II	....	
Do	Chief of Staff	Joan M. DeBoer	NA	ES	....	....	
Do	Deputy Chief of Staff	Marlise A. Streitmatter	NA	ES	....	....	
Do	White House Liaison	Nathaniel S. Turnbull	SC	GS	15	....	
Do	Counselor to the Secretary of Transportation	Vacant	....	ES	....	....	
Do	Counselor to the Deputy Secretary	Joseph F. Peraino	SC	GS	15	....	
Do	Assistant to the Secretary for Policy	Vacant	....	ES	....	....	
Do	Associate Director for Scheduling and Advance.	Georgette N. Brammer	SC	GS	12	....	
Do	Scheduler	Maria Elena Juarez	SC	GS	9	....	
Do	Special Assistant for Scheduling and Advance	Ryan M. Lynch	SC	GS	9	....	
Do	Advance Specialist	Amani K. Kancey	SC	GS	7	....	
Do	Under Secretary of Transportation for Policy	Vacant	PAS	EX	II	....	
	Executive Secretariat						
Do	Director	Carol C. Darr	NA	ES	....	....	
	Civil Rights						
Do	Director	Camille M. Hazeur	NA	ES	....	....	
Do	Deputy Director	Career Incumbent	CA	ES	....	....	
	Small and Disadvantaged Business Utilization						
Do	Director	Brandon T. Neal	NA	ES	....	....	
	Chief Information Officer						
Do	Chief Information Officer	Nitin Pradhan	NA	ES	....	....	
Do	Associate Chief Information Officer for IT Policy Oversight.	Vacant	....	ES	....	....	
Do	Associate Chief Information Officer for Information Technology Shared Services.	Career Incumbent	CA	ES	....	....	
Do	Associate Director for IT Strategy and Technology Projects.	Francisco Reinoso	SC	GS	13	....	
	Public Affairs						
Do	Assistant to the Secretary and Director of Public Affairs.	Aleksandra J. Johnson	NA	ES	....	....	
Do	Deputy Director of Public Affairs	Meghan A. Keck	SC	GS	15	....	
Do	Press Secretary	Justin C. Nisly	SC	GS	12	....	
Do	Deputy Press Secretary	Susan E. Hendrick	SC	GS	11	....	
Do	Associate Director for Speechwriting	Ashley Nash-Hahn	SC	GS	11	....	
	General Counsel						
Do	General Counsel	Robert S. Rivkin	PAS	EX	IV	....	
Do	Deputy General Counsel	Career Incumbent	CA	ES	....	....	
Do	......do	James Cole, Jr.	NA	ES	....	....	
Do	Associate General Counsel	Amy C. Tovar	SC	GS	15	....	
Do	Special Assistant to the General Counsel	Michael J. Hallock	SC	GS	9	....	
Do	Assistant General Counsel for Operations	Career Incumbent	CA	ES	....	....	
Do	Assistant General Counsel for General Law ...	......do	CA	ES	....	....	
Do	Assistant General Counsel for Litigation	......do	CA	ES	....	....	
Do	Assistant General Counsel for Legislation	......do	CA	ES	....	....	
Do	Assistant General Counsel for Regulation and Enforcement.	......do	CA	ES	....	....	
Do	Assistant General Counsel for International Law.	......do	CA	ES	....	....	
Do	Assistant General Counsel for Aviation Enforcement and Proceedings.	......do	CA	ES	....	....	
	Assistant Secretary for Budget and Programs						
Do	Assistant Secretary	Christopher P. Bertram	PAS	EX	IV	....	
Do	Deputy Assistant Secretary	Career Incumbent	CA	ES	....	....	
Do	Deputy Assistant Secretary for Management and Budget.	Sylvia Garcia	SC	GS	15	....	
Do	Director, Office of Financial Management	Career Incumbent	CA	ES	....	....	
Do	Director, Office of Budget and Program Performance.	......do	CA	ES	....	....	
Do	Deputy Director, Office of Budget and Program Performance.	......do	CA	ES	....	....	
	Assistant Secretary for Transportation Policy						
Do	Assistant Secretary	Polly E. Trottenberg	PAS	EX	IV	....	
Do	Deputy Assistant Secretary for Transportation Policy.	Career Incumbent	CA	ES	....	....	
Do	......do	Beth D. Osborne	NA	ES	....	....	

DEPARTMENT OF TRANSPORTATION—Continued

Location	Position	Name of Incumbent	Type of Appt.	Pay Plan	Level, Grade, or Pay	Tenure	Expires
Washington, DC	Deputy Assistant Secretary for Transportation Policy.	Amy M. Scarton	NA	ES	....	....	
Do	Director, Office of Economic and Strategic Analysis.	Career Incumbent	CA	ES	....	....	
Do	Director, Office of Infrastructure, Finance and Innovation.	......do	CA	ES	....	....	
Do	Senior Advisor for Accessible Transportation	Richard A. Devylder	SC	GS	15	....	
Do	Director of Public Engagement	Bryna L. Helfer	SC	GS	15	....	
Do	Deputy Director of Public Engagement	Cheron V. Wicker	SC	GS	14	....	
Do	Associate Director for Transportation Policy ..	Vincent White	SC	GS	12	....	
	Assistant Secretary for Governmental Affairs						
Do	Assistant Secretary	Dana G. Gresham	PAS	EX	IV	....	
Do	Deputy Assistant Secretary	Amit Bose	SC	GS	15	....	
Do	......do	Joanna Liberman Turner ..	SC	GS	15	....	
Do	......do	Patricia B. Readinger	SC	GS	14	....	
Do	Associate Director for Governmental Affairs ..	Federico de Jesus	SC	GS	12	....	
Do	......do	Alexander Friendly	SC	GS	11	....	
Do	......do	Peter C. Gould	SC	GS	9	....	
Do	......do	Aaron P. Rosenthal	SC	GS	9	....	
Do	......do	Michael L. Daley	SC	GS	7	....	
	Assistant Secretary for Aviation and International Affairs						
Do	Assistant Secretary	Susan L. Kurland	PAS	EX	IV	....	
Do	Deputy Assistant Secretary	Career Incumbent	CA	ES	....	....	
Do	......do	Robert Letteney	NA	ES	....	....	
Do	Director, Office of International Transportation and Trade.	Career Incumbent	CA	ES	....	....	
Do	Director, Office of International Aviation	......do	CA	ES	....	....	
Do	Director, Office of Aviation Analysis	......do	CA	ES	....	....	
	Assistant Secretary for Administration						
Do	Deputy Assistant Secretary	Brodi L. Fontenot	NA	ES	....	....	
Do	Advisor to Deputy Assistant Secretary	Career Incumbent	CA	ES	....	....	
Do	Director, Departmental Office of Human Resource Management.	......do	CA	ES	....	....	
Do	Deputy Director, Departmental Office of Human Resource Management.	......do	CA	ES	....	....	
Do	Special Assistant to the Director, Departmental Office of Human Resource Management.	Stephen Gomez	TA	ES	....	....	02/15/15
Do	Director, Office of Security	Career Incumbent	CA	ES	....	....	
Do	Director, Office of Financial Management	......do	CA	ES	....	....	
Do	Director, Office of Facilities, Information and Asset Management.	......do	CA	ES	....	....	
	FEDERAL AVIATION ADMINISTRATION						
	Administrator						
Washington, DC	Administrator	Vacant	PAS	EX	II	....	
Do	Deputy Administrator	Michael Huerta	PAS	EX	IV	....	
Do	Counselor to the Administrator	Vacant	XS	OT	....	....	
	Chief Counsel						
Do	Chief Counsel	Kathryn B. Thomson	XS	OT	....	....	
	Communications						
Do	Assistant Administrator	Brie N. Sachse	SC	GS	15	....	
	Airports						
Do	Associate Administrator	Christa Fornarotto	XS	OT	....	....	
	Aviation Policy, International Affairs and Environment						
Do	Assistant Administrator	Julie Oettinger	XS	OT	....	....	
	Government and Industry						
Do	Assistant Administrator	Roderick D. Hall	SC	GS	15	....	
	FEDERAL HIGHWAY ADMINISTRATION						
	Administrator						
Washington, DC	Administrator	Victor M. Mendez	PAS	EX	II	....	
Do	Deputy Administrator	Gregory G. Nadeau	NA	ES	....	....	
Do	Program Manager for the Intelligent Transportation Systems Programs Office.	Career Incumbent	CA	ES	....	....	
	Chief Counsel						
Do	Chief Counsel	Fred R. Wagner	NA	ES	....	....	

DEPARTMENT OF TRANSPORTATION—Continued

Location	Position	Name of Incumbent	Type of Appt.	Pay Plan	Level, Grade, or Pay	Tenure	Expires
Washington, DC	Deputy Chief Counsel	Career Incumbent	CA	ES	....	....	
Do	Assistant Chief Counsel for Legislation, Regulations and General Law Division.	......do	CA	ES	....	....	
	Administration						
Do	Associate Administrator	Vacant	....	ES	....	....	
Do	Director, Office of Human Resources	Career Incumbent	CA	ES	....	....	
	Infrastructure						
Do	Associate Administrator	......do	CA	ES	....	....	
Do	Director, Office of Program Administration	......do	CA	ES	....	....	
Do	Director, Office of Bridge Technology	......do	CA	ES	....	....	
Do	Director, Office of Pavement Technology	......do	CA	ES	....	....	
Do	Director, Office of Asset Management	......do	CA	ES	....	....	
	Operations						
Do	Associate Administrator	......do	CA	ES	....	....	
Do	Director, Office of Freight Management and Operations.	Vacant	....	ES	....	....	
Do	Director, Office of Transportation Management.	Career Incumbent	CA	ES	....	....	
Do	Director, Office of Transportation Operations	......do	CA	ES	....	....	
	Planning, Environment and Realty						
Do	Associate Administrator	......do	CA	ES	....	....	
Do	Director, Office of Project Development and Environmental Review.	......do	CA	ES	....	....	
Do	Director, Office of Natural Environment	......do	CA	ES	....	....	
Do	Director, Office of Human Environment	Vacant	....	ES	....	....	
Do	Director, Office of Planning	Career Incumbent	CA	ES	....	....	
	Safety						
Do	Director, Office of Safety Integration	......do	CA	ES	....	....	
Do	Director, Office of Safety Programs	......do	CA	ES	....	....	
	Research, Development and Technology						
Do	Associate Administrator	......do	CA	ES	....	....	
Do	Director, Office of Infrastructure Research, Development and Technology.	......do	CA	ES	....	....	
McLean, VA	Director, Office of Operations Research, Development and Technology.	......do	CA	ES	....	....	
Do	Director, Office of Corporate Research, Technology and Innovation Management.	......do	CA	ES	....	....	
	Federal Lands Highway Programs						
Washington, DC	Associate Administrator	......do	CA	ES	....	....	
Sterling, VA	Federal Lands Highway Division Engineer, Eastern.	......do	CA	ES	....	....	
Lakewood, CO	Federal Lands Highway Division Engineer, Central.	......do	CA	ES	....	....	
Vancouver, WA	Federal Lands Highway Division Engineer, Western.	......do	CA	ES	....	....	
	Policy and Governmental Affairs						
Washington, DC	Associate Administrator	David S. Kim	SC	GS	15	....	
Do	Director, Office of International Programs	Career Incumbent	CA	ES	....	....	
Do	Director, Office of Highway Policy Information.	......do	CA	ES	....	....	
Do	Director, Office of Transportation Policy Studies.	......do	CA	ES	....	....	
Do	Director, Office of Legislative Affairs and Policy Communications.	Vacant	....	ES	....	....	
Do	Afghanistan Transportation Counselor	Career Incumbent	CA	ES	....	....	
	Civil Rights						
Do	Associate Administrator	......do	CA	ES	....	....	
	Public Affairs						
Do	Associate Administrator for Public Affairs	Catherine St. Denis	NA	ES	....	....	
	Field Services						
Atlanta, GA	Director of Field Services - South	Career Incumbent	CA	ES	....	....	
Salt Lake City, UT	Director of Field Services - West	......do	CA	ES	....	....	
Baltimore, MD	Director of Field Services - North	Vacant	....	ES	....	....	
Chicago, IL	Director of Field Services - Mid-America	......do	....	ES	....	....	
Sacramento, CA	Division Administrator, California	Career Incumbent	CA	ES	....	....	
Tallahassee, FL	Division Administrator, Florida	......do	CA	ES	....	....	
Austin, TX	Division Administrator, Texas	Vacant	....	ES	....	....	
Albany, NY	Division Administrator, New York	Career Incumbent	CA	ES	....	....	
Lakewood, CO	Director of Technical Services	......do	CA	ES	....	....	

DEPARTMENT OF TRANSPORTATION—Continued

Location	Position	Name of Incumbent	Type of Appt.	Pay Plan	Level, Grade, or Pay	Tenure	Expires
	FEDERAL MOTOR CARRIER SAFETY ADMINISTRATION						
	Administrator						
Washington, DC	Administrator	Anne S. Ferro	PAS	EX	III	....	
Do	Deputy Administrator	William A. Bronrott	NA	ES		....	
Do	Director for Governmental Affairs	John W. Drake	SC	GS	15	....	
Do	Director of Communications	Candice Tolliver	SC	GS	14	....	
	Chief Counsel						
Do	Chief Counsel	Vacant	....	ES		....	
Do	Deputy Chief Counsel	Career Incumbent	CA	ES		....	
	Administration						
Do	Associate Administrator for Administration ...	......do	CA	ES		....	
	Research, Technology and Information Management and Chief Information Officer						
Do	Associate Administrator	......do	CA	ES		....	
Do	Director, Office of Analysis Research and Technology.	......do	CA	ES		....	
	Policy and Program Development						
Do	Associate Administrator	......do	CA	ES		....	
Do	Director, Office of Policy, Plans and Regulations.	Vacant	....	ES		....	
	Enforcement and Program Delivery						
Do	Associate Administrator	Career Incumbent	CA	ES		....	
Do	Director, Office of Motor Carrier Safety Programs.	......do	CA	ES		....	
	Field Operations						
Do	Associate Administrator for Field Operations	......do	CA	ES		....	
Baltimore, MD	Field Administrator - Eastern Region	Vacant	....	ES		....	
Lakewood, CO	Field Administrator - Western Region	Career Incumbent	CA	ES		....	
	FEDERAL RAILROAD ADMINISTRATION						
	Administrator						
Washington, DC	Administrator	Joseph C. Szabo	PAS	EX	III	....	
Do	Deputy Administrator	Karen J. Hedlund	NA	ES		....	
	Chief Counsel						
Do	Chief Counsel	Melissa L. Porter	NA	ES		....	
Do	Deputy Chief Counsel	Career Incumbent	CA	ES		....	
	Communication and Legislative Affairs						
Do	Associate Administrator	Kevin F. Thompson	SC	GS	15	....	
Do	Associate Director of Congressional Affairs	Nathan J. Robinson	SC	GS	12	....	
	Administration and Finance						
Do	Associate Administrator for Administration ...	Career Incumbent	CA	ES		....	
	Railroad Policy and Development						
Do	Associate Administrator	......do	CA	ES		....	
Do	Director, Office of Research and Development	......do	CA	ES		....	
Do	Director, Rail Project Development and Delivery.	......do	CA	ES		....	
Do	Senior Project Manager for California High-Speed Rail Corridor.	Vacant	....	ES		....	
Do	Director, Office of Passenger and Freight Programs.	......do	....	ES		....	
	Railroad Safety						
Do	Deputy Associate Administrator for Safety Compliance and Program Implementation.	......do	....	ES		....	
Do	Deputy Associate Administrator for Regulatory and Legislative Operations.	Career Incumbent	CA	ES		....	
Do	Director, Office of Safety Compliance and Assurance.	......do	CA	ES		....	
Do	Director, Office of Safety Analysis, Risk Reduction and Crossing/Trespasser Programs.	......do	CA	ES		....	
	FEDERAL TRANSIT ADMINISTRATION						
	Administrator						
Washington, DC	Administrator	Peter M. Rogoff	PAS	EX	III	....	
Do	Deputy Administrator	Therese W. McMillan	NA	ES		....	
Do	Executive Director	Career Incumbent	CA	ES		....	

DEPARTMENT OF TRANSPORTATION—Continued

Location	Position	Name of Incumbent	Type of Appt.	Pay Plan	Level, Grade, or Pay	Tenure	Expires
Washington, DC	Associate Administrator for Communications and Legislative Affairs.	Brian D. Farber	SC	GS	15	....	
	Chief Counsel						
Do	Chief Counsel	Dorval R. Carter, Jr.	NA	ES	....	....	
Do	Deputy Chief Counsel	Career Incumbent	CA	ES	....	....	
Do	Attorney Advisor (Special Counsel)	......do	CA	ES	....	....	
	Planning and Environment						
Do	Associate Administrator	......do	CA	ES	....	....	
	Program Management						
Do	Associate Administrator	......do	CA	ES	....	....	
	Research, Demonstration and Innovation						
Do	Associate Administrator	......do	CA	ES	....	....	
	Budget and Policy						
Do	Associate Administrator	......do	CA	ES	....	....	
	Administration						
Do	Associate Administrator	......do	CA	ES	....	....	
	Regional Administrator						
Cambridge, MA	Regional Administrator, Region 1	......do	CA	ES	....	....	
New York, NY	Regional Administrator, Region 2	......do	CA	ES	....	....	
Philadelphia, PA	Regional Administrator, Region 3	......do	CA	ES	....	....	
Atlanta, GA	Regional Administrator, Region 4	......do	CA	ES	....	....	
Chicago, IL	Regional Administrator, Region 5	......do	CA	ES	....	....	
Dallas, TX	Regional Administrator, Region 6	......do	CA	ES	....	....	
Kansas City, MO ...	Regional Administrator, Region 7	......do	CA	ES	....	....	
Denver, CO	Regional Administrator, Region 8	Vacant	....	ES	....	....	
San Francisco, CA	Regional Administrator, Region 9	Career Incumbent	CA	ES	....	....	
Seattle, WA	Regional Administrator, Region 10	......do	CA	ES	....	....	
	MARITIME ADMINISTRATION						
	Administrator						
Washington, DC	Administrator	David T. Matsuda	PAS	EX	III	....	
Do	Deputy Administrator	Vacant	....	ES	....	....	
Do	Associate Administrator for Budget and Programs/Chief Financial Officer.	Career Incumbent	CA	ES	....	....	
Do	Director, Office of Policy and Plans	......do	CA	ES	....	....	
Do	Senior Policy Advisor for Community Initiatives.	......do	CA	ES	....	....	
	Chief Counsel						
Do	Chief Counsel	Franklin R. Parker	NA	ES	....	....	
	Administration						
Do	Associate Administrator	Vacant	....	ES	....	....	
	Business and Workforce Development						
Do	Associate Administrator	Career Incumbent	CA	ES	....	....	
Do	Director, Office of Cargo Preference	......do	CA	ES	....	....	
	Intermodal System Development						
Do	Associate Administrator	......do	CA	ES	....	....	
Do	Deputy Associate Administrator	......do	CA	ES	....	....	
	National Security						
Do	Associate Administrator	......do	CA	ES	....	....	
	Merchant Marine Academy						
Kings Point, NY ...	Superintendent	Vacant	....	ES	....	....	
Do	Deputy Superintendent	......do	....	ES	....	....	
	NATIONAL HIGHWAY TRAFFIC SAFETY ADMINISTRATION						
	Administrator						
Washington, DC	Administrator	David L. Strickland	PAS	EX	III	....	
Do	Deputy Administrator	Ronald L. Medford	NA	ES	....	....	
Do	Director, Office of Governmental Affairs, Policy and Strategic Planning.	Chan D. Lieu	SC	GS	15	....	
Do	Director of Communications	Lynda C. Tran Reamy	SC	GS	15	....	
	Chief Counsel						
Do	Chief Counsel	Oakley Kevin Vincent	NA	ES	....	....	
Do	Assistant Chief Counsel (Rulemaking)	Career Incumbent	CA	ES	....	....	
Do	Assistant Chief Counsel (Litigation)	......do	CA	ES	....	....	
Do	Assistant Chief Counsel (Legislation and General Law).	......do	CA	ES	....	....	

DEPARTMENT OF TRANSPORTATION—Continued

Location	Position	Name of Incumbent	Type of Appt.	Pay Plan	Level, Grade, or Pay	Tenure	Expires
	Traffic Injury Control						
Washington, DC	Senior Associate Administrator	Career Incumbent	CA	ES	....	....	
Do	Associate Administrator for Program Development and Delivery.	......do	CA	ES	....	....	
Do	Associate Administrator for Regional Operations and Program Delivery.	......do	CA	ES	....	....	
Do	Director, Office of Impaired Driving and Occupant Protection.	......do	CA	ES	....	....	
Do	Director, Office of Safety Programs, Traffic Injury Control.	......do	CA	ES	....	....	
	Policy and Operations						
Do	Senior Associate Administrator	......do	CA	ES	....	....	
Do	Associate Administrator for Planning, Administrative and Financial Management.	Vacant	....	ES	....	....	
Do	Associate Administrator for Communications and Consumer Information.	Career Incumbent	CA	ES	....	....	
Do	Chief Information Officer	......do	CA	ES	....	....	
	Vehicle Safety						
Do	Senior Associate Administrator	......do	CA	ES	....	....	
Do	Associate Administrator for Rulemaking	......do	CA	ES	....	....	
Do	Associate Administrator for Vehicle Safety Research.	......do	CA	ES	....	....	
Do	Associate Administrator for the National Center for Statistics and Analysis.	......do	CA	ES	....	....	
Do	Director, Strategic Planning and Domestic and Global Integration Vehicle Safety.	......do	CA	ES	....	....	
Do	Director, Office of Crash Avoidance Standards	......do	CA	ES	....	....	
Do	Director, International Harmonization Policy, Fuel, Economy and Consumer Programs.	......do	CA	ES	....	....	
Columbus, OH	Director, Vehicle Research and Test Center (Ohio).	......do	CA	ES	....	....	
Washington, DC	Director, Office of Crash Avoidance and Electronic Controls.	Vacant	....	ES	....	....	
Do	Director, Office of Regulatory Analysis and Evaluation.	Career Incumbent	CA	ES	....	....	
	PIPELINE AND HAZARDOUS MATERIALS SAFETY ADMINISTRATION						
	Administrator						
Washington, DC	Administrator	Cynthia L. Quarterman	PAS	EX	III	....	
Do	Deputy Administrator	Timothy P. Butters	NA	ES	....	....	
Do	Associate Administrator for Governmental, International and Public Affairs.	Jeannie A. Layson	SC	GS	15	....	
	Chief Counsel						
Do	Chief Counsel	Vanessa Sutherland	NA	ES	....	....	
Do	Deputy Chief Counsel	Vacant	....	ES	....	....	
	Pipeline Safety						
Do	Deputy Associate Administrator for Policy and Programs.	Career Incumbent	CA	ES	....	....	
	Hazardous Materials Safety						
Do	Associate Administrator	......do	CA	ES	....	....	
	Administration / Chief Financial Officer						
Do	Associate Administrator for Finance, Budget and Performance Integration/Chief Financial Officer.	......do	CA	ES	....	....	
Do	Deputy Associate Administrator for Finance, Budget and Performance Integration/Deputy Chief Financial Officer.	......do	CA	ES	....	....	
	RESEARCH AND INNOVATIVE TECHNOLOGY ADMINISTRATION						
	Administrator						
Washington, DC	Administrator	Vacant	PAS	EX	III	....	
Do	Deputy Administrator	Gregory D. Winfree	NA	ES	....	....	
Do	Director, Office of Governmental, International and Public Affairs.	Jane E. Mellow	SC	GS	15	....	
	Chief Counsel						
Do	Chief Counsel	Ellen L. Partridge	NA	ES	....	....	

DEPARTMENT OF TRANSPORTATION—Continued

Location	Position	Name of Incumbent	Type of Appt.	Pay Plan	Level, Grade, or Pay	Tenure	Expires
	Administration						
Washington, DC	Associate Administrator	Career Incumbent	CA	ES	....	....	
	Research, Development and Technology						
Do	Associate Administrator	......do	CA	ES	....	....	
Do	Director, National Space Based Position Navigation and Timing Office.	......do	CA	ES	....	....	
	Volpe National Transportation Systems Center						
Cambridge, MA	Associate Administrator	......do	CA	ES	....	....	
Do	Deputy Associate Administrator for Operations.	......do	CA	ES	....	....	
Do	Deputy Associate Administrator for Research, Innovation and Technology.	......do	CA	ES	....	....	
Do	Deputy Associate Administrator for Aviation Innovation.	......do	CA	ES	....	....	
Do	Director, Center for Safety Management Systems.	Vacant	....	ES	....	....	
	Bureau of Transportation Statistics						
Washington, DC	Associate Administrator and Director	Career Incumbent	CA	ES	....	....	
Do	Deputy Associate Administrator and Deputy Director.	Vacant	....	ES	....	....	
	SAINT LAWRENCE SEAWAY DEVELOPMENT CORPORATION						
	Administrator						
Washington, DC	Administrator	Vacant	PAS	EX	IV	....	
Do	Deputy Administrator	Career Incumbent	CA	ES	....	....	
Massena, NY	Associate Administrator for Strategic Planning and Programs.	Carol Fenton	TA	ES	....	....	11/19/14
	Associate Administrator						
Do	Associate Administrator/Resident Manager	Career Incumbent	CA	ES	....	....	
	SURFACE TRANSPORTATION-BOARD						
	Chairman						
Washington, DC	Chairman	Daniel R. Elliott III	PAS	EX	III	....	12/31/13
	Board Member						
Do	Vice Chairman	Francis P. Mulvey	PAS	EX	IV	....	12/31/12
Do	Board Member	Ann Dawn Begeman	PAS	EX	IV	....	12/31/15
	Public Assistance, Governmental Affairs and Compliance						
Do	Director	Career Incumbent	CA	ES	....	....	
	General Counsel						
Do	General Counsel	......do	CA	ES	....	....	
Do	Deputy General Counsel	......do	CA	ES	....	....	
	Office of Proceedings						
Do	Director	......do	CA	ES	....	....	

DEPARTMENT OF TRANSPORTATION OFFICE OF THE INSPECTOR GENERAL

Location	Position	Name of Incumbent	Type of Appt.	Pay Plan	Level, Grade, or Pay	Tenure	Expires
Washington, DC	**OFFICE OF INSPECTOR GENERAL** Inspector General	Calvin L. Scovel III	PAS	OT	$170,259	....	

DEPARTMENT OF THE TREASURY

Location	Position	Name of Incumbent	Type of Appt.	Pay Plan	Level, Grade, or Pay	Tenure	Expires
	OFFICE OF THE SECRETARY						
Washington, DC	Secretary	Timothy F. Geithner	PAS	EX	I	....	
Do	Deputy Secretary	Neal S. Wolin	PAS	EX	II	....	
Do	Senior Advisor	Sarah Beth Miller	SC	GS	15	....	
Do	Special Assistant	Lauren E. Mandelker	SC	GS	12	....	
Do	Counselor to the Secretary	Randall James Devalk	NA	ES	....	....	
Do	Chief of Staff	Mark Patterson	NA	ES	....	....	
Do	Deputy Chief of Staff	Adewale Olabimeji Adeyemo.	NA	ES	....	....	
Do	White House Liaison	Margaret Buford	SC	GS	15	....	
Do	Director of Scheduling and Advance	Julie Huffman Herr	SC	GS	15	....	
Do	Deputy Director, Scheduling and Advance	Bhumi Haresh Shah	SC	GS	12	....	
Do	Advance Specialist	Natalie J. Reese	SC	GS	9	....	
Do	.....do	Antonio Jaquis White	SC	GS	9	....	
Do	Staff Assistant	Daniel K. Balke	SC	GS	7	....	
Do	Executive Secretary	Rebecca Henszey Ewing	NA	ES	....	....	
Do	Deputy Executive Secretary	Sam I. Valverde	SC	GS	15	....	
Do	.....do	David George Clunie	SC	GS	15	....	
Do	Special Assistant	Million Fikre	SC	GS	12	....	
Do	.....do	Elizabeth A. Hipple	SC	GS	11	....	
Do	.....do	Breanna Nicole Zwart	SC	GS	11	....	
	OFFICE OF THE GENERAL COUNSEL						
Do	General Counsel	Vacant	PAS	EX	IV	....	
Do	Principal Deputy General Counsel	Christopher J. Meade	NA	ES	....	....	
Do	Assistant General Counsel (General Law and Ethics).	Career Incumbent	CA	ES	....	....	
Do	Deputy Assistant General Counsel (General Law and Regulation).	.....do	CA	ES	....	....	
Do	Deputy Assistant General Counsel (Ethics)	.....do	CA	ES	....	....	
Do	Assistant General Counsel (Banking and Finance).	.....do	CA	ES	....	....	
Do	Deputy Assistant General Counsel (Banking and Finance).	Vacant	....	ES	....	....	
Do	Assistant General Counsel (International Affairs).	Career Incumbent	CA	ES	....	....	
Do	Deputy Assistant General Counsel (International Affairs).	Vacant	....	ES	....	....	
Do	Assistant General Counsel (Enforcement and Intelligence).	.....do	....	ES	....	....	
Do	Deputy Assistant General Counsel (Enforcement and Intelligence).	Career Incumbent	CA	ES	....	....	
Do	Chief Counsel, Office of Foreign Assets Control.	Vacant	....	ES	....	....	
Do	Special Counsel for Tax, Trade, and Tariff	Career Incumbent	CA	ES	....	....	
Do	Chief Counsel, Office of Financial Stability	Vacant	....	ES	....	....	
	OFFICE OF THE UNDER SECRETARY FOR INTERNATIONAL AFFAIRS						
Do	Under Secretary	Lael Brainard	PAS	EX	III	....	
Do	Senior Advisor	Sameera Fazili	SC	GS	15	....	
Do	.....do	Lyndsay N. Huot	SC	GS	14	....	
Do	Executive Secretary and Senior Coordinator for China Affairs and the Strategic and Economic Dialogue.	Vacant	....	ES	....	....	
Do	Managing Director for China Operations	Paige M. Gebhardt	SC	GS	14	....	
Do	Special Assistant	Elizabeth S. Van Heuvelen	SC	GS	12	....	
	Office of the Assistant Secretary for International Finance						
Do	Deputy Under Secretary/Designated Assistant Secretary.	Charles Valentine A. Collyns.	PAS	EX	IV	....	
Do	Deputy Assistant Secretary for International Monetary and Financial Policy.	Career Incumbent	CA	ES	....	....	
Do	Director, Office of International Monetary Policy.	.....do	CA	ES	....	....	
Do	Director, Office of International Banking and Securities Markets.	.....do	CA	ES	....	....	
Do	Senior Advisor	.....do	CA	ES	....	....	
Do	Deputy Assistant Secretary for Western Hemisphere.	Leonardo Martinez	NA	ES	....	....	
Do	Director, Office of Western Hemisphere	Career Incumbent	CA	ES	....	....	
Do	Deputy Assistant Secretary for South and East Asia.	.....do	CA	ES	....	....	
Do	Director, Office of South and South Asian Nations.	.....do	CA	ES	....	....	
Do	Director, Office of African Nations	Vacant	....	ES	....	....	

DEPARTMENT OF THE TREASURY—Continued

Location	Position	Name of Incumbent	Type of Appt.	Pay Plan	Level, Grade, or Pay	Tenure	Expires
Tokyo, Japan	Treasury Attaché (Tokyo)	Career Incumbent	CA	ES			
Beijing, China	Economic and Financial Emissary to China	......do	CA	ES			
Washington, DC	Deputy Assistant Secretary for Middle East and Africa.	......do	CA	ES			
Do	Director, Office of Middle East and North Africa.	......do	CA	ES			
Do	Deputy Assistant Secretary for Europe and Eurasia.	Christopher Smart	NA	ES			
Do	Deputy Assistant Secretary for International Economic Analysis.	Bradley Wayne Setser	NA	ES			
Do	Director, Markets Room	Vacant		ES			
	Office of the Assistant Secretary for International Markets and Development						
Do	Assistant Secretary	Maria Louise Lago	PAS	EX	IV		
Do	Deputy Assistant Secretary for Investment Security.	Career Incumbent	CA	ES			
Do	Deputy Assistant Secretary for Trade and Investment Policy.	Sharon H. Yuan	NA	ES			
Do	Director, Office of Trade Finance	Career Incumbent	CA	ES			
Do	Director, Office of International Trade	Vacant		ES			
Do	Deputy Assistant Secretary for Technical Assistance Policy.	Career Incumbent	CA	ES			
Do	Director, Office of Technical Assistance	......do	CA	ES			
Do	Deputy Assistant Secretary for Environment and Energy.	Vacant		ES			
Do	Deputy Assistant Secretary for International Development Policy.	Scott Allen Morris	NA	ES			
Do	Director, Office of Multilateral Development Banks.	Career Incumbent	CA	ES			
	OFFICE OF THE UNDER SECRETARY FOR DOMESTIC FINANCE						
Do	Under Secretary	Mary John Miller	PAS	EX	III		
Do	Senior Advisor	Barrett Hester	SC	GS	15		
Do	Executive Assistant	Sarah Anne Wrennall-Montes.	SC	GS	13		
Do	Member, Financial Stability Oversight Council.	Samuel Roy Woodall, Jr.	PAS	EX	III		
Do	Deputy Assistant Secretary for Financial Stability Oversight Council.	Amias Moore Gerety	NA	ES			
Do	Counselor to the Secretary	Richard B. Berner	NA	ES			
Do	Director, Office of Financial Research	Vacant	PAS	EX	III		
	Office of the Fiscal Assistant Secretary						
Do	Director, Office of Fiscal Projections	Career Incumbent	CA	ES			
Do	Director, Office of Financial Innovation and Transformation.	......do	CA	ES			
Do	Director, Office of Financial Services and Operations.	......do	CA	ES			
Do	Executive Architect	......do	CA	ES			
Do	Chief Counsel, Financial Management Service.	......do	CA	ES			
Do	Chief Counsel, Bureau of the Public Debt	......do	CA	ES			
Kansas City, MO	Project Manager, Information Technology Consolidation.	Carlos Usera	TA	ES			11/20/13
	Office of the Assistant Secretary for Financial Markets						
Washington, DC	Assistant Secretary	Vacant	PAS	EX	IV		
Do	Deputy Assistant Secretary for Federal Finance.	Matthew Starbuck Rutherford.	NA	ES			
Do	Deputy Assistant Secretary for Capital Markets.	Timothy J. Bowler	NA	ES			
Do	Deputy Assistant Secretary for Government Financial Policy.	Career Incumbent	CA	ES			
Do	Director, Office of Policy and Legislative Review.	......do	CA	ES			
Do	Director, Office of Debt Management	Vacant		ES			
	Office of the Assistant Secretary for Financial Institutions						
Do	Assistant Secretary	Cyrus Amir-Mokri	PAS	EX	IV		
Do	Senior Advisor	Katheryn Estelle Rosen	SC	GS	15		
Do	Deputy Assistant Secretary for Small Business, Community Development, and Affordable Housing Policy.	Donet Dominic Graves, Jr.	NA	ES			

DEPARTMENT OF THE TREASURY—Continued

Location	Position	Name of Incumbent	Type of Appt.	Pay Plan	Level, Grade, or Pay	Tenure	Expires
Washington, DC	Director, Small Business Community Development and Affordable Housing Policy.	Career Incumbent	CA	ES	....	....	
Do	Deputy Assistant Secretary for Financial Education, Financial Access, and Consumer Protection.	Melissa S. Koide	NA	ES	....	....	
Do	Deputy Assistant Secretary for Financial Institutions and Government Sponsored Enterprises Policy.	Vacant	....	ES	....	....	
Do	Director, Office of Financial Institutions Policy.	......do	....	ES	....	....	
Do	Deputy Director, Office of Financial Institutions Policy.	......do	....	ES	....	....	
Do	Director, Office of Critical Infrastructure Protection and Compliance Policy.	Career Incumbent	CA	ES	....	....	
Do	Director, Community Development Financial Institutions Fund.	......do	CA	ES	....	....	
Do	Deputy Director, Community Development Financial Institutions Fund.	......do	CA	ES	....	....	
	Office of the Assistant Secretary for Financial Stability						
Do	Assistant Secretary	Timothy G. Massad	PAS	EX	IV	....	
Do	Senior Advisor	John D. Grom	SC	GS	15	....	
Do	Chief Financial Officer	Career Incumbent	CA	ES	....	....	
Do	Assistant Chief Financial Officer	Mark Neil Seiler	TA	ES	....	....	12/17/14
Do	Chief Investment Officer	Mathew Michael Pendo	TA	ES	....	....	11/09/13
Do	Chief Homeownership Preservation Officer	Darius Radcliffe Kingsley ..	TA	ES	....	....	01/14/14
Do	Chief Compliance Officer	Frederick Benjamin Purser	TA	ES	....	....	12/31/14
Do	Chief of Management and Operations	Violette Nicole Bynum	TA	ES	....	....	12/17/14
Do	Director of Internal Review	Career Incumbent	CA	ES	....	....	
	OFFICE OF THE UNDER SECRETARY FOR TERRORISM AND FINANCIAL INTELLIGENCE						
Do	Under Secretary for Terrorism and Financial Crimes.	David S. Cohen	PAS	EX	III	....	
Do	Director, Office of Foreign Assets Control	Career Incumbent	CA	ES	....	....	
Do	Deputy Director, Office of Foreign Assets Control.	......do	CA	ES	....	....	
Do	Associate Director, Office of Program Policy and Implementation.	......do	CA	ES	....	....	
Do	Associate Director, Office of Resource Management.	......do	CA	ES	....	....	
Do	Associate Director, Office of Enforcement	......do	CA	ES	....	....	
Do	Associate Director, Office of Global Targeting	Vacant	....	ES	....	....	
	Office of the Assistant Secretary for Terrorist Financing and Financial Crimes						
Do	Assistant Secretary for Terrorist Financing ...	Daniel L. Glaser	PAS	EX	IV	....	
Do	Senior Advisor	Elizabeth S. Rosenberg	SC	GS	15	....	
Do	Deputy Assistant Secretary for Terrorist Financing and Financial Crimes.	Luke A. Bronin	NA	ES	....	....	
Do	Director, Office of Strategic Policy	Career Incumbent	CA	ES	....	....	
Do	Director, Office of Global Affairs	Vacant	....	ES	....	....	
	Office of the Assistant Secretary for Intelligence and Analysis						
Do	Assistant Secretary	Susan Leslie Ireland	PAS	EX	IV	....	
Do	Deputy Assistant Secretary for Analysis and Production.	Career Incumbent	CA	ES	....	....	
Do	Director, Office of Middle East and Europe	Vacant	....	ES	....	....	
Do	Director, Office of Transnational Issues	Career Incumbent	CA	ES	....	....	
Do	Deputy Assistant Secretary for Intelligence Community Integration.	......do	CA	ES	....	....	
	OFFICE OF THE ASSISTANT SECRETARY FOR LEGISLATIVE AFFAIRS						
Do	Deputy Under Secretary/Designated Assistant Secretary.	Alastair Fitzpayne	PAS	EX	IV	....	
Do	Deputy Assistant Secretary for Legislative Affairs (Housing, Small Business, and Troubled Assets Relief Program).	Megan O. Moore	NA	ES	....	....	
Do	Deputy Assistant Secretary for Legislative Affairs (Appropriations and Management).	Lisa Lorelei Pena	NA	ES	....	....	
Do	Deputy Assistant Secretary for Legislative Affairs (International Affairs).	Stephane J. Lebouder	NA	ES	....	....	

DEPARTMENT OF THE TREASURY—Continued

Location	Position	Name of Incumbent	Type of Appt.	Pay Plan	Level, Grade, or Pay	Tenure	Expires
Washington, DC	Deputy Assistant Secretary for Legislative Affairs (Banking and Finance, and Terrorism and Financial Intelligence).	Kathleen Lynch Mellody	NA	ES	....	....	
Do	Deputy Assistant Secretary for Legislative Affairs (Tax and Budget).	Sandra Salstrom	NA	ES	....	....	
Do	Senior Advisor	Patrick Thomas Maloney ...	SC	GS	15	....	
Do	Special Assistant	Cara Vaile Camacho	SC	GS	12	....	
Do	......do	Julian Drew Colbert	SC	GS	11	....	
Do	......do	Andrea Brazille Ambriz	SC	GS	11	....	
Do	......do	Namrata A. Mujumdar	SC	GS	11	....	
	OFFICE OF THE ASSISTANT SECRETARY FOR PUBLIC AFFAIRS						
Do	Assistant Secretary	Jenni Rane Lecompte	PAS	EX	IV	....	
Do	Deputy Assistant Secretary	Natalie Wyeth	NA	ES	....	....	
Do	......do	Anthony Dion Coley	NA	ES	....	....	
Do	Deputy Assistant Secretary for Business Affairs and Public Liaison.	Victoria S. Palomo	NA	ES	....	....	
Do	Senior Advisor	Marissa Hopkins	SC	GS	14	....	
Do	......do	Eric L. Dash	SC	GS	14	....	
Do	Senior Speechwriter	Mark Francis Cohen	SC	GS	14	....	
Do	Speechwriter	Jonathan Posen	SC	GS	12	....	
Do	Spokesperson	Suzanne Michelle Elio	SC	GS	13	....	
Do	......do	John Lawrence Sullivan	SC	GS	13	....	
Do	......do	Kara S. Alaimo	SC	GS	13	....	
Do	Special Assistant	Edward Lance Williams II	SC	GS	12	....	
Do	Spokesperson	Matthew C. Anderson	SC	GS	12	....	
Do	......do	Sabrina Nadia Siddiqui	SC	GS	12	....	
Do	Media Affairs Specialist	Charles Daniel Anderson ..	SC	GS	12	....	
Do	......do	Matthew Ira Weil	SC	GS	11	....	
Do	Press Assistant	Stephanie Ma	SC	GS	7	....	
	OFFICE OF THE ASSISTANT SECRETARY FOR ECONOMIC POLICY						
Do	Assistant Secretary	Janice C. Eberly	PAS	EX	IV	....	
Do	Special Assistant	Lisa Ann Abraham	SC	GS	9	....	
Do	Deputy Assistant Secretary for Macroeconomic Analysis.	Vacant	....	ES	....	....	
Do	Director, Office of Macroeconomic Analysis ...	......do	....	ES	....	....	
Do	Deputy Assistant Secretary for Microeconomic Analysis.	Alexander Michael Gelber	SC	GS	15	....	
Do	Director, Office of Microeconomic Analysis	Vacant	....	ES	....	....	
Do	Deputy Assistant Secretary for Policy Coordination.	Aaron Klein	NA	ES	....	....	
	OFFICE OF THE ASSISTANT SECRETARY FOR TAX POLICY						
Do	Assistant Secretary	Vacant	PAS	EX	IV	....	
Do	Senior Advisor	Jason Levitis	SC	GS	15	....	
Do	Deputy Assistant Secretary	Emily McMahon	NA	ES	....	....	
Do	Tax Legislative Counsel	Career Incumbent	CA	ES	....	....	
Do	Deputy Tax Legislative Counsel	......do	CA	ES	....	....	
Do	International Tax Counsel	......do	CA	ES	....	....	
Do	Deputy International Tax Counsel	Vacant	....	ES	....	....	
Do	Benefits Tax Counsel	Career Incumbent	CA	ES	....	....	
Do	Deputy Benefits Tax Counsel	......do	CA	ES	....	....	
Do	Deputy Assistant Secretary for Tax Analysis	......do	CA	ES	....	....	
Do	Director, Office of Tax Analysis	......do	CA	ES	....	....	
Do	Director, Revenue Estimating	......do	CA	ES	....	....	
Do	Director, Individual Taxation	......do	CA	ES	....	....	
Do	Director, Receipts Forecasting	......do	CA	ES	....	....	
Do	Director, Business and International Taxation.	......do	CA	ES	....	....	
Do	Deputy Assistant Secretary for International Tax Affairs.	Manal S. Corwin	NA	ES	....	....	
Do	Senior Advisor to the Secretary and Deputy Assistant Secretary for Retirement and Health Policy.	J. Mark Iwry	NA	ES	....	....	
Do	Deputy Assistant Secretary for Tax, Trade, and Tariff Policy.	Career Incumbent	CA	ES	....	....	
	Alcohol and Tobacco Tax and Trade Bureau						
Do	Chief Counsel	Vacant	....	ES	....	....	
	OFFICE OF THE ASSISTANT SECRETARY FOR MANAGEMENT						
Do	Assistant Secretary	......do	PAS	EX	IV	....	
Do	Chief Financial Officer	Daniel Mark Tangherlini ...	PAS	EX	IV	....	

DEPARTMENT OF THE TREASURY—Continued

Location	Position	Name of Incumbent	Type of Appt.	Pay Plan	Level, Grade, or Pay	Tenure	Expires
Washington, DC	Senior Advisor	Kevin J. Donahue	SC	GS	15		
Do	Deputy Assistant Secretary for Management and Budget.	Nani A. Coloretti	NA	ES			
Do	Departmental Budget Director	Career Incumbent	CA	ES			
Do	Director, Strategic Planning and Performance Improvement.	......do	CA	ES			
Do	Director, Office of Financial Management	Vacant		ES			
Do	Director, Office of Accounting and Internal Control.	Career Incumbent	CA	ES			
Do	Director, Office of Special Entity Accounting	......do	CA	ES			
Do	Deputy Assistant Secretary for Human Resources and Chief Human Capital Officer.	......do	CA	ES			
Do	Principal Associate Chief Human Capital Officer for Civil Rights and Diversity.	......do	CA	ES			
Do	Associate Chief Human Capital Officer for Human Capital Strategic Management.	......do	CA	ES			
Do	Associate Chief Human Capital Officer for Human Capital Development and Performance/Chief Learning Officer.	Vacant		ES			
Do	Associate Chief Human Capital Officer for Human Capital Services.	Career Incumbent	CA	ES			
Do	Director, Office of District of Columbia Pensions.	......do	CA	ES			
Do	Deputy Assistant Secretary and Chief Information Officer.	......do	CA	ES			
Do	Associate Chief Information Officer for Architecture and Planning.	Vacant		ES			
Do	Associate Chief Information Officer for Infrastructure Operations.	Career Incumbent	CA	ES			
Do	Associate Chief Information Officer for Cyber Security.	......do	CA	ES			
Do	Associate Chief Information Officer for Planning and Management.	Vacant		ES			
Do	Associate Chief Information Officer for Human Resources Connect.	Career Incumbent	CA	ES			
Do	Deputy Assistant Secretary for Privacy and Treasury Records.	......do	CA	ES			
Do	Director, Departmental Offices Operations	Vacant		ES			
Do	Program Executive Officer, Homeland Security Presidential Directive 12 Operations.	Career Incumbent	CA	ES			
	TREASURER OF THE UNITED STATES						
Do	Treasurer of the United States	Rosa Gumataotao Rios	PAS	SL			
Do	Advanced Counterfeit Deterrence Program Director.	Career Incumbent	CA	ES			
	United States Mint						
Do	Director of the Mint	Vacant	PAS	SL		5 Years	
Do	Deputy Director	Career Incumbent	CA	ES			
Do	Chief Counsel	......do	CA	ES			
	Bureau of Engraving and Printing						
Do	Director	......do	CA	ES			
Do	Deputy Director	......do	CA	ES			
Do	Associate Director (Corporate Planning)	......do	CA	ES			
Do	Associate Director (Management)	......do	CA	ES			
Do	Associate Director (Chief Financial Officer)	......do	CA	ES			
Do	Associate Director (Chief Information Officer)	......do	CA	ES			
Do	Associate Director (Product and Technology Development).	......do	CA	ES			
Do	Associate Director (Eastern Currency Facility).	......do	CA	ES			
Do	Associate Director (Western Currency Facility).	......do	CA	ES			
Do	Chief Counsel, Bureau of Engraving and Printing.	......do	CA	ES			
	INTERNAL REVENUE SERVICE						
Do	Commissioner of Internal Revenue	Douglas H. Shulman	PAS	EX	III	5 Years	11/12/12
Do	Chief Counsel, Internal Revenue Service	William J. Wilkins, Jr.	PAS	EX	V		
	INTERNAL REVENUE SERVICE OVERSIGHT BOARD						
Do	Member	Deborah L. Wince Smith	PAS	AD	$30,000	5 Years	09/14/10
Do	......do	Vacant	PAS	AD	$30,000	5 Years	
Do	......do	Robert Tobias	PAS	AD	$30,000	5 Years	09/14/10
Do	......do	Paul Cherecwich	PAS	AD	$30,000	5 Years	09/14/09
Do	......do	Raymond T. Wagner, Jr.	PAS	AD	$30,000	5 Years	09/14/09

DEPARTMENT OF THE TREASURY—Continued

Location	Position	Name of Incumbent	Type of Appt.	Pay Plan	Level, Grade, or Pay	Tenure	Expires
Washington, DC	Member	Vacant	PAS	AD	$30,000	5 Years	
Do	......do	Earl Edwin Eck II	PAS	AD	$30,000	5 Years	09/14/13
	COMPTROLLER OF THE CURRENCY						
Do	Comptroller of the Currency	Thomas J. Curry	PAS	EX	IV	5 Years	04/01/17

DEPARTMENT OF THE TREASURY OFFICE OF THE INSPECTOR GENERAL

Location	Position	Name of Incumbent	Type of Appt.	Pay Plan	Level, Grade, or Pay	Tenure	Expires
Washington, DC	Inspector General	Eric M. Thorson	PAS	OT	$170,259	....	
Do	Deputy Inspector General	Vacant	....	ES	....	....	
Do	Senior Advisor to the Inspector General	Susan Marshall	TA	ES	....	3 Years	10/24/13
Do	Special Inspector General for Small Business Lending Fund.	Career Incumbent	CA	ES	....	....	

DEPARTMENT OF THE TREASURY INSPECTOR GENERAL FOR TAX ADMINISTRATION

Location	Position	Name of Incumbent	Type of Appt.	Pay Plan	Level, Grade, or Pay	Tenure	Expires
Washington, DC	Inspector General	J. Russell George	PAS	OT	$170,259	....	

DEPARTMENT OF THE TREASURY SPECIAL INSPECTOR GENERAL FOR THE TROUBLED ASSET RELIEF PROGRAM

Location	Position	Name of Incumbent	Type of Appt.	Pay Plan	Level, Grade, or Pay	Tenure	Expires
Washington, DC	Special Inspector General	Christy Lynne Romero	PAS	OT	$170,259	....	
Do	Deputy Special Inspector General	Career Incumbent	CA	ES	....	....	
Do	Chief of Staff	......do	CA	ES	....	....	
Do	Senior Policy Advisor	Brian Joseph Sano	TA	ES	....	3 Years	06/18/15

DEPARTMENT OF VETERANS AFFAIRS

Location	Position	Name of Incumbent	Type of Appt.	Pay Plan	Level, Grade, or Pay	Tenure	Expires
	OFFICE OF THE SECRETARY AND DEPUTY						
Washington, DC	Secretary	Eric K. Shinseki	PAS	EX	I	....	
Do	Deputy Secretary	W. S. Gould	PAS	EX	II	....	
Do	Chief of Staff	John R. Gingrich	NA	ES	....	....	
Do	Deputy Chief of Staff	Career Incumbent	CA	ES	....	....	
Do	Director, Center for Minority Veterans	Vacant	....	ES	....	....	
Do	Director, Center for Women Veterans	Irene Trowell-Harris	NA	ES	....	....	
Do	Senior Advisor to the Secretary	John J. Spinelli	NA	ES	....	....	
Do	Executive Secretary to the Department	Career Incumbent	CA	ES	....	....	
Do	Senior Advisor	Peter L. Levin	NA	ES	....	....	
Do	......do	Vacant	....	ES	....	....	
Do	......do	Lindsey Davis Stover	NA	ES	....	....	
Do	......do	Mary Carstensen	NA	ES	....	....	
Do	......do	Jonah J. Czerwinski	NA	ES	....	....	
Do	......do	Gregory Kammerer	TA	ES	....	....	05/11/14
Do	Executive Director, Senior Executive Leader Development Program.	Career Incumbent	CA	ES	....	....	
Do	Special Assistant	Clare Hall Reed	SC	GS	13	....	
Do	......do	Charlyn A. Isaac	SC	GS	11	....	
Do	Special Assistant to the Secretary	Drew M. Brookie	SC	GS	13	....	
Do	Director, Center for Faith Based Community Initiatives.	Evna T. Lavelle	SC	GS	15	....	
Do	Special Assistant to the Deputy Secretary	Joel Spangenberg	SC	GS	15	....	
Do	Special Assistant	Allen J. Gill	SC	GS	15	....	
Do	Special Assistant, White House Liaison	Michelle C. Dominguez	SC	GS	12	....	
	OFFICE OF ACQUISITIONS, LOGISTICS AND CONSTRUCTION						
Do	Executive Director	Career Incumbent	CA	ES	....	....	
Frederick, MD	Chancellor, VA Acquisition Academy	Vacant	....	ES	....	....	
	Office of Acquisition and Materiel Management						
Washington, DC	Associate Deputy Assistant Secretary Logistics and Supply Chain Management.	Career Incumbent	CA	ES	....	....	
	BOARD OF VETERANS' APPEALS						
Do	Chairman	Vacant	PAS	EX	IV	....	
	OFFICE OF THE GENERAL COUNSEL						
Do	General Counsel	Will A. Gunn	PAS	EX	IV	....	
Do	Deputy General Counsel	Career Incumbent	CA	ES	....	....	
Do	Assistant General Counsel, Group I	......do	CA	ES	....	....	
Do	Assistant General Counsel, Group II	......do	CA	ES	....	....	
Do	Assistant General Counsel, Group III	......do	CA	ES	....	....	
Do	Assistant General Counsel, Group IV	......do	CA	ES	....	....	
Do	Assistant General Counsel, Group V	......do	CA	ES	....	....	
Do	Assistant General Counsel, Group VI	......do	CA	ES	....	....	
Do	Assistant General Counsel, Group VII	......do	CA	ES	....	....	
Do	Associate General Counsel (Ethics)	......do	CA	ES	....	....	
Do	Associate General Counsel	......do	CA	ES	....	....	
	OFFICE OF THE ASSISTANT SECRETARY FOR MANAGEMENT						
Do	Assistant Secretary for Management	Vacant	PAS	EX	IV	....	
Do	Executive Director	Career Incumbent	CA	ES	....	....	
Do	Director, Office of Performance Management	......do	CA	ES	....	....	
	Office of Budget						
Do	Deputy Assistant Secretary for Budget	......do	CA	ES	....	....	
Do	Associate Deputy Assistant Secretary, Budget Operations.	......do	CA	ES	....	....	
Do	Associate Deputy Assistant Secretary, Program Budgets.	......do	CA	ES	....	....	
	Office of Finance						
Do	Deputy Assistant Secretary	......do	CA	ES	....	....	
Do	Associate Deputy Assistant Secretary for Financial Policy.	......do	CA	ES	....	....	
Do	Associate Deputy Assistant Secretary for Financial Process Improvement and Audit Readiness.	......do	CA	ES	....	....	
	Office of Asset Enterprise Management						
Do	Director, Asset Enterprise Management	......do	CA	ES	....	....	

DEPARTMENT OF VETERANS AFFAIRS—Continued

Location	Position	Name of Incumbent	Type of Appt.	Pay Plan	Level, Grade, or Pay	Tenure	Expires
	OFFICE OF THE ASSISTANT SECRETARY FOR POLICY AND PLANNING						
Washington, DC	Assistant Secretary	Raul Perea-Henze	PAS	EX	IV	....	
Do	Director, National Center for Veterans Analysis and Statistics.	Career Incumbent	CA	ES	....	....	
Do	Executive Director of the VA/DoD Collaboration Service.	John P. Medve	TA	ES	....	....	11/18/12
Do	Principal Deputy Assistant Secretary	Career Incumbent	CA	ES	....	....	
Do	Deputy Assistant Secretary for Data Governance and Analysis.	......do	CA	ES	....	....	
Do	Executive Director	......do	CA	ES	....	....	
	Office of Policy						
Do	Deputy Assistant Secretary	......do	CA	ES	....	....	
Do	Director, Corporate Analysis and Evaluation	......do	CA	ES	....	....	
Do	Executive Director	......do	CA	ES	....	....	
Do	......do	Vacant	....	ES	....	....	
	OFFICE OF THE ASSISTANT SECRETARY FOR HUMAN RESOURCES AND ADMINISTRATION						
Do	Assistant Secretary	John U. Sepulveda	PAS	EX	IV	....	
Do	Principal Deputy Assistant Secretary	Career Incumbent	CA	ES	....	....	
Do	Executive Director	Joseph A. Viani	TA	ES	....	....	09/11/13
	Office of Human Resources Management						
Do	Deputy Assistant Secretary	Career Incumbent	CA	ES	....	....	
Do	Deputy Assistant Secretary for Labor-Management Relations.	......do	CA	ES	....	....	
Do	Associate Deputy Assistant Secretary for Human Resources Management Operations.	......do	CA	ES	....	....	
	Office of Diversity Management and Equal Employment Opportunity						
Do	Deputy Assistant Secretary	......do	CA	ES	....	....	
	Office of Administration						
Do	Executive Director	......do	CA	ES	....	....	
Do	Associate Deputy Assistant Secretary	......do	CA	ES	....	....	
	Office of Resolution Management						
Do	Deputy Assistant Secretary	......do	CA	ES	....	....	
Do	Associate Deputy Assistant Secretary	Vacant	....	ES	....	....	
	Office of Corporate Senior Executive Management						
Do	Deputy Assistant Secretary	Career Incumbent	CA	ES	....	....	
	VA Learning University						
Do	Dean	......do	CA	ES	....	....	
	OFFICE OF THE ASSISTANT SECRETARY FOR PUBLIC AND INTERGOVERNMENTAL AFFAIRS						
Do	Assistant Secretary	Vacant	PAS	EX	IV	....	
Do	Director, Homeless Veterans Program Office	Career Incumbent	CA	ES	....	....	
Do	Executive Director, Public and Intergovernmental Affairs.	......do	CA	ES	....	....	
	Office of Public Affairs						
Do	Director	Nathan B. Naylor	NA	ES	....	....	
Do	Press Secretary	Joshua Taylor	SC	GS	14	....	
	Office of Intergovernmental Affairs						
Do	Director	John M. Garcia	NA	ES	....	....	
Do	Director, Office of Tribal Government Relations.	Career Incumbent	CA	ES	....	....	
	OFFICE OF THE ASSISTANT SECRETARY FOR CONGRESSIONAL AND LEGISLATIVE AFFAIRS						
Do	Assistant Secretary	Joan M. Mooney	PAS	EX	IV	....	
Do	Associate Deputy Assistant Secretary	Career Incumbent	CA	ES	....	....	
Do	Director for Congressional Affairs	Vacant	....	ES	....	....	
Do	Special Assistant	Janko Mitric	SC	GS	14	....	
Do	......do	Sean Thomas Foertsch	SC	GS	15	....	

DEPARTMENT OF VETERANS AFFAIRS—Continued

Location	Position	Name of Incumbent	Type of Appt.	Pay Plan	Level, Grade, or Pay	Tenure	Expires
	OFFICE OF THE ASSISTANT SECRETARY FOR INFORMATION AND TECHNOLOGY						
Washington, DC	Assistant Secretary	Roger W. Baker	PAS	EX	IV	....	
Do	Principal Deputy Assistant Secretary	Career Incumbent	CA	ES	....	....	
Do	Assistant Deputy Chief Information Officer for Project Management.	......do	CA	ES	....	....	
Vancouver, WA	Executive Director (Field Operations)	......do	CA	ES	....	....	
New York, NY	Executive Director (Systems Engineering)	......do	CA	ES	....	....	
Washington, DC	Deputy Chief Information Officer for Product Development.	......do	CA	ES	....	....	
Do	Deputy Assistant Secretary for Information Security.	......do	CA	ES	....	....	
Do	Associate Deputy Assistant Secretary for Policy, Privacy and Incident Management.	......do	CA	ES	....	....	
Do	Deputy Chief Information Officer for Architecture, Strategy, and Design.	......do	CA	ES	....	....	
Do	Deputy Director	......do	CA	ES	....	....	
Do	Assistant Deputy Chief Information Officer for Enterprise Development Software Engineering.	......do	CA	ES	....	....	
Do	Assistant Deputy Chief Information Officer for Enterprise Development Software Development.	......do	CA	ES	....	....	
Do	Executive Director (Acquisition Strategy and Business Relationships).	......do	CA	ES	....	....	
Do	Program Manager, Customer Advocate for Corporate.	......do	CA	ES	....	....	
Do	Executive Director (Enterprise Risk Management).	......do	CA	ES	....	....	
Do	Assistant Deputy Chief Information Officer for Product Management.	......do	CA	ES	....	....	
Do	Senior Advisor, VA Innovation Initiative (VAI2).	Michael D. O'Neill	TA	ES	....	....	04/04/14
Do	Interim Deputy Assistant Secretary Information Security.	Career Incumbent	CA	ES	....	....	
Do	Deputy Chief Information Officer	Vacant	....	ES	....	....	
Do	Program Management Officer	Susan A. Perez	TA	ES	....	....	02/11/14
	OFFICE OF THE ASSISTANT SECRETARY FOR OPERATIONS, SECURITY AND PREPAREDNESS						
Do	Assistant Secretary	Jose D. Riojas	PAS	EX	IV	....	
Do	Director, Office of Personnel Security and Identity Management.	Career Incumbent	CA	ES	....	....	
	NATIONAL CEMETERY ADMINISTRATION						
Do	Under Secretary for Memorial Affairs	Steve Louis Muro	PAS	EX	III	....	
Do	Director, Field Programs Service	Career Incumbent	CA	ES	....	....	
Do	Deputy Under Secretary for Memorial Affairs	Vacant	....	ES	....	....	
Do	Associate Director, Office of Field Programs ..	Career Incumbent	CA	ES	....	....	
Do	Associate Deputy Under Secretary for Management.	......do	CA	ES	....	....	
Do	Director, Memorial Program Service	......do	CA	ES	....	....	
Philadelphia, PA	Memorial Service Network Director	......do	CA	ES	....	....	
Decatur, GA	......do	......do	CA	ES	....	....	
Indianapolis, IN	......do	......do	CA	ES	....	....	
Lakewood, CO	......do	......do	CA	ES	....	....	
Oakland, CA	......do	......do	CA	ES	....	....	
	VETERANS BENEFITS ADMINISTRATION						
Washington, DC	Under Secretary for Benefits	Allison Hickey	PAS	EX	III	....	
Do	Deputy Under Secretary for Benefits	Career Incumbent	CA	ES	....	....	
Do	Deputy Under Secretary for Disability Assistance.	......do	CA	ES	....	....	
Do	Deputy Under Secretary for Economic Opportunity.	......do	CA	ES	....	....	
Do	Director, Compensation and Pension Service	......do	CA	ES	....	....	
Do	Director, Loan Guaranty Service	......do	CA	ES	....	....	
Do	Director, Vocational Rehabilitation and Employment.	......do	CA	ES	....	....	
Do	Director, Education Service	......do	CA	ES	....	....	
Do	Chief of Staff	......do	CA	ES	....	....	
Do	Director, Employee Development and Training.	......do	CA	ES	....	....	

DEPARTMENT OF VETERANS AFFAIRS—Continued

Location	Position	Name of Incumbent	Type of Appt.	Pay Plan	Level, Grade, or Pay	Tenure	Expires
Washington, DC	Associate Deputy Under Secretary for Field Operations.	Career Incumbent	CA	ES	....	....	
Do	Director, Office of Management	......do	CA	ES	....	....	
Do	Director, Office of Performance Analysis and Integrity.	......do	CA	ES	....	....	
Do	Director, Office of Facilities, Access and Administration.	Vacant	....	ES	....	....	
Do	Director, Benefits Assistance Service	Career Incumbent	CA	ES	....	....	
Do	Director, Veterans Benefits Management System Program Management Office.	......do	CA	ES	....	....	
Do	Director, Office of Veterans Relationship Management Program Office.	......do	CA	ES	....	....	
Do	Director, Office of Strategic Planning	......do	CA	ES	....	....	
Do	Director, Pension and Fiduciary Service	......do	CA	ES	....	....	
Philadelphia, PA ...	Director, Insurance Service	......do	CA	ES	....	....	
Washington, DC	Director, VBA/DoD Programs	......do	CA	ES	....	....	
	Area Directors						
Muskogee, OK	Area Director - Central	......do	CA	ES	....	....	
Nashville, TN	Area Director - South	......do	CA	ES	....	....	
Phoenix, AZ	Area Director - West	......do	CA	ES	....	....	
Detroit, MI	Area Director - East	......do	CA	ES	....	....	
	Regional Office Directors						
Boston, MA	Director, Regional Office	......do	CA	ES	....	....	
New York, NY	......do	......do	CA	ES	....	....	
Atlanta, GA	......do	......do	CA	ES	....	....	
St. Petersburg, FL	......do	......do	CA	ES	....	....	
Winston Salem, NC	......do	......do	CA	ES	....	....	
Cleveland, OH	......do	......do	CA	ES	....	....	
Chicago, IL	......do	......do	CA	ES	....	....	
Detroit, MI	......do	......do	CA	ES	....	....	
Oakland, CA	......do	......do	CA	ES	....	....	
Los Angeles, CA ...	......do	......do	CA	ES	....	....	
Waco, TX	......do	......do	CA	ES	....	....	
Houston, TX	......do	......do	CA	ES	....	....	
Philadelphia, PA ...	......do	......do	CA	ES	....	....	
St. Paul, MN	......do	......do	CA	ES	....	....	
St. Louis, MO	......do	......do	CA	ES	....	....	
Seattle, WA	......do	......do	CA	ES	....	....	
Lakewood, CO	......do	......do	CA	ES	....	....	
Montgomery, AL	......do	......do	CA	ES	....	....	
Roanoke, VA	......do	......do	CA	ES	....	....	
Nashville, TN	......do	Vacant	....	ES	....	....	
Indianapolis, IN	......do	Career Incumbent	CA	ES	....	....	
New Orleans, LA ...	......do	......do	CA	ES	....	....	
Muskogee, OK	......do	......do	CA	ES	....	....	
Buffalo, NY	......do	......do	CA	ES	....	....	
Phoenix, AZ	......do	......do	CA	ES	....	....	
Milwaukee, WI	......do	......do	CA	ES	....	....	
Pittsburgh, PA	......do	......do	CA	ES	....	....	
Columbia, SC	......do	Career Incumbent	CA	ES	....	....	
Louisville, KY	......do	......do	CA	ES	....	....	
Little Rock, AR	......do	Vacant	....	ES	....	....	
San Juan, Puerto Rico.	......do	Career Incumbent	CA	ES	....	....	
Portland, OR	......do	......do	CA	ES	....	....	
Baltimore, MD	......do	......do	CA	ES	....	....	
Jackson, MS	......do	......do	CA	ES	....	....	
San Diego, CA	......do	......do	CA	ES	....	....	
Lincoln, NE	......do	......do	CA	ES	....	....	
Salt Lake City, UT	......do	......do	CA	ES	....	....	
Manila, Philippines	Director, Regional Office and Outpatient Clinic.	Vacant	....	ES	....	....	
	VETERANS HEALTH ADMINISTRATION						
Washington, DC	Under Secretary for Health	Robert A. Petzel, M.D.	PAS	EX	III	....	
Do	Deputy Under Secretary for Health for Operations and Management.	William C. Schoenhard	NA	ES	....	....	
Do	Assistant Deputy Under Secretary for Health for Operations and Management.	Career Incumbent	CA	ES	....	....	
Do	Assistant Deputy Under Secretary for Health for Organizational Integration.	......do	CA	ES	....	....	
Do	Assistant Deputy Under Secretary for Health for Policy and Planning.	......do	CA	ES	....	....	
Do	Assistant Deputy Under Secretary of Health for Workforce Services.	......do	CA	ES	....	....	

DEPARTMENT OF VETERANS AFFAIRS—Continued

Location	Position	Name of Incumbent	Type of Appt.	Pay Plan	Level, Grade, or Pay	Tenure	Expires
Washington, DC	Assistant Deputy Under Secretary for Health for Informatics and Analytics.	Career Incumbent	CA	ES	....	....	
Do	Chief Workforce Management and Consulting Officer.	Vacant	....	ES	....	....	
Do	Chief of Staff	Career Incumbent	CA	ES	....	....	
Do	Director, Policy, Analysis, and Forecasting	Career Incumbent	CA	ES	....	....	
Do	Chief Information Officer	......do	CA	ES	....	....	
Do	Associate Chief Financial Officer for Resource Management.	......do	CA	ES	....	....	
Do	Chief Communication Officer	......do	CA	ES	....	....	
Do	Director, Readjustment Counseling Service	......do	CA	ES	....	....	
Do	Director, Strategic Planning and Analysis	......do	CA	ES	....	....	
Do	Chief Business Officer	......do	CA	ES	....	....	
Denver, CO	Deputy Chief Business Officer for Revenue Operations.	......do	CA	ES	....	....	
Washington, DC	Director, Network Support (Central)	......do	CA	ES	....	....	
Do	Deputy Chief Business Officer for Purchased Care.	Vacant	....	ES	....	....	
Topeka, KS	Deputy Chief Business Officer for Member Services.	Career Incumbent	CA	ES	....	....	
Washington, DC	Deputy Chief Officer, Workforce Management and Consulting Office.	......do	CA	ES	....	....	
Ann Arbor, MI	Health Systems Administrator (Director, Organizational Health Initiative).	......do	CA	ES	....	....	
Washington, DC	Deputy Chief of Staff	......do	CA	ES	....	....	
Vallejo, CA	Director of Special Projects, National Center for Organizational Development.	......do	CA	ES	....	....	
Washington, DC	Deputy Chief Learning Officer	Vacant	....	ES	....	....	
Do	Director, Office of Rural Health	Career Incumbent	CA	ES	....	....	
Do	Chief Learning Officer	Vacant	....	ES	....	....	
Do	Special Assistant	Career Incumbent	CA	ES	....	....	
Do	Executive Director, Consolidated Patient Account Centers.	......do	CA	ES	....	....	
Pittsburgh, PA	Director, Service Area Office	......do	CA	ES	....	....	
Cincinnati, OH	Director, National Center for Organizational Development.	......do	CA	ES	....	....	
Washington, DC	Project Executive	......do	CA	ES	....	....	
	Medical Center Directors						
Albany, NY	Director, Veterans Affairs Medical Center	......do	CA	ES	....	....	
Albuquerque, NM ..	Director, New Mexico Veterans Affairs Healthcare System.	......do	CA	ES	....	....	
Alexandria, LA	Director, Veterans Affairs Medical Center	......do	CA	ES	....	....	
Altoona, PA	......do	......do	CA	ES	....	....	
Amarillo, TX	Director, Amarillo Veterans Affairs Health Care System.	......do	CA	ES	....	....	
Ann Arbor, MI	Director, Veterans Affairs Medical Center	......do	CA	ES	....	....	
Asheville, NC	......do	......do	CA	ES	....	....	
Atlanta, GA	......do	......do	CA	ES	....	....	
Augusta, GA	......do	Vacant	....	ES	....	....	
Bath, NY	......do	Career Incumbent	CA	ES	....	....	
Battle Creek, MI ...	......do	Vacant	....	ES	....	....	
Bay Pines, FL	......do	Career Incumbent	CA	ES	....	....	
Beckley, WV	......do	......do	CA	ES	....	....	
Bedford, MA	......do	Vacant	....	ES	....	....	
Big Spring, TX	Director, West Texas Veterans Affairs Healthcare System.	Career Incumbent	CA	ES	....	....	
Biloxi, MS	Director, Veterans Affairs Medical Center	Vacant	....	ES	....	....	
Birmingham, AL	......do	......do	....	ES	....	....	
Boise, ID	......do	Career Incumbent	CA	ES	....	....	
Boston, MA	Director, Veterans Affairs Boston Healthcare System.	......do	CA	ES	....	....	
New York -Bronx, NY.	Director, Veterans Affairs Medical Center	......do	CA	ES	....	....	
New York, NY	Director, Veterans Affairs New York Harbor Health Care System.	......do	CA	ES	....	....	
Orlando, FL	Director, Veterans Affairs East Central Florida Healthcare System.	......do	CA	ES	....	....	
Buffalo, NY	Director, Veterans Affairs Western New York Healthcare System.	......do	CA	ES	....	....	
Butler, PA	Director, Veterans Affairs Medical Center	......do	CA	ES	....	....	
Canandaigua, NY ..	......do	......do	CA	ES	....	....	
Charleston, SC	......do	......do	CA	ES	....	....	
Cheyenne, WY	Director, Veterans Affairs Medical and Regional Office Center.	......do	CA	ES	....	....	
Dallas, TX	Health System Administrator	......do	CA	ES	....	....	

DEPARTMENT OF VETERANS AFFAIRS—Continued

Location	Position	Name of Incumbent	Type of Appt.	Pay Plan	Level, Grade, or Pay	Tenure	Expires
Chicago, IL	Director, Veterans Affairs Chicago Health Care System.	Career Incumbent	CA	ES	....	....	
Chillicothe, OH	Director, Veterans Affairs Medical Center	......do	CA	ES	....	....	
Cincinnati, OH	......do	......do	CA	ES	....	....	
Clarksburg, WV	......do	......do	CA	ES	....	....	
Cleveland, OH	......do	......do	CA	ES	....	....	
Columbia, MO	......do	......do	CA	ES	....	....	
Columbia, SC	......do	......do	CA	ES	....	....	
Dallas, TX	Director, Veterans Affairs North Texas Health Care System.	......do	CA	ES	....	....	
Dayton, OH	Director, Veterans Affairs Medical Center	......do	CA	ES	....	....	
Des Moines, IA	Director, Veterans Affairs Central Iowa Healthcare System.	......do	CA	ES	....	....	
Dublin, GA	Director, Veterans Affairs Medical Center	......do	CA	ES	....	....	
Durham, NC	......do	......do	CA	ES	....	....	
East Orange, NJ	......do	......do	CA	ES	....	....	
El Paso, TX	Director, El Paso Veterans Affairs Health Care System.	Vacant	....	ES	....	....	
Fargo, ND	Director, Veterans Affairs Medical and Regional Office Center.	Career Incumbent	CA	ES	....	....	
St. Cloud, MN	Director, Veterans Affairs Medical Center	......do	CA	ES	....	....	
Fayetteville, NC	......do	......do	CA	ES	....	....	
Fort Harrison, MT	Director, Veterans Affairs Medical and Regional Office Center.	......do	CA	ES	....	....	
Fort Meade, SD	Director, Veterans Affairs Black Hills Health Care System.	......do	CA	ES	....	....	
Fresno, CA	Director, Veterans Affairs Central California Health Care System.	Vacant	....	ES	....	....	
Grand Junction, CO.	Director, Veterans Affairs Medical Center	Career Incumbent	CA	ES	....	....	
Hampton, VA	......do	Vacant	....	ES	....	....	
Hines, IL	......do	Career Incumbent	CA	ES	....	....	
Houston, TX	......do	......do	CA	ES	....	....	
Huntington, WV	......do	......do	CA	ES	....	....	
Indianapolis, IN	......do	......do	CA	ES	....	....	
Iowa City, IA	......do	......do	CA	ES	....	....	
Iron Mountain, MI	......do	......do	CA	ES	....	....	
Jackson, MS	......do	......do	CA	ES	....	....	
Kansas City, MO ...	......do	......do	CA	ES	....	....	
Gainesville, FL	Director, Veterans Affairs North Florida/South Georgia Healthcare System.	......do	CA	ES	....	....	
Las Vegas, NV	Director, Veterans Affairs Southern Nevada Health Care System.	......do	CA	ES	....	....	
Lebanon, PA	Director, Veterans Affairs Medical Center	......do	CA	ES	....	....	
Lexington, KY	......do	......do	CA	ES	....	....	
Little Rock, AR	Director, Veterans Affairs Central Arkansas Veterans Healthcare System.	......do	CA	ES	....	....	
Loma Linda, CA	Director, Veterans Affairs Medical Center	......do	CA	ES	....	....	
Long Beach, CA	Director, Veterans Affairs Long Beach Healthcare System.	......do	CA	ES	....	....	
Louisville, KY	Director, Veterans Affairs Medical Center	......do	CA	ES	....	....	
Marion, IL	......do	......do	CA	ES	....	....	
Fort Wayne, IN	Director, Veterans Affairs Northern Indiana Healthcare System.	......do	CA	ES	....	....	
Martinsburg, WV ...	Director, Veterans Affairs Medical Center	......do	CA	ES	....	....	
Memphis, TN	......do	......do	CA	ES	....	....	
Miami, FL	......do	......do	CA	ES	....	....	
Montrose, NY	Director, Veterans Affairs Hudson Valley Health Care System.	......do	CA	ES	....	....	
Johnson City, TN ..	Director, Veterans Affairs Medical Center	......do	CA	ES	....	....	
Nashville, TN	Director, Veterans Affairs Tennessee Valley Healthcare System.	......do	CA	ES	....	....	
Muskogee, OK	Director, Veterans Affairs Medical Center	......do	CA	ES	....	....	
New Orleans, LA ...	......do	......do	CA	ES	....	....	
North Chicago, IL ..	......do	......do	CA	ES	....	....	
Coatesville, PA	......do	......do	CA	ES	....	....	
Northport, NY	......do	......do	CA	ES	....	....	
Omaha, NE	Director, Veterans Affairs Nebraska/Western Iowa Health Care System.	......do	CA	ES	....	....	
Palo Alto, CA	Director, Veterans Affairs Palo Alto Health Care System.	......do	CA	ES	....	....	
Philadelphia, PA	Director, Veterans Affairs Medical Center	......do	CA	ES	....	....	
Pittsburgh, PA	Director, Veterans Affairs Pittsburgh Health Care System.	......do	CA	ES	....	....	
Poplar Bluff, MO ...	Director, Veterans Affairs Medical Center	......do	CA	ES	....	....	
Portland, OR	......do	......do	CA	ES	....	....	

DEPARTMENT OF VETERANS AFFAIRS—Continued

Location	Position	Name of Incumbent	Type of Appt.	Pay Plan	Level, Grade, or Pay	Tenure	Expires
Prescott, AZ	Director, Northern Arizona Veterans Affairs Health Care System.	Career Incumbent	CA	ES	....	....	
Providence, RI	Director, Veterans Affairs Medical Center	......do	CA	ES	....	....	
Richmond, VA	......do	......do	CA	ES	....	....	
Roseburg, OR	......do	......do	CA	ES	....	....	
Saginaw, MI	......do	......do	CA	ES	....	....	
Salisbury, NC	......do	Vacant	....	ES	....	....	
Salt Lake City, UT	......do	Career Incumbent	CA	ES	....	....	
San Antonio, TX	......do	......do	CA	ES	....	....	
Chicago, IL	Director, Veterans Affairs Illiana Health Care System.	......do	CA	ES	....	....	
San Juan, Puerto Rico.	Director, Veterans Affairs Medical Center	......do	CA	ES	....	....	
Seattle, WA	......do	......do	CA	ES	....	....	
Los Angeles, CA	Director, Veterans Affairs Greater Los Angeles Health Care System.	......do	CA	ES	....	....	
Sheridan, WY	Director, Veterans Affairs Medical Center	......do	CA	ES	....	....	
Shreveport, LA	......do	......do	CA	ES	....	....	
Sioux Falls, SD	......do	......do	CA	ES	....	....	
Spokane, WA	......do	......do	CA	ES	....	....	
St. Louis, MO	......do	......do	CA	ES	....	....	
Syracuse, NY	......do	......do	CA	ES	....	....	
Temple, TX	Director, Veterans Affairs Central Texas Health Care System.	......do	CA	ES	....	....	
Togus, ME	Director, Veterans Affairs Medical and Regional Office Center.	Vacant	....	ES	....	....	
Tomah, WI	Director, Veterans Affairs Medical Center	Career Incumbent	CA	ES	....	....	
Topeka, KS	Director, Veterans Affairs Eastern Kansas Health Care System.	Vacant	....	ES	....	....	
Tucson, AZ	Director, Veterans Affairs Medical Center	Career Incumbent	CA	ES	....	....	
Tuscaloosa, AL	......do	......do	CA	ES	....	....	
Walla Walla, WA ...	......do	......do	CA	ES	....	....	
Washington, DC	......do	......do	CA	ES	....	....	
West Haven, CT	Director, Veterans Affairs Connecticut Healthcare System.	......do	CA	ES	....	....	
White City, OR	Director, Veterans Affairs Medical Center	Vacant	....	ES	....	....	
White River Junction, VT.	Director, Veterans Affairs Medical and Regional Office Center.	......do	....	ES	....	....	
Wichita, KS	......do	......do	....	ES	....	....	
Wilkes-Barre, PA ...	Director, Veterans Affairs Medical Center	Career Incumbent	CA	ES	....	....	
Wilmington, DE	......do	Vacant	....	ES	....	....	
Milwaukee, WI	......do	Career Incumbent	CA	ES	....	....	
Northampton, MA	......do	......do	CA	ES	....	....	
Tampa, FL	......do	......do	CA	ES	....	....	
Madison, WI	......do	......do	CA	ES	....	....	
Baltimore, MD	......do	......do	CA	ES	....	....	
Phoenix, AZ	......do	......do	CA	ES	....	....	
San Diego, CA	......do	......do	CA	ES	....	....	
Oklahoma City, OK	......do	Vacant	....	ES	....	....	
Tuskegee, AL	Director, Central Alabama Healthcare System.	......do	....	ES	....	....	
San Francisco, CA	Director, Veterans Affairs Medical Center	Career Incumbent	CA	ES	....	....	
West Palm Beach, FL.	......do	......do	CA	ES	....	....	
Anchorage, AK	Director, Veterans Affairs Operations Clinic and Regional Office.	......do	CA	ES	....	....	
Denver, CO	Director, Veterans Affairs Eastern Colorado Health Care System.	......do	CA	ES	....	....	
	Veterans Integrated Service Network Directors						
Albany, NY	Director, Veterans Integrated Service Network.	......do	CA	ES	....	....	
New York -Bronx, NY.	......do	......do	CA	ES	....	....	
Pittsburgh, PA	......do	......do	CA	ES	....	....	
Linthicum Heights, MD.	......do	......do	CA	ES	....	....	
Denver, CO	......do	......do	CA	ES	....	....	
Durham, NC	......do	......do	CA	ES	....	....	
Atlanta, GA	......do	Vacant	....	ES	....	....	
Bay Pines, FL	......do	Career Incumbent	CA	ES	....	....	
Nashville, TN	......do	......do	CA	ES	....	....	
Cincinnati, OH	......do	......do	CA	ES	....	....	
Ann Arbor, MI	......do	......do	CA	ES	....	....	
Kansas City, MO ...	......do	Vacant	....	ES	....	....	
Jackson, MS	......do	Career Incumbent	CA	ES	....	....	

DEPARTMENT OF VETERANS AFFAIRS—Continued

Location	Position	Name of Incumbent	Type of Appt.	Pay Plan	Level, Grade, or Pay	Tenure	Expires
Dallas, TX	Director, Veterans Integrated Service Network.	Career Incumbent	CA	ES	....	....	
Phoenix, AZ	......do	......do	CA	ES	....	....	
Portland, OR	......do	Vacant	....	ES	....	....	
San Francisco, CA	......do	Career Incumbent	CA	ES	....	....	
Long Beach, CA	......do	......do	CA	ES	....	....	
Minneapolis, MN ...	......do	Career Incumbent	CA	ES	....	....	
Do	Chief Operations Officer	Vacant	....	ES	....	....	
Washington, DC	Deputy Network Director	Career Incumbent	CA	ES	....	....	
	Title 38 Positions						
Do	Associate Deputy Chief Medical Director	Vacant	XS	OT	....	....	
Hampton, VA	Director, Chaplain Service	......do	XS	OT	....	....	
Washington, DC	National Director, Nutrition and Food Service	Ellen M. Bosley	XS	OT	$148,773	....	
Do	Chief Nursing Officer	Catherine J. Rick	XS	OT	$179,700	....	
Do	Chief Consultant, Pharmacy Benefits Management Services.	Michael A. Valentino	XS	OT	$198,360	....	
Linthicum Heights, MD.	Chief Medical Officer	Archna N. Sharma, M.D. ...	XS	OT	$230,834	....	
Washington, DC	Assistant Under Secretary for Health for Dentistry.	Timothy O. Ward	XS	OT	$216,099	....	
Ann Arbor, MI	Chief Patient Safety Officer	James P. Bagian, M.D.	XS	OT	$242,326	....	
Pittsburgh, PA	Chief Medical Officer	David S. MacPherson, M.D..	XS	OT	$211,099	....	
Washington, DC	Deputy Director, Clinical Science Research and Development Service.	Cheryl J. Oros	XS	OT	$152,265	....	
Ann Arbor, MI	National Program Director, Nuclear Medicine and Radiation Safety Service.	Milton D. Gross, M.D.	XS	OT	$226,596	....	
Washington, DC	Deputy Chief Research and Development Officer.	Holly Birdsall	XS	OT	$258,294	....	
Do	National Director, Anesthesia Services	Sam T. Sum-Ping	XS	OT	$334,929	....	
Seattle, WA	Chief Consultant, Spinal Cord Injury and Disorders.	Margaret C. Hammond, M.D..	XS	OT	$238,127	....	
Washington, DC	Director for Internal and External Collaborations.	Alexander E.K. Ommaya ...	XS	OT	$158,500	....	
Do	Chief Consultant, Women Veterans Health Strategic Health Care Group.	Patricia M. Hayes	XS	OT	$149,989	....	
New Orleans, LA ...	Director, Healthcare Retention and Recruitment Office.	Marisa W. Palkuti	XS	OT	$139,285	....	
Cincinnati, OH	Supervisory Psychologist	Vacant	XS	OT	....	....	
Detroit, MI	Director, Veterans Affairs Medical Center	Pamela J. Reeves	XS	OT	$217,836	....	
Columbus, OH	Director, Outpatient Clinic	Lilian M. Thome	XS	OT	$215,200	....	
Reno, NV	Director, Veterans Affairs Sierra Nevada Healthcare System.	Kurt W. Schlegelmilch	XS	OT	$226,487	....	
Honolulu, HI	Director, Veterans Affairs Pacific Islands Healthcare System.	James E. Hastings, M.D. ...	XS	OT	$230,000	....	
Sacramento, CA	Health System Administrator	Brian J. O'Neill, M.D.	XS	OT	$230,000	....	
Boston, MA	Director, Veterans Integrated Service Network.	Michael F. May-Smith, M.D..	XS	OT	$228,215	....	
Hines, IL	......do	Jeffrey A. Murawsky, M.D.	XS	OT	$232,000	....	
Washington, DC	Director, Emergency Management	Vacant	XS	OT	....	....	
Do	Chief Consultant, Rehabilitation Services	Lucille B. Beck	XS	OT	$158,500	....	
Do	Deputy Chief Academics Officer	Karen Sanders	XS	OT	$230,839	....	
Do	Chief Consultant	Antonette M. Zeiss	XS	OT	$154,698	....	
Do	Chief Consultant, Geriatrics and Extended Care Services.	James Burris	XS	OT	$234,397	....	
Do	Deputy to the Assistant Deputy Under Secretary for Health, Clinical Operations.	Vacant	XS	OT	....	....	
Do	Chief Public Health and Environmental Hazards Officer.	Victoria Davey	XS	OT	$163,411	....	
Fayetteville, AR	Director, Veterans Affairs Medical Center	Mark Enderle	XS	OT	$239,700	....	
Kansas City, MO ...	Director, Veterans Integrated Service Network.	William Patterson	XS	OT	$239,390	....	
Washington, DC	Deputy Chief Consultant, Mental Health Strategic Healthcare Group.	Vacant	XS	OT	....	....	
Do	Deputy Chief Officer, Office of Research Oversight.	Min-Fu Tsan, M.D.	XS	OT	$225,000	....	
Do	Senior Health Policy Program Director	Sherrie L. Hans	XS	OT	$144,266	....	
Bay Pines, FL	Senior Advisor on Legislative and Congressional Affairs.	Thomas G. Bowman	XS	OT	$165,300	....	
Washington, DC	Associate Chief Patient Care Services Officer	Vacant	XS	OT	....	....	
Do	Chief Consultant for Care Coordination	Adam W. Darkins	XS	OT	$158,500	....	
Do	Director, HIV and HCV Prevention Service	Kim W. Hamlett-Berry	XS	OT	$148,773	....	
Do	Chief Consultant, Rehabilitation Strategic Healthcare Group, Audiology and Speech Pathology Service.	Vacant	XS	OT	....	....	

DEPARTMENT OF VETERANS AFFAIRS—Continued

Location	Position	Name of Incumbent	Type of Appt.	Pay Plan	Level, Grade, or Pay	Tenure	Expires
Washington, DC	Director, Environmental Agents Service	Mark A. Brown	XS	OT	$144,266	....	
Do	Director, Clinical/Quality Liaison	Vacant	XS	OT		....	
Martinsburg, WV ...	Chief Consultant, Emergency Management Strategic Healthcare.	Daniel Bochicchio	XS	OT	$235,000	....	
Washington, DC	Associate Clinical/Quality Liaison	Mary T. Roseborough	XS	OT	$158,500	....	
Do	Director, Environmental Epidemiology Service.	Han K. Kang	XS	OT	$158,500	....	
Boston, MA	Epidemiology Program Director, Quality and Performance Office.	Steven M. Wright	XS	OT	$150,767	....	
Kansas City, MO ...	Assistant Deputy Under Secretary for Health for Quality and Safety.	Peter L. Almenoff	XS	OT	$228,088	....	
Washington, DC	Deputy Clinical Prosthetics Officer	Billie Jane Randolph	XS	OT	$159,665	....	
Do	Chief Consultant for Human Resources	Elias Hernandez	XS	OT	$154,285	....	
Do	Director, Human Resources and Staffing Services.	Makki Mohamad	XS	OT	$149,590	....	
Do	Director, Enterprise Systems Management	Susan Lloyd	XS	OT	$165,300	....	
Do	Director, Healthcare Talent Management Office.	Diane L. Rogers	XS	OT	$137,620	....	
Do	Transformation Initiative Lead, Health Care Efficiency.	Susan Kane	XS	OT	$125,000	....	
Hines, IL	Chief Medical Officer	Joan McInerney	XS	OT	$225,000	....	
Washington, DC	Director, Rehabilitation Research and Development.	Michael E. Selzer, M.D.	XS	OT	$217,288	....	
Houston, TX	National Director, Radiation Oncology Program.	P. G. Shankar Giri, M.D. ...	XS	OT	$320,000	....	
Washington, DC	Chief Consultant, Medical and Surgical Service.	Robert L. Jesse	XS	OT	$277,820	....	
Do	Director, Biomedical Laboratory Research and Clinical Science Research and Development Service.	Timothy J. O'Leary	XS	OT	$223,491	....	
Ann Arbor, MI	Clinical Management Officer	Alan J. Pawlow, M.D.	XS	OT	$226,342	....	
Bedford, MA	Chief Medical Officer	Fuller F. George	XS	OT	....		
Washington, DC	Director, Health Data and Information	Marcia Insley	XS	OT	$154,828	....	
Do	Deputy Director, VA/DoD Vision Center of Excellence.	Mary Lawrence	XS	OT	$228,000	....	
Do	Chief Officer, Office of Quality and Performance.	Joseph Francis, M.D.	XS	OT	$230,000	....	
Do	Chief Officer, Office of Research Oversight	John T. Puglisi	XS	OT	$165,300	....	
Silver Spring, MD	Director, Veterans Affairs/Department of Defense Health Information Sharing Service.	William C. Freeman	XS	OT	$159,665	....	
Washington, DC	Deputy Chief Learning Officer for Business Operations.	Sheree Cramer	XS	OT	$159,665	....	
Do	Director, Organizational Integrity and Information Synchronization.	Caitlin A. O'Brien	XS	OT	$179,700	....	
Do	Deputy Chief, Patient Care Service Office	Gerald A. Cross, M.D.	XS	OT	$288,394	....	
Durham, NC	Chief Diagnostics Services/National Director, Radiology Services.	Charles M. Anderson	XS	OT	$317,717	....	
Washington, DC	Assistant Deputy Under Secretary for Health for Policy and Services.	Stanlie M. Daniels	XS	OT	$173,600	....	
Do	Deputy Chief Officer, Office of Public Health	Richard A. Kaslow	XS	OT	$245,000	....	
Do	Director, Health Services Research and Development Service.	Seth A. Eisen	XS	OT	$231,036	....	
Do	Associate Chief Officer for Assistant Deputy Under Secretary for Health Operations.	Terry A. Ross	XS	OT	$149,989	....	
Ann Arbor, MI	Deputy Chief Patient Safety Officer	Robin R. Hemphill, M.D. ...	XS	OT	$227,500	....	
Washington, DC	Chief Medical Officer, Veterans Integrated Services Network.	Michael H. Bonner, M.D. ...	XS	OT	$200,000	....	
Do	Deputy Chief Officer, Office of Legislative, Regulatory, and Intergovernmental Affairs.	Karen T. Malebranche	XS	OT	$165,300	....	
Do	Assistant Under Secretary for Health for Dentistry.	Patricia E. Arola	XS	OT	$218,085	....	
Do	Assistant Deputy Chief, Patient Care Services.	Sonja Batten	XS	OT	$149,989	....	
Fort Howard, MD ..	Director, Optometry Service	John C. Townsend	XS	AD	$165,300	....	
Cleveland, OH	Director, Podiatry Service	Jeffrey M. Robbins	XS	AD	$160,829	....	
Cheyenne, WY	Director, Regional Office Medical Center	David M. Kilpatrick, M.D. .	XS	AD	$210,618	....	
Manchester, NH	Director, Veterans Affairs Medical Center	Marc F. Levenson, M.D.	XS	AD	$208,215	....	
Erie, PA	......do	Michael D. Adelman	XS	OT	$210,000	....	

DEPARTMENT OF VETERANS AFFAIRS OFFICE OF THE INSPECTOR GENERAL

Location	Position	Name of Incumbent	Type of Appt.	Pay Plan	Level, Grade, or Pay	Tenure	Expires
	IMMEDIATE OFFICE OF THE INSPECTOR GENERAL						
Washington, DC	Inspector General	George Joseph Opfer	PAS	OT	$170,259	....	

INDEPENDENT AGENCIES AND GOVERNMENT CORPORATIONS

ADMINISTRATIVE CONFERENCE OF THE UNITED STATES

Location	Position	Name of Incumbent	Type of Appt.	Pay Plan	Level, Grade, or Pay	Tenure	Expires
Washington, DC	Chairman	Paul Verkuil	PAS	EX	II		
Do	Member	Preeta D. Bansal	PA	WC			
Do	......do	Ronald A. Cass	PA	WC			
Do	......do	Mariano-Florentino Cuellar	PA	WC			
Do	......do	Theodore B. Olson	PA	WC			
Do	......do	Jane C. Sherburne	PA	WC			
Do	Executive Director	Career Incumbent	CA	ES			
Do	General Counsel	......do	CA	ES			
Do	Research Director	......do	CA	ES			

ADVISORY COUNCIL ON HISTORIC PRESERVATION

Location	Position	Name of Incumbent	Type of Appt.	Pay Plan	Level, Grade, or Pay	Tenure	Expires
Sacramento, CA	Council Member (Chairman)	Milford Wayne Donaldson	PA	OT	$100	4 Years	06/10/13
Newark, NJ	Council Member (Vice Chairman)	Clement A. Price	PA	OT	$100	3 Years	06/10/13
Seattle, WA	Council Member (Expert)	Horace H. Foxall, Jr.	PA	OT	$100	4 Years	06/10/14
Chicago, IL	......do	Theresa M. Guen-Murray	PA	OT	$100	4 Years	06/10/15
Arlington, VA	......do	Dorothy T. Lippert	PA	OT	$100	4 Years	06/10/15
Seattle, WA	......do	John G. Williams III	PA	OT	$100	4 Years	06/10/12
Charleston, WV	Council Member (General Public)	Mark A. Sadd	PA	OT	$100	4 Years	06/10/12
Evanston, IL	......do	Bradford J. White	PA	OT	$100	4 Years	06/10/14
Washington, DC	Council Member (Governor)	Vacant	PA	OT	$100	4 Years	
Columbus, OH	Council Member (Mayor)	Michael B. Coleman	PA	OT	$100	4 Years	06/10/13
Quapaw, OK	Council Member (Native American/Native Hawaiian).	John L. Berrey	PA	OT	$100	4 Years	06/10/12

AFRICAN DEVELOPMENT FOUNDATION

Location	Position	Name of Incumbent	Type of Appt.	Pay Plan	Level, Grade, or Pay	Tenure	Expires
Washington, DC	President and Chief Executive Officer	Rodney James MacAlister	XS	AD			

AMERICAN BATTLE MONUMENTS COMMISSION

Location	Position	Name of Incumbent	Type of Appt.	Pay Plan	Level, Grade, or Pay	Tenure	Expires
Arlington, VA	Commissioner, Chairman	Merrill A. McPeak	PA	WC			
Do	Commissioner	Cynthia F. Campbell	PA	WC			
Do	......do	Barbaralee Diamonstein-Spielvogel.	PA	WC			
Do	......do	Darrell L. Dorgan	PA	WC			
Do	......do	John L. Estrada	PA	WC			
Do	......do	Evelyn P. Foote	PA	WC			
Do	......do	Rolland E. Kidder	PA	WC			
Do	......do	Richard L. Klass	PA	WC			
Do	......do	Nstance A. Morella	PA	WC			
Do	......do	Ike N. Skelton	PA	WC			
Do	......do	Maura C. Sullivan	PA	WC			
Do	Secretary	Joseph Maxwell Cleland	PA	AD	$165,300		

APPALACHIAN REGIONAL COMMISSION

Location	Position	Name of Incumbent	Type of Appt.	Pay Plan	Level, Grade, or Pay	Tenure	Expires
Washington, DC	Federal Co-Chairman	Earl Gohl	PAS	EX	III	....	
Do	Alternate Federal Co-Chairman	Vacant	PAS	EX	V	....	

ARCHITECTURAL AND TRANSPORTATION BARRIERS COMPLIANCE BOARD (UNITED STATES ACCESS BOARD)

Location	Position	Name of Incumbent	Type of Appt.	Pay Plan	Level, Grade, or Pay	Tenure	Expires
Washington, DC	Member	Regina Blye	PA	AD	....	....	12/03/14
Do	......do	John G. Box	PA	AD	....	....	12/03/10
Do	......do	Karen Louise Braitmayer ..	PA	AD	....	....	12/03/13
Do	......do	Phillip Demal Jenkins	PA	AD	....	....	12/03/12
Do	......do	Christopher S. Hart	PA	AD	....	....	12/03/14
Do	......do	Mathew Ronie McCollough	PA	AD	....	....	12/03/14
Do	......do	Melick K. Neil	PA	AD	....	....	12/03/11
Do	......do	Howard A. Rosenblum	PA	AD	....	....	12/03/13
Do	......do	Deborah A. Ryan	PA	AD	....	....	12/03/13
Do	......do	Nancy Ann Starnes	PA	AD	....	....	12/03/12
Do	......do	Gary L. Talbot	PA	AD	....	....	12/03/11
Do	......do	Hans A. Van Winkle	PA	AD	....	....	12/03/12
Do	......do	Vacant	PA	AD	....	....	

ARMED FORCES RETIREMENT HOME

Location	Position	Name of Incumbent	Type of Appt.	Pay Plan	Level, Grade, or Pay	Tenure	Expires
Washington, DC	Deputy Chief Operating Officer and Chief Financial Officer.	Vacant	....	ES	....	....	

ARCTIC RESEARCH COMMISSION

Location	Position	Name of Incumbent	Type of Appt.	Pay Plan	Level, Grade, or Pay	Tenure	Expires
Washington, DC	Chair	Frances A. Ulmer	PA	PD	$587	4 Years	02/26/15
Do	Member	David Benton	PA	PD	$587	4 Years	02/26/16
Do	......do	Mary C. Pete	PA	PD	$587	4 Years	02/26/13
Do	......do	Warren M. Zapol	PA	PD	$587	4 Years	02/26/16
Do	......do	Charles J. Vorosmarty	PA	PD	$587	4 Years	02/26/16
Do	......do	Vacant	PA	PD	....	....	
Do	......do	......do	PA	PD	....	....	
	OFFICE OF THE EXECUTIVE DIRECTOR						
Do	Executive Director	Career Incumbent	CA	ES	....	....	

BARRY GOLDWATER SCHOLARSHIP AND EXCELLENCE IN EDUCATION FOUNDATION

Location	Position	Name of Incumbent	Type of Appt.	Pay Plan	Level, Grade, or Pay	Tenure	Expires
Springfield, VA	Chairman	Peggy Goldwater-Clay	PAS	WC	....	....	
Do	Member	Gwendolyn E. Boyd	PAS	WC	....	....	
Do	......do	Marcos Edward Galindo	PAS	WC	....	....	
Do	......do	Charles R. Korsmo	PAS	WC	....	....	
Do	......do	Laurie A. Nichols	PAS	WC	....	....	
Do	......do	Maria E. Rengifo-Ruess	PAS	WC	....	....	
Do	......do	Charles P. Ruch	PAS	WC	....	....	
Do	......do	John H. Yopp	PAS	WC	....	....	
	OFFICE OF THE EXECUTIVE SECRETARY						
Do	President	W. Frank Gilmore	NA	ES	....	....	

BROADCASTING BOARD OF GOVERNORS

Location	Position	Name of Incumbent	Type of Appt.	Pay Plan	Level, Grade, or Pay	Tenure	Expires
	BOARD OF GOVERNORS						
Washington, DC	Chairman	Vacant	PAS	AD			
Do	Member	Susan McCue	PAS	AD			08/13/11
Do	......do	Dana Perino	PAS	AD			08/13/12
Do	......do	Vacant	PAS	AD			
Do	......do	Dennis M. Mulhaupt	PAS	AD			08/13/11
Do	......do	Michael P. Meehan	PAS	AD			08/13/10
Do	......do	Michael Lynton	PAS	AD			08/13/12
Do	......do	Victor H. Ashe	PAS	AD			08/13/10
	INTERNATIONAL BROADCASTING BUREAU						
Do	Director	Richard M. Lobo	PAS	EX	IV		
Do	Deputy Director	Career Incumbent	CA	ES			
Do	Chief of Staff	......do	CA	ES			
Do	General Counsel	Vacant		ES			
Do	Deputy General Counsel	Career Incumbent	CA	ES			
Do	Chief Financial Officer	......do	CA	ES			
Do	Director, Communications and External Affairs.	......do	CA	ES			
Do	Director, Office of Technology Services and Innovation.	......do	CA	ES			
Do	Deputy for Engineering and Transmission Services.	......do	CA	ES			
Do	Director, Performance Review	......do	CA	ES			
Do	Director, Media and Social Innovation Center	Robert J. Bole	TA	ES			06/26/14
Do	Director, Strategy and Development	Bruce Andrew Sherman	TA	ES			01/24/15
Do	Senior Advisor	Career Incumbent	CA	ES			
Tinang Island, Philippines.	Station Manager	......do	CA	FE			
Kuwait, Kuwait	......do	......do	CA	FE			
	Voice of America						
Washington, DC	Director, Voice of America	David Ensor	NA	ES			
Do	Chief of Staff	Career Incumbent	CA	ES			
Do	Executive Editor	......do	CA	ES			
Do	Associate Director for Language Programming.	......do	CA	ES			
Do	Associate Director for Operations	......do	CA	ES			
	Office of Cuba Broadcasting						
Miami, FL	Director	Carlos Garcia-Perez	NA	ES			
Do	General Manager	Guillermo M. Santa Cruz ..	SC	GS	15		
Do	Confidential Assistant	Ivonne Silva	SC	GS	12		

CENTRAL INTELLIGENCE AGENCY

Location	Position	Name of Incumbent	Type of Appt.	Pay Plan	Level, Grade, or Pay	Tenure	Expires
	OFFICE OF THE DIRECTOR						
Washington, DC	Director	David H. Petraeus	PAS	EX	II	5 Years	09/08/16
Do	Deputy Director	Michael J. Morell	PA	EX	II	5 Years	05/06/15
Do	Statutory Inspector General	David B. Buckley	PAS	EX	III	5 Years	10/06/15
Do	General Counsel	Stephen W. Preston	PAS	EX	III	5 Years	07/01/14

CHEMICAL SAFETY AND HAZARD INVESTIGATION BOARD

Location	Position	Name of Incumbent	Type of Appt.	Pay Plan	Level, Grade, or Pay	Tenure	Expires
Washington, DC	Board Chairperson	Rafael Moure-Eraso	PAS	EX	IV		06/24/15
Do	Board Member	John S. Bresland	PAS	EX	IV		03/14/13
Do	......do	Mark A. Griffon	PAS	EX	IV		06/24/15
Do	......do	Vacant	PAS	EX	IV		
Do	......do	......do	PAS	EX			
Do	General Counsel	Career Incumbent	CA	ES			
Do	Chief Operating Officer	Vacant		ES			
Do	Special Assistant - Deepwater Horizon	Daniel Horowitz	TA	ES		3 Months	04/22/15

CHRISTOPHER COLUMBUS FELLOWSHIP FOUNDATION

Location	Position	Name of Incumbent	Type of Appt.	Pay Plan	Level, Grade, or Pay	Tenure	Expires
Newton, MA	Chairman	Maria Lombardo-Trifiletti	PA	AD		6 Years	10/02/14
Canton, MS	Vice Chairman	James H. Herring	PA	AD		6 Years	10/02/12
New Orleans, LA	Member, Board of Trustees	Cynthia Butler-Mcintyre	PA	AD		6 Years	01/19/15
Las Vegas, NV	......do	Warren G. Hioki	PA	AD		6 Years	12/25/15
Phoenix, AZ	......do	Kimberly A. Owens	PA	AD		6 Years	01/19/15
Williamsburg, VA	......do	Ronald B. Rapoport	PA	AD		6 Years	10/19/14
Seattle, WA	......do	Sima F. Sarrafan	PA	AD		6 Years	01/19/17
Washington, DC	......do	Peter C. Schaumber	PA	AD		6 Years	10/02/16
Woodstock, MD	......do	Anthony C. Wisniewski	PA	AD		6 Years	03/23/13
Auburn, NY	......do	Vacant	PA	AD		6 Years	
Do	......do	......do	PA	AD		6 Years	
Do	......do	......do	PA	AD		6 Years	
Do	......do	......do	PA	AD		6 Years	

COMMISSION ON CIVIL RIGHTS

Location	Position	Name of Incumbent	Type of Appt.	Pay Plan	Level, Grade, or Pay	Tenure	Expires
	COMMISSIONERS						
San Francisco, CA	Chairman	Martin R. Castro	PA	EX	IV		
Concord, MA	Commissioner	Michael Yaki	XS	EX	IV		
Las Vegas, NV	......do	David Kladney	XS	EX	IV		
Washington, DC	......do	Gail Heriot	XS	EX	IV		
Cleveland, OH	......do	Peter N. Kirsanow	PA	EX	IV		
River Forest, IL	......do	Roberta Achtenberg	PA	EX	IV		
Washington, DC	......do	Todd Francis Gaziano	XS	EX	IV		
Do	Special Assistant	John Robert Martin	SC	GS	14		
Do	Vice Chairman	Abigail Thernstrom	PA	EX	IV		
Do	Special Assistant	Alison E. Somin	SC	GS	13		
North Tonawanda, NY.	Special Assistant to the Commissioner	Alec Haniford Deull	SC	GS	14		
Washington, DC	Special Assistant	Nicholas Jeremy Colten	SC	GS	11		
Do	Special Assistant to the Commissioner	Richard S. Schmechel	SC	GS	14		
Do	Special Assistant to the Chairman	Marlene Sallo	SC	GS	14		
Do	Special Assistant to the Commissioner	Tim Fay	SC	GS	14		
	STAFF MEMBERS						
Do	Assistant Staff Director for Civil Rights Evaluation.	Vacant		ES			
Do	Acting Staff Director	......do		ES			
Do	General Counsel	......do		ES			
Do	Staff Director	......do		ES			

COMMISSION OF FINE ARTS

Location	Position	Name of Incumbent	Type of Appt.	Pay Plan	Level, Grade, or Pay	Tenure	Expires
Washington, DC	Chairman	Earl A. Powell III	PA	WC		4 Years	
Do	Vice Chairman	Elizabeth Plater-Zyberk	PA	WC		4 Years	
Do	Commissioner Member	Diana Balmori	PA	WC		4 Years	
Do	......do	Witold Rybczynski	PA	WC		4 Years	
Do	......do	Teresita Fernandez	PA	WC		4 Years	
Do	......do	Philip Freelon	PA	WC		4 Years	
Do	......do	Edwin Schlossberg	PA	WC		4 Years	
	OFFICE OF THE SECRETARY						
Do	Secretary of the Commission	Career Incumbent	CA	ES			

COMMITTEE FOR PURCHASE FROM PEOPLE WHO ARE BLIND OR SEVERELY DISABLED

Location	Position	Name of Incumbent	Type of Appt.	Pay Plan	Level, Grade, or Pay	Tenure	Expires
Arlington, VA	Chairperson	J. Anthony Poleo	PA	WC			
Do	Vice Chairperson	James M. Kesteloot	PA	PD		5 Years	07/29/15
Do	Member	Robert Terence Kelly, Jr.	PA	PD		5 Years	05/02/13
Do	......do	Vacant	PA	WC			
Do	......do	Jan Frye	PA	WC			
Do	......do	Mark F. Heinrich	PA	WC			

COMMITTEE FOR PURCHASE FROM PEOPLE WHO ARE BLIND OR SEVERELY DISABLED—
Continued

Location	Position	Name of Incumbent	Type of Appt.	Pay Plan	Level, Grade, or Pay	Tenure	Expires
Arlington, VA	Member	Paul Laird	PA	WC	....	....	
Do	......do	Pamela Schwenke	PA	WC	....	....	
Do	......do	William Sisk	PA	WC	....	....	
Do	......do	Vacant	PA	WC	....	....	
Do	......do	Anil Lewis	PA	PD	....	5 Years	05/30/12
Do	......do	Karen J. McCulloh	PA	PD	....	5 Years	10/05/16
Do	......do	Lisa Wilusz	PA	WC	....	....	
Do	......do	Perry Edward Anthony	PA	WC	....	....	
Do	......do	Kathleen Martinez	PA	WC	....	....	
Do	Executive Director	Career Incumbent	CA	ES	....	....	

COMMODITY FUTURES TRADING COMMISSION

Location	Position	Name of Incumbent	Type of Appt.	Pay Plan	Level, Grade, or Pay	Tenure	Expires
	OFFICE OF THE CHAIRPERSON						
Washington, DC	Chairperson	Gary Gensler	PAS	EX	III	....	
Do	Commissioner	Scott D. O'Malia	PAS	EX	IV	....	
Do	......do	Bart H. Chilton	PAS	EX	IV	....	
Do	......do	Jill E. Sommers	PAS	EX	IV	....	
Do	......do	Vacant	PAS	OT	....	....	
Chicago, IL	Staff Advisor to the Chief of Staff	Vacant	....	ES	....	....	
Washington, DC	Special Assistant to the Commissioner	Clay L. Pederson	SC	OT	$150,000	....	
Do	Administrative Assistant to the Commissioner.	Shonneice Jones	SC	OT	$61,956	....	
Do	Administrative Assistant	Danielle Nicole Barrett	SC	OT	$62,000	....	
Do	Administrative Assistant to the Commissioner.	Sharon Jean Floyd	SC	OT	$66,848	....	
Do	Director of Legislative Affairs	John Patrick Riley	SC	OT	$182,000	....	
Do	Director, Office of Public Affairs	Steven W. Adamske	SC	OT	$171,825	....	
Do	Public Affairs Specialist (Speechwriter)	Stephanie Allen	SC	OT	$148,511	....	
	DIVISION OF ENFORCEMENT						
Do	Director	Vacant	....	ES	....	....	
	DIVISION OF TRADING AND MARKETS						
Do	Director	......do	....	ES	....	....	

CONSUMER FINANCIAL PROTECTION BUREAU

Location	Position	Name of Incumbent	Type of Appt.	Pay Plan	Level, Grade, or Pay	Tenure	Expires
Washington, DC	Director	Richard Cordray	PAS	EX	II	....	

CONSUMER PRODUCT SAFETY COMMISSION

Location	Position	Name of Incumbent	Type of Appt.	Pay Plan	Level, Grade, or Pay	Tenure	Expires
	OFFICE OF THE CHAIRMAN						
Bethesda, MD	Chairman	Inez M. Tenenbaum	PAS	EX	III	7 Years	10/26/13
Do	Chief of Staff (Legal)	Matthew R. Howsare	SC	GS	15	....	
Do	Special Assistant (Legal)	Elliot F. Kaye	SC	GS	15	....	
Do	......do	Anupama C. Connor	SC	GS	15	....	
Do	Executive Assistant	Dorothy S. Lee	SC	GS	13	....	
	Office of Legislative Affairs						
Do	Director	Christopher R. Day	SC	GS	15	....	
	Office of the General Counsel						
Do	General Counsel	Career Incumbent	CA	ES	....	....	
	Office of Communications						
Do	Director	Scott J. Wolfson	SC	GS	15	....	
	OFFICE OF COMMISSIONERS						
Do	Commissioner	Nancy A. Nord	PAS	EX	IV	7 Years	10/26/12
Do	Special Assistant (Legal)	Joseph J. Martyak	SC	GS	15	....	

CONSUMER PRODUCT SAFETY COMMISSION—Continued

Location	Position	Name of Incumbent	Type of Appt.	Pay Plan	Level, Grade, or Pay	Tenure	Expires
Bethesda, MD	Special Assistant (Legal)	Nathan S. Cardon	SC	GS	13	....	
Do	Staff Assistant	Timothy M. Reggev	SC	GS	9	....	
Do	Commissioner	Anne M. Northup	PAS	EX	IV	7 Years	10/26/11
Do	Special Assistant (Legal)	Gregg S. Avitabile	SC	GS	15	....	
Do	......do	Kelly K. Pearson	SC	GS	15	....	
Do	Staff Assistant	Mark S. Fellin	SC	GS	11	....	
Do	Commissioner	Robert S. Adler	PAS	EX	IV	7 Years	10/26/14
Do	Special Assistant (Legal)	Jason K. Levine	SC	GS	15	....	
Do	......do	Jana L. Fong-Swamidoss ...	SC	GS	15	....	
Do	Executive Assistant	Ophelia McCardell	SC	GS	12	....	
Do	Commissioner	Vacant	PAS	EX	IV	7 Years	10/26/17
	OFFICE OF EXECUTIVE DIRECTOR						
Do	Executive Director	Kenneth R. Hinson	NA	ES	....	....	
Do	Deputy Executive Director, Operations Support.	Career Incumbent	CA	ES	....	....	
Do	Deputy Executive Director, Safety Operations	......do	CA	ES	....	....	
	Office of Hazard Identification and Reduction						
Do	Assistant Executive Director, Hazard Identification and Reduction.	......do	CA	ES	....	....	
Do	Associate Executive Director, Economic Analysis.	......do	CA	ES	....	....	
Rockville, MD	Associate Executive Director, Laboratory Sciences.	......do	CA	ES	....	....	
Bethesda, MD	Associate Executive Director, Epidemiology ...	......do	CA	ES	....	....	
Rockville, MD	Associate Executive Director, Engineering Sciences.	......do	CA	ES	....	....	
Bethesda, MD	Associate Executive Director, Health Sciences	......do	CA	ES	....	....	
	Office of Compliance						
Do	Assistant Executive Director	Vacant	....	ES	....	....	
Do	Deputy Director	Career Incumbent	CA	ES	....	....	
	Office of Information and Technology Services						
Do	Chief Information Officer	......do	CA	ES	....	....	
	Office of Financial Management, Planning, and Evaluation						
Do	Chief Financial Officer	......do	CA	ES	....	....	
	Office of Education, Global Outreach and Small Business Ombudsman						
Do	Director	......do	CA	ES	....	....	
	Office of Import Surveillance						
Do	Director	Vacant	....	ES	....	....	

CONSUMER PRODUCT SAFETY COMMISSION OFFICE OF THE INSPECTOR GENERAL

Location	Position	Name of Incumbent	Type of Appt.	Pay Plan	Level, Grade, or Pay	Tenure	Expires
Bethesda, MD	Inspector General	Career Incumbent	CA	ES	....	....	

CORPORATION FOR NATIONAL AND COMMUNITY SERVICE

Location	Position	Name of Incumbent	Type of Appt.	Pay Plan	Level, Grade, or Pay	Tenure	Expires
	BOARD OF DIRECTORS						
Washington, DC	Member, Chair	Laysha Ward	PAS	WC	....	5 Years	12/27/12
Do	Member, Vice Chair	Eric J. Tanenblatt	PAS	WC	....	5 Years	10/06/12
Do	Member	Rick Christman	PAS	WC	....	5 Years	10/16/12
Do	......do	Julie Fisher Cummings	PAS	WC	....	5 Years	09/14/12
Do	......do	Jane Hartley	PAS	WC	....	5 Years	10/06/14
Do	......do	Hyepin Im	PAS	WC	....	5 Years	10/06/13
Do	......do	Marguerite Kondracke	PAS	WC	....	5 Years	06/10/14
Do	......do	Matthew McCabe	PAS	WC	....	5 Years	10/06/13
Do	......do	James Palmer	PAS	WC	....	5 Years	10/06/12
Do	......do	Lisa Garcia Quiroz	PAS	WC	....	5 Years	02/08/14
Do	......do	Phyllis N. Segal	PAS	WC	....	5 Years	10/06/13
Do	......do	Stan Soloway	PAS	WC	....	5 Years	10/06/12

CORPORATION FOR NATIONAL AND COMMUNITY SERVICE—Continued

Location	Position	Name of Incumbent	Type of Appt.	Pay Plan	Level, Grade, or Pay	Tenure	Expires
	DEPARTMENT OF THE CHIEF EXECUTIVE OFFICER						
Washington, DC	Chief Executive Officer	Wendy M. Spencer	PAS	EX	III	....	
Do	Chief of Staff	Vacant	XS	OT	....	....	
Do	Deputy Chief of Staff for Policy	Asim Mishra	XS	OT	....	....	
Do	Special Assistant	Vacant	XS	OT	....	....	
Do	......do	......do	XS	OT	....	....	
Do	Director of Scheduling and Advance, Senior Advisor for CEO Engagement.	Daniel S. Holt	XS	OT	....	....	
Do	Executive Assistant and Scheduler	Vacant	XS	OT	....	....	
	Office of General Counsel						
Do	General Counsel	Valerie E. Green	XS	OT	....	....	
Do	Executive Assistant	Phyllis Rae Green	XS	OT	....	....	
	Office of Government Relations						
Do	Director	Vacant	XS	OT	....	....	
Do	Deputy Director	Rebecca Claster	XS	OT	....	....	
Do	Deputy Director, Intergovernmental Relations	Kimberly L. Allman	XS	OT	....	....	
Do	Senior Legislative Assistant	Collin E. Burton	XS	OT	....	....	
	Office of Strategy and Special Initiatives						
Do	Chief Strategy Officer	Vacant	XS	OT	....	....	
Do	Senior Advisor	Susannah Laleh Washburn	XS	OT	....	....	
	Office of External Affairs						
Do	Chief	James L. Fetig	XS	OT	....	....	
Do	Director of Public Affairs	Vacant	XS	OT	....	....	
Do	Senior Communications Advisor	Alexander McCandless Scott.	XS	OT	....	....	
Do	Public Affairs Specialist	Tess Hetzel	XS	OT	....	....	
Do	Press Secretary	Vacant	XS	OT	....	....	
Do	Deputy Press Secretary	Kate E. Enos	XS	OT	....	....	
Do	Speech Writer	Larae N. Booker	XS	OT	....	....	
Do	Director of Digital Media	Sacha Cohen	XS	OT	....	....	
Do	Senior Advisor to the CEO and Director of Partnerships and Engagement.	John D. Kelly	XS	OT	....	....	
Do	Assistant Director, Faith Based and Neighborhood Partnerships.	Clay N. Middleton	XS	OT	....	....	
	DEPARTMENT OF THE CHIEF OF PROGRAM OPERATIONS						
Do	Chief of Program Operations	Idara Umoh Nickelson	XS	OT	....	....	
Do	Senior Advisor for Wounded Warrior, Veteran and Military Family Initiatives.	Koby J. Langley	XS	OT	....	....	
	Office of AmeriCorps VISTA						
Do	Director	Mary W. Strasser	XS	OT	....	....	
	Office of AmeriCorps State and National						
Do	Director of AmeriCorps	William C. Basl	XS	OT	....	....	
	Office of National Senior Service Corps						
Do	Director of Senior Corps/Strategic Advisor for Veterans and Military Families.	Erwin J. Tan	XS	OT	....	....	
	Office of Social Innovation Fund						
Lawrence, KS	Director	Paul L. Carttar	XS	OT	....	....	
Washington, DC	Deputy Director	Vacant	XS	OT	....	....	
	OFFICE OF THE INSPECTOR GENERAL						
Do	Inspector General	Deborah J. Jeffrey	PAS	EX	III	....	

COUNCIL OF INSPECTORS GENERAL ON INTEGRITY AND EFFICIENCY

Location	Position	Name of Incumbent	Type of Appt.	Pay Plan	Level, Grade, or Pay	Tenure	Expires
Washington, DC	Executive Director	Career Incumbent	CA	ES	....	....	
Do	Executive Director for the Inspector General Training Institute.	Vacant	....	ES	....	....	

COURT SERVICES AND OFFENDER SUPERVISION AGENCY FOR THE DISTRICT OF COLUMBIA

Location	Position	Name of Incumbent	Type of Appt.	Pay Plan	Level, Grade, or Pay	Tenure	Expires
Washington, DC	Director	Nancy M. Ware	PAS	EX	IV	....	
	PRETRIAL SERVICES AGENCY						
Do	Director	Vacant	....	ES	....	....	

DEFENSE NUCLEAR FACILITIES SAFETY BOARD

Location	Position	Name of Incumbent	Type of Appt.	Pay Plan	Level, Grade, or Pay	Tenure	Expires
Washington, DC	Chairman	Peter S. Winokur	PAS	EX	III	....	
Do	Vice Chairman	Jessie H. Roberson	PAS	EX	III	....	
Do	Member	Vacant	PAS	EX	III	....	
Do	......do	Joseph F. Bader	PAS	EX	III	....	
Do	......do	John E. Mansfield	PAS	EX	III	....	
Do	General Counsel	Vacant	....	ES	....	....	
Do	General Manager	......do	....	ES	....	....	
Do	Senior Counsel for Nuclear Safety Engineering.	......do	XS	SL	....	....	

DELTA REGIONAL AUTHORITY

Location	Position	Name of Incumbent	Type of Appt.	Pay Plan	Level, Grade, or Pay	Tenure	Expires
Clarksdale, MS	Federal Co-Chairman	Christopher A. Masingill ...	PAS	EX	V	4 Years	
Do	Alternate Federal Co-Chairman	Michael G. Marshall	PA	EX	IV	4 Years	

DWIGHT D. EISENHOWER MEMORIAL COMMISSION

Location	Position	Name of Incumbent	Type of Appt.	Pay Plan	Level, Grade, or Pay	Tenure	Expires
Washington, DC	Chairman	Rocco C. Siciliano	PA	WC	....	....	
Do	Commissioner	Alfred Geduldig	PA	WC	....	....	
Do	......do	Susan Banes Harris	PA	WC	....	....	
Do	Executive Director	Carl W. Reddel	XS	AD	$155,500	....	

ENVIRONMENTAL PROTECTION AGENCY

Location	Position	Name of Incumbent	Type of Appt.	Pay Plan	Level, Grade, or Pay	Tenure	Expires
	OFFICE OF THE ADMINISTRATOR						
Washington, DC	Administrator	Lisa P. Jackson	PAS	EX	II	....	
Do	Deputy Administrator	Robert W. Perciasepe	PAS	EX	III	....	
Do	Chief of Staff	Diane E. Thompson	NA	ES	....	....	
Do	Deputy Chief of Staff	Career Incumbent	CA	ES	....	....	
Do	Deputy Chief of Staff (Operations)	Jose T. Lozano	NA	ES	....	....	
Do	Senior Climate Policy Counsel	Vacant	....	ES	....	....	
Do	Special Assistant to the Senior Climate Policy Counsel.	Charles S. Imohiosen	SC	GS	15	....	
Do	Senior Policy Counsel to the Administrator	Robert M. Sussman	NA	ES	....	....	
Do	Senior Advisor to the Administrator	Vacant	....	ES	....	....	
Do	Counselor to the Administrator for Agricultural Policy.	Lawrence E. Elworth	NA	ES	....	....	
Do	Director, Office of Gulf Coast Ecosystem Restoration.	John H. Hankinson, Jr.	NA	ES	....	....	
Do	Deputy Director, Office of Gulf Coast Ecosystem Restoration.	Vacant	....	ES	....	....	
Do	White House Liaison	Jon Monger	SC	GS	12	....	
Do	Deputy White House Liaison	Kelley S. Smith	SC	GS	11	....	
Do	Policy Analyst	Christopher L. Busch	SC	GS	12	....	
Do	Trip Coordinator	Katharine M. Bluhm	SC	GS	11	....	
Do	Special Representative	Shalini Vajjhala	SC	GS	15	....	
	Scheduling Staff						
Do	Director of Scheduling and Advance	Elizabeth A. Ashwell	SC	GS	14	....	
Do	Deputy Director of Scheduling	Ryan M. Robison	SC	GS	11	....	

ENVIRONMENTAL PROTECTION AGENCY—Continued

Location	Position	Name of Incumbent	Type of Appt.	Pay Plan	Level, Grade, or Pay	Tenure	Expires
	Advance Staff						
Washington, DC	Deputy Director for Advance	Adrian K. Collins	SC	GS	12	....	
Do	Advance Specialist	Jeffrey Tate	SC	GS	11	....	
	Office of the Executive Services						
Do	Director	Eric E. Wachter	SC	GS	15	....	
	Office of Regional Operations						
Do	Director	Janet L. Woodka	NA	ES		....	
	Office of Homeland Security						
Do	Deputy Associate Administrator	Career Incumbent	CA	ES		....	
Do	Associate Administrator	Deborah Y. Dietrich	NA	ES		....	
	Office of Children's Health Protection						
Do	Director	Career Incumbent	CA	ES		....	
	Office of Federal Advisory Committee Management and Outreach						
Do	Director	Vacant	....	ES		....	
	Office of Civil Rights						
Do	Director	Career Incumbent	CA	ES		....	
	Office of Small and Disadvantaged Business Utilization						
Do	Director	......do	CA	ES		....	
	Science Advisory Board						
Do	Director	......do	CA	ES		....	
	Office of Congressional and Intergovernmental Relations						
Do	Associate Administrator	Arvin R. Ganesan	NA	ES		....	
Do	Principal Deputy Associate Administrator	Career Incumbent	CA	ES		....	
Do	Deputy Associate Administrator for Office of Congressional Affairs.	Laura E. Vaught	SC	GS	15	....	
Do	Deputy Associate Administrator for Intergovernmental Relations.	Sarah H. Pallone	SC	GS	15	....	
Do	Special Assistant	Marcus K. McClendon	SC	GS	13	....	
	Office of External Affairs and Environmental Education						
Do	Associate Administrator	Vacant	....	ES		....	
Do	Principal Deputy Associate Administrator	......do		ES		....	
Do	Deputy Associate Administrator	Stephanie A. Owens	NA	ES		....	
Do	Deputy Associate Administrator	Brendan C. Gilfillan	SC	GS	14	....	
Do	Director, Office of Environmental Education ..	Vacant	....	ES		....	
Do	Director, Office of Public Engagement	Drucilla Ealons	SC	GS	15	....	
Do	Senior Speech Writer	Michael Moats	SC	GS	14	....	
Do	Deputy Press Secretary	Alisha R. Johnson	SC	GS	12	....	
Do	Assistant Press Secretary	Robert K. Delp, Jr.	SC	GS	9	....	
Do	......do	Andra M. Belknap	SC	GS	9	....	
Do	Special Assistant to the Associate Administrator.	Shira A. Sternberg	SC	GS	12	....	
	Office of Policy						
Do	Associate Administrator	Michael L. Goo	NA	ES		....	
Do	Principal Deputy Associate Administrator for Policy, Economics and Innovation.	Vacant	....	ES		....	
Do	Deputy Associate Administrator for Policy	Bernice I. Corman	NA	ES		....	
Do	Senior Advisor	Vacant	....	ES		....	
Do	Director, National Center for Environmental Economics.	Career Incumbent	CA	ES		....	
Do	Director, National Center for Environmental Innovation.	Vacant	....	ES		....	
Do	Director, Office of Regulatory Policy and Management.	Career Incumbent	CA	ES		....	
Do	Director, Office of Strategic Environmental Management.	......do	CA	ES		....	
Do	Special Assistant to the Associate Administrator for Policy, Economics and Innovation.	Sarah Dale	SC	GS	12	....	
	OFFICE OF THE CHIEF FINANCIAL OFFICER						
Do	Chief Financial Officer	Barbara Bennett	PAS	EX	IV	....	
	OFFICE OF ENVIRONMENTAL INFORMATION						
Do	Assistant Administrator	Malcolm D. Jackson	PAS	EX	IV	....	
Do	Principal Deputy Assistant Administrator	Career Incumbent	CA	ES		....	

ENVIRONMENTAL PROTECTION AGENCY—Continued

Location	Position	Name of Incumbent	Type of Appt.	Pay Plan	Level, Grade, or Pay	Tenure	Expires
Washington, DC	Deputy Assistant Administrator	Vacant	....	ES	....	....	
	Office of Information Analysis and Access						
Do	Director	Career Incumbent	CA	ES	....	....	
Do	Deputy Director	Vacant	....	ES	....	....	
	Office of Information Collection						
Do	Director	Career Incumbent	CA	ES	....	....	
Do	Deputy Director	Vacant	....	ES	....	....	
	Office of Technology Operations and Planning						
Do	Director	Career Incumbent	CA	ES	....	....	
Do	Deputy Director	......do	CA	ES	....	....	
	OFFICE OF ADMINISTRATION AND RESOURCES MANAGEMENT						
Do	Assistant Administrator	Craig E. Hooks	PAS	EX	IV	....	
Do	Principal Deputy Assistant Administrator	Career Incumbent	CA	ES	....	....	
Do	Federal Environmental Executive	Jonathan P. Powers	NA	ES	....	....	
	OFFICE OF ENFORCEMENT AND COMPLIANCE ASSURANCE						
Do	Assistant Administrator	Cynthia Giles	PAS	EX	IV	....	
Do	Principal Deputy Assistant Administrator	Career Incumbent	CA	ES	....	....	
Do	Deputy Assistant Administrator	Steven Chester	NA	ES	....	....	
Do	Deputy Associate Assistant Administrator for Environmental Justice.	Career Incumbent	CA	ES	....	....	
Do	Senior Legal Advisor	Vacant	....	ES	....	....	
Do	Senior Enforcement Counsel	......do	....	ES	....	....	
	Office of Administration and Policy						
Do	Director	Career Incumbent	CA	ES	....	....	
	Office of Compliance						
Do	Senior Enforcement Counsel	Vacant	....	ES	....	....	
	Office of Criminal Enforcement, Forensics and Training						
Do	Program Advisor	......do	....	ES	....	....	
	Office of Federal Activities						
Do	Director	Career Incumbent	CA	ES	....	....	
	OFFICE OF THE GENERAL COUNSEL						
Do	General Counsel	C. Scott Fulton	PAS	EX	IV	....	
Do	Principal Deputy General Counsel	Career Incumbent	CA	ES	....	....	
Do	Deputy General Counsel	Tseming Yang	NA	ES	....	....	
Do	......do	Avi S. Garbow	NA	ES	....	....	
Do	Principal Associate General Counsel	Vacant	....	ES	....	....	
Do	Principal Associate General Counsel for Special Litigation and Emergency Response.	......do	....	ES	....	....	
	Air and Radiation Law Office						
Do	Associate General Counsel	Career Incumbent	CA	ES	....	....	
	Alternative Dispute Resolution Law Office						
Do	Director	......do	CA	ES	....	....	
	Civil Rights and Finance Law Office						
Do	Associate General Counsel	......do	CA	ES	....	....	
	Cross-Cutting Law Office						
Do	Associate General Counsel	......do	CA	ES	....	....	
	Pesticides and Toxic Substances Law Office						
Do	Associate General Counsel	......do	CA	ES	....	....	
	Solid Waste and Emergency Response Law Office						
Do	Associate General Counsel	......do	CA	ES	....	....	
	Water Law Office						
Do	Associate General Counsel	......do	CA	ES	....	....	
	General Law Office						
Do	Associate General Counsel	......do	CA	ES	....	....	
	OFFICE OF INTERNATIONAL AND TRIBAL AFFAIRS						
Do	Assistant Administrator	Michelle DePass	PAS	EX	IV	....	
Do	Principal Deputy Assistant Administrator	Vacant	....	ES	....	....	
Do	Deputy Assistant Administrator	Career Incumbent	CA	ES	....	....	
Do	Senior Advisor	Vacant	....	ES	....	....	

ENVIRONMENTAL PROTECTION AGENCY—Continued

Location	Position	Name of Incumbent	Type of Appt.	Pay Plan	Level, Grade, or Pay	Tenure	Expires
Washington, DC	Senior Counsel (Environmental Governance)	Career Incumbent	CA	ES	....	....	
	Office of Global Affairs and Policy						
Do	Director	......do	CA	ES	....	....	
	Office of Management Operations						
Do	Director, Office of Management and International Services.	......do	CA	ES	....	....	
	Office of Regional and Bilateral Affairs						
Do	Director	......do	CA	ES	....	....	
	American Indian Environmental Office						
Do	Director	......do	CA	ES	....	....	
	OFFICE OF WATER						
Do	Assistant Administrator	Vacant	PAS	EX	IV	....	
Do	Deputy Assistant Administrator	Nancy Stoner	NA	ES	....	....	
Do	.......do	Career Incumbent	CA	ES	....	....	
Do	Associate Assistant Administrator	Vacant	....	ES	....	....	
Do	Senior Advisor	Kenneth J. Kopocis	TA	ES	....	....	12/03/12
	Office of Ground Water and Drinking Water						
Do	Director	Vacant	....	ES	....	....	
Do	Deputy Director	Career Incumbent	CA	ES	....	....	
	Office of Science and Technology						
Do	Director	.....do	CA	ES	....	....	
Do	Deputy Director	.....do	CA	ES	....	....	
	Office of Waste Water Management						
Do	Director	Vacant	....	ES	....	....	
Do	Deputy Director	Career Incumbent	CA	ES	....	....	
	Office of Wetlands, Oceans and Watersheds						
Do	Director	......do	CA	ES	....	....	
Do	Deputy Director	......do	CA	ES	....	....	
	OFFICE OF SOLID WASTE AND EMERGENCY RESPONSE						
Do	Assistant Administrator	Mathy Stanislaus	PAS	EX	IV	....	
Do	Principal Deputy Assistant Administrator	Career Incumbent	CA	ES	....	....	
Do	Deputy Assistant Administrator	Elisabeth G. Feldt	NA	ES	....	....	
Do	Associate Assistant Administrator	Vacant	....	ES	....	....	
	Federal Facilities Restoration and Reuse Office						
Arlington, VA	Director	Career Incumbent	CA	ES	....	....	
	Office of Emergency Management						
Washington, DC	Director	......do	CA	ES	....	....	
Do	Deputy Director	......do	CA	ES	....	....	
	Office of Brownfields Cleanup and Redevelopment						
Do	Director	......do	CA	ES	....	....	
	Office of Program Management						
Do	Director	Vacant	....	ES	....	....	
	Office of Superfund Remediation and Technology Innovation						
Arlington, VA	Director	Career Incumbent	CA	ES	....	....	
Do	Deputy Director	......do	CA	ES	....	....	
	Office of Resource Conservation and Recovery						
Do	Director	......do	CA	ES	....	....	
Do	Deputy Director	......do	CA	ES	....	....	
	OFFICE OF AIR AND RADIATION						
Washington, DC	Assistant Administrator	Regina McCarthy	PAS	EX	IV	....	
Do	Principle Deputy Assistant Administrator	Janet G. McCabe	NA	ES	....	....	
Do	Deputy Assistant Administrator	Career Incumbent	CA	ES	....	....	
Do	Associate Assistant Administrator	Joel C. Beauvais	NA	ES	....	....	
Do	Senior Advisor	Vacant	....	ES	....	....	
Do	Senior Counsel	Joseph M. Goffman	SC	GS	15	....	
	Office of Air Quality Planning and Standards						
Durham, NC	Director	Career Incumbent	CA	ES	....	....	
	Office of Transportation and Air Quality						
Washington, DC	Director	.....do	CA	ES	....	....	
Ann Arbor, MI	Deputy Director	.....do	CA	ES	....	....	

ENVIRONMENTAL PROTECTION AGENCY—Continued

Location	Position	Name of Incumbent	Type of Appt.	Pay Plan	Level, Grade, or Pay	Tenure	Expires
	Office of Radiation and Indoor Air						
Arlington, VA	Director	Career Incumbent	CA	ES	....	....	
	Office of Atmospheric Programs						
Washington, DC	Director	......do	CA	ES	....	....	
	OFFICE OF CHEMICAL SAFETY AND POLLUTION PREVENTION						
Do	Assistant Administrator	Vacant	PAS	EX	IV	....	
Do	Principal Deputy Assistant Administrator	Career Incumbent	CA	ES		....	
Do	Deputy Assistant Administrator	Vacant	....	ES		....	
Do	......do	......do	....	ES		....	
	Office of Pesticide Programs						
Arlington, VA	Director	Career Incumbent	CA	ES		....	
Do	Deputy Director (Programs)	Vacant	....	ES		....	
Do	Deputy Director (Management)	Career Incumbent	CA	ES		....	
	Office of Pollution Prevention and Toxics						
Washington, DC	Director	......do	CA	ES		....	
Do	Deputy Director (Program Management)	......do	CA	ES		....	
Do	Deputy Director (Programs)	......do	CA	ES		....	
	Office of Science Coordination and Policy						
Do	Director	......do	CA	ES		....	
	OFFICE OF RESEARCH AND DEVELOPMENT						
Do	Assistant Administrator	Vacant	PAS	EX	IV	....	
Do	Principal Deputy Assistant Administrator	Career Incumbent	CA	ES		....	
Do	Deputy Assistant Administrator (Science)	Vacant	....	ES		....	
Do	Associate Assistant Administrator	Career Incumbent	CA	ES		....	
Do	Senior Advisor	......do	CA	ES		....	
Durham, NC	......do	......do	CA	ES		....	
Washington, DC	Director for Sustainable Development	......do	CA	ES		....	
	Office of the Science Advisor						
Do	Chief Scientist to the Science Advisor	......do	CA	ES		....	
Do	Earth Observation Systems Executive	Vacant	....	ES		....	
	Office of Science Policy						
Do	Director	Career Incumbent	CA	ES		....	
	REGIONAL OFFICES						
	Region 1- Boston, Massachusetts						
Boston, MA	Regional Administrator	H. Curtis Spalding	NA	ES		....	
Do	Deputy Regional Administrator	Career Incumbent	CA	ES		....	
	Region 2 - New York, New York						
New York, NY	Regional Administrator	Judith Enck	NA	ES		....	
Do	Deputy Regional Administrator	Career Incumbent	CA	ES		....	
Do	Regional Climate Change Program Advisor ...	Paul F. Simon	TA	ES		....	10/22/13
	Region 3 - Philadelphia, Pennsylvania						
Philadelphia, PA	Regional Administrator	Shawn Garvin	NA	ES		....	
Do	Deputy Regional Administrator	Career Incumbent	CA	ES		....	
	Region 4 - Atlanta, Georgia						
Atlanta, GA	Regional Administrator	Gwendolyn R. Keyes Fleming.	NA	ES		....	
Do	Deputy Regional Administrator	Career Incumbent	CA	ES		....	
	Region 5 - Chicago, Illinois						
Chicago, IL	Regional Administrator	Susan J. Hedman	NA	ES		....	
Do	Deputy Regional Administrator	Career Incumbent	CA	ES		....	
	Region 6 - Dallas, Texas						
Dallas, TX	Regional Administrator	Vacant	....	ES		....	
Do	Deputy Regional Administrator	Career Incumbent	CA	ES		....	
Do	Senior Advisor for Coastal Restoration, Climate Change and Public Outreach.	William K. Honker	TA	ES		....	06/04/13
Do	Senior Advisor for US/Mexico Border and Emerging Programs.	William L. Luthans	TA	ES		....	06/18/13
	Region 7 - Kansas City, Kansas						
Kansas City, KS	Regional Administrator	Karl B. Brooks	NA	ES		....	
Do	Deputy Regional Administrator	Vacant		ES		....	
	Region 8 - Denver, Colorado						
Denver, CO	Regional Administrator	James B. Martin	NA	ES		....	
Do	Deputy Regional Administrator	Career Incumbent	CA	ES		....	

ENVIRONMENTAL PROTECTION AGENCY—Continued

Location	Position	Name of Incumbent	Type of Appt.	Pay Plan	Level, Grade, or Pay	Tenure	Expires
Denver, CO	Assistant Regional Administrator for Enforcement, Compliance and Environmental Justice.	Career Incumbent	CA	ES	....	....	
Do	Senior Interagency Project Advisor	Eddie A. Sierra	TA	ES	....	....	06/04/13
	Region 9 - San Francisco, California						
San Francisco, CA	Regional Administrator	Jared Blumenfeld	NA	ES	....	....	
Do	Deputy Regional Administrator	Vacant	....	ES	....	....	
Do	Senior Policy Advisor	Nancy J. Ryerson	TA	ES	....	....	06/25/13
	Region 10 - Seattle, Washington						
Seattle, WA	Regional Administrator	Dennis J. McLerran	NA	ES	....	....	
Do	Deputy Regional Administrator	Career Incumbent	CA	ES	....	....	

ENVIRONMENTAL PROTECTION AGENCY OFFICE OF THE INSPECTOR GENERAL

Location	Position	Name of Incumbent	Type of Appt.	Pay Plan	Level, Grade, or Pay	Tenure	Expires
Washington, DC	Inspector General	Arthur A. Elkins, Jr.	PAS	EX	III	....	

EQUAL EMPLOYMENT OPPORTUNITY COMMISSION

Location	Position	Name of Incumbent	Type of Appt.	Pay Plan	Level, Grade, or Pay	Tenure	Expires
	OFFICE OF THE CHAIR						
Washington, DC	Chairman	Jacqueline A. Berrien	PAS	EX	III	....	
Do	Commissioner	Chai R. Feldblum	PAS	EX	IV	....	
Do	......do	Victoria A. Lipnic	PAS	EX	IV	....	
Do	......do	Constance S. Barker	PAS	EX	IV	....	
Do	......do	Vacant	PAS	EX	IV	....	
Do	Chief Operating Officer	Claudia A. Withers	NA	ES	....	....	
Do	Senior Advisor	Vacant	....	ES	....	....	
Do	Senior Advisor (Information Technology)	......do	....	ES	....	....	
Do	Director, Policy Management and Coordination.	......do	....	ES	....	....	
Do	Senior Attorney Advisor (Senior Counsel)	Patrick Olen Patterson	NA	ES	....	....	
Do	Senior Policy Analyst	Joi Olivia Chaney	SC	GS	15	....	
	OFFICE OF THE GENERAL COUNSEL						
Do	General Counsel	Patrick David Lopez	PAS	EX	V	....	
Do	Associate General Counsel for Litigation Management Services.	Career Incumbent	CA	ES	....	....	
Do	Deputy General Counsel	......do	CA	ES	....	....	
Do	Associate General Counsel for Appellate Services.	Vacant	....	ES	....	....	
Do	Associate General Counsel for Systemic Litigation Services.	Career Incumbent	CA	ES	....	....	
Do	Senior Litigation Project Manager	Vacant	....	ES	....	....	
Do	Senior Litigation Project Manager	......do	....	ES	....	....	
	OFFICE OF HUMAN RESOURCES						
Do	Chief Human Capital Officer	Career Incumbent	CA	ES	....	....	
	OFFICE OF COMMUNICATIONS AND LEGISLATIVE AFFAIRS						
Do	Director	Todd A. Cox	NA	ES	....	....	
	OFFICE OF RESEARCH, INFORMATION AND PLANNING						
Do	Director	Career Incumbent	CA	ES	....	....	
	OFFICE OF INFORMATION TECHNOLOGY						
Do	Chief Information Officer	......do	CA	ES	....	....	
	OFFICE OF LEGAL COUNSEL						
Do	Associate Legal Counsel	Vacant	....	ES	....	....	
Do	Legal Counsel	Career Incumbent	CA	ES	....	....	
Do	Deputy Legal Counsel	Vacant	....	ES	....	....	
	OFFICE OF CHIEF FINANCIAL OFFICER						
Do	Chief Financial Officer	Career Incumbent	CA	ES	....	....	

EQUAL EMPLOYMENT OPPORTUNITY COMMISSION—Continued

Location	Position	Name of Incumbent	Type of Appt.	Pay Plan	Level, Grade, or Pay	Tenure	Expires
	OFFICE OF FEDERAL OPERATIONS						
Washington, DC	Director	Career Incumbent	CA	ES	....	....	
Do	Director, Federal Sector Programs	......do	CA	ES	....	....	
Do	Director, Appelate Review Programs	Vacant	....	ES	....	....	
	OFFICE OF FIELD PROGRAMS						
Do	Director	Career Incumbent	CA	ES	....	....	
Do	Chief Administrative Judge	Vacant	....	ES	....	....	
Do	National Legal/Enforcement Executive Advisor.	Career Incumbent	CA	ES	....	....	
	State and Local Programs						
Do	Director	......do	CA	ES	....	....	
Dallas, TX	Program Manager	......do	CA	ES	....	....	
Houston, TX	......do	......do	CA	ES	....	....	
Indianapolis, IN	......do	......do	CA	ES	....	....	
Los Angeles, CA	......do	......do	CA	ES	....	....	
Memphis, TN	......do	......do	CA	ES	....	....	
Miami, FL	......do	......do	CA	ES	....	....	
New York, NY	......do	......do	CA	ES	....	....	
Philipsburg, PA	......do	......do	CA	ES	....	....	
Phoenix, AZ	......do	......do	CA	ES	....	....	
San Francisco, CA	......do	......do	CA	ES	....	....	
St. Louis, MO	......do	......do	CA	ES	....	....	
Charlotte, NC	......do	......do	CA	ES	....	....	
Birmingham, AL	......do	......do	CA	ES	....	....	
Atlanta, GA	......do	......do	CA	ES	....	....	
Chicago, IL	......do	......do	CA	ES	....	....	

EQUAL EMPLOYMENT OPPORTUNITY COMMISSION OFFICE OF THE INSPECTOR GENERAL

Location	Position	Name of Incumbent	Type of Appt.	Pay Plan	Level, Grade, or Pay	Tenure	Expires
Washington, DC	Inspector General	Career Incumbent	CA	ES	....	....	

EXPORT-IMPORT BANK

Location	Position	Name of Incumbent	Type of Appt.	Pay Plan	Level, Grade, or Pay	Tenure	Expires
	Office of the Chairman						
Washington, DC	President and Chairman	Fred P. Hochberg	PAS	EX	III	4 Years	01/20/13
Do	Executive Vice President and Chief Operating Officer.	Alice P. Albright	SC	SL	....	3 Years	
Do	Chief of Staff	Kevin P. Varney	SC	SL	....	....	
Do	Deputy Chief of Staff	Mona K. Jabbour	SC	GS	14	3 Years	
Do	Special Assistant to the Chief of Staff	Kenneth E. Milstead	SC	GS	10	....	
Do	Senior Advisor to the Chairman	Peter R. Arulanantham	SC	GS	15	....	
Do	Executive Secretary	David R. Brooks	SC	GS	13	3 Years	
	BOARD OF DIRECTORS						
Do	First Vice President and Vice Chairman	Wanda F. Felton	PAS	EX	IV	2 Years	01/20/13
Do	Member	Patricia M. Loui-Schmicker	PAS	EX	IV	4 Years	01/20/15
Do	......do	Larry W. Walther	PAS	EX	IV	2 Years	01/20/13
Do	......do	Sean R. Mulvaney	PAS	EX	IV	4 Years	01/20/15
	OFFICE OF COMMUNICATIONS						
Do	Senior Vice President for Communications	Daniel W. Reilly	SC	SL	....	....	
Do	Senior Advisor	Jamie Elizabeth Radice	SC	GS	14	....	
Do	Director of Scheduling	Carolyn J. Schopp	SC	GS	13	....	
Do	Speechwriter	Robert B. Rackleff	SC	GS	14	....	
	OFFICE OF THE GENERAL COUNSEL						
Do	Senior Vice President and General Counsel ...	Angela Mariana Freyre	SC	SL	....	3 Years	
	OFFICE OF CONGRESSIONAL AFFAIRS						
Do	Senior Vice President for Congressional Affairs.	Scott P. Schloegel	SC	SL	....	3 Years	
	EXPORT FINANCE GROUP						
Do	Senior Vice President	John A. McAdams	SC	SL	....	....	

EXPORT-IMPORT BANK—Continued

Location	Position	Name of Incumbent	Type of Appt.	Pay Plan	Level, Grade, or Pay	Tenure	Expires
	Office of Inspector General (OIG)						
Washington, DC	Inspector General	Osvaldo L. Gratacos	PAS	EX	III	....	

FARM CREDIT ADMINISTRATION

Location	Position	Name of Incumbent	Type of Appt.	Pay Plan	Level, Grade, or Pay	Tenure	Expires
	OFFICE OF THE BOARD						
McLean, VA	Chairman	Leland Anders Strom	PAS	EX	III	6 Years	10/13/12
Do	Member	Jill L. Long Thompson	PAS	EX	IV	6 Years	05/21/14
Do	.....do	Kenneth A. Spearman	PAS	EX	IV	6 Years	05/21/16
Do	Executive Assistant to the Member	Inga P. Smulkstys	SC	VH	....	....	
	Office of Chief Executive Officer						
Do	Director	Michael Alan Stokke	SC	VH	$209,501	....	
Do	Associate Director of Congressional Affairs	James Russell Middleton ...	SC	VH	$191,104	....	

FEDERAL COMMUNICATIONS COMMISSION

Location	Position	Name of Incumbent	Type of Appt.	Pay Plan	Level, Grade, or Pay	Tenure	Expires
	OFFICE OF THE CHAIRMAN						
Washington, DC ...	Chairman	Julius M. Genachowski	PAS	EX	III	....	
Do	Commissioner	Robert McDowell	PAS	EX	IV	....	
Do	.....do	Mignon L. Clyburn	PAS	EX	IV	....	
Do	.....do	Jessica Rosenworcel	PAS	EX	IV	....	
Do	.....do	Ajit V. Pai	PAS	EX	IV	....	
Do	Chief of Staff	Zachary Katz	NA	ES	....	....	
Do	Senior Advisor to the Chairman	Sherrese M. Smith	XS	SL	$165,300	....	
Do	Senior Advisor to the Commissioner	Angela E. Giancarlo	XS	SL	$165,300	....	
Do	.....do	Vacant	XS	SL		....	
Do	.....do	Matthew B. Berry	XS	SL	$165,300	....	
Do	.....do	David Grimaldi	XS	SL	$163,000	....	
	OFFICE OF LEGISLATIVE AFFAIRS						
Do	Deputy Director, OLA	Christopher J. Lewis	SC	GS	14	....	
	INTERNATIONAL BUREAU						
Do	Bureau Chief	Career Incumbent	CA	ES		....	
Do	Deputy Bureau Chief	......do	CA	ES		....	
	OFFICE OF STRATEGIC PLANNING AND POLICY ANALYSIS						
Do	Director	Vacant		ES	....	....	
Do	Deputy Director	.....do		ES	....	....	
Do	.....do	Career Incumbent	CA	ES	....	....	
Do	Senior Legal Advisor	......do	CA	SL	....	....	
Do	Senior Economic Advisor	......do	CA	SL	....	....	
Do	.....do	......do	CA	SL	....	....	
Do	Advisor	Russell Caditz-Peck	SC	GS	11	....	
	OFFICE OF THE MANAGING DIRECTOR						
Do	Managing Director	Career Incumbent	CA	ES	....	....	
Do	Deputy Managing Director	......do	CA	ES	....	....	
Do	.....do	......do	CA	ES	....	....	
Do	.....do	......do	CA	ES	....	....	
Do	Chief Financial Officer	......do	CA	ES	....	....	
Do	Chief Information Officer	......do	CA	ES	....	....	
Do	Chief Human Capital Officer	......do	CA	ES	....	....	
	OFFICE OF ENGINEERING AND TECHNOLOGY						
Do	Chief	......do	CA	ES	....	....	
Do	Deputy Chief	......do	CA	ES	....	....	
	OFFICE OF GENERAL COUNSEL						
Do	General Counsel	Vacant		ES	....	....	
Do	Deputy General Counsel	Sean A. Lev	NA	ES	....	....	
Do	.....do	Career Incumbent	CA	ES	....	....	
Do	.....do	Vacant		ES	....	....	

FEDERAL COMMUNICATIONS COMMISSION—Continued

Location	Position	Name of Incumbent	Type of Appt.	Pay Plan	Level, Grade, or Pay	Tenure	Expires
Washington, DC	Associate General Counsel (Litigation)	Career Incumbent	CA	ES	....	....	
Do	Associate General Counsel (Administrative Law).	......do	CA	ES	....	....	
Do	Senior Legal Advisor (Ethics)	......do	CA	SL	....	....	
Do	Deputy Associate General Counsel	......do	CA	SL	....	....	
	WIRELESS TELECOMMUNICATIONS BUREAU						
Do	Bureau Chief	......do	CA	ES	....	....	
Do	Deputy Bureau Chief	......do	CA	ES	....	....	
Do	......do	......do	CA	ES	....	....	
Do	Associate Bureau Chief	......do	CA	ES	....	....	
Do	Chief Engineer	......do	CA	SL	....	....	
	OFFICE OF MEDIA RELATIONS						
Do	Communications Director	Tammy Fang-Yi Sun	SC	GS	15	....	
	ENFORCEMENT BUREAU						
Do	Chief	Career Incumbent	CA	ES	....	....	
Do	Deputy Bureau Chief	......do	CA	ES	....	....	
Do	Chief of Staff	......do	CA	ES	....	....	
Do	Assistant Bureau Chief, Economics	......do	CA	ES	....	....	
	WIRELINE COMPETITION BUREAU						
Do	Bureau Chief	......do	CA	ES	....	....	
Do	Deputy Bureau Chief	......do	CA	ES	....	....	
Do	......do	......do	CA	ES	....	....	
	MEDIA BUREAU						
Do	Bureau Chief	......do	CA	ES	....	....	
Do	Deputy Bureau Chief	......do	CA	ES	....	....	
Do	......do	......do	CA	ES	....	....	
Do	......do	......do	CA	ES	....	....	
Do	Chief, Video Division	......do	CA	ES	....	....	
	CONSUMER AND GOVERNMENTAL AFFAIRS BUREAU						
Do	Chief	......do	CA	ES	....	....	
Do	Deputy Bureau Chief	......do	CA	ES	....	....	
Do	......do	......do	CA	ES	....	....	
	PUBLIC SAFETY AND HOMELAND SECURITY BUREAU						
Do	Bureau Chief	David S. Turetsky	NA	ES	....	....	
Do	Deputy Bureau Chief	Career Incumbent	CA	ES	....	....	
Do	......do	......do	CA	ES	....	....	
Do	Division Chief, Public Communications Outreach and Operations Division.	......do	CA	ES	....	....	

FEDERAL DEPOSIT INSURANCE CORPORATION

Location	Position	Name of Incumbent	Type of Appt.	Pay Plan	Level, Grade, or Pay	Tenure	Expires
Washington, DC	Chairman	Vacant	PAS	EX	....	....	
Do	Vice Chairman	Martin J. Gruenberg	PAS	EX	IV	....	
Do	Member of the Board of Directors	Thomas Hoenig	PAS	EX	IV	....	
Do	......do	Jeremiah Norton	PAS	EX	IV	....	
Do	Inspector General	Jon T. Rymer	PAS	EX	IV	....	
Do	Writer-Editor	Michele A. Heller	SC	OT	....	....	

FEDERAL ELECTION COMMISSION

Location	Position	Name of Incumbent	Type of Appt.	Pay Plan	Level, Grade, or Pay	Tenure	Expires
Washington, DC	Commissioner Member	Cynthia L. Bauerly	PAS	EX	IV	....	
Do	Executive Assistant	Eric Hallstrom	XS	GS	15	....	
Do	......do	Sarah Rozensky	XS	GS	15	....	
Do	Commissioner Member	Caroline C. Hunter	PAS	EX	IV	....	
Do	Executive Assistant	Eric S. Brown	XS	GS	15	....	
Do	......do	Vacant	XS	GS	15	....	
Do	......do	Rebekah Miller	XS	GS	13	....	
Do	Special Assistant	Jill A. Moschak	XS	GS	13	....	
Do	Commissioner Member	Donald F. McGahn	PAS	EX	IV		

FEDERAL ELECTION COMMISSION—Continued

Location	Position	Name of Incumbent	Type of Appt.	Pay Plan	Level, Grade, or Pay	Tenure	Expires
Washington, DC	Executive Assistant	Gary Lawkowski	XS	GS	15	....	
Do	......do	Vacant	XS	GS	15	....	
Do	Commissioner Member	Matthew S. Petersen	PAS	EX	IV	....	
Do	Executive Assistant	Kevin J. Plummer	XS	GS	15	....	
Do	....do	Jonathan D. Borrowman ...	XS	GS	15	....	
Do	Commissioner Member	Steven T. Walther	PAS	EX	IV	....	
Do	Executive Assistant	Brad C. Deutsch	XS	GS	15	....	
Do	......do	Vacant	XS	GS	15	....	
Do	Commissioner Member	Ellen L. Weintraub	PAS	EX	IV	....	
Do	Executive Assistant	Julia Richardson	XS	GS	15	....	
Do	......do	Alexander Tausanovitch	XS	GS	15	....	
Do	......do	Daniel Weiner	XS	GS	15	....	
Do	......do	Nicole Zeitler	XS	GS	15	....	
Do	Staff Director	D. Alec Palmer	XS	EX	IV	....	
Do	General Counsel	Anthony Herman	XS	EX	V	....	

FEDERAL ENERGY REGULATORY COMMISSION

Location	Position	Name of Incumbent	Type of Appt.	Pay Plan	Level, Grade, or Pay	Tenure	Expires
	OFFICE OF THE CHAIRMAN						
Washington, DC	Chairman	Jon Wellinghoff	PAS	EX	III	5 Years	06/30/13
Do	Chief of Staff	Career Incumbent	CA	ES	....	....	
Do	Senior Advisor	Vacant		ES	....	....	
Do	Confidential Assistant	Mae C. Davis	SC	GS	13	....	
	Office of Member						
Do	Member	Anthony T. Clark	PAS	EX	IV	4 Years	06/30/16
Do	......do	Cheryl A. Lafleur	PAS	EX	IV	4 Years	06/30/14
Do	......do	John R. Norris	PAS	EX	IV	5 Years	06/30/17
Do	......do	Philip D. Moeller	PAS	EX	IV	5 Years	06/30/15
Do	Confidential Assistant	Brian Morgan	SC	GS	11	....	
Do	Program Analyst	Laura Vendetta	SC	GS	9	....	
Do	Confidential Assistant	Jennifer A. Murray	SC	GS	12	....	
	Office of External Affairs						
Do	Director	Vacant		ES	....	....	
	Office of General Counsel						
Do	General Counsel	Career Incumbent	CA	ES	....	....	
Do	Deputy General Counsel	......do	CA	ES	....	....	
Do	Associate General Counsel, General and Administrative Law.	Vacant		ES	....	....	
Do	Associate General Counsel, Energy Projects ...	Career Incumbent	CA	ES	....	....	
Do	Deputy Associate General Counsel, Energy Projects.	......do	CA	ES	....	....	
Do	Associate General Counsel	......do	CA	ES	....	....	
Do	......do	......do	CA	ES	....	....	
Do	Solicitor	......do	CA	ES	....	....	
	Office of Energy Market Regulation						
Do	Director	......do	CA	ES	....	....	
Do	Deputy Director	......do	CA	ES	....	....	
Do	Director, Division of Electric Power Regulation- Central.	......do	CA	ES	....	....	
Do	Director, Division of Electric Power Regulation- West.	......do	CA	ES	....	....	
Do	Director, Division of Tariffs and Market Development - East.	......do	CA	ES	....	....	
Do	Director, Division of Pipeline Regulation	......do	CA	ES	....	....	
	Office of Energy Projects						
Do	Director	......do	CA	ES	....	....	
Do	Deputy Director	......do	CA	ES	....	....	
Do	Director, Hydropower Licensing	Vacant		ES	....	....	
Do	Director, Hydropower Administration and Compliance.	Career Incumbent	CA	ES	....	....	
Do	Director, Gas Environment and Engineering	......do	CA	ES	....	....	
	Office of Enforcement						
Do	Director	Norman C. Bay	NA	ES	....	....	
Do	Deputy Director	Career Incumbent	CA	ES	....	....	
Do	Director, Investigations	......do	CA	ES	....	....	
Do	Director and Chief Accountant, Audits Division.	......do	CA	ES	....	....	

FEDERAL ENERGY REGULATORY COMMISSION—Continued

Location	Position	Name of Incumbent	Type of Appt.	Pay Plan	Level, Grade, or Pay	Tenure	Expires
Washington, DC	Director, Division of Energy Market Oversight.	Career Incumbent	CA	ES	....	....	
Do	Director, Division of Analytics and Surveillance.	......do	CA	ES	....	....	
	Office of Electric Reliability						
Do	Director	......do	CA	ES	....	....	
Do	Deputy Director	......do	CA	ES	....	....	
Do	Director, Division of Compliance	......do	CA	ES	....	....	
Do	Director, Division of Logistics and Security	......do	CA	ES	....	....	
Do	Director, Division of Reliability Standards	......do	CA	ES	....	....	
Do	Director, Division of Engineering, Planning, and Operations.	......do	CA	ES	....	....	
	Office of Administrative Litigation						
Do	Director	......do	CA	ES	....	....	
Do	Director, Technical Division I	......do	CA	ES	....	....	
Do	Director, Technical Division II	......do	CA	ES	....	....	
Do	Director, Legal Division	......do	CA	ES	....	....	
	Office of the Executive Director						
Do	Executive Director	......do	CA	ES	....	....	
Do	Deputy Executive Director	Vacant	....	ES	....	....	
Do	Chief Information Officer	Career Incumbent	CA	ES	....	....	
Do	Chief Human Capital Officer	......do	CA	ES	....	....	
Do	Chief Financial Officer	......do	CA	ES	....	....	
	Office of Energy Policy and Innovation						
Do	Director	......do	CA	ES	....	....	
Do	Deputy Director	......do	CA	ES	....	....	
Do	Director, Economic and Technical Analysis	......do	CA	ES	....	....	
Do	Director, Policy Development	......do	CA	ES	....	....	
	Office of the Secretary						
Do	Secretary of the Commission	......do	CA	ES	....	....	

FEDERAL FINANCIAL INSTITUTIONS EXAMINATION COUNCIL

Location	Position	Name of Incumbent	Type of Appt.	Pay Plan	Level, Grade, or Pay	Tenure	Expires
Washington, DC	**APPRAISAL SUBCOMMITTEE** Executive Director	Career Incumbent	CA	SL	$158,329	....	

FEDERAL HOUSING FINANCE AGENCY

Location	Position	Name of Incumbent	Type of Appt.	Pay Plan	Level, Grade, or Pay	Tenure	Expires
Washington, DC	Director	Vacant	PAS	EX	....	....	
Do	Confidential Assistant	Joyce L. Lewis	SC	OT	$99,500	....	07/12/12

FEDERAL LABOR RELATIONS AUTHORITY

Location	Position	Name of Incumbent	Type of Appt.	Pay Plan	Level, Grade, or Pay	Tenure	Expires
Washington, DC	**OFFICE OF THE CHAIRMAN** Chairman	Carol W. Pope	PAS	EX	IV	5 Years	07/01/09
Do	**OFFICE OF MEMBER** Member	Ernest W. Dubester	PAS	EX	V	5 Years	07/29/12
Do	......do	Vacant	PAS	EX	V	5 Years	07/01/15
Do	**OFFICE OF THE GENERAL COUNSEL** General Counsel	Julia Akins Clark	PAS	EX	V	5 Years	08/07/14
Do	**FEDERAL SERVICE IMPASSES PANEL** Chair, Federal Service Impasses Panel	Mary E. Jacksteit	PA	SL	$162,900	5 Years	01/10/14
Do	Member, Federal Service Impasses Panel	Vacant	PA	SL	$162,900	5 Years	01/10/17
Do	......do	......do	PA	SL	$162,900	5 Years	01/10/17
Do	......do	Barbara B. Franklin	PA	SL	$162,900	5 Years	01/10/15

FEDERAL LABOR RELATIONS AUTHORITY—Continued

Location	Position	Name of Incumbent	Type of Appt.	Pay Plan	Level, Grade, or Pay	Tenure	Expires
Washington, DC	Member, Federal Service Impasses Panel	Edward F. Hartfield	PA	SL	$162,900	5 Years	01/10/15
Do	......do	Martin Howard Malin	PA	SL	$162,900	5 Years	01/10/14
Do	......do	Donald S. Wasserman	PA	SL	$162,900	5 Years	01/10/14
	FOREIGN SERVICE LABOR RELATIONS						
Do	Member	Earle W. Hockenberry, Jr.	XS	SL	$162,900	3 Years	08/16/15
Do	......do	Stephen R. Ledford	XS	SL	$162,900	3 Years	08/16/15

FEDERAL MARITIME COMMISSION

Location	Position	Name of Incumbent	Type of Appt.	Pay Plan	Level, Grade, or Pay	Tenure	Expires
Washington, DC	**OFFICE OF THE MEMBERS** Chairman	Richard A. Lidinsky, Jr.	PAS	EX	III	5 Years	
Do	Member	Joseph E. Brennan	PAS	EX	IV	5 Years	
Do	......do	Mario Cordero	PAS	EX	IV	5 Years	
Do	......do	Michael A. Khouri	PAS	EX	IV	5 Years	
Do	......do	Rebecca F. Dye	PAS	EX	IV	5 Years	
Do	Chief of Staff	Vacant	....	ES			
Do	Counsel to the Commissioner	Edward L. Lee, Jr.	SC	GS	15	....	
Do	Counsel	Steven Najarian	SC	GS	15	....	
Do	*Office of the General Counsel* General Counsel	Career Incumbent	CA	ES	....	....	
Do	**OFFICE OF THE MANAGING DIRECTOR** Managing Director	......do	CA	ES	....	....	

FEDERAL MEDIATION AND CONCILIATION SERVICE

Location	Position	Name of Incumbent	Type of Appt.	Pay Plan	Level, Grade, or Pay	Tenure	Expires
Washington, DC	**OFFICE OF THE DIRECTOR** Director	George H. Cohen	PAS	EX	III	....	
Do	Deputy Director (Field Operations)	Career Incumbent	CA	ES	....	....	
Do	Chief Financial Officer	......do	CA	ES	....	....	
Do	National Representative	Vacant	....	ES	....	....	
Independence, OH	*Office of the Deputy Director* Director of Field Operations	......do	....	ES	....	....	

FEDERAL MINE SAFETY AND HEALTH REVIEW COMMISSION

Location	Position	Name of Incumbent	Type of Appt.	Pay Plan	Level, Grade, or Pay	Tenure	Expires
Washington, DC	**OFFICE OF THE CHAIRMAN** Chairman	Mary Lucille Jordan	PA	EX	III	....	08/30/14
Do	Senior Policy Advisor	John McWilliam	TA	ES	....	....	01/29/14
Do	Confidential Assistant	Mariel L. De la Cruz	SC	GS	9	....	08/30/14
Do	Attorney Advisor (General)	Elizabeth Sarah Symonds	SC	GS	15	....	08/30/14
Do	**OFFICE OF THE COMMISSIONERS** Commissioner	Michael G. Young	PAS	EX	IV	....	08/30/14
Do	......do	Robert F. Cohen, Jr.	PAS	EX	IV	....	08/30/12
Do	......do	Michael F. Duffy	PAS	EX	IV	....	08/30/12
Do	......do	Patrick K. Nakamura	PAS	EX	IV	....	08/30/16
Do	Confidential Assistant	Pamela I. Chisholm	SC	GS	11	....	08/30/16
Do	**OFFICE OF THE GENERAL COUNSEL** General Counsel	Career Incumbent	CA	ES	....	....	

FEDERAL RESERVE SYSTEM

Location	Position	Name of Incumbent	Type of Appt.	Pay Plan	Level, Grade, or Pay	Tenure	Expires
Washington, DC	Chairman	Ben Bernanke	PAS	EX	I	4 Years	01/31/14
Do	Vice Chairman	Janet Yellen	PAS	EX	II	4 Years	
Do	Governor	Jerome Powell	PAS	EX	II	14 Years	01/31/14
Do	......do	Sarah Raskin	PAS	EX	II	14 Years	01/31/16
Do	......do	Jeremy Stein	PAS	EX	II	14 Years	01/31/18
Do	......do	Elizabeth Duke	PAS	EX	II	14 Years	
Do	......do	Daniel Tarullo	PAS	EX	II	14 Years	01/31/22

FEDERAL RETIREMENT THRIFT INVESTMENT BOARD

Location	Position	Name of Incumbent	Type of Appt.	Pay Plan	Level, Grade, or Pay	Tenure	Expires
Washington, DC	Board Chairman	Michael D. Kennedy	PAS	OT		4 Years	09/25/14
Do	Board Member	Terrance A. Duffy	PAS	OT		3 Years	10/11/07
Do	......do	Dana K. Bilyeu	PAS	OT		3 Years	10/11/15
Do	......do	Ronald McCray	PAS	OT		3 Years	09/25/16
Do	......do	David Jones	PAS	OT		3 Years	10/11/14
Do	Executive Director	Gregory Long	XS	EX	III		
Do	General Counsel	Career Incumbent	CA	ES			
Do	Director of External Affairs	......do	CA	ES			
Do	Director, Office of Enterprise Planning	......do	CA	ES			
Do	Director, Office of Investments	......do	CA	ES			
Do	Director, Office of Benefits	......do	CA	ES			
Do	Chief Information Officer	......do	CA	ES			

FEDERAL TRADE COMMISSION

Location	Position	Name of Incumbent	Type of Appt.	Pay Plan	Level, Grade, or Pay	Tenure	Expires
	OFFICE OF THE CHAIRMAN						
Washington, DC	Chairman	Jonathan D. Leibowitz	PAS	EX	III	7 Years	09/25/17
Do	Commissioner	Maureen K. Ohlhausen	PAS	EX	IV	7 Years	09/25/18
Do	......do	Julie S. Brill	PAS	EX	IV	7 Years	09/25/16
Do	......do	Edith Ramirez	PAS	EX	IV	7 Years	09/25/15
Do	......do	J. Thomas Rosch	PAS	EX	IV	7 Years	09/25/12
Do	Secretary	Career Incumbent	CA	ES			
Do	Director, Office of Policy Planning	Vacant		ES			
Do	Director, Office of Public Affairs	Cecelia J. Prewett	NA	ES			
Do	Confidential Assistant	June R. Young	SC	GS	12		
	OFFICE OF EXECUTIVE DIRECTOR						
Do	Executive Director	Career Incumbent	CA	ES			
Do	Deputy Executive Director	......do	CA	ES			
Do	Chief Financial Officer	......do	CA	ES			
Do	Chief Human Capital Officer	......do	CA	ES			
	OFFICE OF THE GENERAL COUNSEL						
Do	General Counsel	Willard K. Tom	NA	ES			
Do	Principal Deputy General Counsel	Career Incumbent	CA	ES			
Do	Deputy General Counsel for Litigation	......do	CA	ES			
Do	Deputy General Counsel for Legal Counsel ...	......do	CA	ES			
	OFFICE OF INTERNATIONAL AFFAIRS						
Do	Director, Office of International Affairs	......do	CA	ES			
Do	Deputy Director for International Technical Assistance.	......do	CA	ES			
	BUREAU OF COMPETITION						
Do	Director, Bureau of Competition	Richard A. Feinstein	NA	ES			
Do	Deputy Director, Bureau of Competition	Peter J. Levitas	NA	ES			
Do	......do	Norman A. Armstrong, Jr.	NA	ES			
Do	Assistant Director for Policy and Coordination.	Career Incumbent	CA	ES			
Do	Assistant Director for Mergers I	......do	CA	ES			
Do	Assistant Director for Mergers II	......do	CA	ES			
Do	Assistant Director for Mergers III	......do	CA	ES			
Do	Assistant Director for Mergers IV	......do	CA	ES			
Do	Assistant Director for Health Care	Vacant		ES			
Do	Assistant Director for Compliance	Career Incumbent	CA	ES			
Do	Assistant Director for Anticompetitive Practices.	......do	CA	ES			

FEDERAL TRADE COMMISSION—Continued

Location	Position	Name of Incumbent	Type of Appt.	Pay Plan	Level, Grade, or Pay	Tenure	Expires
	BUREAU OF CONSUMER PROTECTION						
Washington, DC	Director, Bureau of Consumer Protection	Vacant	....	ES	....	....	
Do	Deputy Director, Bureau of Consumer Protection.	......do	....	ES	....	....	
Do	......do	Charles A. Harwood	NA	ES	....	....	
Do	Associate Director for Privacy and Identity Protection.	Career Incumbent	CA	ES	....	....	
Do	Associate Director for Advertising Practices ...	......do	CA	ES	....	....	
Do	Associate Director for Marketing Practices	......do	CA	ES	....	....	
Do	Associate Director for Financial Practices	......do	CA	ES	....	....	
Do	Associate Director for Consumer and Business Education.	......do	CA	ES	....	....	
Do	Associate Director for Planning and Information.	......do	CA	ES	....	....	
Do	Associate Director for Enforcement	......do	CA	ES	....	....	
	BUREAU OF ECONOMICS						
Do	Director, Bureau of Economics	Vacant	....	ES	....	....	
Do	Deputy Director for Research and Development and Operations.	Career Incumbent	CA	ES	....	....	
Do	Deputy Director for Antitrust	......do	CA	ES	....	....	
Do	Deputy Director for Consumer Protection	......do	CA	ES	....	....	

GENERAL SERVICES ADMINISTRATION

Location	Position	Name of Incumbent	Type of Appt.	Pay Plan	Level, Grade, or Pay	Tenure	Expires
	OFFICE OF THE ADMINISTRATOR						
Washington, DC	Administrator	Vacant	PAS	EX	III	....	
Do	Deputy Administrator	Susan F. Brita	NA	ES	....	....	
Do	Chief of Staff	Michael J. Robertson	NA	ES	....	....	
Do	Senior Advisor to the Administrator and Chief Acquisition Officer.	Anne E. Rung	NA	ES	....	....	
Do	White House Liaison	Gregory M. Mecher	SC	GS	15	....	
Do	Communications Director	Betsaida Alcantara	SC	GS	15	....	
Do	Deputy Press Secretary	Daniel Cruz	SC	GS	12	....	
Do	Director of Policy - Emergency Management ..	Matthew T. Toner	SC	GS	14	....	
Do	Director of Public Engagement	Jonathan A. Shapiro	SC	GS	12	....	
Do	Special Assistant to the Chief of Staff	Faith A. Rogers	SC	GS	9	....	
	FEDERAL ACQUISITION SERVICE						
Arlington, VA	Commissioner	Career Incumbent	CA	ES	....	....	
Do	Deputy Commissioner	......do	CA	ES	....	....	
Do	Associate Commissioner for Strategic Innovations.	Lena E. Trudeau	TA	ES	....	....	10/30/14
	PUBLIC BUILDINGS SERVICE						
Washington, DC	Commissioner	Vacant	....	ES	....	....	
Do	Deputy Commissioner	Career Incumbent	CA	ES	....	....	
Do	Associate Commissioner	Desa Sealy	NA	ES	....	....	
Do	......do	David H. Ehrenwerth	NA	ES	....	....	
	OFFICE OF GOVERNMENTWIDE POLICY						
Do	Associate Administrator	Career Incumbent	CA	ES	....	....	
Do	Principal Deputy Associate Administrator	Vacant	....	ES	....	....	
	OFFICE OF ADMINISTRATIVE SERVICES						
Do	Chief Administrative Services Officer	Career Incumbent	CA	ES	....	....	
Do	Deputy Chief Administrative Services Officer	......do	CA	ES	....	....	
Do	Special Advisor to the Chief Administrative Services Officer.	Bianca M. Oden	SC	GS	13	....	
	OFFICE OF COMMUNICATIONS AND MARKETING						
Do	Associate Administrator	Vacant	....	ES	....	....	
	OFFICE OF CITIZEN SERVICES AND INNOVATIVE TECHNOLOGIES						
Do	Associate Administrator	David L. McClure	NA	ES	....	....	
Do	Principal Deputy Associate Administrator	Kathy P. Conrad	NA	ES	....	....	
Do	Deputy Associate Administrator for Citizen Services.	Career Incumbent	CA	ES	....	....	
Do	Senior Advisor for Information Technology	......do	CA	ES	....	....	

GENERAL SERVICES ADMINISTRATION—Continued

Location	Position	Name of Incumbent	Type of Appt.	Pay Plan	Level, Grade, or Pay	Tenure	Expires
	OFFICE OF GENERAL COUNSEL						
Washington, DC	General Counsel	Kris E. Durmer	NA	ES			
Do	Deputy General Counsel	Career Incumbent	CA	ES			
Do	Associate General Counsel, General Law	.....do	CA	ES			
Do	Associate General Counsel, Real Property	.....do	CA	ES			
Do	Associate General Counsel, Personal Property	.....do	CA	ES			
Do	Regional Counsel	.....do	CA	ES			
San Francisco, CA	.....do	.....do	CA	ES			
	OFFICE OF CONGRESSIONAL AND INTERGOVERNMENTAL AFFAIRS						
Washington, DC	Associate Administrator	Rodney P. Emery	NA	ES			
Do	Deputy Associate Administrator for Legislative Affairs.	Lisa A. Austin	SC	GS	15		
Do	Legislative Policy Advisor	Brett J. Prather	SC	GS	13		
Do	Special Assistant	Joan M. Currie	SC	GS	13		
	OFFICE OF THE CHIEF INFORMATION OFFICER						
Do	Chief Information Officer	Career Incumbent	CA	ES			
Do	Deputy Chief Information Officer	.....do	CA	ES			
	OFFICE OF SMALL BUSINESS UTILIZATION						
Do	Associate Administrator	Jiyoung C. Park	NA	ES			
Do	Special Assistant	Allison C. Pulliam	SC	GS	9		
	OFFICE OF CIVIL RIGHTS						
Do	Associate Administrator	Career Incumbent	CA	ES			
	REGIONAL ADMINISTRATORS						
	National Capital Region						
Washington, DC	Regional Administrator	Julia E. Hudson	NA	ES			
Do	Project Executive for Campus Development	Shapour Ebadi	TA	ES			08/28/13
	New England Region						
Boston, MA	Regional Administrator	Robert C. Zarnetske III	SC	GS	15		
Do	Special Assistant	Samir L. Randolph	SC	GS	11		
	Northeast and Caribbean Region						
New York, NY	Regional Administrator	Denise L. Pease	SC	GS	15		
Do	Special Assistant	Gita J. Stulberg	SC	GS	11		
	Mid-Atlantic Region						
Philadelphia, PA	Regional Administrator	Sara Manzano-Diaz	SC	GS	15		
	Southeast Sunbelt Region						
Atlanta, GA	Regional Administrator	Shyamsundar K. Reddy	SC	GS	15		
	Great Lakes Region						
Chicago, IL	Regional Administrator	Ann Lata P. Kalayil	SC	GS	15		
Do	Special Assistant	LaDarius R. Curtis	SC	GS	12		
	The Heartland Region						
Kansas City, MO ...	Regional Administrator	Jason O. Klumb	SC	GS	15		
Do	Special Assistant	Tanner D. Banion	SC	GS	11		
	Greater Southwest Region						
Fort Worth, TX	Special Assistant	Trista R. Allen	SC	GS	13		
	Rocky Mountain Region						
Denver, CO	Regional Administrator	Susan B. Damour	SC	GS	15		
	Pacific Rim Region						
San Francisco, CA	Regional Administrator	Ruth F. Cox	SC	GS	15		
Do	Special Assistant	Vannarith T. Tamom, Jr.	SC	GS	11		
	Northwest/Arctic Region						
Auburn, WA	Regional Administrator	George E. Northcroft	SC	GS	15		

GENERAL SERVICES ADMINISTRATION OFFICE OF THE INSPECTOR GENERAL

Location	Position	Name of Incumbent	Type of Appt.	Pay Plan	Level, Grade, or Pay	Tenure	Expires
Washington, DC	Inspector General	Brian D. Miller	PAS	EX	III		

HARRY S. TRUMAN SCHOLARSHIP FOUNDATION

Location	Position	Name of Incumbent	Type of Appt.	Pay Plan	Level, Grade, or Pay	Tenure	Expires
Washington, DC	**OFFICE OF EXECUTIVE SECRETARY** Executive Secretary	Andrew Owen Rich	XS	ES	....	....	

UNITED STATES INTERAGENCY COUNCIL ON HOMELESSNESS

Location	Position	Name of Incumbent	Type of Appt.	Pay Plan	Level, Grade, or Pay	Tenure	Expires
Washington, DC	Executive Director	Barbara J. Poppe	XS	AD	$145,700	....	

INTER-AMERICAN FOUNDATION

Location	Position	Name of Incumbent	Type of Appt.	Pay Plan	Level, Grade, or Pay	Tenure	Expires
Arlington, VA	President	Robert Kaplan	XS	EX	IV	....	
Washington, DC	Board Member (Chair)	John P. Salazar	PAS	OT	....	6 Years	
Do	Board Member (Vice Chair)	Thomas J. Dodd	PAS	OT	....	6 Years	
Do	Board Member	Eduardo Arriola	PAS	OT	....	6 Years	
Do	......do	J. Kelly Ryan	PAS	OT	....	6 Years	
Do	......do	Jack C. Vaughn, Jr.	PAS	OT	....	6 Years	
Do	......do	Roger W. Wallace	PAS	OT	....	6 Years	
Do	......do	Vacant	PAS	OT	....	6 Years	
Do	......do	......do	PAS	OT	....	6 Years	
Do	......do	......do	PAS	OT	....	6 Years	

INTERNATIONAL BOUNDARY AND WATER COMMISSION

Location	Position	Name of Incumbent	Type of Appt.	Pay Plan	Level, Grade, or Pay	Tenure	Expires
El Paso, TX	Commissioner	Edward Drusina	PA	EX	III	....	

INTERNATIONAL BOUNDARY COMMISSION: UNITED STATES AND CANADA

Location	Position	Name of Incumbent	Type of Appt.	Pay Plan	Level, Grade, or Pay	Tenure	Expires
Washington, DC	Commissioner	Vacant	PA	OT	....	....	

INTERSTATE COMMISSION ON THE POTOMAC RIVER BASIN

Location	Position	Name of Incumbent	Type of Appt.	Pay Plan	Level, Grade, or Pay	Tenure	Expires
Rockville, MD	Federal Commissioner	Jane Graeffe Witheridge ...	PA	OT	....	....	
Do	......do	George Wesley Reiger	PA	OT	....	....	
Do	......do	Vacant	PA	OT	....	....	

INTERNATIONAL JOINT COMMISSION

Location	Position	Name of Incumbent	Type of Appt.	Pay Plan	Level, Grade, or Pay	Tenure	Expires
Washington, DC	Commissioner (Chair)	Lana B. Pollack	PAS	AD	....	....	
Rockville, MD	Commissioner	Dereth Glance	PAS	AD	....	....	
Do	......do	Richard Moy	PAS	AD	....	....	

JAMES MADISON MEMORIAL FELLOWSHIP FOUNDATION

Location	Position	Name of Incumbent	Type of Appt.	Pay Plan	Level, Grade, or Pay	Tenure	Expires
Washington, DC	President	Lewis Larsen	XS	GS	15	....	

JAPAN-UNITED STATES FRIENDSHIP COMMISSION

Location	Position	Name of Incumbent	Type of Appt.	Pay Plan	Level, Grade, or Pay	Tenure	Expires
Washington, DC	**JAPAN-UNITED STATES FRIENDSHIP COMMISSION** Executive Director	Career Incumbent	CA	ES	....	....	

JOHN F. KENNEDY CENTER

Location	Position	Name of Incumbent	Type of Appt.	Pay Plan	Level, Grade, or Pay	Tenure	Expires
Washington, DC	Trustee	Colleen Bell	PAS	WC	....	6 Years	09/01/13
Do	......do	Judith Ann Eisenberg	PAS	WC	....	6 Years	09/01/13
Do	......do	C. Michael Kojaian	PAS	WC	....	6 Years	09/01/13
Do	......do	Donna G. Marriott	PAS	WC	....	6 Years	09/01/13
Do	......do	William Charles Powers	PAS	WC	....	6 Years	09/01/13
Do	......do	Leonard Sands	PAS	WC	....	6 Years	09/01/13
Do	......do	Nancy Goodman Brinker ...	PAS	WC	....	6 Years	09/01/14
Do	......do	Donald J. Hall, Jr.	PAS	WC	....	6 Years	09/01/14
Do	......do	Joan E. Hotchkis	PAS	WC	....	6 Years	09/01/14
Do	......do	Herbert V. Kohler, Jr.	PAS	WC	....	6 Years	09/01/14
Do	......do	Carl Lindner III	PAS	WC	....	6 Years	09/01/14
Do	......do	Marilyn Carlson Nelson	PAS	WC	....	6 Years	09/01/14
Do	......do	Robert F. Pence	PAS	WC	....	6 Years	09/01/14
Do	......do	Duane R. Roberts	PAS	WC	....	6 Years	09/01/14
Do	......do	David Rubenstein	PAS	WC	....	6 Years	09/01/14
Do	......do	Shirley Ryan	PAS	WC	....	6 Years	09/01/14
Do	......do	Marc Stern	PAS	WC	....	6 Years	09/01/14
Do	......do	Vacant	PAS	WC	....	6 Years	
Do	......do	Gordon J. Davis	PAS	WC	....	6 Years	09/01/16
Do	......do	Fred Eychaner	PAS	WC	....	6 Years	09/01/16
Do	......do	Victoria Reggie Kennedy ...	PAS	WC	....	6 Years	09/01/16
Do	......do	Cappy R. McGarr	PAS	WC	....	6 Years	09/01/16
Do	......do	Charles B. Ortner	PAS	WC	....	6 Years	09/01/16
Do	......do	Penny Pritzker	PAS	WC	....	6 Years	09/01/16
Do	......do	Adrienne Arsht	PAS	WC	....	6 Years	09/01/18
Do	......do	David C. Bohnett	PAS	WC	....	6 Years	09/01/18
Do	......do	Giselle Fernandez	PAS	WC	....	6 Years	09/01/18
Do	......do	Norma Lee Funger	PAS	WC	....	6 Years	09/01/18
Do	......do	Caroline Kennedy	PAS	WC	....	6 Years	09/01/18
Do	......do	Rebecca Pohlad	PAS	WC	....	6 Years	09/01/18
Do	......do	Romesh Wadhwani	PAS	WC	....	6 Years	09/01/18
Do	......do	Anthony Welters	PAS	WC	....	6 Years	09/01/18
Do	......do	Elaine Wynn	PAS	WC	....	6 Years	09/01/18
Do	......do	Vacant	PAS	WC	....	6 Years	
Do	......do	......do	PAS	WC	....	6 Years	
Do	......do	......do	PAS	WC	....	6 Years	

MARINE MAMMAL COMMISSION

Location	Position	Name of Incumbent	Type of Appt.	Pay Plan	Level, Grade, or Pay	Tenure	Expires
Bethesda, MD	Chairman	Daryl Boness	PAS	AD	....	....	
Sausalito, CA	Commissioner	Frances Gulland	PAS	AD	....	....	
Encinitas, CA	......do	Michael F. Tillman	PAS	AD	....	....	
Washington, DC	Executive Director	Timothy J. Ragen	XS	AD	$179,700	....	

MEDICAID AND CHIP PAYMENT AND ACCESS COMMISSION

Location	Position	Name of Incumbent	Type of Appt.	Pay Plan	Level, Grade, or Pay	Tenure	Expires
Washington, DC	Executive Director	Vacant	XS	AD	....	....	
Do	Deputy Director, Operations, Finance and Mgmt.	Erin D. Singshinsuk	XS	AD	$163,000	....	
Do	Director, Long-Term Services and Support	Ellen S. O'Brien	XS	AD	$155,000	....	
Do	Director, Eligibility, Enrollment, and Benefits	Christopher L. Peterson	XS	AD	$160,000	....	
Do	Principal Analyst	Mary E. Stahlman	XS	AD	$164,299	....	

MEDICARE PAYMENT ADVISORY COMMISSION

Location	Position	Name of Incumbent	Type of Appt.	Pay Plan	Level, Grade, or Pay	Tenure	Expires
Washington, DC	Executive Director	Mark E. Miller	XS	AD	$171,000	....	
Do	Deputy Director	James E. Mathews	XS	AD	$162,800	....	
Do	Principal Policy Analyst	Carol L. Carter	XS	AD	$161,000	....	
Do	......do	David V. Glass	XS	AD	$148,000	....	
Do	......do	Scott C. Harrison	XS	AD	$156,000	....	
Do	......do	Kevin J. Hayes	XS	AD	$157,600	....	
Do	......do	Nancy F. Ray	XS	AD	$157,600	....	
Do	......do	John M. Richardson	XS	AD	$151,000	....	
Do	......do	Jeffrey T. Stensland	XS	AD	$155,000	....	

MERIT SYSTEMS PROTECTION BOARD

Location	Position	Name of Incumbent	Type of Appt.	Pay Plan	Level, Grade, or Pay	Tenure	Expires
	OFFICE OF THE BOARD, CHAIRMAN						
Washington, DC	Chairman	Susan Tsui Grundmann	PAS	EX	III	....	03/01/16
Do	Chief of Staff	Steven V. Lenkart	NA	ES	....	....	
Do	Chief Counsel	Lynore M. Carnes	NA	ES	....	....	
Do	Special Advisor to the Board	Career Incumbent	CA	ES	....	....	
	Office of the Board, Vice Chairman						
Do	Vice Chairman	Anne Marie Wagner	PAS	EX	IV	....	03/01/14
Do	Chief Counsel	Bernard E. Doyle	NA	ES	....	....	
	Office of the Board, Member						
Do	Member	Mark A. Robbins	PAS	EX	IV	....	03/01/18
Do	Chief Counsel	Vacant	....	ES	....	....	
	Office of Appeals Counsel						
Do	Director	......do	....	ES	....	....	
	Office of the General Counsel						
Do	General Counsel	James M. Eisenmann	NA	ES	....	....	

MILLENNIUM CHALLENGE CORPORATION

Location	Position	Name of Incumbent	Type of Appt.	Pay Plan	Level, Grade, or Pay	Tenure	Expires
Washington, DC	Board Member	Mark A. Green	PAS	OT	$155,500	3 Years	12/28/13
Do	......do	Alan J. Patricof	PAS	OT	$155,500	2 Years	12/28/12
Do	......do	Vacant	PAS	OT	....	....	
Do	......do	......do	PAS	OT	....	....	
	OFFICE OF THE CHIEF EXECUTIVE OFFICER						
Do	Chief Executive Officer	Daniel W. Yohannes	PAS	EX	II	....	
Do	Senior Advisor to CEO	Cassandra Q. Butts	PA	AD	$172,500	....	
Do	Senior Investment Risk Officer	Frances S. Reid	XS	AD	$172,000	....	
Do	Chief of Staff	Steven M. Kaufmann	PA	AD	$175,000	....	
	DEPARTMENT OF POLICY AND EVALUATION						
Do	Vice President	Sheila W. Herrling	PA	AD	$173,500	....	
Do	Deputy Vice President	James F. Parks	PA	AD	$170,200	....	
	OFFICE OF THE GENERAL COUNSEL						
Do	Vice President and General Counsel	Melvin F. Williams	PA	AD	$172,500	....	
Do	Deputy General Counsel	Henry C. Pitney	XS	OT	$170,200	....	

MILLENNIUM CHALLENGE CORPORATION—Continued

Location	Position	Name of Incumbent	Type of Appt.	Pay Plan	Level, Grade, or Pay	Tenure	Expires
	DEPARTMENT OF ADMINISTRATION AND FINANCE						
Washington, DC	Vice President	Chantale Y. Wong	PA	AD	$172,000	....	
Do	Deputy Vice President	Margaret L. Yao	PA	AD	$170,200	....	
	DEPARTMENT OF CONGRESSIONAL AND PUBLIC AFFAIRS						
Do	Vice President	Thomas C. Cooper	PA	AD	$171,500	....	
Do	Managing Director (Public Affairs)	Nasserie M. Carew	XS	AD	$150,000	....	
Do	Managing Director (Congressional Affairs)	James Mazzarella	XS	AD	$165,060	....	
	DEPARTMENT OF COMPACT DEVELOPMENT						
Do	Vice President	Patrick C. Fine	PA	AD	$175,000	....	
Do	Deputy Vice President (ESA)	Andrew J. Mayock	PA	AD	$165,000	....	
Do	Deputy Vice President (EAPLA)	Thomas F. Hurley	XS	AD	$170,200	....	
Do	Deputy Vice President (WA)	Jonathan O. Bloom	XS	AD	$170,200	....	

MORRIS K. UDALL AND STEWART L. UDALL FOUNDATION

Location	Position	Name of Incumbent	Type of Appt.	Pay Plan	Level, Grade, or Pay	Tenure	Expires
Tucson, AZ	Trustee	Eric D. Eberhard	PAS	WC	....	6 Years	
Do	......do	Anne J. Udall	PAS	WC	....	6 Years	
Do	......do	Robert Lance Boldrey	PAS	WC	....	6 Years	05/26/13
Do	......do	Michael A. Butler	PAS	WC	....	6 Years	
Do	......do	Diane J. Humetewa	PAS	WC	....	6 Years	
Do	......do	Stephen M. Prescott, M.D. ..	PAS	WC	....	6 Years	
Do	......do	D. Michael Rappoport	PAS	WC	....	6 Years	
Do	......do	Bradley Udall	PAS	WC	....	6 Years	
Do	......do	Vacant	PAS	WC	....	6 Years	

NATIONAL AERONAUTICS AND SPACE ADMINISTRATION

Location	Position	Name of Incumbent	Type of Appt.	Pay Plan	Level, Grade, or Pay	Tenure	Expires
	OFFICE OF THE ADMINISTRATOR						
Washington, DC	Administrator	Charles F. Bolden, Jr.	PAS	EX	II	....	
Do	Deputy Administrator	Lori B. Garver	PAS	EX	III	....	
Do	Chief of Staff	David P. Radzanowski	NA	ES	....		
Do	Deputy Chief of Staff	Michael French	NA	ES	....		
Do	White House Liaison	Vacant	....	ES	....		
Do	Executive Officer	Brett E. Silcox	SC	GS	14	3 Years	
Do	Senior Advisor	James Terry Edmonds	SC	GS	15	3 Years	
	OFFICE OF THE CHIEF FINANCIAL OFFICER						
Do	Chief Financial Officer	Elizabeth Mayer Robinson	PAS	EX	IV	....	
	OFFICE OF THE CHIEF INFORMATION OFFICER						
Do	Chief Information Officer	Career Incumbent	CA	ES	....		
	OFFICE OF THE CHIEF HEALTH AND MEDICAL OFFICER						
Do	Chief Health and Medical Officer	......do	CA	ES	....		
	OFFICE OF DIVERSITY AND EQUAL OPPORTUNITY						
Do	Associate Administrator	......do	CA	ES	....		
	OFFICE OF EDUCATION						
Do	Associate Administrator	......do	CA	ES	....		
	OFFICE OF GENERAL COUNSEL						
Do	General Counsel	......do	CA	ES	....		
Do	Deputy General Counsel	Vacant	....	ES	....		
Do	Associate General Counsel (General Law Practice Group).	Career Incumbent	CA	ES	....		
Do	Associate General Counsel (Contracts)	......do	CA	ES	....		
Do	Associate General Counsel (Commercial/Intellectual Property Law Group).	......do	CA	ES	....		
Do	Special Assistant	William J. Donovan	SC	GS	11	....	

NATIONAL AERONAUTICS AND SPACE ADMINISTRATION—Continued

Location	Position	Name of Incumbent	Type of Appt.	Pay Plan	Level, Grade, or Pay	Tenure	Expires
	OFFICE OF LEGISLATIVE AND INTERGOVERNMENTAL AFFAIRS						
Washington, DC	Associate Administrator	Lance S. Statler	NA	ES	....	....	
Do	Legislative Affairs Specialist	Rashawn L. Mitchell	SC	GS	9	3 Years	
Do	......do	Shannon Gabrielle Valley ..	SC	GS	9	3 Years	
	OFFICE OF COMMUNICATIONS						
Do	Associate Administrator	David Scott Weaver	NA	ES	....	....	
Do	Deputy Associate Administrator for Public Outreach.	Alan Michael Ladwig	NA	ES	....	....	
Do	Deputy Assistant Administrator for Public Affairs.	Career Incumbent	CA	ES	....	....	
Do	Managing Editor	......do	CA	ES	....	....	
Do	Special Assistant	Sarah Rebecca Ramsey	SC	GS	14	3 Years	
Do	Press Secretary	Lauren Brooke Worley	SC	GS	12	3 Years	
	OFFICE OF SMALL BUSINESS PROGRAMS						
Do	Associate Administrator	Career Incumbent	CA	ES	....	....	
	AERONAUTICS RESEARCH MISSION DIRECTORATE						
Do	Associate Administrator	......do	CA	ES	....	....	
	SCIENCE MISSION DIRECTORATE						
Do	Associate Administrator	John Mace Grunsfeld	TA	ES	....	....	01/05/13
	HUMAN EXPLORATION AND OPERATIONS MISSION DIRECTORATE						
Do	Associate Administrator	Career Incumbent	CA	ES	....	....	
	MISSION SUPPORT DIRECTORATE						
	Office of Internal Controls and Management Systems						
Washington, DC	Assistant Administrator	Career Incumbent	CA	GS	15	....	
	AMES RESEARCH CENTER						
Moffett Field, CA ...	Director	......do	CA	ES	....	....	
Do	Chief Counsel	......do	CA	ES	....	....	
	DRYDEN FLIGHT RESEARCH CENTER						
Edwards Air Force Base, CA.	Director	......do	CA	ES	....	....	
Do	Chief Counsel	......do	CA	ES	....	....	
	GLENN RESEARCH CENTER						
Cleveland, OH	Director	......do	CA	ES	....	....	
Do	Chief Counsel	......do	CA	ES	....	....	
	GODDARD SPACE FLIGHT CENTER						
Greenbelt, MD	Director	......do	CA	ES	....	....	
Do	Chief Counsel	......do	CA	ES	....	....	
	JOHNSON SPACE CENTER						
Houston, TX	Director	......do	CA	ES	....	....	
Do	Chief Counsel	......do	CA	ES	....	....	
	KENNEDY SPACE CENTER						
Kennedy Space Center, FL.	Director	......do	CA	ES	....	....	
Do	Chief Counsel	......do	CA	ES	....	....	
	LANGLEY RESEARCH CENTER						
Hampton, VA	Director	......do	CA	ES	....	....	
Do	Chief Counsel	......do	CA	ES	....	....	
	MARSHALL SPACE FLIGHT CENTER						
Huntsville, AL	Director	......do	CA	ES	....	....	
Do	Chief Counsel	......do	CA	ES	....	....	
	STENNIS SPACE CENTER						
Bay St. Louis, MS	Director	......do	CA	ES	....	....	
Do	Chief Counsel	Vacant	....	ES	....	....	

NATIONAL AERONAUTICS AND SPACE ADMINISTRATION OFFICE OF THE INSPECTOR GENERAL

Location	Position	Name of Incumbent	Type of Appt.	Pay Plan	Level, Grade, or Pay	Tenure	Expires
Washington, DC	Inspector General	Paul K. Martin	PAS	ES	....	....	

NATIONAL ARCHIVES AND RECORDS ADMINISTRATION

Location	Position	Name of Incumbent	Type of Appt.	Pay Plan	Level, Grade, or Pay	Tenure	Expires
	ARCHIVIST OF UNITED STATES AND DEPUTY ARCHIVIST OF THE UNITED STATES						
College Park, MD ..	Archivist of the United States	David Sean Ferriero	PAS	EX	III	....	
	General Counsel						
Do	General Counsel	Career Incumbent	CA	ES	....	....	
	Congressional and Legislative Affairs Staff						
Do	Director	......do	CA	ES	....	....	
	Office of the Chief Operating Officer						
Washington, DC	Director, Information Security Oversight Office.	......do	CA	ES	....	....	
College Park, MD ..	Director, Records Center Programs	......do	CA	ES	....	....	
Do	Deputy Chief Information Officer	Vacant	....	ES	....	....	
Do	Director, Preservation Programs	Career Incumbent	CA	ES	....	....	
Do	Director, Office of Government Information Services.	......do	CA	ES	....	....	
Do	Director, National Declassification Center	......do	CA	ES	....	....	
Atlanta, GA	Director, Jimmy Carter Library	Jay E. Hakes	XS	SL	$165,300	....	
Simi Valley, CA	Director, Ronald Reagan Library	R. Duke Blackwood	XS	SL	$165,300	....	
Boston, MA	Director, John F. Kennedy Library	Thomas J. Putnam	XS	SL	$148,225	....	
Ann Arbor, MI	Director, Gerald R. Ford Library	Elaine K. Didier	XS	SL	$163,554	....	
College Station, TX	Director, George Bush Library	Warren Finch	XS	SL	$143,303	....	
Austin, TX	Director, Lyndon B. Johnson Library	Mark Updegrove	XS	SL	$165,300	....	
Little Rock, AR	Director, William J. Clinton Library	Mary T. Garner	XS	SL	$140,679	....	
Yorba Linda, CA ...	Director, Richard M. Nixon Library	Vacant	XS	SL	....	....	
Lewisville, TX	Director, George W. Bush Library	Alan C. Lowe	XS	SL	$165,300	....	
West Branch, IA	Director, Herbert Hoover Library	Thomas F. Schwartz	XS	SL	$135,000	....	

NATIONAL CAPITAL PLANNING COMMISSION

Location	Position	Name of Incumbent	Type of Appt.	Pay Plan	Level, Grade, or Pay	Tenure	Expires
Washington, DC	Chairman	L. Preston Bryant, Jr.	PA	OT	....	....	01/01/13
Do	Commission Member	John M. Hart	PA	OT	....	....	01/04/15
Do	......do	Elizabeth Ann White	PA	OT	....	....	01/01/17

NATIONAL COUNCIL ON DISABILITY

Location	Position	Name of Incumbent	Type of Appt.	Pay Plan	Level, Grade, or Pay	Tenure	Expires
Washington, DC	Chairman	Jonathan M. Young	PAS	OT	....	3 Years	
Do	Member	Gary H. Blumenthal	PAS	OT	....	3 Years	
Do	......do	Sara A. Gelser	PAS	OT	....	3 Years	
Do	......do	Matan A. Koch	PAS	OT	....	3 Years	
Do	......do	Ari Ne'Eman	PAS	OT	....	3 Years	
Do	......do	Clyde E. Terry	PAS	OT	....	3 Years	
Do	......do	Linda Wetters	PAS	OT	....	3 Years	
Do	......do	Stephanie Orlando	PAS	OT	....	3 Years	
Do	......do	Chester A. Finn	PAS	OT	....	3 Years	
Do	......do	Lonnie C. Moore	PAS	OT	....	3 Years	
Do	......do	Fernando M. Torres-Gil	PAS	OT	....	3 Years	
Do	......do	Kamilah O. Martin-Proctor	PAS	OT	....	3 Years	
Do	......do	Pamela Y. Holmes	PAS	OT	....	3 Years	
Do	......do	Dongwoo J. Pak	PAS	OT	....	3 Years	
Do	......do	Janice L. Lehrer-Stein	PAS	OT	....	3 Years	

NATIONAL CREDIT UNION ADMINISTRATION

Location	Position	Name of Incumbent	Type of Appt.	Pay Plan	Level, Grade, or Pay	Tenure	Expires
	OFFICE OF THE CHAIRMAN						
Alexandria, VA	Chairman	Deborah Matz	PAS	EX	III	6 Years	
Do	Chief of Staff	John Steven Bosack	SC	OT	$191,155	....	
Do	Director, Public and Congressional Affairs/ Chief Policy Advisor to the Chairman.	Todd M. Harper	SC	OT	$234,999	....	
Do	Staff Assistant	Angela Sanders	SC	OT	$84,049		
	OFFICE OF THE BOARD						
Do	Board Member (Vice Chair)	Christiane Gigi Hyland	PAS	EX	IV	6 Years	
Do	Board Member	Michael E. Fryzel	PAS	EX	IV	6 Years	
Do	Senior Policy Advisor	Gary Kohn	SC	OT	$191,155	....	
Do	.....do	Sarah Dee Vega	SC	OT	$191,155	....	
Do	Staff Assistant	Donna G. Giobbi	SC	OT	$80,121	....	
Do	.....do	Katie M. Supples	SC	OT	$60,091	....	

NATIONAL FOUNDATION ON THE ARTS AND HUMANITIES

Location	Position	Name of Incumbent	Type of Appt.	Pay Plan	Level, Grade, or Pay	Tenure	Expires
	INSTITUTE OF MUSEUM AND LIBRARY SERVICES						
Washington, DC	Director	Susan Hodge Hildreth	PAS	EX	III	4 Years	01/23/15
	National Museum and Library Services Board						
Do ....:...	Member	Katherine M B Berger	PAS	OT	$100	5 Years	12/29/12
Do	.....do	Julia W. Bland	PAS	OT	$100	5 Years	03/17/13
Do	.....do	Karen Brosius	PAS	OT	....	5 Years	12/29/12
Do	.....do	Janet G. Cellucci	PAS	OT	$100	5 Years	03/17/13
Do	.....do	John Francis Coppola	PAS	OT	$100	5 Years	06/24/15
Do	.....do	William J. Hagenah	PAS	OT	$100	5 Years	03/17/13
Do	.....do	Carla Diane Hayden	PAS	OT	$100	5 Years	06/24/15
Do	.....do	Mark Y. Herring	PAS	OT	$100	5 Years	03/17/13
Do	.....do	Ioannis N. Miaoulis	PAS	OT	$100	5 Years	01/02/13
Do	.....do	Mary Rose Minow	PAS	OT	$100	5 Years	10/18/15
Do	.....do	Douglas G. Myers	PAS	OT	$100	5 Years	11/30/12
Do	.....do	Christina Orr-Cahall	PAS	OT	$100	5 Years	01/02/13
Do	.....do	Jeffrey H. Patchen	PAS	OT	....	5 Years	12/11/12
Do	.....do	Lotsee F. Patterson	PAS	OT	....	5 Years	11/18/12
Do	.....do	Harry Robinson, Jr.	PAS	OT	$100	5 Years	02/15/11
Do	.....do	Lawrence Joseph Pijeaux, Jr..	PAS	OT	$100	5 Years	06/24/15
Do	.....do	Katina Strauch	PAS	OT	$100	5 Years	12/20/12
Do	.....do	D. Winston Tabb	PAS	OT	$100	5 Years	06/24/15
Do	.....do	Robert Wedgeworth, Jr.	PAS	OT	$100	5 Years	06/24/15
Do	.....do	Sandra J. Pickett	PAS	OT	$100	5 Years	05/18/12
	NATIONAL ENDOWMENT FOR THE ARTS						
Do	Chairman	Fredric Landesman	PAS	EX	III	....	
Do	Executive Director, Presidents Committee on the Arts and the Humanities.	Vacant	....	ES	...........:........	....	
Do	Chief of Staff and Director of Public Affairs ...	Jamie L. Bennett	NA	ES	....	....	
Do	Senior Deputy Chairman	Joan Shigekawa	NA	ES	....	....	
Do	Senior Advisor for Program Innovation	William O Brien	NA	ES	....	....	
Do	Arts Education Counselor to the Senior Deputy Chairman.	Elisabeth F. Leach	SC	GS	15	....	
Do	Scheduler	Wendy G. Beren	SC	GS	11	....	
Do	White House and Congressional Liaison	Michael John Griffin	SC	GS	14	....	
Do	Special Assistant for Congressional Affairs	Elizabeth Miller	SC	GS	9	....	
Do	Confidential Assistant to the Chief of Staff	Sasha Daniela Burger	SC	GS	9	....	
Do	Senior Advisor to the Chairman and Director of Strategic Partnerships.	Daniel Berman Lurie	SC	GS	15	....	
	Presidents Committee on the Arts and Humanities						
Do	Executive Director	Rachel Eva Goslins	NA	ES	....	....	
	NATIONAL ENDOWMENT FOR THE HUMANITIES						
Do	Chairman	James A. Leach	PAS	EX	III	4 Years	
Do	Deputy Chairman	Career Incumbent	CA	ES	....	....	
Do	General Counsel	......do	CA	ES	....	....	
Do	Assistant Chairman for Programs	......do	CA	ES	....	....	

NATIONAL FOUNDATION ON THE ARTS AND HUMANITIES—Continued

Location	Position	Name of Incumbent	Type of Appt.	Pay Plan	Level, Grade, or Pay	Tenure	Expires
Washington, DC	Assistant Chairman for Partnership and Strategic Initiatives.	Evagren O. Caldera	NA	ES	....	....	
Do	Chief Information Officer	......do	CA	ES	....	....	
Do	Director, Office of Challenge Grants	......do	CA	ES	....	....	
Do	Director, Federal/State Partnership	......do	CA	ES	....	....	
Do	Director, Division of Preservation and Access ..	......do	CA	ES	....	....	
Do	Director, Division of Public Programs	Vacant	....	ES	....	....	
Do	Director, Division of Research Programs	......do	....	ES	....	....	
Do	Deputy Director, President's Committee on the Arts and the Humanities.	Career Incumbent	CA	ES	....	....	
Do	Director, White House and Congressional Affairs.	Courtney M. Chapin	NA	ES	....	....	
Do	Director of Communications	Judith M. Havemann	SC	GS	15	....	
Do	Special Assistant	Claire Elliott Noble	SC	GS	7	....	
Do	......do	Andrew Simon	SC	GS	7	....	
Do	Council Member	Rolena K. Adorno	PAS	AD	....	....	
Do	......do	Adele L. Alexander	PAS	AD	....	....	
Do	......do	Albert J. Beveridge	PAS	AD	....	....	
Do	......do	Allison Blakely	PAS	AD	....	....	
Do	......do	Constance M. Carroll	PAS	AD	....	....	
Do	......do	Jamsheed Chosky	PAS	AD	....	....	
Do	......do	Cathy N. Davidson	PAS	AD	....	....	
Do	......do	Dawn H. Delbanco	PAS	AD	....	....	
Do	......do	Jane M. Doggett	PAS	AD	....	....	
Do	......do	Paula B. Duffy	PAS	AD	....	....	
Do	......do	Jean B. Elshtain	PAS	AD	....	....	
Do	......do	Gary D. Glenn	PAS	AD	....	....	
Do	......do	Allen Guelzo	PAS	AD	....	....	
Do	......do	Mary Habeck	PAS	AD	....	....	
Do	......do	David M. Hertz	PAS	AD	....	....	
Do	......do	Marvin Krislov	PAS	AD	....	....	
Do	......do	Iris Love	PAS	AD	....	....	
Do	......do	Robert S. Martin	PAS	AD	....	....	
Do	......do	Wilfred M. McClay	PAS	AD	....	....	
Do	......do	Ricardo J. Quinones	PAS	AD	....	....	
Do	......do	Carol M. Swain	PAS	AD	....	....	
Do	......do	Martha W. Weinberg	PAS	AD	....	....	
Do	......do	Kenneth R. Weinstein	PAS	AD	....	....	
Do	......do	Jay Winik	PAS	AD	....	....	
Do	......do	Christopher Merrill	PAS	AD	....	....	

NATIONAL ENDOWMENT FOR THE HUMANITIES OFFICE OF THE INSPECTOR GENERAL

Location	Position	Name of Incumbent	Type of Appt.	Pay Plan	Level, Grade, or Pay	Tenure	Expires
Washington, DC	Inspector General	Vacant	....	ES	....	....	

NATIONAL LABOR RELATIONS BOARD

Location	Position	Name of Incumbent	Type of Appt.	Pay Plan	Level, Grade, or Pay	Tenure	Expires
	OFFICE OF THE BOARD MEMBERS						
Washington, DC	Chairman	Mark Gaston Pearce	PAS	EX	III	....	
Do	Board Member	Terence Francis Flynn	PAS	EX	IV	....	
Do	......do	Richard Griffin, Jr.	PAS	EX	IV	....	
Do	......do	Sharon I. Block	PAS	EX	IV	....	
Do	......do	Brian E. Hayes	PAS	EX	IV	....	
Do	Chief Counsel to Board Member (Chairman)	Kent Y. Hirozawa	NA	ES	....	....	
Do	Chief Counsel to Board Member	James R. Murphy	NA	ES	....	....	
Do	......do	John F. Colwell	NA	ES	....	....	
Do	......do	Peter J. Carlton	NA	ES	....	....	
Do	......do	Peter D. Winkler	NA	ES	....	....	
Do	Deputy Chief Counsel to Board Member	Career Incumbent	CA	ES	....	....	
Do	Director, Office Representation Appeals and Advice.	......do	CA	ES	....	....	
Do	Solicitor	......do	CA	ES	....	....	
Do	Deputy Chief Counsel to Board Member	......do	CA	ES	....	....	
Do	......do	......do	CA	ES	....	....	
Do	......do	......do	CA	ES	....	....	
Do	......do	......do	CA	ES	....	....	

NATIONAL LABOR RELATIONS BOARD—Continued

Location	Position	Name of Incumbent	Type of Appt.	Pay Plan	Level, Grade, or Pay	Tenure	Expires
Washington, DC	Executive Assistant to the Chairman	Robert Schiff	NA	ES	....	....	
Do	Deputy Chief Counsel to Chairman	Career Incumbent	CA	ES	....	....	
Do	Deputy Chief Counsel to Board Member	......do	CA	ES	....	....	
Do	......do	......do	CA	ES	....	....	
	OFFICE OF THE GENERAL COUNSEL						
Do	Acting General Counsel	Lafe E. Solomon	PAS	EX	IV	....	
Do	Deputy General Counsel	Career Incumbent	CA	ES	....	....	
Do	Assistant General Counsel (Legal) (Chair, NLRB Restructuring Committee).	Jennifer Ann Abruzzo	TA	ES	....	....	04/06/13
Do	Associate General Counsel, Division of Enforcement Litigation.	Career Incumbent	CA	ES	....	....	

NATIONAL MEDIATION BOARD

Location	Position	Name of Incumbent	Type of Appt.	Pay Plan	Level, Grade, or Pay	Tenure	Expires
Washington, DC	Chairman	Linda A. Puchala	PAS	EX	III	....	
Do	Board Member	Harry R. Hoglander	PAS	EX	IV	....	
Do	......do	Vacant	PAS	EX	....	....	
Do	General Counsel	Career Incumbent	CA	ES	....	....	
Do	Confidential Assistant	Olybia Mandes Angelopoulos.	SC	GS	12	....	
Do	......do	Robin Ann Stein	SC	GS	12	....	

NATIONAL SCIENCE FOUNDATION

Location	Position	Name of Incumbent	Type of Appt.	Pay Plan	Level, Grade, or Pay	Tenure	Expires
	OFFICE OF THE DIRECTOR						
Arlington, VA	Director	Subra Suresh	PAS	EX	II	....	10/17/16
Do	Deputy Director	Cora B. Marrett	PAS	EX	III	....	
Do	Senior Advisor	Career Incumbent	CA	ES	....	....	
Do	......do	......do	CA	ES	....	....	
Do	Senior Advisor for Strategic Initiatives	Dedric Antonio Carter	TA	ES	....	....	01/13/15
	Office of Cyberinfrastructure						
Do	Office Head	Vacant	....	ES	....	....	
Do	Deputy Office Head	Mark A. Suskin	TA	ES	....	....	07/20/13
	Office of the General Counsel						
Do	General Counsel	Career Incumbent	CA	ES	....	....	
	Office of Legislative and Public Affairs						
Do	Office Head	Judith B. Gan	TA	ES	....	....	12/02/14
Do	Director, Division of Legislative Affairs	Vacant	....	ES	....	....	
Do	Director, Division of Public Affairs	......do	....	ES	....	....	
Do	Senior Advisor	......do	....	ES	....	....	
	Office of Integrative Activities						
Do	Office Head	......do	....	ES	....	....	
Do	Senior Advisor	......do	....	ES	....	....	
Do	Head Experimental Programs to Stimulate Competitive Research.	......do	....	ES	....	....	
	Office of International Science and Engineering						
Do	Office Head	Career Incumbent	CA	ES	....	....	
Do	Executive Officer	David M. Stonner	TA	ES	....	....	07/20/13
	OFFICE OF POLAR PROGRAMS						
Do	Office Head	Career Incumbent	CA	ES	....	....	
Do	Deputy Office Head	Vacant	....	ES	....	....	
	Antarctic Infrastructure and Logistics Division						
Do	Deputy Division Director	......do	....	ES	....	....	
	Antarctic Sciences Division						
Do	Division Director	Career Incumbent	CA	ES	....	....	
	Arctic Sciences Division						
Do	Division Director	......do	CA	ES	....	....	

NATIONAL SCIENCE FOUNDATION—Continued

Location	Position	Name of Incumbent	Type of Appt.	Pay Plan	Level, Grade, or Pay	Tenure	Expires
Arlington, VA	Deputy Division Director	Career Incumbent	CA	ES	....	....	
	Polar Environment, Health and Safety Office						
Do	Office Head	......do	CA	ES	....	....	
	NATIONAL SCIENCE BOARD						
Do	Executive Officer	......do	CA	ES	....	....	
Do	Senior Scientist	Vacant	....	ES	....	....	
	DIRECTORATE FOR BIOLOGICAL SCIENCES						
Do	Assistant Director	......do	....	ES	....	....	
Do	Senior Science Advisor	......do	....	ES	....	....	
	Division of Biological Infrastructure						
Do	Division Director	......do	....	ES	....	....	
Do	Deputy Division Director	Career Incumbent	CA	ES	....	....	
	Division of Environmental Biology						
Do	Division Director	Vacant	....	ES	....	....	
	Division of Integrative Organismal Systems						
Do	Division Director	Career Incumbent	CA	ES	....	....	
	Division of Molecular and Cellular Biosciences						
Do	Division Director	......do	CA	ES	....	....	
Do	Deputy Division Director	Vacant	....	ES	....	....	
	DIRECTORATE FOR COMPUTER AND INFORMATION SCIENCE AND ENGINEERING						
Do	Assistant Director	......do	....	ES	....	....	
Do	Senior Science Advisor	Career Incumbent	CA	ES	....	....	
	Division of Computer and Network Systems						
Do	Division Director	Vacant	....	ES	....	....	
Do	Deputy Division Director	......do	....	ES	....	....	
	Division of Computing and Communication Foundations						
Do	Division Director	......do	....	ES	....	....	
Do	Deputy Division Director	Tracy J. Kimbrel	TA	ES	....	....	01/11/12
	Division of Information and Intelligent Systems						
Do	Division Director	Vacant	....	ES	....	....	
Do	Deputy Division Director	Career Incumbent	CA	ES	....	....	
	DIRECTORATE FOR EDUCATION AND HUMAN RESOURCES						
Do	Assistant Director	......do	CA	ES	....	....	
Do	Deputy Assistant Director	......do	CA	ES	....	....	
	Division of Graduate Education						
Do	Division Director	......do	CA	ES	....	....	
Do	Deputy Division Director	Valerie Petit Wilson	TA	ES	....	....	08/03/13
	Division of Human Resource Development						
Do	Division Director	Vacant	....	ES	....	....	
Do	Deputy Division Director	......do	....	ES	....	....	
	Division of Research on Learning in Formal and Informal Settings						
Do	Division Director	......do	....	ES	....	....	
Do	Deputy Division Director	Career Incumbent	CA	ES	....	....	
	Division of Undergraduate Education						
Do	Division Director	Vacant	....	ES	....	....	
Do	Deputy Division Director	Katherine Jean Denniston	TA	ES	....	....	10/01/12
	DIRECTORATE FOR ENGINEERING						
Do	Assistant Director	Vacant	....	ES	....	....	
Do	Deputy Assistant Director	Career Incumbent	CA	ES	....	....	
	Division of Engineering Education and Centers						
Do	Division Director	Vacant	....	ES	....	....	
Do	Deputy Division Director (Centers)	Career Incumbent	CA	ES	....	....	
	Division of Chemical, Bioengineering, Environmental, and Transport Systems						
Do	Division Director	Vacant	....	ES	....	....	

NATIONAL SCIENCE FOUNDATION—Continued

Location	Position	Name of Incumbent	Type of Appt.	Pay Plan	Level, Grade, or Pay	Tenure	Expires
	Division of Civil, Mechanical, and Manufacturing Innovation						
Arlington, VA	Division Director	Career Incumbent	CA	ES	....	....	
	Division of Electrical, Communication and Cyber Systems						
Do	Division Director	Vacant	....	ES	....	....	
	Division of Industrial Innovation and Partnerships						
Do	Division Director	Jinliu Wang	TA	ES	....	....	02/01/14
	DIRECTORATE FOR GEOSCIENCES						
Do	Assistant Director	Vacant	....	ES	....	....	
Do	Deputy Assistant Director	Career Incumbent	CA	ES	....	....	
Do	Senior Staff Associate	......do	CA	ES	....	....	
	Division of Atmospheric and Geospace Sciences						
Do	Division Director	Vacant	....	ES	....	....	
Do	Head, Upper Atmosphere Research Section ...	Career Incumbent	CA	ES	....	....	
Do	Section Head, Atmosphere Section	David Joseph Verardo	TA	ES	....	....	07/20/13
	Division of Earth Sciences						
Do	Division Director	Vacant	....	ES	....	....	
Do	Head, Surface Earth Processes Section	Career Incumbent	CA	ES	....	....	
	Division of Ocean Sciences						
Do	Division Director	Vacant	....	ES	....	....	
Do	Head, Marine Geosciences Section	Career Incumbent	CA	ES	....	....	
Do	Head, Oceans Section	Vacant	....	ES	....	....	
	DIRECTORATE FOR MATHEMATICAL AND PHYSICAL SCIENCES						
Do	Assistant Director	......do	....	ES	....	....	
	Division of Astronomical Sciences						
Do	Division Director	James Scott Ulvestad	TA	ES	....	....	07/02/13
Do	Deputy Division Director	Vacant	....	ES	....	....	
	Division of Chemistry						
Do	Division Director	......do	....	ES	....	....	
Do	Deputy Division Director	Career Incumbent	CA	ES	....	....	
	Division of Materials Research						
Do	Division Director	Vacant	....	ES	....	....	
Do	Deputy Division Director	Career Incumbent	CA	ES	....	....	
	Division of Mathematical Sciences						
Do	Division Director	Vacant	....	ES	....	....	
	Division of Physics						
Do	Division Director	Career Incumbent	CA	ES	....	....	
Do	Deputy Division Director	......do	CA	ES	....	....	
	DIRECTORATE FOR SOCIAL, BEHAVIORAL AND ECONOMIC SCIENCES						
Do	Assistant Director	Vacant	....	ES	....	....	
	Division of Behavioral and Cognitive Sciences						
Do	Division Director	Career Incumbent	CA	ES	....	....	
Do	Deputy Division Director	Amber L. Story	TA	ES	....	....	10/24/12
	National Center for Science and Engineering Statistics						
Do	Division Director	Vacant	....	ES	....	....	
Do	Deputy Division Director	Career Incumbent	CA	ES	....	....	
	Division of Social and Economic Sciences						
Do	Division Director	Vacant	....	ES	....	....	
Do	Deputy Division Director	Kellina M. Craig-Henderson.	TA	ES	....	....	01/28/14
	OFFICE OF BUDGET, FINANCE AND AWARD MANAGEMENT						
Do	Deputy Director, Large Facility Projects	Career Incumbent	CA	ES	....	....	
	OFFICE OF INFORMATION AND RESOURCE MANAGEMENT						
Do	Senior Advisor	......do	CA	ES	....	....	
Do	......do	......do	CA	ES	....	....	
Do	Chief Information Officer	......do	CA	ES	....	....	

NATIONAL SCIENCE FOUNDATION—Continued

Location	Position	Name of Incumbent	Type of Appt.	Pay Plan	Level, Grade, or Pay	Tenure	Expires
	Division of Information Systems						
Arlington, VA	Division Director	Vacant	....	ES	....	....	

NATIONAL TRANSPORTATION SAFETY BOARD

Location	Position	Name of Incumbent	Type of Appt.	Pay Plan	Level, Grade, or Pay	Tenure	Expires
	OFFICE OF BOARD MEMBERS						
Washington, DC	Chairman	Deborah A.P. Hersman (D)	PAS	EX	III	2 Years	12/31/13
Do	Vice Chairman	Christopher A. Hart (D)	PAS	EX	IV	2 Years	12/31/12
Do	Member	Mark R. Rosekind (D)	PAS	EX	IV	5 Years	12/31/14
Do	......do	Robert L. Sumwalt (R)	PAS	EX	IV	5 Years	12/31/16
Do	......do	Earl F. Weener (R)	PAS	EX	IV	5 Years	12/31/15
Do	Executive Director	Vacant	....	ES	....	....	
Do	Special Assistant	Mary Cresence Stafford	SC	GS	15	....	
Do	......do	Patrick J. Lally	SC	GS	15	....	
Do	......do	Sean Dalton	SC	GS	15	....	
Do	......do	Louis H. Mayo, Jr.	SC	GS	15	....	
	Office of the General Counsel						
Do	General Counsel	Career Incumbent	CA	ES	....	....	
	Office of Communications						
Do	Director	Thomas E. Zoeller	NA	ES	....	....	

NORTHERN BORDER REGIONAL COMMISSION

Location	Position	Name of Incumbent	Type of Appt.	Pay Plan	Level, Grade, or Pay	Tenure	Expires
Bangor, ME	Federal Co-Chairperson	Sanford Blitz	PAS	EX	III	....	

NUCLEAR REGULATORY COMMISSION

Location	Position	Name of Incumbent	Type of Appt.	Pay Plan	Level, Grade, or Pay	Tenure	Expires
	OFFICE OF THE CHAIRMAN						
Rockville, MD	Chairman	Allison M. Macfarlane	PAS	EX	II	5 Years	06/30/13
Do	Chief of Staff	Phillip A. Niedzielski-Eichner.	NA	ES	....	....	
Do	Deputy Chief of Staff	Jacob Zimmerman	XS	OT	$165,300	....	
Do	Legal Counsel	Susan H. Vrahoretis	XS	OT	$144,385	....	
Do	Director of Communications	Vacant	XS	OT	....	....	
Do	Director of External Engagement	Mary J. Woollen	XS	OT	$125,109	....	
Do	Policy Advisor for Corporate Management	Clare V. Kasputys	XS	OT	$163,275	....	
Do	Policy Advisor for Security	Marshall D. Kohen	XS	OT	$140,259	....	
Do	Policy Advisor for Reactors	John R. Jolicoeur	XS	OT	$163,275	....	
Do	......do	Nathan T. Sanfilippo	XS	OT	$140,259	....	
Do	Policy Advisor for Materials	Heather M. Astwood	XS	OT	$163,275	....	
Do	......do	Andrew S. Imboden	XS	OT	$144,385	....	
	OFFICE OF COMMISSIONER SVINICKI						
Do	Commissioner	Kristine L. Svinicki	PAS	EX	III	5 Years	06/30/17
Do	Chief of Staff	Jeffry M. Sharkey	XS	OT	$165,300	....	
Do	Legal Counsel	Vacant	XS	OT	....	....	
Do	Technical Assistant for Reactors	Patrick I. Castleman	XS	OT	$163,995	....	
Do	Technical Assistant for Materials	Alan L. Frazier	XS	OT	$155,500	....	
	OFFICE OF COMMISSIONER APOSTOLAKIS						
Do	Commissioner	George Apostolakis	PAS	EX	III	5 Years	06/30/14
Do	Chief of Staff	Belkys Sosa	XS	OT	$165,300	....	
Do	Legal Counsel	Roger K. Davis	XS	OT	$165,300	....	
Do	Technical Assistant for Reactors	Nanette V. Gilles	XS	OT	$165,300	....	
Do	Technical Assistant for Materials	Steven L. Baggett	XS	OT	$165,300	....	
	OFFICE OF COMMISSIONER MAGWOOD						
Do	Commissioner	William D. Magwood IV	PAS	EX	III	5 Years	06/30/15

NUCLEAR REGULATORY COMMISSION—Continued

Location	Position	Name of Incumbent	Type of Appt.	Pay Plan	Level, Grade, or Pay	Tenure	Expires
Rockville, MD	Chief of Staff	Patrice M. Bubar	XS	OT	$165,300	....	
Do	Legal Counsel	Margaret J. Bupp	XS	OT	$148,675	....	
Do	Technical Assistant for Reactors	William T. Orders	XS	OT	$165,300	....	
Do	Technical Assistant for Materials	Rebecca Tadesse	XS	OT	$158,830	....	
	OFFICE OF COMMISSIONER OSTENDORFF						
Do	Commissioner	William C. Ostendorff	PAS	EX	III	5 Years	06/30/16
Do	Chief of Staff	John R. Tappert	XS	OT	$165,300	....	
Do	Legal Counsel	Kimberly Ann Sexton	XS	OT	$115,731	....	
Do	Technical Assistant for Reactors	Michael X. Franovich	XS	OT	$160,000	....	
Do	Technical Assistant for Materials	Andrea L. Kock	XS	OT	$160,000	....	
	ADVISORY COMMITTEE ON REACTOR SAFEGUARDS						
Do	Executive Director	Career Incumbent	CA	ES	....	....	
	OFFICE OF THE SECRETARY						
Do	Secretary of the Commission	......do	CA	ES	....	....	
	OFFICE OF THE CHIEF FINANCIAL OFFICER						
Do	Chief Financial Officer	......do	CA	ES	....	....	
	OFFICE OF THE GENERAL COUNSEL						
Do	General Counsel	Vacant	....	ES	....	....	
Do	Deputy General Counsel	......do	....	ES	....	....	
	Associate General Counsel for Licensing and Regulation						
Do	Associate General Counsel	Career Incumbent	CA	ES	....	....	
Do	Assistant General Counsel for Legal Counsel, Legislation, and Special Projects.	......do	CA	ES	....	....	
Do	Assistant General Counsel for Reactor and Materials Rulemaking.	......do	CA	ES	....	....	
Do	Assistant General Counsel for High-Level Waste, Fuel Cycle, and Nuclear Security.	......do	CA	ES	....	....	
	Associate General Counsel for Hearings, Enforcement, and Administration						
Do	Associate General Counsel	......do	CA	ES	....	....	
Do	Assistant General Counsel for Administration	......do	CA	ES	....	....	
Do	Assistant General Counsel for Materials Litigation and Enforcement.	......do	CA	ES	....	....	
Do	Assistant General Counsel for New Reactor Programs.	......do	CA	ES	....	....	
Do	Assistant General Counsel for Operating Reactors.	......do	CA	ES	....	....	
	OFFICE OF CONGRESSIONAL AFFAIRS						
Do	Director	......do	CA	ES	....	....	
	OFFICE OF PUBLIC AFFAIRS						
Do	Director	......do	CA	ES	....	....	
	OFFICE OF INTERNATIONAL PROGRAMS						
Do	Director	......do	CA	ES	....	....	
Do	Deputy Director	......do	CA	ES	....	....	
	OFFICE OF THE EXECUTIVE DIRECTOR FOR OPERATIONS						
Do	Executive Director for Operations	......do	CA	ES	....	....	
Do	Deputy Executive Director for Reactor and Preparedness Programs.	......do	CA	ES	....	....	
Do	Deputy Executive Director for Materials, Waste, Research, State, Tribal, and Compliance Programs.	......do	CA	ES	....	....	
Do	Deputy Executive Director for Corporate Management/Chief Information Officer.	......do	CA	ES	....	....	
Do	Assistant for Operations	......do	CA	ES	....	....	
	OFFICE OF ENFORCEMENT						
Do	Director	......do	CA	ES	....	....	
	OFFICE OF INVESTIGATIONS						
Do	Director	......do	CA	ES	....	....	
	OFFICE OF ADMINISTRATION						
Do	Director	......do	CA	ES	....	....	

NUCLEAR REGULATORY COMMISSION—Continued

Location	Position	Name of Incumbent	Type of Appt.	Pay Plan	Level, Grade, or Pay	Tenure	Expires
	OFFICE OF THE CHIEF HUMAN CAPITAL OFFICER						
Rockville, MD	Chief Human Capital Officer	Career Incumbent	CA	ES	....	....	
Do	Deputy Chief Human Capital Officer	......do	CA	ES	....	....	
Do	Associate Director for Human Resources Training and Development/Chief Learning Officer.	......do	CA	ES	....	....	
Do	Associate Director for Human Resources Operations and Policy.	......do	CA	ES	....	....	
	OFFICE OF INFORMATION SERVICES						
Do	Director, Office of Information Services/Deputy Chief Information Officer.	......do	CA	ES	....	....	
	OFFICE OF NUCLEAR SECURITY AND INCIDENT RESPONSE						
Do	Director	......do	CA	ES	....	....	
	OFFICE OF NUCLEAR REACTOR REGULATION						
Do	Director	......do	CA	ES	....	....	
	OFFICE OF NEW REACTORS						
Do	Director	......do	CA	ES	....	....	
	OFFICE OF NUCLEAR MATERIAL SAFETY AND SAFEGUARDS						
Do	Director	......do	CA	ES	....	....	
Do	Deputy Director	......do	CA	ES	....	....	
	OFFICE OF FEDERAL AND STATE MATERIALS AND ENVIRONMENTAL MANAGEMENT PROGRAMS						
Do	Director	......do	CA	ES	....	....	
	OFFICE OF NUCLEAR REGULATORY RESEARCH						
Do	Director	......do	CA	ES	....	....	
Do	Deputy Director	......do	CA	ES	....	....	
	REGION I						
King of Prussia, PA	Regional Administrator	......do	CA	ES	....	....	
	REGION II						
Atlanta, GA	Regional Administrator	......do	CA	ES	....	....	
	REGION III						
Lisle, IL	Regional Administrator	......do	CA	ES	....	....	
	REGION IV						
Arlington, TX	Regional Administrator	......do	CA	ES	....	....	

NUCLEAR REGULATORY COMMISSION OFFICE OF THE INSPECTOR GENERAL

Location	Position	Name of Incumbent	Type of Appt.	Pay Plan	Level, Grade, or Pay	Tenure	Expires
Rockville, MD	Inspector General	Hubert T. Bell	PAS	OT	....	....	
Do	Deputy Inspector General	David C. Lee	NA	ES	....	....	

NUCLEAR WASTE TECHNICAL REVIEW BOARD

Location	Position	Name of Incumbent	Type of Appt.	Pay Plan	Level, Grade, or Pay	Tenure	Expires
Arlington, VA	Chairman	Rodney C. Ewing	PA	AD	....	....	
Do	Board Member	Jean M. Bahr	PA	AD	....	....	
Do	......do	Steven M. Becker	PA	AD	....	....	
Do	......do	Susan L. Brantley	PA	AD	....	....	
Do	......do	Sue B. Clark	PA	AD	....	....	
Do	......do	Efi G. Foufoula	PA	AD	....	....	
Do	......do	Gerald S. Frankel	PA	AD	....	....	
Do	......do	Linda K. Nozick	PA	AD	....	....	
Do	......do	Kenneth L. Peddicord	PA	AD	....	....	
Do	......do	Paul J. Turinsky	PA	AD	....	....	
Do	......do	Mary Lou Zoback	PA	AD	....	....	

NUCLEAR WASTE TECHNICAL REVIEW BOARD—Continued

Location	Position	Name of Incumbent	Type of Appt.	Pay Plan	Level, Grade, or Pay	Tenure	Expires
Arlington, VA	Executive Director	Career Incumbent	CA	ES	....	....	

OCCUPATIONAL SAFETY AND HEALTH REVIEW COMMISSION

Location	Position	Name of Incumbent	Type of Appt.	Pay Plan	Level, Grade, or Pay	Tenure	Expires
Washington, DC	**OFFICE OF COMMISSIONERS** Commission Member (Chairman)	Thomasina V. Rogers	PAS	EX	III	....	
Do	Commission Member	Vacant	PAS	EX	IV	....	
Do	......do	Cynthia L. Attwood	PAS	EX	IV	....	
Do	Counsel	Janice L. Glick	SC	GS	15	....	
Do	Chief of Staff and Legal Counsel to the Chairman.	Richard L. Huberman, Esq.	NA	ES	....	....	
Do	Confidential Assistant to the Chairman	Saint M. Ahmir-Abdul	SC	GS	13	....	
Do	**OFFICE OF THE GENERAL COUNSEL** General Counsel	Career Incumbent	CA	ES	....	....	

OFFICE OF THE FEDERAL COORDINATOR ALASKA NATURAL GAS TRANSPORTATION PROJECTS

Location	Position	Name of Incumbent	Type of Appt.	Pay Plan	Level, Grade, or Pay	Tenure	Expires
Washington, DC	Federal Coordinator	Larry Persily	PAS	EX	III	....	

OFFICE OF GOVERNMENT ETHICS

Location	Position	Name of Incumbent	Type of Appt.	Pay Plan	Level, Grade, or Pay	Tenure	Expires
Washington, DC	Director	Vacant	PAS	EX	III	....	
Do	General Counsel	Career Incumbent	CA	ES	....	....	

OFFICE OF NAVAJO AND HOPI INDIAN RELOCATION

Location	Position	Name of Incumbent	Type of Appt.	Pay Plan	Level, Grade, or Pay	Tenure	Expires
Flagstaff, AZ	Commissioner	Vacant	PAS	EX	IV	....	
Do	Executive Director	Career Incumbent	CA	ES	....	....	
Do	Deputy Executive Director	Vacant	....	ES	....	....	

OFFICE OF PERSONNEL MANAGEMENT

Location	Position	Name of Incumbent	Type of Appt.	Pay Plan	Level, Grade, or Pay	Tenure	Expires
Washington, DC	**OFFICE OF THE DIRECTOR** Director	John M. Berry	PAS	EX	II	4 Years	04/03/13
Do	Deputy Director	Vacant	PAS	EX	III	....	
Do	Chief of Staff and Director of External Affairs	Elizabeth A. Montoya	NA	ES	....	....	
Do	Senior Advisor to the Director	Michael A. Grant	NA	ES	....	....	
Do	Senior Advisor for Pay Reform and Federal Prevailing Rate Advisory Committee Chair.	Sheldon Ira Friedman	TA	ES	....	....	02/28/13
Do	Chief Operating Officer	Career Incumbent	CA	ES	....	....	
Do	Deputy Chief of Staff for Programs and Initiatives.	Justin R. Johnson	NA	ES	....	....	
Do	......do	Jennifer I. Mason	NA	ES	....	....	
Do	Executive Director, CHCO Council	Kathryn M. Medina	SC	GS	15	....	
Do	Counselor to the Director	Victor J. Basile	SC	GS	15	....	
Do	Director of Advance	Katie M. Pennell	SC	GS	12	....	
Do	Senior Advisor to the Director and Deputy PIO for Innovation.	Matthew Wesley Collier	SC	GS	15	....	

OFFICE OF PERSONNEL MANAGEMENT—Continued

Location	Position	Name of Incumbent	Type of Appt.	Pay Plan	Level, Grade, or Pay	Tenure	Expires
	Executive Secretariat and Ombudsman						
Washington, DC	Director	Career Incumbent	CA	ES	....	....	
	COMMUNICATIONS AND PUBLIC LIAISON						
Do	Director	Thomas Joseph Robert Richards.	NA	ES	....	....	
Do	Deputy Director	Catherine Hand	SC	GS	15	....	
Do	Press Secretary	Sedelta D. Verble	SC	GS	15	....	
Do	Strategic Communications Specialist	John Hamer Marble, Jr.	SC	GS	12	....	
Do	Communications Specialist	Joseph Peter Resnek	SC	GS	9	....	
Do	Speechwriter	John A. La Rue	SC	GS	12	....	
	OFFICE OF THE GENERAL COUNSEL						
Do	General Counsel	Elaine D. Kaplan	NA	ES	....	....	
Do	Deputy General Counsel	Career Incumbent	CA	ES	....	....	
Do	......do	......do	CA	ES	....	....	
Do	Deputy General Counsel for Policy	Robert Harry Shriver III ...	NA	ES	....	....	
Do	Attorney-Advisor	Mauro Albert Morales	SC	GS	15	....	
	CONGRESSIONAL AND LEGISLATIVE AFFAIRS						
Do	Director	Tania Alexia Shand	NA	ES	....	....	
Do	Senior Advisor for Learning and Mentoring ...	Neal Malik Walker	SC	GS	13	....	
Do	Congressional Relations Officer	Christopher T. Medley	SC	GS	12	....	
	PLANNING AND POLICY ANALYSIS						
Do	Director	Jonathan Rockwell Foley ...	NA	ES	....	....	
Do	Deputy Director	Career Incumbent	CA	ES	....	....	
Do	Deputy Performance Improvement Officer	Bernhard Sigmund Kluger	SC	GS	15	....	
	HEALTHCARE AND INSURANCE						
Do	Director	John Joseph O'Brien	TA	ES	....	....	01/04/13
Do	Deputy Director	Career Incumbent	CA	ES	....	....	
Do	Assistant Director, National Healthcare Operations.	......do	CA	ES	....	....	
	EMPLOYEE SERVICES						
Do	Associate Director, Employee Services and Chief Human Capital Officer.	......do	CA	ES	....	....	
Do	Deputy Associate Director	......do	CA	ES	....	....	
Do	Deputy Associate Director, Recruitment and Hiring.	......do	CA	ES	....	....	
Do	Assistant Director, Veterans Services	......do	CA	ES	....	....	
Do	Assistant Director, Agency Support and Technical Assistance.	......do	CA	ES	....	....	
Do	Deputy Associate Director, Pay and Leave	......do	CA	ES	....	....	
Do	Deputy Associate Director, Partnership and Labor Relations.	......do	CA	ES	....	....	
Do	Deputy Associate Director, OPM Human Resources and Deputy Chief Human Capital Officer.	......do	CA	ES	....	....	
Do	Deputy Associate Director, Executive Resources and Employee Development.	......do	CA	ES	....	....	
Do	Director of External Veterans/Military Affairs and Community Outreach.	Michele S. Jones	NA	ES	....	....	
	MERIT SYSTEM AUDIT AND COMPLIANCE						
Do	Associate Director	Career Incumbent	CA	ES	....	....	
Do	Director, Combined Federal Campaign Operations.	......do	CA	ES	....	....	
Do	Director, Internal Oversight and Compliance	......do	CA	ES	....	....	
	FEDERAL INVESTIGATIVE SERVICES						
Boyers, PA	Associate Director	......do	CA	ES	....	....	
Washington, DC ...	Deputy Associate Director, External Affairs ...	......do	CA	ES	....	....	
Do	Deputy Associate Director, Technical Services	Vacant	....	ES	....	....	
Do	Deputy Associate Director, Administrative Services.	Career Incumbent	CA	ES	....	....	
Boyers, PA	Senior Advisor	......do	CA	ES	....	....	
	HUMAN RESOURCES SOLUTIONS						
Charlottesville, VA	Director, Federal Executive Institute	......do	CA	ES	....	....	
Washington, DC	Associate Director	......do	CA	ES	....	....	
Do	Deputy Associate Director, Leadership and Talent Management Solutions.	Vacant		ES	....	....	
Do	Deputy Associate Director, Emerging Solutions/HR Innovations.	Career Incumbent	CA	ES	....	....	

OFFICE OF PERSONNEL MANAGEMENT—Continued

Location	Position	Name of Incumbent	Type of Appt.	Pay Plan	Level, Grade, or Pay	Tenure	Expires
Washington, DC	Assistant Director, HR Management Solutions.	Vacant	....	ES	....	....	
Do	Assistant Director, Leadership and HR Development Solutions.	Career Incumbent	CA	ES	....	....	
Do	Assistant Director, HR Strategy and Evaluation Solutions.	......do	CA	ES	....	....	
Do	Assistant Director, Account Management	......do	CA	ES	....	....	
Do	Deputy Associate Director, Human Resources Solutions.	......do	CA	ES	....	....	
Do	Deputy Assistant Director, Leadership and HR Development Solutions.	......do	CA	ES	....	....	
	OFFICE OF THE CHIEF FINANCIAL OFFICER						
Do	Associate Chief Financial Officer, Budget and Performance.	......do	CA	ES	....	....	
Do	Associate Chief Financial Officer, Center for Financial Systems Management.	......do	CA	ES	....	....	
	CHIEF INFORMATION OFFICER						
Do	Deputy Chief Information Officer	......do	CA	ES	....	....	
Do	Deputy Chief Information Officer for Operations.	......do	CA	ES	....	....	
Do	Assistant Director, Integrated Hiring Solutions.	......do	CA	ES	....	....	
	DIVERSITY AND INCLUSION						
Do	Director, Office of Diversity and Inclusion	......do	CA	ES	....	....	

OFFICE OF PERSONNEL MANAGEMENT OFFICE OF THE INSPECTOR GENERAL

Location	Position	Name of Incumbent	Type of Appt.	Pay Plan	Level, Grade, or Pay	Tenure	Expires
Washington, DC	**OFFICE OF THE INSPECTOR GENERAL** Inspector General	Patrick E. McFarland	PAS	OT	$170,259	....	

OFFICE OF SPECIAL COUNSEL

Location	Position	Name of Incumbent	Type of Appt.	Pay Plan	Level, Grade, or Pay	Tenure	Expires
	HEADQUARTERS, OFFICE OF SPECIAL COUNSEL						
Washington, DC	Special Counsel	Carolyn N. Lerner	PAS	EX	IV	....	
Do	Deputy Special Counsel	Mark P. Cohen	NA	ES	....	....	
Do	Senior Associate Special Counsel (SASC)	Vacant	....	ES	....	....	
Do	Associate Special Counsel (IPD)	Bruce D. Fong	TA	ES	....	....	05/01/15
Do	Director, Office of Planning and Analysis	Vacant	....	ES	....	....	
Do	Director, Administrative Services	......do	....	ES	....	....	
Do	Office of General Counsel	......do	....	ES	....	....	

OFFICE OF THE DIRECTOR OF NATIONAL INTELLIGENCE

Location	Position	Name of Incumbent	Type of Appt.	Pay Plan	Level, Grade, or Pay	Tenure	Expires
Washington, DC	Director	James R. Clapper	PAS	EX	I	5 Years	
Do	Principal Deputy Director	Stephanie L. O'Sullivan	PAS	EX	II	5 Years	
Do	Director, National Counterterrorism Center ..	Matthew Glen Olsen	PAS	EX	II	5 Years	
Do	Intelligence Community Inspector General	Irvin Charles McCullough III.	PAS	EX	II	5 Years	
Do	General Counsel	Robert Litt	PAS	EX	IV	5 Years	
Do	Intelligence Community Chief Information Officer.	Adolfo Tarasiuk, Jr.	PA	ES	$179,690	5 Years	
Do	Program Manager - Information Sharing Environment.	Kshemendra N. Paul	PA	ES	$176,998	5 Years	

OVERSEAS PRIVATE INVESTMENT CORPORATION

Location	Position	Name of Incumbent	Type of Appt.	Pay Plan	Level, Grade, or Pay	Tenure	Expires
Washington, DC	President	Elizabeth Lascelles Littlefield.	PAS	EX	III	....	
Do	Executive Vice President	Mimi Ewnet Alemayehou ..	PAS	EX	IV	....	
Do	Board Member	Katherine M. Gehl	PAS	EX	IV	....	
Do	......do	Michael James Warren	PAS	EX	IV	....	
Do	......do	Roberto R. Herencia	PAS	EX	IV	....	
Do	......do	Maxwell T. Kennedy	PAS	EX	IV	....	
Do	......do	Terry Lewis	PAS	EX	IV	....	
Do	......do	Kevin G. Nealer	PAS	EX	IV	....	
Do	......do	James A. Torrey	PAS	EX	IV	....	
Do	Chief of Staff	Matthew Todd Schneider ..	XS	AD	$175,218	....	
Do	Deputy Chief of Staff and Senior Advisor to President.	Jacqueline Strasser Higgins.	XS	AD	$169,700	....	
Do	Managing Director, Investment Development Coordination.	John F. Moran	XS	AD	$164,830	....	
Do	Vice President, External Affairs	Judith Delzoppo Pryor	XS	AD	$175,218	....	
Do	Vice President, Investment Policy	John E. Morton	XS	AD	$175,218	....	
Do	Vice President, Investment Funds	Jay Koh	XS	AD	$175,218	....	
Do	Vice President and General Counsel	Don S. De Amicis	XS	AD	$175,218	....	
Do	Advisor, Office of the President	Maria Paula Garcia Tufro	XS	AD	$100,000	....	
Do	Communications Director	Nancy Sue Payne	XS	AD	$152,635	....	
Do	Director, Congressional Affairs	Aysha R. House-Moshi	XS	AD	$127,883	....	
Do	Special Assistant	Gabriel J. Bitol	XS	AD	$90,000	....	
Do	......do	Allison M. Carragher	XS	AD	$60,648	....	
Do	Executive Assistant	Alexander W. Hirschhorn ..	XS	AD	$62,467	....	
Do	......do	Rebecca E. Barnes	XS	AD	$87,350	....	

PEACE CORPS

Location	Position	Name of Incumbent	Type of Appt.	Pay Plan	Level, Grade, or Pay	Tenure	Expires
	OFFICE OF THE DIRECTOR						
Washington, DC	Director	Aaron S. Williams	PAS	EX	III	....	
Do	Counselor / White House Liaison	Elisa D. Montoya	XS	FE	....	3 Years	
Do	Special Assistant	Conor Sanchez	XS	FP	....	3 Years	
	Office of the General Counsel						
Do	General Counsel	Michael W. Rubin	XS	FE	....	....	
	Office of the Chief Financial Officer						
Do	Chief Financial Officer	Joseph L. Hepp	XS	FE	....	....	
	Office of Congressional Relations						
Do	Director	Paul C. Weinberger	XS	FE	....	....	
	Office of Innovation						
Do	Director	Cynthia McVay	XS	FE	....	....	
Do	Special Assistant	Patrick M. Choquette	XS	FP	....	3 Years	
	OFFICE OF THE DEPUTY DIRECTOR						
Do	Deputy Director	Carolyn H. Radelet	PAS	EX	IV	....	
	Office of Global Operations						
Do	Associate Director	Esther T. Benjamin	XS	FE	....	3 Years	
Do	Regional Director	Carlos Torres	XS	FE	....	....	
Do	......do	Helen A. Lowman	XS	FE	....	....	
Do	......do	Richard C. Day	XS	FE	....	3 Years	
Do	Director of Peace Corps Response	Sarah E. Morgenthau	XS	FE	....	3 Years	
	Office of Strategic Information, Research and Planning						
Do	Director	Cathryn L. Thorup	XS	FE	....	3 Years	
	Office of Volunteer Recruitment and Selection						
Do	Associate Director	Earl Yates	XS	FE	....	3 Years	
	Office of Volunteer Support						
Do	Associate Director	Jules M. Delaune	XS	FE	....	....	
	Office of Communications						
Do	Director	Maureen Bridget Knightly	XS	FE	....	....	
Do	Press Director	Vacant	XS	FP	....	....	
	OFFICE OF THE CHIEF OF STAFF						
Do	Chief of Staff	William Stacy Rhodes	XS	FE	....	....	

PEACE CORPS—Continued

Location	Position	Name of Incumbent	Type of Appt.	Pay Plan	Level, Grade, or Pay	Tenure	Expires
	Office of Management						
Washington, DC	Associate Director	Vacant	XS	FE	....	....	
	Office of Strategic Partnerships						
Do	Associate Director	......do	XS	FE	....	....	
Do	Director of Intergovernmental Affairs and Global Partnerships.	Nicole Katherine Mlade	XS	FP	....	3 Years	
Do	Director of Gifts and Grants Management	Jennifer L. Chavez Rubio ..	XS	FP	....	3 Years	
Do	Director of University and Domestic Partnerships.	Vacant	XS	FP	....	....	
Do	Special Assistant to the Director of Gifts and Grants Management.	......do	XS	FP	....	....	
	Office of the Chief Information Officer						
Do	Chief Information Officer	Dorine C. Andrews	XS	FE	....	3 Years	
	Office of Compliance						
Do	Special Assistant to Chief of Staff on Compliance.	Jennifer Parrish Taylor	XS	FP	....	3 Years	

PENSION BENEFIT GUARANTY CORPORATION

Location	Position	Name of Incumbent	Type of Appt.	Pay Plan	Level, Grade, or Pay	Tenure	Expires
	OFFICE OF THE DIRECTOR						
Washington, DC	Director	Joshua Gotbaum	PAS	EX	III	....	
	Office of Policy and External Affairs						
Do	Deputy Director, Policy	Laricke D. Blanchard	SC	SL	....	....	
Do	Director, Communications and Public Affairs Department.	John Jioni Palmer	SC	GS	15	....	

POSTAL REGULATORY COMMISSION

Location	Position	Name of Incumbent	Type of Appt.	Pay Plan	Level, Grade, or Pay	Tenure	Expires
Washington, DC	Chairman	Ruth Y. Goldway	PAS	EX	IV	6 Years	11/22/14
Do	Commissioner	Nanci E. Langley	PAS	EX	IV	6 Years	11/22/12
Do	......do	Mark Acton	PAS	EX	IV	6 Years	10/14/16
Do	......do	Tony Hammond	PAS	EX	IV	6 Years	10/14/12
Do	......do	Robert G. Taub	PAS	EX	IV	6 Years	10/14/16

PRESIDENT'S COMMISSION ON WHITE HOUSE FELLOWSHIPS

Location	Position	Name of Incumbent	Type of Appt.	Pay Plan	Level, Grade, or Pay	Tenure	Expires
Washington, DC	Director	Cindy S. Moelis	NA	ES	....	....	
Do	Deputy Director	Erika J. Henderson	SC	GS	13	....	
Do	Special Assistant	Sophia B. Kim	SC	GS	12	....	

PRESIDIO TRUST

Location	Position	Name of Incumbent	Type of Appt.	Pay Plan	Level, Grade, or Pay	Tenure	Expires
San Francisco, CA	Chairman, Board of Directors	Nancy Bechtle	PA	WC	....	4 Years	05/04/15
Do	Member, Board of Directors	David H. Grubb	PA	WC	....	4 Years	05/04/13
Do	......do	William R. Hambrecht	PA	WC	....	4 Years	05/04/13
Do	......do	Charlene Harvey	PA	WC	....	4 Years	05/04/13
Do	......do	John Reynolds	NA	WC	....	4 Years	05/13/13
Do	......do	Alexander Mehran	PA	WC	....	4 Years	05/04/15
Do	......do	Paula Collins	PA	WC	....	4 Years	05/04/15
Do	Executive Director	Craig Middleton	XS	AD	....	....	

RAILROAD RETIREMENT BOARD

Location	Position	Name of Incumbent	Type of Appt.	Pay Plan	Level, Grade, or Pay	Tenure	Expires
	BOARD MEMBERS						
Chicago, IL	Chairman	Michael S. Schwartz	PAS	EX	III	5 Years	08/28/12
Do	Member of Board	Jerome F. Kever	PAS	EX	IV	5 Years	08/28/08
Do	......do	Walter A. Barrows	PAS	EX	IV	5 Years	08/28/14

RAILROAD RETIREMENT BOARD OFFICE OF THE INSPECTOR GENERAL

Location	Position	Name of Incumbent	Type of Appt.	Pay Plan	Level, Grade, or Pay	Tenure	Expires
Chicago, IL	Inspector General	Martin Dickman	PAS	OT			

RECOVERY ACCOUNTABILITY AND TRANSPARENCY BOARD

Location	Position	Name of Incumbent	Type of Appt.	Pay Plan	Level, Grade, or Pay	Tenure	Expires
Washington, DC	Director of Communications	Edward T. Pound	XS	AD	$155,500		
Do	Information Technology Specialist	Donald I. Cox	XS	AD	$146,000		

SECURITIES AND EXCHANGE COMMISSION

Location	Position	Name of Incumbent	Type of Appt.	Pay Plan	Level, Grade, or Pay	Tenure	Expires
	OFFICE OF THE CHAIRMAN						
Washington, DC	Chairman	Mary L. Schapiro	PAS	EX	III		
Do	Commissioner	Daniel M. Gallagher, Jr.	PAS	EX	IV		
Do	......do	Elisse B. Walter	PAS	EX	IV		
Do	......do	Luis A. Aguilar	PAS	EX	IV		
Do	......do	Troy A. Paredes	PAS	EX	IV		
Do	Chief of Staff	Didem A. Nisanci	SC	OT	$230,700		
Do	Director of Communications	Myron L. Marlin	SC	OT	$230,700		
Do	Confidential Assistant	Ammani V. Nagesh	SC	OT	$103,550		
Do	Special Assistant	Leidy Valencia	SC	OT	$69,466		
Do	Confidential Assistant	Awilda Santiago	SC	OT	$55,179		
Do	......do	Mary E. Christ	SC	OT	$106,125		
Do	......do	Kathleen Gallagher	SC	OT	$97,375		
Do	......do	Diana Lynn Carpenter	SC	OT	$86,920		
Do	......do	Jule Konick	SC	OT	$91,770		
Do	Legislative and Intergovernmental Affairs Specialist.	Anne-Marie Kelley	SC	OT	$143,928		
	OFFICE OF THE CHIEF OPERATING OFFICER						
Do	Chief Operating Officer	Jeff Heslop	SC	OT	$230,700		
Philadelphia, PA	Executive Staff Assistant	Rachel E. Hurnyak	SC	OT	$70,183		
	OFFICE OF THE GENERAL COUNSEL						
Washington, DC	Confidential Assistant	Shara Brooks	SC	OT	$64,425		
	DIVISION OF ENFORCEMENT						
Do	Secretary	Sheila A. Russell	SC	OT	$89,797		
	DIVISION OF CORPORATION FINANCE						
Do	Managing Executive	Peter M. Uhlmann	SC	OT	$230,700		
Do	Confidential Assistant	Janet S. Schmautz	SC	OT	$77,646		
	DIVISION OF INVESTMENT MANAGEMENT						
Do	Confidential Assistant	Sandra M. Hult	SC	OT	$77,901		
	OFFICE OF COMPLIANCE INSPECTIONS AND EXAMINATIONS						
Do	Confidential Assistant	Joan M. Forrester	SC	OT	$64,425		

SELECTIVE SERVICE SYSTEM

Location	Position	Name of Incumbent	Type of Appt.	Pay Plan	Level, Grade, or Pay	Tenure	Expires
	OFFICE OF THE DIRECTOR						
Arlington, VA	Director	Lawrence G Romo	PAS	EX	IV	....	
Do	Deputy Director	Edward T. Allard III	NA	ES	....	....	

SMALL BUSINESS ADMINISTRATION

Location	Position	Name of Incumbent	Type of Appt.	Pay Plan	Level, Grade, or Pay	Tenure	Expires
	OFFICE OF THE ADMINISTRATOR						
Washington, DC	Administrator	Karen Gordon Mills	PAS	EX	III	....	
Do	Deputy Administrator	Marie Collins Johns	PAS	EX	IV	....	
Do	Chief Operating Officer	Career Incumbent	CA	ES	....	....	
Do	Senior Advisor to the Chief Operating Officer	Megan K. Smith	SC	GS	12	....	
Do	Chief of Staff	Jonathan Swain	NA	ES	....	....	
Do	Deputy Chief of Staff	Michele Chang	NA	ES	....	....	
Do	White House Liaison	Daniel S. Jones	SC	GS	14	....	
Do	Special Advisor to the Deputy Administrator	Joseph L. Tansey III	SC	GS	11	....	
Do	Senior Advisor to the Deputy Administrator ..	Marisa Renee Lee	SC	GS	14	....	
Do	Director of Scheduling and Operations	Emily Buttrey	SC	GS	13	....	
Do	Special Assistant to the Administrator	Rachel R. Thomas	SC	GS	7	....	
Do	Senior Policy Advisor	Jessica A. Milano	SC	GS	15	....	
	Office of Advocacy						
Do	Chief Counsel for Advocacy	Winslow L. Sargeant	PAS	EX	IV	....	
	Office of the General Counsel						
Do	General Counsel	Sara Lipscomb	NA	ES	....	....	
	Office of Congressional and Legislative Affairs						
Do	Assistant Administrator	Nicholas J. Coutsos	NA	ES	....	....	
Do	Deputy Assistant Administrator	Jordan Montgomery Haas ..	SC	GS	14	....	
Do	.....do	Thaddeus W. Inge	SC	GS	14	....	
Do	Special Assistant	Meina Banh	SC	GS	11	....	
	Office of Field Operations						
Do	Assistant Associate Administrator	Career Incumbent	CA	ES	....	....	
Do	Associate Administrator	Robert Scott Hill	NA	ES	....	....	
Do	Deputy Associate Administrator	Career Incumbent	CA	ES	....	....	
Do	Assistant Administrator for Non-Contiguous States and Territories and District Director for Puerto Rico.	Vacant	....	ES	....	....	
New York, NY	Regional Administrator, Region II	Silva-Puras P. Jorge	SC	GS	15	....	
Atlanta, GA	Regional Administrator for Region IV	Cassius F. Butts	SC	GS	15	....	
Chicago, IL	Regional Administrator, Region V	Marianne O'Brien Markowitz.	SC	GS	15	....	
Dallas, TX	Regional Administrator, Region VI	Yolanda Garcia Olivarez ..	SC	GS	15	....	
Kansas City, MO ...	Regional Administrator, Region VII	Patricia I. Brown-Dixon	SC	GS	15	....	
Los Angeles, CA	Regional Administrator, Region IX	Elizabeth B. Echols	SC	GS	15	....	
Seattle, WA	Regional Administrator, Region X	Calvin William Goings	SC	GS	15	....	05/11/10
	Executive Office of Disaster Strategic Planning and Operations						
Washington, DC	Chief	Career Incumbent	CA	ES	....	....	
	Office of Communications and Public Liaison						
Do	Assistant Administrator	Frederick Joseph Baldassaro, Jr..	SC	GS	15	....	
Do	Deputy Assistant Administrator	Career Incumbent	CA	ES	....	....	
Do	Deputy Assistant Administrator for Communications and Public Liaison.	Hayley Kitt Meadvin	SC	GS	14	....	
Do	Press Secretary	Emily Elizabeth Cain	SC	GS	13	....	
Do	Senior Speechwriter	Scott Evan Frotman	SC	GS	15	....	
Do	Deputy Press Secretary	Nina S. Smith	SC	GS	12	....	
	Office of the Chief Financial Officer						
Denver, CO	Director of Denver Finance Center	Vacant	....	ES	....	....	
	Office of Veterans' Business Development						
Washington, DC	Associate Administrator	Matthew R. Jeppson	NA	ES	....	....	
	Office of Capital Access						
Do	Associate Administrator	Jeanne Anderson Hulit	NA	ES	....	....	
Do	Director, Capital Access Loan Processing Systems.	Career Incumbent	CA	ES	....	....	12/10/08
Do	Director, Credit Risk Management	.....do	CA	ES	....	....	

SMALL BUSINESS ADMINISTRATION—Continued

Location	Position	Name of Incumbent	Type of Appt.	Pay Plan	Level, Grade, or Pay	Tenure	Expires
Washington, DC	Deputy Associate Administrator for Capital Access.	John P. Kelley	SC	GS	15	....	
Do	Special Advisor	Hosheus D. Isaac	SC	GS	14	....	
	Office of Entrepreneurial Development						
Do	Associate Administrator	Michael A. Chodos	NA	ES	....	....	
Do	Associate Administrator for Small Business Development Centers.	Vacant	....	ES	....	....	
Do	Assistant Administrator for Women's Business Ownership and Executive Director of the Council on Underserved Communities.	Ana R. Harvey	NA	ES	....	....	
Do	Senior Advisor to the Associate Administrator	Brian M. Compagnone	SC	GS	14	....	
Do	Director of Clusters and Skills Initiatives	Erin E. Andrew	SC	GS	14	....	
	Office of Management and Administration						
Do	Deputy Associate Administrator	Career Incumbent	CA	ES	....	....	
	Office of the Chief Information Officer						
Do	Chief Information Officer	.....do	CA	ES	....	....	
	Office of Government Contracting and Business Development						
Do	Director	.....do	CA	ES	....	....	
Do	Deputy Associate Deputy Administrator	.....do	CA	ES	....	....	
Do	Associate Administrator	Ali John Shoraka	NA	ES	....	....	
Do	Special Advisor to the Associate Administrator.	John J. Spears	SC	GS	13	....	
Do	.....do	Aditi Sharma Dussault	SC	GS	12	....	
	Office of the Ombudsman						
Do	National Ombudsman and Assistant Administrator for Regulatory Enforcement Fairness.	Vacant	....	ES	....	....	
	Office of Faith-Based and Community Initiatives						
Do	Assistant Administrator	Gerard Cox Flavin	SC	GS	15	....	
	OFFICE OF DISASTER ASSISTANCE						
Do	Associate Administrator	Career Incumbent	CA	ES	....	....	
Do	Deputy Associate Administrator	.....do	CA	ES	....	....	
	OFFICE OF INTERNATIONAL TRADE						
Do	Associate Administrator	Dario J. Gomez	SC	GS	15	....	
Do	Deputy Associate Administrator	Career Incumbent	CA	ES	....	....	
	OFFICE OF INVESTMENT						
Do	Associate Administrator	Sean J. Greene	NA	ES	....	....	
	OFFICE OF NATIVE AMERICAN AFFAIRS						
Do	Assistant Administrator	Christopher Lee James	SC	GS	15	....	

SMALL BUSINESS ADMINISTRATION OFFICE OF THE INSPECTOR GENERAL

Location	Position	Name of Incumbent	Type of Appt.	Pay Plan	Level, Grade, or Pay	Tenure	Expires
Washington, DC	Inspector General	Peggy Elizabeth Gustafson	PAS	OT	....	....	

SMITHSONIAN INSTITUTION

Location	Position	Name of Incumbent	Type of Appt.	Pay Plan	Level, Grade, or Pay	Tenure	Expires
	OFFICE OF THE SECRETARY						
	Woodrow Wilson International Center for Scholars						
Washington, DC	Deputy Director	Samuel F. Wells, Jr.	XS	OT	$128,199	....	
Do	Deputy Director for Planning and Management.	Dean W. Anderson	XS	OT	$130,200	....	

SOCIAL SECURITY ADMINISTRATION

Location	Position	Name of Incumbent	Type of Appt.	Pay Plan	Level, Grade, or Pay	Tenure	Expires
	OFFICE OF THE COMMISSIONER						
Washington, DC	Commissioner	Michael J. Astrue	PAS	EX	I	6 Years	01/19/13
Do	Deputy Commissioner of Social Security	Carolyn W. Colvin	PAS	EX	II	6 Years	01/19/13
Woodlawn, MD	Chief of Staff	Career Incumbent	CA	ES	....	....	
Washington, DC	Deputy Chief of Staff	......do	CA	ES	....	....	
Do	Executive Secretary	Vacant	....	ES	....	....	
Woodlawn, MD	Senior Advisor to the Deputy Commissioner ..	Career Incumbent	CA	ES	....	....	
Washington, DC	......do	......do	CA	ES	....	....	
Woodlawn, MD	......do	Stacy L. Rodgers	SC	GS	15	....	
	Office of International Programs						
Do	Associate Commissioner for International Programs.	Career Incumbent	CA	ES	....	....	
	Social Security Advisory Board						
Washington, DC	Chairman	Marsha R. Katz	XS	PD	$596	6 Years	09/30/12
Do	Member	Jagadeesh Gokhale	XS	PD	$596	6 Years	09/30/15
Do	......do	Dorcas R. Hardy	XS	PD	$596	6 Years	09/30/16
Do	......do	Barbara B. Kennelly	XS	PD	$596	6 Years	09/30/17
Do	......do	Mark J. Warshawsky	PA	PD	$596	6 Years	09/30/12
Do	......do	Vacant	PA	PD	....	....	
Do	......do	......do	PA	PD	....	....	
Do	Staff Director	Deborah K. Sullivan	XS	AD	....	....	
Do	Deputy Staff Director	Vacant	XS	AD	....	....	
Do	Professional Staff Member	Joel A. Feinleib	XS	AD	....	....	
Do	......do	Beverly K. Rollins	XS	AD	....	....	
Do	......do	David D. Warner	XS	AD	....	....	
Do	......do	Jacqueline L. Chapin	XS	AD	....	....	
Do	......do	Jeremy P. Elder	XS	AD	....	....	
Do	Staff Assistant	Roberta A. Walker	XS	AD	....	....	
	OFFICE OF BUDGET, FINANCE AND MANAGEMENT						
Woodlawn, MD	Deputy Commissioner	Career Incumbent	CA	ES	....	....	
Do	Senior Advisor	......do	CA	ES	....	....	
	Office of Facilities and Supply Management						
Do	Associate Commissioner	......do	CA	ES	....	....	
Do	Deputy Associate Commissioner	......do	CA	ES	....	....	
	Office of Security and Emergency Preparedness						
Do	Associate Commissioner	Vacant	....	ES	....	....	
	OFFICE OF COMMUNICATIONS						
Do	Deputy Commissioner	James J. Courtney, Jr.	NA	ES	....	....	
Do	Assistant Deputy Commissioner	Career Incumbent	CA	ES	....	....	
Do	Press Officer	Vacant	....	ES	....	....	
	Office of External Affairs						
Do	Associate Commissioner	......do	....	ES	....	....	
	Office of Communications Planning and Technology						
Do	Associate Commissioner	......do	....	ES	....	....	
	Office of Public Inquiries						
Do	Associate Commissioner	Career Incumbent	CA	ES	....	....	
	Office of Open Government						
Do	Associate Commissioner	......do	CA	ES	....	....	
	OFFICE OF DISABILITY ADJUDICATION AND REVIEW						
Falls Church, VA ...	Senior Advisor to the Deputy Commissioner ..	......do	CA	ES	....	....	
	Office of Executive Operations and Human Resources						
Do	Associate Commissioner	......do	CA	ES	....	....	
Woodlawn, MD	Deputy Associate Commissioner	......do	CA	ES	....	....	
	Office of Budget, Facilities and Security						
Falls Church, VA ...	Associate Commissioner	......do	CA	ES	....	....	
Do	Deputy Associate Commissioner	......do	CA	ES	....	....	
	Office of Electronic Services and Strategic Information						
Do	Associate Commissioner	......do	CA	ES	....	....	
Do	Deputy Associate Commissioner	Vacant	....	ES	....	....	

SOCIAL SECURITY ADMINISTRATION—Continued

Location	Position	Name of Incumbent	Type of Appt.	Pay Plan	Level, Grade, or Pay	Tenure	Expires
	OFFICE OF THE GENERAL COUNSEL						
Woodlawn, MD	General Counsel	David F. Black	NA	ES	....	....	
Do	Deputy General Counsel	Career Incumbent	CA	ES	....	....	
	Office of Regional Chief Counsels						
New York, NY	Regional Chief Counsel	......do	CA	ES	....	....	
Atlanta, GA	......do	......do	CA	ES	....	....	
Chicago, IL	......do	......do	CA	ES	....	....	
Dallas, TX	......do	......do	CA	ES	....	....	
Kansas City, MO ...	......do	......do	CA	ES	....	....	
Richmond, CA	......do	Vacant	....	ES	....	....	
Philadelphia, PA	......do	Career Incumbent	CA	ES	....	....	
Boston, MA	......do	Vacant	....	ES	....	....	
Denver, CO	......do	Career Incumbent	CA	ES	....	....	
Seattle, WA	......do	......do	CA	ES	....	....	
	Office of Program Law						
Woodlawn, MD	Associate General Counsel	......do	CA	ES	....	....	
	OFFICE OF HUMAN RESOURCES						
Do	Deputy Commissioner	......do	CA	ES	....	....	
Do	Assistant Deputy Commissioner	......do	CA	ES	....	....	
Do	Senior Advisor	......do	CA	ES	....	....	
	Office of Learning						
Do	Associate Commissioner	......do	CA	ES	....	....	
	OFFICE OF LEGISLATION AND CONGRESSIONAL AFFAIRS						
Washington, DC	Deputy Commissioner	Scott L. Frey	NA	ES	....	....	
Do	Assistant Deputy	Career Incumbent	CA	ES	....	....	
Do	Senior Advisor	Scott E. Daniels	SC	GS	15	....	
	Office of Legislative Development and Operations						
Woodlawn, MD	Associate Commissioner	Career Incumbent	CA	ES	....	....	
Do	Deputy Associate Commissioner	Vacant	....	ES	....	....	
	OFFICE OF OPERATIONS						
Do	Deputy Commissioner	Career Incumbent	CA	ES	....	....	
Do	Assistant Deputy Commissioner	......do	CA	ES	....	....	
	Office of Regional Commissioners						
Boston, MA	Regional Commissioner, Region I	......do	CA	ES	....	....	
Do	Deputy Regional Commissioner, Region I	Vacant	....	ES	....	....	
Do	Assistant Regional Commissioner for Management and Operations Support.	Career Incumbent	CA	ES	....	....	
New York, NY	Regional Commissioner, Region II	......do	CA	ES	....	....	
Do	Deputy Regional Commissioner, Region II	......do	CA	ES	....	....	
Do	Assistant Regional Commissioner for Management and Operations Support.	......do	CA	ES	....	....	
Do	Assistant Regional Commissioner for Processing Center Operations (New York).	......do	CA	ES	....	....	
Philadelphia, PA	Regional Commissioner, Region III	......do	CA	ES	....	....	
Do	Deputy Regional Commissioner, Region III	Vacant	....	ES	....	....	
Do	Assistant Regional Commissioner for Management and Operations Support.	Career Incumbent	CA	ES	....	....	
Do	Assistant Regional Commissioner for Processing Center Operations (Philadelphia).	......do	CA	ES	....	....	
Atlanta, GA	Regional Commissioner, Region IV	......do	CA	ES	....	....	
Do	Deputy Regional Commissioner, Region IV	......do	CA	ES	....	....	
Do	Assistant Regional Commissioner for Management and Operations Support.	......do	CA	ES	....	....	
Birmingham, AL	Assistant Regional Commissioner for Processing Center Operations (Atlanta).	......do	CA	ES	....	....	
Chicago, IL	Regional Commissioner, Region V	......do	CA	ES	....	....	
Do	Deputy Regional Commissioner, Region V	......do	CA	ES	....	....	
Do	Assistant Regional Commissioner for Management and Operations Support.	Vacant	....	ES	....	....	
Do	Assistant Regional Commissioner for Processing Center Operations (Chicago).	Career Incumbent	CA	ES	....	....	
Dallas, TX	Regional Commissioner, Region VI	......do	CA	ES	....	....	
Do	Deputy Regional Commissioner, Region VI	......do	CA	ES	....	....	
Do	Assistant Regional Commissioner for Management and Operations Support.	......do	CA	ES	....	....	
Kansas City, MO ...	Regional Commissioner, Region VII	......do	CA	ES	....	....	
Do	Deputy Regional Commissioner, Region VII ...	......do	CA	ES	....	....	
Do	Assistant Regional Commissioner for Management and Operations Support.	......do	CA	ES	....	....	

SOCIAL SECURITY ADMINISTRATION—Continued

Location	Position	Name of Incumbent	Type of Appt.	Pay Plan	Level, Grade, or Pay	Tenure	Expires
Kansas City, MO ...	Assistant Regional Commissioner for Processing Center Operations (Kansas City).	Career Incumbent	CA	ES	....	....	
Denver, CO	Regional Commissioner, Region VIII	......do	CA	ES	....	....	
Do	Deputy Regional Commissioner, Region VIII	......do	CA	ES	....	....	
Do	Assistant Regional Commissioner for Management and Operations Support.	......do	CA	ES	....	....	
San Francisco, CA	Regional Commissioner, Region IX	......do	CA	ES	....	....	
Do	Deputy Regional Commissioner, Region IX	......do	CA	ES	....	....	
Do	Assistant Regional Commissioner for Management and Operations Support.	......do	CA	ES	....	....	
Do	Assistant Regional Commissioner for Processing Center Operations (San Francisco).	......do	CA	ES	....	....	
Seattle, WA	Regional Commissioner, Region X	......do	CA	ES	....	....	
Do	Deputy Regional Commissioner, Region X	......do	CA	ES	....	....	
Do	Assistant Regional Commissioner for Management and Operations Support.	......do	CA	ES	....	....	
	Office of Central Operations						
Woodlawn, MD	Associate Commissioner	......do	CA	ES	....	....	
Do	Deputy Associate Commissioner	......do	CA	ES	....	....	
Do	Assistant Associate Commissioner for Management and Operations Support.	Vacant		ES	....	....	
Do	Assistant Associate Commissioner for Disability Operations.	Career Incumbent	CA	ES	....	....	
Baltimore, MD	Assistant Associate Commissioner for Earnings Operations.	Vacant		ES	....	....	
Do	Assistant Associate Commissioner for International Operations.	......do		ES	....	....	
	Office Automation Support						
Woodlawn, MD	Associate Commissioner	Career Incumbent	CA	ES	....	....	
Do	Deputy Associate Commissioner	......do	CA	ES	....	....	
	Office of Public Service and Operations Support						
Do	Associate Commissioner	......do	CA	ES	....	....	
Do	Deputy Associate Commissioner	......do	CA	ES	....	....	
	Office of Telephone Services						
Do	Associate Commissioner	......do	CA	ES	....	....	
Do	Deputy Associate Commissioner	......do	CA	ES	....	....	
	Office of Electronic Services						
Do	Associate Commissioner	......do	CA	ES	....	....	
Do	Deputy Associate Commissioner	......do	CA	ES	....	....	
	Office of Disability Determinations						
Do	Deputy Associate Commissioner	......do	CA	ES	....	....	
	OFFICE OF QUALITY PERFORMANCE						
	Office of Quality Review						
Woodlawn, MD	Associate Commissioner	Career Incumbent	CA	ES	....	....	
Do	Deputy Associate Commissioner	......do	CA	ES	....	....	
	Office of Quality Improvement						
Do	Associate Commissioner	......do	CA	ES	....	....	
Do	Deputy Associate Commissioner	Vacant		ES	....	....	
	Office of Quality Data Management						
Do	Associate Commissioner	......do		ES	....	....	
	Office of Field Site Operations						
Do	Associate Commissioner	Career Incumbent	CA	ES	....	....	
	OFFICE OF RETIREMENT AND DISABILITY POLICY						
Do	Deputy Commissioner	......do	CA	ES	....	....	
Do	Assistant Deputy Commissioner	......do	CA	ES	....	....	
	Office of Income Security Programs						
Do	Associate Commissioner	......do	CA	ES	....	....	
Do	Deputy Associate Commissioner	......do	CA	ES	....	....	
	Office of Employment Support Programs						
Do	Associate Commissioner	......do	CA	ES	....	....	
	Office of Disability Programs						
Do	Associate Commissioner	......do	CA	ES	....	....	
Do	Deputy Associate Commissioner	Vacant		ES	....	....	

SOCIAL SECURITY ADMINISTRATION—Continued

Location	Position	Name of Incumbent	Type of Appt.	Pay Plan	Level, Grade, or Pay	Tenure	Expires
	Office of Program Development and Research						
Woodlawn, MD	Associate Commissioner	Vacant	....	ES	....	....	
	Office of Research, Evaluation and Statistics						
Washington, DC	Associate Commissioner	Career Incumbent	CA	ES	....	....	
	Office of Retirement Policy						
Do	Associate Commissioner	Vacant	....	ES	....	....	
	OFFICE OF SYSTEMS						
Woodlawn, MD	Deputy Commissioner	Career Incumbent	CA	ES	....	....	
Do	Assistant Deputy Commissioner	......do	CA	ES	....	....	
	Office of Telecommunications and Systems Operations						
Do	Assistant Associate Commissioner for Enterprise Information Technology Operations and Security.	Vacant	....	ES	....	....	
Do	Assistant Associate Commissioner for Infrastructure Architecture and Configuration.	......do		ES	....	....	
	Office of Enterprise Support, Architecture and Engineering						
Do	Associate Commissioner	Career Incumbent	CA	ES	....	....	
Do	Deputy Associate Commissioner	......do	CA	ES	....	....	
	Office of Retirement and Survivors Insurance Systems						
Do	Associate Commissioner	......do	CA	ES	....	....	
Do	Deputy Associate Commissioner	Vacant	....	ES	....	....	
	Office of Earnings, Enumeration and Administrative Systems						
Do	Associate Commissioner	Career Incumbent	CA	ES	....	....	
Do	Deputy Associate Commissioner	Vacant	....	ES	....	....	
	Office of Systems Electronic Services						
Do	Associate Commissioner	Career Incumbent	CA	ES	....	....	
Do	Deputy Associate Commissioner	......do	CA	ES	....	....	
	Office of Applications and Supplemental Security Income Systems						
Do	Associate Commissioner	......do	CA	ES	....	....	
Do	Deputy Associate Commissioner	......do	CA	ES	....	....	
	Office of Disability Systems						
Do	Associate Commissioner	......do	CA	ES	....	....	
Do	Deputy Associate Commissioner	......do	CA	ES	....	....	

SOCIAL SECURITY ADMINISTRATION OFFICE OF THE INSPECTOR GENERAL

Location	Position	Name of Incumbent	Type of Appt.	Pay Plan	Level, Grade, or Pay	Tenure	Expires
	IMMEDIATE OFFICE OF THE INSPECTOR GENERAL						
Woodlawn, MD	Inspector General	Patrick P. OCarroll	PAS	EX	II	....	
Do	Deputy Inspector General	Career Incumbent	CA	ES	....	....	
	OFFICE OF AUDIT						
Do	Assistant Inspector General	......do	CA	ES	....	....	
Do	Deputy Assistant Inspector General - Financial Systems and Operations Audits.	......do	CA	ES	....	....	
Do	Deputy Assistant Inspector General - Program Audits and Evaluations.	......do	CA	ES	....	....	
	OFFICE OF COUNSEL						
Do	Counsel to the Inspector General	......do	CA	ES	....	....	
	OFFICE OF EXTERNAL RELATIONS						
Do	Assistant Inspector General	......do	CA	ES	....	....	
	OFFICE OF INVESTIGATIONS						
Do	Assistant Inspector General	......do	CA	ES	....	....	
Do	Deputy Assistant Inspector General - Field Operations.	......do	CA	ES	....	....	

SOCIAL SECURITY ADMINISTRATION OFFICE OF THE INSPECTOR GENERAL—Continued

Location	Position	Name of Incumbent	Type of Appt.	Pay Plan	Level, Grade, or Pay	Tenure	Expires
Woodlawn, MD	**OFFICE OF TECHNOLOGY AND RESOURCE MANAGEMENT** Assistant Inspector General	Career Incumbent	CA	ES	....	....	

TENNESSEE VALLEY AUTHORITY

Location	Position	Name of Incumbent	Type of Appt.	Pay Plan	Level, Grade, or Pay	Tenure	Expires
Knoxville, TN	**BOARD OF DIRECTORS** Chairman, Board of Directors	William B. Sansom	PAS	OT	....	5 Years	05/18/14
Do	Member	Richard Capel Howorth	PAS	OT	....	5 Years	05/18/15
Do	......do	William H. Graves	PAS	OT	....	5 Years	05/18/12
Do	......do	Barbara S. Haskew	PAS	OT	....	5 Years	05/18/14
Do	......do	Neil Gray McBride	PAS	OT	....	5 Years	05/18/13
Do	......do	Marilyn Ann Brown	PAS	OT	....	5 Years	05/18/12
Do	......do	Vacant	PAS	OT	....	5 Years	
Do	......do	......do	PAS	OT	....	5 Years	
Do	......do	......do	PAS	OT	....	5 Years	
Do	Inspector General	Richard W. Moore	PAS	OT	....	....	

TRADE AND DEVELOPMENT AGENCY

Location	Position	Name of Incumbent	Type of Appt.	Pay Plan	Level, Grade, or Pay	Tenure	Expires
Arlington, VA	**OFFICE OF THE DIRECTOR** Director	Leocadia I. Zak	PAS	EX	III	....	
Do	Deputy Director	Career Incumbent	CA	ES	....	....	
Do	Export Promotion Director	Leila Aridi Afas	SC	GS	14	....	
Do	Chief of Staff	Jonathan Phillip Wright	SC	GS	15	....	
Do	Director for Congressional Affairs and Public Relations.	Thomas Hardy	XS	GS	15	....	
Do	Public Affairs Specialist	Christine M. Campigotto ...	SC	GS	12	....	
Do	*Office of the General Counsel* General Counsel	Vacant	....	ES	....	....	

UNITED STATES AGENCY FOR INTERNATIONAL DEVELOPMENT

Location	Position	Name of Incumbent	Type of Appt.	Pay Plan	Level, Grade, or Pay	Tenure	Expires
Washington, DC	**OFFICE OF THE ADMINISTRATOR** Administrator, Agency for International Development.	Rajiv Shah	PAS	EX	II	....	
Do	Deputy Administrator, Agency for International Development.	Donald Steinberg	PAS	EX	III	....	
Do	Chief Operating Officer	Sean Carroll	NA	ES	....	....	
Do	Senior Advisor	Maura L. O'Neill	NA	ES	....	....	
Do	White House Liaison	Kathleen C. Beale	XS	AD	$123,758	....	
Do	Speechwriter	Ariana Berengaut	XS	AD	$64,548	....	
Do	Director, Faith Based Community Initiatives	James M. Brinkmoeller	XS	AD	$152,635	....	
Do	Confidential Assistant	Gregory R. Degen	XS	AD	$51,630	....	
Do	......do	Kathleen F. Dorian	XS	AD	$51,630	....	
Do	Senior Impact Planning Advisor	Thomas Garwin	XS	AD	$165,300	....	
Do	Confidential Assistant	Anna L. Gohmann	XS	AD	$79,864	....	
Do	Program Specialist	Sana L. Hussain	XS	AD	$74,958	....	
Do	Gender Coordinator	Carla Koppell	XS	AD	$165,300	....	
Do	Program Manager	Gideon Maltz	XS	AD	$148,510	....	
Do	Senior Speechwriter	Maany Peyvan	XS	AD	$103,872	....	
Do	Program Specialist	Rachel K. Rose	XS	AD	$60,232	....	
Do	......do	Sandra M. Stonesifer	XS	AD	$97,936	....	
Do	Chief of Staff	Margaret Sullivan	XS	AD	$165,300	....	
Do	Executive Assistant Scheduler	Beatina E. Theopold	XS	AD	$97,936	....	
Do	Executive Director (Global Development Council and Policy Advisor).	Jayne Thomisee	XS	AD	$132,009	....	
Do	Special Assistant	Rosarie G. Tucci	XS	AD	$64,292	....	
Do	......do	Elizabeth Jaff	XS	AD	$62,467	....	

UNITED STATES AGENCY FOR INTERNATIONAL DEVELOPMENT—Continued

Location	Position	Name of Incumbent	Type of Appt.	Pay Plan	Level, Grade, or Pay	Tenure	Expires
Washington, DC	Counselor	Career Incumbent	CA	FE	$176,871	....	
Do	Chief, Operating Officer	Vacant	....	OT	....	....	
	Office of the General Counsel						
Do	General Counsel	Lisa C. Gomer	NA	ES	....	....	
Do	Attorney Advisor General	Donald Gressett	XS	SL	$141,306	....	
	Bureau for Legislative and Public Affairs						
Do	Assistant Administrator	Vacant	PAS	EX	IV	....	
Do	Deputy Assistant Administrator, Legislative Affairs.	Barbara A. Feinstein	TA	ES	....	....	12/18/13
Do	Deputy Assistant Administrator, Legislative and Public Affairs.	Ann L. Doyle	XS	AD	$139,929	....	
Do	Congressional Liaison Officer	Joshua J. Albert	XS	AD	$108,717	....	
Do	Senior Advisor	Ginny J. Barahona	XS	AD	$108,717	....	
Do	Congressional Liaison Officer	Youshea Berry	XS	AD	$105,211	....	
Do	Director for Public Engagement	Kathryn Bunting	XS	AD	$160,886	....	
Do	Special Assistant	Angela Catella	XS	AD	$92,001	....	
Do	Congressional Liaison Officer	Dannie L. Diego	XS	AD	$119,238	....	
Do	Program Manager	Clay Doherty	XS	AD	$126,251	....	
Do	Special Assistant	Katharine B. Gage	XS	AD	$77,368	....	
Do	Director for Public Engagement	Rwaida Gharib	XS	AD	$112,224	....	
Do	Special Assistant	Jay Gilliam	XS	AD	$51,630	....	
Do	Senior Advisor	Barbara Larkin	XS	AD	$165,300	....	
Do	Congressional Liaison Specialist	Jeffrey Mettille	XS	AD	$61,474	....	
Do	Writer Editor	Kelly L. Ramundo	XS	AD	$89,033	....	
Do	Special Assistant	Laura M. Rodriguez	XS	AD	$53,350	....	
Do	Congressional Liaison Officer	Clifford Stammerman	XS	AD	$112,224	....	
Do	Public Affairs Specialist	Abigail Sugrue	XS	AD	$60,274	....	
	Policy, Planning and Learning						
Do	Senior Advisor (Strategy and Communication)	Negar Akhavi	XS	AD	$155,500	....	
Do	Senior Advisor	Thomas G. Beck	XS	AD	$140,259	....	
Do	Senior Advisor (Donor Coordination)	Sohini Chatterjee	XS	AD	$155,500	....	
Do	Office Director	Steven Feldstein	XS	AD	$132,009	....	
Do	Deputy Assistant to the Administrator	Lawrence A. Garber	XS	AD	$165,300	....	
Do	Senior Advisor (Global Engagement)	Nicole R. Goldin	XS	AD	$140,259	....	
Do	Coordinator of Disability and Inclusive Development.	Charlotte McLain-Nhlapo ..	XS	AD	$155,500	....	
Do	Deputy Assistant to the Administrator	Anthony F. Pipa	XS	AD	$153,049	....	
Do	Special Assistant	Jennifer Watts	XS	AD	$68,712	....	
Do	Assistant to the Administrator	Career Incumbent	CA	FE	$157,302	....	
Do	Deputy Assistant Administrator	......do	CA	FE	$163,072	....	
Do	Director, Office of Donor Engagement	......do	CA	FE	$154,627	....	
	Bureau for Asia						
Do	Assistant Administrator	Nisha Desai Biswal	PAS	EX	IV	....	
Do	Deputy Assistant Administrator	Gregory A. Beck	XS	AD	$146,999	....	
Do	......do	Career Incumbent	CA	FE	$147,965	....	
Do	Special Assistant	Pooja Kadakia	XS	AD	$62,467	....	
Do	Senior Policy Advisor	Amy E. Searight	XS	AD	$132,009	....	
Do	Director, Office of Strategic Planning and Operations.	......do	CA	OT	$155,500	....	
	Bureau for Middle East						
Do	Assistant Administrator	Mara E. Rudman	PAS	EX	IV	....	
Do	Deputy Assistant Administrator	Hady A. Amr	XS	AD	$161,175	....	
Do	Special Assistant	William J. Hummel	XS	AD	$79,864	....	
Do	Deputy Assistant Administrator	Career Incumbent	CA	FE	$179,700	....	
Do	Director, Office of Iraq Reconstruction	......do	CA	FE	$162,248	....	
Do	Director, Office of Middle East Affairs	Vacant	....	OT	....	....	
Do	Director, Office of Technical Support	......do	....	OT	....	....	
	Bureau for Democracy, Conflict, and Humanitarian Assistance						
Do	Assistant Administrator	Nancy E. Lindborg	PAS	EX	IV	....	
Do	Special Assistant	Tsehaynesh E. Abebe	XS	AD	$68,712	....	
Do	Program Manager	Mark R. Bartolini	XS	AD	$127,883	....	
Do	Director, Office of Military Affairs	Beth Degrasse	XS	AD	$165,300	....	
Do	Director, Office of Military Affairs	Vacant	....	OT	....	....	
Do	Strategic Communications Advisor	Camille Eiss	XS	AD	$92,001	....	
Do	Director, Office of Food for Peace	Dina Marie Esposito	XS	AD	$152,635	....	
Do	Director, Office of Food for Peace	Vacant	....	OT	....	....	
Do	Senior Advisor	Jonathan Freeman	XS	AD	$87,520	....	
Do	Advisor	Ashley P. Hernreich	XS	AD	$105,211	....	
Do	Deputy Assistant Administrator (DCHA)	Sarah Mendelson	XS	AD	$160,886	....	
Do	Dept Director, OTI	Jennifer N. Parker	XS	AD	$127,883	....	

UNITED STATES AGENCY FOR INTERNATIONAL DEVELOPMENT—Continued

Location	Position	Name of Incumbent	Type of Appt.	Pay Plan	Level, Grade, or Pay	Tenure	Expires
Washington, DC	Program Manager (Tech Lead Conflict Advisor).	Andrew T. Sweet	XS	AD	$108,717	....	
Do	Director DCHA/DG	David Yang	XS	AD	$165,300	....	
Do	Deputy Assistant Administrator	Vacant	....	OT	....	....	
Do	Director, Office of Civil Response	Career Incumbent	CA	OT	$152,207	....	
Do	Director, Office of Program, Policy and Management.	Vacant	....	OT	....	....	
Do	Senior Development Advisor	Career Incumbent	CA	FE	$162,392	....	
	Bureau for Global Health						
Do	Assistant Administrator	Ariel Pablos-Mendez	PAS	EX	IV	....	
Do	Deputy Assistant Administrator	Amie Batson	XS	AD	$165,300	....	
Do	Special Assistant	Leek A. Deng	XS	AD	$51,630	....	
Do	Senior Advisor	Wendy A. Taylor	XS	AD	$165,300	....	
Do	Malaria Coordinator	Robert T. Ziemer	PA	AD	$157,989	....	
Do	Deputy Assistant Administrator	Career Incumbent	CA	FE	$162,392	....	
Do	Director, Office of Health, Infectious Disease and Nutrition.	Vacant	....	OT	....	....	
Do	Director, Office of HIV/AIDS	.....do	....	OT	....	....	
Do	Director, Office of Strategic Planning and Budget.	......do	....	OT	....	....	
	Bureau for Africa						
Do	Assistant Administrator	Earl Gast	PAS	EX	IV	....	
Do	Deputy Assistant Administrator AFR/AA	Linda Etim	XS	AD	$157,936	....	
Do	Deputy Assistant Administrator	Rajakumari Jandhyala	XS	AD	$144,976	....	
Do	Senior Advisor for Economic Growth	Ricardo Michel	XS	AD	$136,134	....	
Do	Senior Advisor	Chloe Schwenke	XS	AD	$140,259	....	
Do	Deputy Assistant Administrator	Career Incumbent	CA	FE	$156,206	....	
Do	Director, Office of East African Affairs	......do	CA	FE	$148,809	....	
Do	Director, Office of Sustainable Development ..	......do	CA	FE	$159,559	....	
Do	Director, Office of Southern Africa Affairs	......do	CA	OT	$155,500	....	
Do	Director, Office of Sudan Programs	......do	CA	OT	$155,500	....	
Do	Director, Office of West African Affairs	......do	CA	OT	$155,500	....	
	Bureau for Europe and Eurasia						
Do	Assistant Administrator	Paige Alexander	PAS	EX	IV	....	
Do	Deputy Assistant Administrator	Jonathan S. Hale	XS	AD	$132,009	....	
Do	Director, Office of Eurasian Affairs	......do	CA	FE	$157,364	....	
	Bureau for Latin America and the Caribbean						
Do	Assistant Administrator	Mark Barry Feierstein	PAS	EX	IV	....	
Do	Senior Advisor	Paloma M Adams	XS	AD	$155,500	....	
Do	International Cooperation Specialist	Mileydi Guilarte	XS	AD	$112,224	....	
Do	Deputy Assistant Administrator	Mark E. Lopes	XS	AD	$153,048	....	
Do	Special Assistant	Oliva A. Lopez	XS	AD	$64,292	....	
Do	Staff Assistant	Lillian W. Trienens	XS	AD	$64,548	....	
Do	Deputy Assistant Administrator	Career Incumbent	CA	FE	$170,571	....	
Do	Director, Office of Programs	Vacant	....	FE	....	....	
Do	Director, Office of Economic Growth	Career Incumbent	CA	FE	$164,830	....	
Do	Director, Office of Democracy, Governance and Social Transition.	......do	CA	FE	$155,500	....	
Do	Deputy Assistant Administrator	......do	CA	FE	$157,364	....	
Do	Director, Strategic and Program Office	Vacant	....	OT	....	....	
Do	Director, Office of Caribbean Affairs	Career Incumbent	CA	FE	$150,284	....	
Do	Director, Office of Regional and Sustainable Development.	......do	CA	OT	$155,500	....	
	Bureau for Management						
Do	Assistant Administrator	Vacant	PAS	EX	....	....	
Do	Special Assistant	Sophia A. Magill	XS	AD	$51,630	....	
Do	Deputy Assistant Administrator	John S. Munzer	XS	AD	$123,758	....	
Do	Deputy Assistant Administrator	Career Incumbent	CA	FE	$153,459	....	
Do	Director, Office of Management Services	......do	CA	OT	$155,500	....	
Do	Chief, Overseas Management Division	......do	CA	OT	$152,207	....	
	Office of Human Resources						
Do	Special Assistant	Anna P. Franklin	XS	AD	$74,872	....	
Do	Chief, Foreign Service Personnel	Career Incumbent	CA	OT	$155,500	....	
	Bureau for Economic Growth, Agriculture and Trade						
Do	Assistant Administrator	Eric Postel	PA	EX	IV	....	
Do	Deputy Assistant Administrator	Wendy E. Abt	XS	AD	$165,300	....	
Do	Global Climate Change Coordinator	Katharine M. Batten	XS	AD	$165,300	....	
Do	Program Manager	Shari Berenbach	XS	AD	$155,500	....	
Do	Policy Advisor	John Comings	XS	AD	$123,758	....	
Do	Senior Advisor (Gender)	Karen J. Frederickson	XS	AD	$148,510	....	
Do	Senior Environment Advisor	Christian Holmes	XS	AD	$165,300	....	

UNITED STATES AGENCY FOR INTERNATIONAL DEVELOPMENT—Continued

Location	Position	Name of Incumbent	Type of Appt.	Pay Plan	Level, Grade, or Pay	Tenure	Expires
Washington, DC	General Business Specialist	Benjamin Hubbard	XS	AD	$135,555		
Do	Special Assistant	Keren O. Johnson	XS	AD	$72,876		
Do	Deputy Assistant Administrator	Career Incumbent	CA	FE	$173,807		
Do	.....do	Vacant		OT			
Do	Director, Office of Economic Growth	Career Incumbent	CA	OT	$155,500		
Do	Director, Office Education	.....do	CA	OT	$126,851		
Do	Director, Office of Infrastructure and Engineering.	Vacant		OT			
Do	Director, Office of Policy, Information, Communication and Outreach.	Career Incumbent	CA	OT	$143,469		
	Bureau for Foreign Assistance						
Do	Regional Director	.....do	CA	OT	$147,773		
	Office of Afghanistan and Pakistan Affairs						
Do	Assistant to the Administrator	Alexander Thier	XS	AD	$157,686		
Do	Program Manager	Vacant		OT			
Do	.....do	Career Incumbent	CA	OT	$131,294		
Do	Supervisory Program Manager	Vacant		OT			
	Bureau for Food Security						
Do	Chief Scientist and Senior Advisor to the Administrator.	Julie A. Howard	XS	AD	$131,183		
Do	Senior Advisor	Sean Maloney	XS	AD	$108,717		
Do	Deputy Coordinator, Development	Tjada D. McKenna	XS	AD	$152,635		
Do	Assistant to the Administrator	Career Incumbent	CA	FE	$175,564		
Do	Deputy Assistant Administrator	.....do	CA	OT	$139,290		
Do	Senior Development Advisor	.....do	CA	OT	$155,500		
Do	Director, Office of Agriculture, Research and Technology.	Vacant		OT			
	Office of Budget and Resource Management						
Do	Budget Advisor	Farrah Barrios	XS	AD	$108,717		
Do	Special Advisor	Nishant Roy	XS	AD	$77,368		
Do	Senior Advisor	Michele M. Sumilas	XS	AD	$155,500		
Do	Assistant to the Administrator	Vacant		OT			
Do	Deputy Assistant Administrator	.....do		OT			
Do	.....do	Career Incumbent	CA	FE	$158,458		
Do	.....do	.....do	CA	FE	$178,796		
Do	Deputy Office Director for Management	Vacant		OT			
Do	Director, Office of Acquisition and Assistance	Career Incumbent	CA	OT	$152,207		
Do	Deputy Director, Office of Acquisition and Assistance.	.....do	CA	OT	$152,207		
	Office of Innovation and Development Alliances						
Do	Senior Communications and Engagement Coordinator.	Cynthia Jasso-Rotunno	XS	AD	$165,300		
Do	Special Assistant for Engagement	Rose K. Kennedy-Townsend.	XS	AD	$53,350		
Do	Special Programs Director	Maureen E. Kinder	XS	AD	$105,211		
Do	Senior Advisor	Claire Lucas	XS	AD	$165,300		
Do	Deputy Director	Vacant		OT			

UNITED STATES AGENCY FOR INTERNATIONAL DEVELOPMENT OFFICE OF THE INSPECTOR GENERAL

Location	Position	Name of Incumbent	Type of Appt.	Pay Plan	Level, Grade, or Pay	Tenure	Expires
Washington, DC	Inspector General	Vacant	PAS	OT			

UNITED STATES - CHINA ECONOMIC AND SECURITY REVIEW COMMISSION

Location	Position	Name of Incumbent	Type of Appt.	Pay Plan	Level, Grade, or Pay	Tenure	Expires
Washington, DC	Chairman	Dennis C. Shea	XS	PD		2 Years	12/31/12
Do	Vice Chairman	William A. Reinsch	XS	PD	0	2 Years	12/31/13
Do	Commissioner	Carolyn Bartholomew	XS	PD	0	2 Years	12/31/13
Do	.....do	Daniel A. Blumenthal	XS	PD	0	2 Years	12/31/13
Do	.....do	Peter T. Brookes	XS	PD	0	2 Years	12/31/13
Do	.....do	Robin Cleveland	XS	PD	0	2 Years	12/31/12
Do	.....do	C. Richard D'Amato	XS	PD	0	2 Years	12/31/12

UNITED STATES - CHINA ECONOMIC AND SECURITY REVIEW COMMISSION—Continued

Location	Position	Name of Incumbent	Type of Appt.	Pay Plan	Level, Grade, or Pay	Tenure	Expires
Washington, DC	Commissioner	Jeffrey L. Fiedler	XS	PD	0	2 Years	12/31/12
Do	......do	Carte P. Goodwin	XS	PD	0	2 Years	12/31/13
Do	......do	Daniel M. Slane	XS	PD	0	2 Years	12/31/13
Do	......do	Michael R. Wessel	XS	PD	0	2 Years	12/31/12
Do	......do	Larry M. Wortzel	XS	PD	0	2 Years	12/31/12

UNITED STATES COMMISSION ON INTERNATIONAL RELIGIOUS FREEDOM

Location	Position	Name of Incumbent	Type of Appt.	Pay Plan	Level, Grade, or Pay	Tenure	Expires
Washington, DC	Commissioner	Vacant	PA	WC	....	2 Years	
Do	......do	Azizah al-Hibri	PA	WC	....	2 Years	
Do	......do	William Shaw	PA	WC	....	2 Years	

UNITED STATES COMMISSION FOR THE PRESERVATION OF AMERICA'S HERITAGE ABROAD

Location	Position	Name of Incumbent	Type of Appt.	Pay Plan	Level, Grade, or Pay	Tenure	Expires
Washington, DC	Chairman	Warren L. Miller	PA	WC	....	....	
Do	Member	Ned W. Bandler	PA	WC	....	....	
Do	......do	Dorothy A. Bennett	PA	WC	....	....	
Do	......do	Herbert Block	PA	WC	....	....	
Do	......do	Tyrone C. Fahner	PA	WC	....	....	
Do	......do	Emil A. Fish	PA	WC	....	....	
Do	......do	Jules Fleischer	PA	WC	....	....	
Do	......do	Martin B. Gold	PA	WC	....	....	
Do	......do	Michael B. Levy	PA	WC	....	....	
Do	......do	Rachmiel Liberman	PA	WC	....	....	
Do	......do	Harley Lippman	PA	WC	....	....	
Do	......do	Michael A. Menis	PA	WC	....	....	
Do	......do	Larry Pressler	PA	WC	....	....	
Do	......do	Jonathan J. Rikoon	PA	WC	....	....	
Do	......do	Harriet Rotter	PA	WC	....	....	
Do	......do	Lee R. Seeman	PA	WC	....	....	
Do	......do	Joan E. Silber	PA	WC	....	....	
Do	......do	Richard Weisberg	PA	WC	....	....	
Do	......do	Lesley Weiss	PA	WC	....	....	
Do	......do	Susan C. York	PA	WC	....	....	
Do	......do	Gary P. Zola	PA	WC	....	....	

UNITED STATES ELECTION ASSISTANCE COMMISSION

Location	Position	Name of Incumbent	Type of Appt.	Pay Plan	Level, Grade, or Pay	Tenure	Expires
Washington, DC	Commissioner	Vacant	PAS	EX	IV	4 Years	
Do	......do	......do	PAS	EX	IV	4 Years	
Do	......do	......do	PAS	EX	IV	4 Years	
Do	......do	......do	PAS	EX	IV	4 Years	

UNITED STATES HOLOCAUST MEMORIAL COUNCIL

Location	Position	Name of Incumbent	Type of Appt.	Pay Plan	Level, Grade, or Pay	Tenure	Expires
Washington, DC	Chairman (Chair has separate appointment as Council Member).	Tom A. Bernstein	PA	PD	$596	5 Years	01/15/17
Do	Vice Chairman (Vice Chair has separate appointment as Council Member).	Joshua B. Bolten	PA	PD	$596	5 Years	01/15/15
Do	Member	Edward I. Koch	PA	PD	$596	5 Years	01/15/10
Do	......do	Debra Abrams	PA	PD	$596	5 Years	01/15/11
Do	......do	Alan I. Casden	PA	PD	$596	2 Years	01/15/11
Do	......do	Norma Lerner	PA	PD	$596	5 Years	01/15/11
Do	......do	J. Philip Rosen	PA	PD	$596	5 Years	01/15/11
Do	......do	Bradley D. Wine	PA	PD	$596	5 Years	01/15/11
Do	......do	Judith Yudof	PA	PD	$596	5 Years	01/15/11
Do	......do	Miriam Adelson	PA	PD	$596	5 Years	01/15/12

UNITED STATES HOLOCAUST MEMORIAL COUNCIL—Continued

Location	Position	Name of Incumbent	Type of Appt.	Pay Plan	Level, Grade, or Pay	Tenure	Expires
Washington, DC	Member	Carol B. Cohen	PA	PD	$596	5 Years	01/15/12
Do	......do	Joel M. Geiderman	PA	PD	$596	5 Years	01/15/12
Do	......do	Michael J. Gerson	PA	PD	$596	5 Years	01/15/12
Do	......do	Zvi Y. Gitelman	PA	PD	$596	5 Years	01/15/12
Do	......do	Marc Goldman	PA	PD	$596	5 Years	01/15/12
Do	......do	William S. Levine	PA	PD	$596	5 Years	01/15/12
Do	......do	Kenneth B. Mehlman	PA	PD	$596	5 Years	01/15/12
Do	......do	Jeffrey S. Wilpon	PA	PD	$596	5 Years	01/15/12
Do	......do	Fred S. Zeidman	PA	PD	$596	5 Years	01/15/12
Do	......do	Norman R. Bobins	PA	PD	$596	5 Years	01/15/13
Do	......do	Joseph M. Brodecki	PA	PD	$596	5 Years	01/15/13
Do	......do	Michael David Epstein	PA	PD	$596	5 Years	01/15/13
Do	......do	Donald Etra	PA	PD	$596	5 Years	01/15/13
Do	......do	David M. Flaum	PA	PD	$596	5 Years	01/15/13
Do	......do	Andrew S. Hochberg	PA	PD	$596	5 Years	01/15/13
Do	......do	Ezra Katz	PA	PD	$596	5 Years	01/15/13
Do	......do	Howard E. Konar	PA	PD	$596	5 Years	01/15/13
Do	......do	Douglas R. Korn	PA	PD	$596	5 Years	01/15/13
Do	......do	Hadassah F. Lieberman	PA	PD	$596	5 Years	01/15/13
Do	......do	Pierre-Richard Prosper	PA	PD	$596	5 Years	01/15/13
Do	......do	Elliott Abrams	PA	PD	$596	5 Years	01/15/14
Do	......do	Michael Chertoff	PA	PD	$596	5 Years	01/15/14
Do	......do	William J. Danhof	PA	PD	$596	5 Years	01/15/14
Do	......do	Sanford L. Gottesman	PA	PD	$596	5 Years	01/15/14
Do	......do	Cheryl F. Halpern	PA	PD	$596	5 Years	01/15/14
Do	......do	J. David Heller	PA	PD	$596	5 Years	01/15/14
Do	......do	Amy Kaslow	PA	PD	$596	5 Years	01/15/14
Do	......do	M. Ronald Krongold	PA	PD	$596	5 Years	01/15/14
Do	......do	Michael B. Mukasey	PA	PD	$596	5 Years	01/15/14
Do	......do	Daniel J. Silva	PA	PD	$596	5 Years	01/15/14
Do	......do	Matthew L. Adler	PA	PD	$596	5 Years	01/15/15
Do	......do	Kitty Dukakis	PA	PD	$596	5 Years	01/15/15
Do	......do	K. Chaya Friedman	PA	PD	$596	5 Years	01/15/15
Do	......do	Mark D. Goodman	PA	PD	$596	5 Years	01/15/15
Do	......do	Joseph D. Gutman	PA	PD	$596	4 Years	01/15/15
Do	......do	Roman D. Kent	PA	PD	$596	4 Years	01/15/15
Do	......do	Deborah E. Lipstadt	PA	PD	$596	4 Years	01/15/15
Do	......do	Ronald Ratner	PA	PD	$596	5 Years	01/15/15
Do	......do	Menachem Z. Rosensaft	PA	PD	$596	5 Years	01/15/15
Do	......do	Kirk A. Rudy	PA	PD	$596	5 Years	01/15/15
Do	......do	Nancy B. Gilbert	PA	PD	$596	5 Years	01/15/16
Do	......do	Marc R. Stanley	PA	PD	$596	5 Years	01/15/16
Do	......do	Howard D. Unger	PA	PD	$596	5 Years	01/15/16
Do	......do	Clemantine Wamariya	PA	PD	$596	5 Years	01/15/16
Do	......do	Elie Wiesel	PA	PD	$596	5 Years	01/15/16
Do	......do	Tom A. Bernstein	PA	PD	$596	5 Years	01/15/12
Do	......do	Joshua B. Bolten	PA	PD	$596	5 Years	01/15/14

UNITED STATES INSTITUTE OF PEACE

Location	Position	Name of Incumbent	Type of Appt.	Pay Plan	Level, Grade, or Pay	Tenure	Expires
Washington, DC	Chairman of the Board of Directors	J. Robinson West	PAS	PD	....	4 Years	
Do	Vice Chairman of the Board of Directors	George E. Moose	PAS	PD	....	4 Years	
Do	Member of the Board of Directors	Judy Ansley	PAS	PD	....	4 Years	
Do	......do	Eric S. Edelman	PAS	PD	....	4 Years	
Do	......do	Kerry Kennedy	PAS	PD	....	4 Years	
Do	......do	Ikram Khan	PAS	PD	....	4 Years	
Do	......do	John A. Lancaster	PAS	PD	....	4 Years	
Do	......do	Stephen D. Krasner	PAS	PD	....	4 Years	
Do	......do	Jeremy Rabkin	PAS	PD	....	4 Years	
Do	......do	Judy Van Rest	PAS	PD	....	4 Years	
Do	......do	Nancy M. Zirkin	PAS	PD	....	4 Years	
Do	......do	Leon E. Panetta	PAS	PD	....	4 Years	
Do	......do	Hillary R. Clinton	PAS	PD	....	4 Years	
Do	......do	Vacant	PAS	PD	....	....	
Do	......do	......do	PAS	PD	....	....	

UNITED STATES INTERNATIONAL TRADE COMMISSION

Location	Position	Name of Incumbent	Type of Appt.	Pay Plan	Level, Grade, or Pay	Tenure	Expires
	OFFICE OF THE CHAIRMAN						
Washington, DC	Chairman	Irving A. Williamson, Esq	PAS	EX	III	....	06/16/14
Do	Vice Chairman	Vacant	PAS	EX	IV	....	
Do	Commissioner	Daniel R. Pearson	PAS	EX	IV	....	06/16/13
Do	.....do	David S. Johanson	PAS	EX	IV	....	
Do	.....do	Dean Arthur Pinkert	PAS	EX	IV	....	
Do	.....do	Shara L. Aranoff	PAS	EX	IV	....	06/24/13
Do	.....do	Deanna T. Okun	PAS	EX	III	....	06/16/13
Do	Chief of Staff	Vacant	....	ES	....	....	
Do	Staff Assistant (Legal)	Dana A. Lofgren	SC	GS	13	....	
Do	.....do	Michael Diehl	SC	GS	15	....	
Do	.....do	Stephanie Lynn Nagel	SC	GS	15	....	
Do	Confidential Assistant	Kasey Caroline Sporck	SC	GS	11	....	
Do	Executive Assistant	Sybia Kea Harrison	SC	GS	13	....	
Do	Staff Assistant	Erin D. Joffre	SC	GS	15	....	
Do	Staff Assistant (Legal)	Michael Joseph Robbins	SC	GS	14	....	
Do	.....do	Stuart M. Weiser	SC	GS	15	....	
Do	.....do	Michael P. Mabile	SC	GS	15	....	
Do	Staff Assistant (Economics)	John H. Davitt	SC	GS	14	....	
Do	Executive Assistant	Sally E. Knight	SC	GS	13	....	
Do	Staff Assistant (Legal)	Jonathan G. Seiger	SC	GS	15	....	
Do	.....do	Karen Veninga Driscoll	SC	GS	15	....	
Do	.....do	William Theodore Kane	SC	GS	15	....	
Do	Confidential Assistant	Cordelia Odessa Stroman-Blair.	SC	GS	12	....	
Do	Executive Assistant	Joyce Rylyk	SC	GS	13	....	
	OFFICE OF ADMINISTRATION						
Do	Director	Career Incumbent	CA	ES	....	....	
	OFFICE OF THE GENERAL COUNSEL						
Do	General Counsel	.....do	CA	ES	....	....	
	OFFICE OF OPERATIONS						
Do	Director	Vacant	....	ES	....	....	
	Office of Economics						
Do	Director	Career Incumbent	CA	ES	....	....	
	Office of Tariff Affairs and Trade Agreements						
Do	Director	.....do	CA	ES	....	....	
	Office of Unfair Import Investigations						
Do	Director	.....do	CA	ES	....	....	

UNITED STATES POSTAL SERVICE

Location	Position	Name of Incumbent	Type of Appt.	Pay Plan	Level, Grade, or Pay	Tenure	Expires
Washington, DC	Chairman, Board of Governors	Thurgood Marshall, Jr	PAS	OT	....	....	
Do	Vice Chairman, Board of Governors	Mickey D. Barnett	PAS	OT	....	....	
Do	Member, Board of Governors	James H. Bilbray	PAS	OT	....	....	
Do	.....do	Louis J. Giuliano	PAS	OT	....	....	
Do	.....do	Dennis J. Toner	PAS	OT	....	....	
Do	.....do	Ellen C. Williams	PAS	OT	....	....	
Do	Postmaster General	Patrick R. Donahoe	XS	OT	....	....	
Do	Deputy Postmaster General	Ronald A. Stroman	XS	OT	....	....	
Do	Chief Operating Officer and Executive Vice President.	Megan J. Brennan	XS	OT	....	....	
Do	Chief Financial Officer and Executive Vice President.	Joseph Corbett	XS	OT	....	....	
Do	General Counsel and Executive Vice President.	Mary A. Gibbons	XS	OT	....	....	
Do	Chief Marketing/Sales Officer and Executive Vice President.	Nagisa Manabe	XS	OT	....	....	
Do	Chief Human Resources Officer and Executive Vice President.	Anthony J. Vegliante	XS	OT	....	....	
Arlington, VA	Deputy Assistant Inspector General for Investigations.	Vacant	....	ES	....	....	
Do	Chief Postal Inspector	Guy J. Cottrell	XS	OT	....	....	
Do	Judicial Officer	William A. Campbell	XS	OT	....	....	
Do	Vice President, Government Relations and Public Policy.	Marie T. Dominguez	XS	OT	....	....	
Do	Vice President, Corporate Communications	Samuel M. Pulcrano	XS	OT	....	....	

UNITED STATES POSTAL SERVICE—Continued

Location	Position	Name of Incumbent	Type of Appt.	Pay Plan	Level, Grade, or Pay	Tenure	Expires
Arlington, VA	Vice President, Consumer and Industry Affairs.	Maura Robinson	XS	OT			
Do	Vice President, Delivery and Post Office Operations.	Dean J. Granholm	XS	OT			
Do	Vice President, Facilities	Tom A. Samra	XS	OT			
Do	Vice President, Network Operations	David E. Williams, Jr	XS	OT			
Do	Vice President, Engineering Systems	Michael J. Amato	XS	OT			
Do	Vice President, Product Information	James P. Cochrane	XS	OT			
Do	Vice President, Information Technology	John T. Edgar	XS	OT			
Do	Vice President, Mail Entry and Payment Technology.	Pritha Mehra	XS	OT			
Do	Vice President, Finance and Planning	Stephen J. Masse	XS	OT			
Do	Vice President, Supply Management	Susan M. Brownell	XS	OT			
Do	Vice President, Controller	Timothy F. O'Reilly	XS	OT			
Do	Vice President, Domestic Products	Gary C. Reblin	XS	OT			
Do	Vice President, Sales	William C. Rucker III	XS	OT			
Do	Vice President, Channel Access	Kelly M. Sigmon	XS	OT			
Do	Vice President, Global Business	Giselle E. Valera	XS	OT			
Do	Vice President, Pricing	Jeffrey C. Williamson	XS	OT			
Do	Vice President, Employee Resource Management.	Deborah M. Giannoni-Jackson.	XS	OT			
Do	Vice President, Labor Relations	Douglas A. Tulino	XS	OT			
Do	Vice President, Digital Solutions	Paul Vogel	XS	OT			
Do	Vice President, Chief Information Officer and Executive Vice President.	Ellis A. Burgoyne	XS	OT			
Do	Vice President, Area Operations Capital Metro Area.	David C. Fields	XS	OT			
Do	Vice President, Area Operations Eastern Area	Jordan M. Small	XS	OT			
Do	Vice President, Area Operations Great Lakes Area.	Jacqueline Krage Strako	XS	OT			
Do	Vice President, Area Operations Northeast Area.	Richard P. Uluski	XS	OT			
Do	Vice President, Area Operations Pacific Area	Drew T. Aliperto	XS	OT			
Do	Vice President, Area Operations Southern Area.	Jo Ann Feindt	XS	OT			
Do	Vice President, Area Operations Western Area.	Sylvester Black	XS	OT			
Do	Deputy Assistant Inspector General (Investigations).	Lavan Griffith	XS	OT			

UTAH RECLAMATION MITIGATION AND CONSERVATION COMMISSION

Location	Position	Name of Incumbent	Type of Appt.	Pay Plan	Level, Grade, or Pay	Tenure	Expires
Salt Lake City, UT	Commissioner Member	Jody L. Williams	PA	PD			
Do	......do	James F. Karpowitz	PA	WC			
Do	......do	Brad T. Barber	PA	PD			
Do	......do	Dallin W. Jensen	PA	PD			
Do	......do	Don A. Christiansen	PA	WC			
Do	Executive Director	Michael C. Weland	XS	GS	15		

VIETNAM EDUCATION FOUNDATION

Location	Position	Name of Incumbent	Type of Appt.	Pay Plan	Level, Grade, or Pay	Tenure	Expires
Washington, DC	Chairman	Isaac F. Silvera	PA	AD			
Do	Member	Sandy Hoa Dang	PA	AD			
Do	......do	David T. Duong	PA	AD			
Do	......do	Marjorie Margolies	PA	AD			
Do	......do	Anhlan P. Nguyen	PA	AD			
Do	......do	Quyen N. Vuong	PA	AD			
Do	Executive Director	Lynne A. McNamara	XS	AD	$155,500		

WOODROW WILSON INTERNATIONAL CENTER FOR SCHOLARS

Location	Position	Name of Incumbent	Type of Appt.	Pay Plan	Level, Grade, or Pay	Tenure	Expires
Washington, DC	Director	Vacant	XS	AD			

WOODROW WILSON INTERNATIONAL CENTER FOR SCHOLARS—Continued

Location	Position	Name of Incumbent	Type of Appt.	Pay Plan	Level, Grade, or Pay	Tenure	Expires
Washington, DC	Associate Director	Vacant	XS	AD	....	....	
Do	Senior Executive Officer	Robert S. Litwak	XS	AD	$155,500	....	

APPENDICES

APPENDIX NO. 1

SUMMARY OF POSITIONS SUBJECT TO NONCOMPETITIVE APPOINTMENT

PAS = Positions Subject to Presidential Appointment with Senate Confirmation
PA = Positions Subject to Presidential Appointment without Senate Confirmation
GEN = Positions Designated as Senior Executive Service "General"
NA = Senior Executive Service General Positions Filled by Noncareer Appointment
TA = Senior Executive Service Positions Filled by Limited Emergency or Limited Term Appointment
SC = Positions Filled by Schedule C Excepted Appointment
XS = Positions Subject to Statutory Excepted Appointment

Agency or Department	PAS	PA	GEN	NA	TA	SC	XS
ADMINISTRATIVE CONFERENCE OF THE UNITED STATES	1	5	3	0	0	0	0
ADVISORY COUNCIL ON HISTORIC PRESERVATION	0	11	0	0	0	0	0
AFRICAN DEVELOPMENT FOUNDATION	0	0	0	0	0	0	1
AMERICAN BATTLE MONUMENTS COMMISSION	0	12	0	0	0	0	0
APPALACHIAN REGIONAL COMMISSION	2	0	0	0	0	0	0
ARCHITECT OF THE CAPITOL	1	0	0	0	0	0	0
ARCHITECTURAL AND TRANSPORTATION BARRIERS COMPLIANCE BOARD (UNITED STATES ACCESS BOARD)	0	13	0	0	0	0	0
ARCTIC RESEARCH COMMISSION	0	7	1	0	0	0	0
ARMED FORCES RETIREMENT HOME	0	0	1	0	0	0	0
BARRY GOLDWATER SCHOLARSHIP AND EXCELLENCE IN EDUCATION FOUNDATION	8	0	0	1	0	0	0
BROADCASTING BOARD OF GOVERNORS	9	0	16	2	2	2	0
CENTRAL INTELLIGENCE AGENCY	3	1	0	0	0	0	0
CHEMICAL SAFETY AND HAZARD INVESTIGATION BOARD	5	0	2	0	1	0	0
CHRISTOPHER COLUMBUS FELLOWSHIP FOUNDATION	0	13	0	0	0	0	0
COMMISSION OF FINE ARTS	0	7	1	0	0	0	0
COMMISSION ON CIVIL RIGHTS	0	4	4	0	0	7	4
COMMITTEE FOR PURCHASE FROM PEOPLE WHO ARE BLIND OR SEVERELY DISABLED	0	15	1	0	0	0	0
COMMODITY FUTURES TRADING COMMISSION	5	0	3	0	0	7	0
CONSUMER FINANCIAL PROTECTION BUREAU	1	0	0	0	0	0	0
CONSUMER PRODUCT SAFETY COMMISSION	5	0	15	1	0	15	0
CONSUMER PRODUCT SAFETY COMMISSION OFFICE OF THE INSPECTOR GENERAL	0	0	1	0	0	0	0
CORPORATION FOR NATIONAL AND COMMUNITY SERVICE	14	0	0	0	0	0	31
COUNCIL OF INSPECTORS GENERAL ON INTEGRITY AND EFFICIENCY	0	0	2	0	0	0	0
COURT SERVICES AND OFFENDER SUPERVISION AGENCY FOR THE DISTRICT OF COLUMBIA	1	0	1	0	0	0	0
DEFENSE NUCLEAR FACILITIES SAFETY BOARD	5	0	2	0	0	0	1
DELAWARE RIVER BASIN COMMISSION	0	1	0	0	0	0	0
DELTA REGIONAL AUTHORITY	1	1	0	0	0	0	0
DEPARTMENT OF AGRICULTURE	13	3	138	39	4	164	0
DEPARTMENT OF AGRICULTURE OFFICE OF THE INSPECTOR GENERAL	1	0	1	0	0	0	0
DEPARTMENT OF COMMERCE	23	0	139	36	1	84	1
DEPARTMENT OF COMMERCE OFFICE OF THE INSPECTOR GENERAL	1	0	0	0	0	0	0
DEPARTMENT OF DEFENSE	(53)	0	(357)	(74)	(13)	(101)	0
OFFICE OF THE SECRETARY OF DEFENSE	31	0	283	61	8	74	0
DEPARTMENT OF THE AIR FORCE	7	0	14	3	0	6	0
DEPARTMENT OF THE ARMY	8	0	35	6	4	11	0
DEPARTMENT OF THE NAVY	7	0	25	4	1	10	0
DEPARTMENT OF EDUCATION	16	1	58	14	0	115	2
DEPARTMENT OF EDUCATION OFFICE OF THE INSPECTOR GENERAL	1	0	0	0	0	0	0
DEPARTMENT OF ENERGY	22	0	443	21	1	69	1

Agency or Department	PAS	PA	GEN	NA	TA	SC	XS
DEPARTMENT OF ENERGY OFFICE OF THE INSPECTOR GENERAL	1	0	0	0	0	0	0
DEPARTMENT OF HEALTH AND HUMAN SERVICES	19	1	372	72	2	68	1
DEPARTMENT OF HEALTH AND HUMAN SERVICES OFFICE OF THE INSPECTOR GENERAL	1	0	0	0	0	0	0
DEPARTMENT OF HOMELAND SECURITY	20	2	122	55	17	83	4
DEPARTMENT OF HOMELAND SECURITY OFFICE OF THE INSPECTOR GENERAL	1	0	0	0	0	0	0
DEPARTMENT OF HOUSING AND URBAN DEVELOPMENT	13	0	96	19	1	47	0
DEPARTMENT OF HOUSING AND URBAN DEVELOPMENT OFFICE OF THE INSPECTOR GENERAL	1	0	0	0	0	0	0
DEPARTMENT OF JUSTICE	224	0	142	49	4	65	0
DEPARTMENT OF JUSTICE OFFICE OF THE INSPECTOR GENERAL	1	0	0	0	0	0	0
DEPARTMENT OF LABOR	17	0	62	24	5	80	0
DEPARTMENT OF LABOR OFFICE OF INSPECTOR GENERAL	1	0	0	0	0	0	0
DEPARTMENT OF STATE	253	5	147	38	8	104	0
DEPARTMENT OF STATE OFFICE OF THE INSPECTOR GENERAL	1	0	1	0	0	0	0
DEPARTMENT OF THE INTERIOR	17	0	195	39	6	46	3
DEPARTMENT OF THE INTERIOR OFFICE OF THE INSPECTOR GENERAL	1	0	0	0	0	0	0
DEPARTMENT OF THE TREASURY	33	0	113	30	6	44	0
DEPARTMENT OF THE TREASURY INSPECTOR GENERAL FOR TAX ADMINISTRATION	1	0	0	0	0	0	0
DEPARTMENT OF THE TREASURY OFFICE OF THE INSPECTOR GENERAL	1	0	2	0	1	0	0
DEPARTMENT OF THE TREASURY SPECIAL INSPECTOR GENERAL FOR THE TROUBLED ASSET RELIEF PROGRAM	1	0	2	0	1	0	0
DEPARTMENT OF TRANSPORTATION	22	0	170	27	2	38	4
DEPARTMENT OF TRANSPORTATION OFFICE OF THE INSPECTOR GENERAL	1	0	0	0	0	0	0
DEPARTMENT OF VETERANS AFFAIRS	14	0	322	10	5	10	85
DEPARTMENT OF VETERANS AFFAIRS OFFICE OF THE INSPECTOR GENERAL	1	0	0	0	0	0	0
DWIGHT D EISENHOWER MEMORIAL COMMISSION	0	3	0	0	0	0	1
ENVIRONMENTAL PROTECTION AGENCY	13	0	115	28	6	23	0
ENVIRONMENTAL PROTECTION AGENCY OFFICE OF THE INSPECTOR GENERAL	1	0	0	0	0	0	0
EQUAL EMPLOYMENT OPPORTUNITY COMMISSION	6	0	38	3	0	1	0
EQUAL EMPLOYMENT OPPORTUNITY COMMISSION OFFICE OF THE INSPECTOR GENERAL	0	0	1	0	0	0	0
EXECUTIVE OFFICE OF THE PRESIDENT	29	106	99	21	1	43	22
EXPORT-IMPORT BANK	6	0	0	0	0	13	0
FARM CREDIT ADMINISTRATION	3	0	0	0	0	3	0
FEDERAL COMMUNICATIONS COMMISSION	5	0	47	3	0	3	5
FEDERAL DEPOSIT INSURANCE CORPORATION	5	0	0	0	0	1	0
FEDERAL ELECTION COMMISSION	6	0	0	0	0	0	18
FEDERAL ENERGY REGULATORY COMMISSION	5	0	47	1	0	4	0
FEDERAL FINANCIAL INSTITUTIONS EXAMINATION COUNCIL	0	0	1	0	0	0	0
FEDERAL HOUSING FINANCE AGENCY	1	0	0	0	0	1	0
FEDERAL LABOR RELATIONS AUTHORITY	4	7	0	0	0	0	2
FEDERAL MARITIME COMMISSION	5	0	3	0	0	2	0
FEDERAL MEDIATION AND CONCILIATION SERVICE	1	0	4	0	0	0	0
FEDERAL MINE SAFETY AND HEALTH REVIEW COMMISSION	4	1	1	0	1	3	0
FEDERAL RESERVE SYSTEM	7	0	0	0	0	0	0
FEDERAL RETIREMENT THRIFT INVESTMENT BOARD	5	0	6	0	0	0	1
FEDERAL TRADE COMMISSION	5	0	32	6	0	1	0
GENERAL SERVICES ADMINISTRATION	1	0	20	11	2	26	0
GENERAL SERVICES ADMINISTRATION OFFICE OF THE INSPECTOR GENERAL	1	0	0	0	0	0	0
GOVERNMENT ACCOUNTABILITY OFFICE	1	0	0	0	0	0	0
GOVERNMENT PRINTING OFFICE	1	0	0	0	0	1	3
HARRY S. TRUMAN SCHOLARSHIP FOUNDATION	0	0	0	0	0	0	1
INTER-AMERICAN FOUNDATION	9	0	0	0	0	0	1
INTERNATIONAL BOUNDARY AND WATER COMMISSION	0	1	0	0	0	0	0
INTERNATIONAL BOUNDARY COMMISSION: UNITED STATES AND CANADA	0	1	0	0	0	0	0
INTERNATIONAL JOINT COMMISSION	3	0	0	0	0	0	0
INTERSTATE COMMISSION ON THE POTOMAC RIVER BASIN	0	3	0	0	0	0	0

Agency or Department	PAS	PA	GEN	NA	TA	SC	XS
JAMES MADISON MEMORIAL FELLOWSHIP FOUNDATION	0	0	0	0	0	0	1
JAPAN UNITED STATES FRIENDSHIP COMMISSION	0	0	1	0	0	0	0
JOHN F. KENNEDY CENTER	36	0	0	0	0	0	0
LIBRARY OF CONGRESS	1	10	0	0	0	0	1
MARINE MAMMAL COMMISSION	3	0	0	0	0	0	1
MEDICAID AND CHIP PAYMENT AND ACCESS COMMISSION	0	0	0	0	0	0	5
MEDICARE PAYMENT ADVISORY COMMISSION	0	0	0	0	0	0	9
MERIT SYSTEMS PROTECTION BOARD	3	0	3	4	0	0	0
MILLENNIUM CHALLENGE CORPORATION	3	10	0	0	0	0	6
MORRIS K. UDALL AND STEWART L. UDALL FOUNDATION	9	0	0	0	0	0	0
NATIONAL AERONAUTICS AND SPACE ADMINISTRATION	3	0	34	5	1	7	0
NATIONAL AERONAUTICS AND SPACE ADMINISTRATION OFFICE OF THE INSPECTOR GENERAL	1	0	0	0	0	0	0
NATIONAL ARCHIVES AND RECORDS ADMINISTRATION	1	0	8	0	0	0	10
NATIONAL CAPITAL PLANNING COMMISSION	0	3	0	0	0	0	0
NATIONAL COUNCIL ON DISABILITY	15	0	0	0	0	0	0
NATIONAL CREDIT UNION ADMINISTRATION	3	0	0	0	0	7	0
NATIONAL ENDOWMENT FOR THE HUMANITIES OFFICE OF THE INSPECTOR GENERAL	0	0	1	0	0	0	0
NATIONAL FOUNDATION ON THE ARTS AND THE HUMANITIES	48	0	11	6	0	9	0
NATIONAL LABOR RELATIONS BOARD	6	0	12	6	1	0	0
NATIONAL MEDIATION BOARD	3	0	1	0	0	2	0
NATIONAL SCIENCE FOUNDATION	2	0	79	0	12	0	0
NATIONAL TRANSPORTATION SAFETY BOARD	5	0	2	1	0	4	0
NORTHERN BORDER REGIONAL COMMISSION	1	0	0	0	0	0	0
NUCLEAR REGULATORY COMMISSION	5	0	43	1	0	0	26
NUCLEAR REGULATORY COMMISSION OFFICE OF THE INSPECTOR GENERAL	1	0	0	1	0	0	0
NUCLEAR WASTE TECHNICAL REVIEW BOARD	0	11	1	0	0	0	0
OCCUPATIONAL SAFETY AND HEALTH REVIEW COMMISSION	3	0	1	1	0	2	0
OFFICE OF GOVERNMENT ETHICS	1	0	1	0	0	0	0
OFFICE OF NAVAJO AND HOPI INDIAN RELOCATION	1	0	2	0	0	0	0
OFFICE OF PERSONNEL MANAGEMENT	2	0	40	10	2	13	0
OFFICE OF PERSONNEL MANAGEMENT OFFICE OF THE INSPECTOR GENERAL	1	0	0	0	0	0	0
OFFICE OF SPECIAL COUNSEL	1	0	4	1	1	0	0
OFFICE OF THE DIRECTOR OF NATIONAL INTELLIGENCE	5	2	0	0	0	0	0
OFFICE OF THE FEDERAL COORDINATOR ALASKA NATURAL GAS TRANSPORTATION PROJECTS	1	0	0	0	0	0	0
OFFICE OF THE SECRETARY OF DEFENSE OFFICE OF THE INSPECTOR GENERAL	1	0	1	0	1	0	0
OVERSEAS PRIVATE INVESTMENT CORPORATION	9	0	0	0	0	0	14
PEACE CORPS	2	0	0	0	0	0	26
PENSION BENEFIT GUARANTY CORPORATION	1	0	0	0	0	2	0
POSTAL REGULATORY COMMISSION	5	0	0	0	0	0	0
PRESIDENTS COMMISSION ON WHITE HOUSE FELLOWSHIPS	0	0	0	1	0	2	0
PRESIDIO TRUST	0	6	0	1	0	0	1
RAILROAD RETIREMENT BOARD	3	0	0	0	0	0	0
RAILROAD RETIREMENT BOARD OFFICE OF THE INSPECTOR GENERAL	1	0	0	0	0	0	0
RECOVERY ACCOUNTABILITY AND TRANSPARENCY BOARD	0	0	0	0	0	0	2
SECURITIES AND EXCHANGE COMMISSION	5	0	0	0	0	18	0
SELECTIVE SERVICE SYSTEM	1	0	0	1	0	0	0
SMALL BUSINESS ADMINISTRATION	3	0	18	11	0	31	0
SMALL BUSINESS ADMINISTRATION OFFICE OF THE INSPECTOR GENERAL	1	0	0	0	0	0	0
SMITHSONIAN INSTITUTION	0	0	0	0	0	0	2
SOCIAL SECURITY ADMINISTRATION	2	3	128	3	0	2	12
SOCIAL SECURITY ADMINISTRATION OFFICE OF THE INSPECTOR GENERAL	1	0	9	0	0	0	0
TENNESSEE VALLEY AUTHORITY	10	0	0	0	0	0	0
TRADE AND DEVELOPMENT AGENCY	1	0	2	0	0	3	1
UNITED STATES - CHINA ECONOMIC AND SECURITY REVIEW COMMISSION	0	0	0	0	0	0	12
UNITED STATES AGENCY FOR INTERNATIONAL DEVELOPMENT	11	2	62	3	1	0	96
UNITED STATES AGENCY FOR INTERNATIONAL DEVELOPMENT OFFICE OF THE INSPECTOR GENERAL	1	0	0	0	0	0	0

Agency or Department	PAS	PA	GEN	NA	TA	SC	XS
UNITED STATES COMMISSION FOR THE PRESERVATION OF AMERICA'S HERITAGE ABROAD	0	21	0	0	0	0	0
UNITED STATES COMMISSION ON INTERNATIONAL RELIGIOUS FREEDOM	0	3	0	0	0	0	0
UNITED STATES ELECTION ASSISTANCE COMMISSION	4	0	0	0	0	0	0
UNITED STATES HOLOCAUST MEMORIAL COUNCIL	0	57	0	0	0	0	0
UNITED STATES INSTITUTE OF PEACE	15	0	0	0	0	0	0
UNITED STATES INTERAGENCY COUNCIL ON HOMELESSNESS	0	0	0	0	0	0	1
UNITED STATES INTERNATIONAL TRADE COMMISSION	7	0	7	0	0	16	0
UNITED STATES POSTAL SERVICE	6	0	1	0	0	0	39
UTAH RECLAMATION MITIGATION AND CONSERVATION COMMISSION	0	5	0	0	0	0	1
VIETNAM EDUCATION FOUNDATION	0	6	0	0	0	0	1
WOODROW WILSON INTERNATIONAL CENTER FOR SCHOLARS	0	0	0	0	0	0	3
TOTAL (8045)	1217	364	3821	680	109	1392	462

APPENDIX NO. 2

SENIOR EXECUTIVE SERVICE

The Senior Executive Service (SES) is a personnel system covering top level policy, supervisory, and managerial positions in most Federal agencies. Positions in Government corporations, the FBI and Drug Enforcement Administration, certain intelligence agencies, certain financial regulatory agencies, and the Foreign Service are exempt from the SES.

The SES includes most Civil Service positions above grade 15 of the General Schedule. An agency may establish an SES position only within an allocation approved by the U.S. Office of Personnel Management (OPM). Currently, there are 8328 SES positions allocated by OPM to agencies.

Types of SES Positions

There are two types of SES positions: Career Reserved and General. About half of the SES positions are designated in each category. Once a position is designated by an agency, the designation may not be changed without prior OPM approval.

SES positions are designated Career Reserved when the need to ensure impartiality, or the public's confidence in the impartiality of the Government, requires that they be filled only by career employees (e.g., law enforcement and audit positions).

The remaining SES positions are designated General. A General position may be filled by a career appointee, a noncareer appointee, or, if the position meets the criteria described below, by a limited term or limited emergency appointee. Because of the limitations on the number of limited appointees, most General positions are filled by career appointees.

A given General position may be filled at one time by a career appointee and at another time by a noncareer or limited appointee, or vice versa. Because of the limitations on the number of noncareer and limited appointees, as discussed below, most General positions are filled by career appointees. This publication lists only General positions since Career Reserved positions must be filled by a career appointee.

Appointments to SES Positions

The legislation establishing the SES provides three methods of appointment. Veterans preference is not applicable in the SES.

(1) Career appointment: Career appointments are made through a Governmentwide or an "all sources" merit staffing (competitive) process, including recruitment through a published announcement, rating and ranking of eligible candidates, approval by the agency of the professional qualifications of the selected candidate, and a further review and approval of the executive/managerial qualifications of the proposed selectee by an OPM-administered SES Qualifications Review Board.

A career appointee serves a 1-year probationary period. Upon completion, the appointee acquires tenure rights and may be removed from the SES only for cause or for poor performance. (A performance appraisal for a career appointee may not be made, however, within 120 days after the beginning of a new Presidential Administration, i.e., one where the President changes.)

When a career appointee is reassigned within an agency, he or she must be given at least a 15-day advance written notice. If the reassignment is to another commuting area, the notice period is 60 days; the agency first must consult with the individual as to the reasons and the individual's preferences.

A career appointee may not be involuntarily reassigned within 120 days after the appointment of a new agency head, or during the same period after the appointment of a noncareer supervisor who has the authority to make an initial appraisal of the career appointee's performance. A career appointee may not be involuntarily transferred to another agency.

Like all career Federal employees, a career SES appointee is entitled to protection against retaliatory or politically motivated personnel actions and may lodge a complaint with the Office of the Special Counsel if a prohibited personnel practice has occurred.

(2) Noncareer appointment: By law, no more than 10 percent of total SES positions Governmentwide may be filled by noncareer appointees. The proportion of noncareer appointees may, however, vary from agency to agency, generally up to a limit of 25 percent of the agency's number of SES positions. OPM approves each use of a noncareer authority by an agency, and the authority reverts to OPM when the noncareer appointee leaves the position.

Noncareer appointees may be appointed to any SES General position. There is no requirement for competitive staffing, but the agency head must certify that the appointee meets the qualifications requirements for the position.

Any noncareer appointee may be removed by the appointing authority (e.g., for loss of confidence or change in policy). There is no appeal right.

(3) Limited appointment: Limited appointments are used in situations where the position is not continuing (e.g., to head a special project), or where the position is established to meet a bona fide, unanticipated, urgent need. Limited term appointments may not exceed 3 years; limited emergency appointments, 18 months.

By law, limited appointments Governmentwide may not exceed 5 percent of total SES positions. The appointments may be made only to General positions. Generally, OPM allocates limited appointment authorities on a case-by-case basis. However, each agency has a small pool of limited authorities equal to 3 percent of their total SES position allocation from OPM. Such pool authorities may be used only for appointment of career or career-type Federal civil service employees. Selection procedures and qualification requirements are determined by the agency, and the incumbent serves at the pleasure of the appointing authority.

By law, the appointment to or removal from any SES position in an independent regulatory commission shall not be subject, directly or indirectly, to review or approval by an officer or entity within the Executive Office of the President.

APPENDIX NO. 3

SCHEDULE C POSITIONS

Schedule C positions are excepted from the competitive service because of their confidential or policy-determining character. Most such positions are at grade 15 of the General Schedule or lower. Schedule C positions above the GS–15 level are either in the Senior Level (SL) personnel system or are specifically authorized in law.

The decision concerning whether to place a position in Schedule C is made by the Director, U.S. Office of Personnel Management, upon agency request. Such requests are considered on a case-by-case basis. In addition to consideration of the justification submitted by the agency, OPM may conduct an independent review and analysis. In addition to the Schedule C positions authorized by the OPM Director, a limited number of positions may be placed under Schedule C by Executive Order of the President or by legislation.

Requests for Schedule C exception are appropriate when:

(1) The position involves making or approving substantive policy recommendations; or

(2) The work of the position can be performed successfully only by someone with a thorough knowledge of and sympathy with the goals, priorities, and preferences of an official who has a confidential or policy determining relationship with the President or the agency head. There are special requirements for the types of superiors who are eligible for Schedule C secretaries.

The immediate supervisor of a Schedule C position must be a Presidential appointee, a Senior Executive Service appointee (career or noncareer) occupying a General position, or a Schedule C appointee. The immediate supervisor may not occupy a position in the competitive service or a Career Reserved position in the Senior Executive Service.

The only time when OPM approval is not required for a Schedule C position is when a position is filled by a temporary Schedule C appointment during a Presidential transition, a change of agency head, or establishment of a new agency. Temporary Schedule C positions may be established for 120 days, with one extension of 120 days, under conditions prescribed by OPM. There is a limit on the number of such positions that can be established by an agency. New appointments may be made only during the 1-year period beginning on the date of the agency head's appointment, a new Administration or establishment of a new agency.

By law, the agency head must certify to OPM that both Schedule C and temporary Schedule C positions are not being requested for the sole purpose of detailing the incumbent to the White House.

Agencies may fill Schedule C positions noncompetitively. Because of the confidential or policy-determining nature of Schedule C positions, the incumbents serve at the pleasure of the appointing authority (usually the agency head) and may be removed at any time. They are not covered under conduct-based or performance-removal procedures that apply to certain other excepted Service appointees.

Schedule C positions authorized by OPM are automatically revoked when the incumbent leaves the position (i.e., there is no such thing as a "vacant" Schedule C position).

APPENDIX NO. 4

FEDERAL SALARY SCHEDULES FOR 2012

The information in the body of this report reflects grades or salaries in effect on the first pay period on or after January 1, 2012.

EXECUTIVE SCHEDULE (EX)

Level I	$199,700
Level II	$179,700
Level III	$165,300
Level IV	$155,500
Level V	$145,700

SENIOR EXECUTIVE SERVICE SCHEDULE (ES)

Pay ranges for the Senior Executive Service (SES) are established by law. The minimum is 120 percent of the rate of basic pay for GS–15, step 1. For agencies without a certified SES performance appraisal system, SES members' pay may not exceed the rate payable for level III of the Executive Schedule. For agencies with a certified SES performance appraisal system, SES members' pay may not exceed the rate payable for level II of the Executive Schedule. SES members are not entitled to locality-based comparability payments.**

Structure of the SES Pay System	Minimum	Maximum
Agencies with a Certified SES Performance Appraisal System	$119,554	$179,700
Agencies without a Certified SES Performance Appraisal System	119,554	165,300

SENIOR LEVEL (SL)

The minimum pay for SL positions is 120 percent of the rate of basic pay for GS–15, step 1. For agencies without a certified SL performance appraisal system, SL members' pay may not exceed the rate payable for level III of the Executive Schedule. For agencies with a certified SL performance appraisal system, SL members' pay may not exceed the rate payable for level II of the Executive Schedule. SL members are not entitled to locality-based comparability payments.**

Structure of the SL Pay System	Minimum	Maximum
Agencies with a Certified SES Performance Appraisal System	$119,554	$179,700
Agencies without a Certified SES Performance Appraisal System	119,554	165,300

**Certain SES and SL employees in Non-Foreign Areas receive locality pay under provisions of the Non-Foreign Area Retirement Equity Assurance (AREA) Act (as contained in the National Defense Authorization Act for Fiscal Year 2010 [Pub. L. 111–84, October 28, 2009]).

GENERAL SCHEDULE (GS)

Initial appointments to positions under the General Schedule are normally made at the minimum rate of the grade, although under certain circumstances, individuals with superior qualifications or fulfilling a special agency need may be paid at a rate above the minimum rate.

Step increases are granted to GS employees at the end of 52 weeks of service in steps 1, 2, and 3 of each grade; at the end of 104 weeks of service in steps 4, 5, and 6; and at the end of 156 weeks of service in steps 7, 8, and 9. An employee's work must be determined to be of an acceptable level of competence before granting a step increase. In addition to the periodic step increase, an employee whose work is outstanding may be advanced to the next higher step rate no more than once every 52 weeks. In addition to the 2012 basic pay rates listed below, GS employees are entitled to locality-based comparability payments for their respective locality pay area. The employee's locality rate of pay may not exceed the rate payable for level IV of the Executive Schedule. Certain GS employees may receive higher special rates instead of locality rates established to address significant recruitment or retention problems.

GENERAL SCHEDULE

Grade	2012 Annual Rates and Steps									
	1	2	3	4	5	6	7	8	9	10
GS–1	$17,803	$18,398	$18,990	$19,579	$20,171	$20,519	$21,104	$21,694	$21,717	$22,269
GS–2	20,017	20,493	21,155	21,717	21,961	22,607	23,253	23,899	24,545	25,191
GS–3	21,840	22,568	23,296	24,024	24,752	25,480	26,208	26,936	27,664	28,392
GS–4	24,518	25,335	26,152	26,969	27,786	28,603	29,420	30,237	31,054	31,871
GS–5	27,431	28,345	29,259	30,173	31,087	32,001	32,915	33,829	34,743	35,657
GS–6	30,577	31,596	32,615	33,634	34,653	35,672	36,691	37,710	38,729	39,748
GS–7	33,979	35,112	36,245	37,378	38,511	39,644	40,777	41,910	43,043	44,176
GS–8	37,631	38,885	40,139	41,393	42,647	43,901	45,155	46,409	47,663	48,917
GS–9	41,563	42,948	44,333	45,718	47,103	48,488	49,873	51,258	52,643	54,028
GS–10	45,771	47,297	48,823	50,349	51,875	53,401	54,927	56,453	57,979	59,505
GS–11	50,287	51,963	53,639	55,315	56,991	58,667	60,343	62,019	63,695	65,371
GS–12	60,274	62,283	64,292	66,301	68,310	70,319	72,328	74,337	76,346	78,355
GS–13	71,674	74,063	76,452	78,841	81,230	83,619	86,008	88,397	90,786	93,175
GS–14	84,697	87,520	90,343	93,166	95,989	98,812	101,635	104,458	107,281	110,104
GS–15	99,628	102,949	106,270	109,591	112,912	116,233	119,554	122,875	126,196	129,517

2012 LOCALITY PAY AREAS AND RATES

Atlanta-Sandy Springs-Gainesville, GA–AL	19.29%
Boston-Worcester-Manchester, MA–NH–RI–ME	24.80%
Buffalo-Niagara-Cattaraugus, NY	16.98%
Chicago-Naperville-Michigan City, IL–IN–WI	25.10%
Cincinnati-Middletown-Wilmington, OH–KY–IN	18.55%
Cleveland-Akron-Elyria, OH	18.68%
Columbus-Marion-Chillicothe, OH	17.16%
Dallas-Fort Worth, TX	20.67%
Dayton-Springfield-Greenville, OH	16.24%
Denver-Aurora-Boulder, CO	22.52%
Detroit-Warren-Flint, MI	24.09%
Hartford-West Hartford-Willimantic, CT–MA	25.82%
Houston-Baytown-Huntsville, TX	28.71%
Huntsville-Decatur, AL	16.02%
Indianapolis-Anderson-Columbus, IN	14.68%
Los Angeles-Long Beach-Riverside, CA	27.16%
Miami-Fort Lauderdale-Pompano Beach, FL	20.79%
Milwaukee-Racine-Waukesha, WI	18.10%
Minneapolis-St. Paul-St. Cloud, MN–WI	20.96%
New York-Newark-Bridgeport, NY–NJ–CT–PA	28.72%
Philadelphia-Camden-Vineland, PA–NJ–DE–MD	21.79%
Phoenix-Mesa-Scottsdale, AZ	16.76%
Pittsburgh-New Castle, PA	16.37%
Portland-Vancouver-Beaverton, OR–WA	20.35%
Raleigh-Durham-Cary, NC	17.64%
Richmond, VA	16.47%
Sacramento-Arden-Arcade-Yuba City, CA–NV	22.20%
San Diego-Carlsbad-San Marcos, CA	24.19%
Seattle-Tacoma-Olympia, WA	21.81%
Washington-Baltimore-Northern Virginia, DC–MD–VA–WV–PA	24.22%
Rest of U.S.	14.16%

Note: Locality pay areas are defined in 5 CFR 531.603(b) and are available on the Office of Personnel Management Web site at http://www.opm.gov/oca/12tables/locdef.asp.

WASHINGTON–BALTIMORE–NORTHERN VIRGINIA, DC–MD–VA–WV–PA LOCALITY PAY SCHEDULE

The following salary tables reflect the locality pay rates for the Washington-Baltimore-Northern Virginia, DC–MD–VA–WV–PA locality pay area in 2012. The tables incorporate a locality payment of 24.22 percent.

GENERAL SCHEDULE

Grade	2012 Annual Rates and Steps									
	1	2	3	4	5	6	7	8	9	10
GS–1	$22,115	$22,854	$23,589	$24,321	$25,056	$25,489	$26,215	$26,948	$26,977	$27,663
GS–2	24,865	25,456	26,279	26,977	27,280	28,082	28,885	29,687	30,490	31,292
GS–3	27,130	28,034	28,938	29,843	30,747	31,651	32,556	33,460	34,364	35,269
GS–4	30,456	31,471	32,486	33,501	34,516	35,531	36,546	37,560	38,575	39,590
GS–5	34,075	35,210	36,346	37,481	38,616	39,752	40,887	42,022	43,158	44,293
GS–6	37,983	39,249	40,514	41,780	43,046	44,312	45,578	46,843	48,109	49,375
GS–7	42,209	43,616	45,024	46,431	47,838	49,246	50,653	52,061	53,468	54,875
GS–8	46,745	48,303	49,861	51,418	52,976	54,534	56,092	57,649	59,207	60,765
GS–9	51,630	53,350	55,070	56,791	58,511	60,232	61,952	63,673	65,393	67,114
GS–10	56,857	58,752	60,648	62,544	64,439	66,335	68,230	70,126	72,022	73,917
GS–11	62,467	64,548	66,630	68,712	70,794	72,876	74,958	77,040	79,122	81,204
GS–12	74,872	77,368	79,864	82,359	84,855	87,350	89,846	92,341	94,837	97,333
GS–13	89,033	92,001	94,969	97,936	100,904	103,872	106,839	109,807	112,774	115,742
GS–14	105,211	108,717	112,224	115,731	119,238	122,744	126,251	129,758	133,264	136,771
GS–15	123,758	127,883	132,009	136,134	140,259	144,385	148,510	152,635	155,500	155,500

SPECIAL LAW ENFORCEMENT OFFICER (LEO) PAY SCHEDULES

Law enforcement officers at grades GS–3 through GS–10 are entitled to special base rates that are higher than General Schedule base rates. Such LEOs receive the locality payments applicable in their locality pay area on top of these special base rates. The locality pay area definitions and pay percentages are the same as those used for regular General Schedule employees.

SPECIAL SALARY RATES FOR LEOS

Grade	2012 Annual Rates and Steps									
	1	2	3	4	5	6	7	8	9	10
GS–3	$26,208	$26,936	$27,664	$28,392	$29,120	$29,848	$30,576	$31,304	$32,032	$32,760
GS–4	29,420	30,237	31,054	31,871	32,688	33,505	34,322	35,139	35,956	36,773
GS–5	33,829	34,743	35,657	36,571	37,485	38,399	39,313	40,227	41,141	42,055
GS–6	35,672	36,691	37,710	38,729	39,748	40,767	41,786	42,805	43,824	44,843
GS–7	38,511	39,644	40,777	41,910	43,043	44,176	45,309	46,442	47,575	48,708
GS–8	40,139	41,393	42,647	43,901	45,155	46,409	47,663	48,917	50,171	51,425
GS–9	42,948	44,333	45,718	47,103	48,488	49,873	51,258	52,643	54,028	55,413
GS–10	47,297	48,823	50,349	51,875	53,401	54,927	56,453	57,979	59,505	61,031

NOTE: These special base rates for law enforcement officers (as defined in 5 U.S.C. 5541(3) and 5 CFR 550.103) are authorized by section 403 of the Federal Employees Pay Comparability Act of 1990, as amended. By law, these rates must be the basis for computing locality payments. (5 CFR part 531, subpart F.)

THE FOREIGN SERVICE SCHEDULE

	Class								
	1	2	3	4	5	6	7	8	9
Step 1	$99,628	$80,728	$65,413	$53,003	$42,948	$38,394	$34,324	$30,684	$27,431
Step 2	102,617	83,150	67,375	54,593	44,236	39,546	35,354	31,605	28,254
Step 3	105,695	85,644	69,397	56,231	45,564	40,732	36,414	32,553	29,102
Step 4	108,866	88,214	71,479	57,918	46,930	41,954	37,507	33,529	29,975
Step 5	112,132	90,860	73,623	59,655	48,338	43,213	38,632	34,535	30,874
Step 6	115,496	93,586	75,832	61,445	49,789	44,509	39,791	35,571	31,800
Step 7	118,961	96,393	78,107	63,288	51,282	45,844	40,985	36,638	32,754
Step 8	122,530	99,285	80,450	65,187	52,821	47,220	42,214	37,737	33,737
Step 9	126,206	102,264	82,863	67,143	54,405	48,636	43,481	38,870	34,749
Step 10	129,517	105,332	85,349	69,157	56,037	50,095	44,785	40,036	35,791
Step 11	129,517	108,492	87,910	71,232	57,719	51,598	46,129	41,237	36,865
Step 12	129,517	111,746	90,547	73,369	59,450	53,146	47,512	42,474	37,971
Step 13	129,517	115,099	93,263	75,570	61,234	54,741	48,938	43,748	39,110
Step 14	129,517	118,552	96,061	77,837	63,071	56,383	50,406	45,060	40,283

SENIOR FOREIGN SERVICE SCHEDULE

The Senior Foreign Service (SFS) pay system is an open-range, performance-based pay system that is linked to the SES pay system. SFS members, like SES members, are not entitled to automatic across-the-board increases and locality-based comparability payments. Instead, pay adjustments are based on a member's individual performance and/or contribution to the agency's performance.

The Executive order prescribes three SFS salary classes that are linked to the SES as follows:

(1) Career Minister (CM) with a range from 94 percent of the rate payable to level III of the Executive Schedule to 100 percent of the rate payable to level II of the Executive Schedule (Note: Career Ambassador (CA) SFS members are also paid within the CM rate range);

(2) Minister-Counselor (MC) with a range from 90 percent of the rate payable to level III of the Executive Schedule to 100 percent of the rate payable to level III of the Executive Schedule; and

(3) Counselor (OC), with a range from 120 percent of the rate payable to GS–15, step 1 to 100 percent of the rate payable to level III of the Executive Schedule.

The 2012 pay ranges for the SFS classes are:

SFS Class	Minimum	Maximum
OC	$119,554	$165,300
MC	$119,554	$165,300
CM, CA	$119,554	$179,700

DEPARTMENT OF VETERANS AFFAIRS, VETERANS HEALTH ADMINISTRATION FEDERAL SALARY SCHEDULES EFFECTIVE ON THE FIRST DAY OF THE FIRST APPLICABLE PAY PERIOD BEGINNING ON OR AFTER JANUARY 1, 2012

SCHEDULE FOR THE OFFICE OF THE UNDER SECRETARY FOR HEALTH
(38 U.S.C. 7306)*

	Minimum	Maximum
Assistant Under Secretaries for Health		$157,279**
(Only applies to incumbents who are not physicians or dentists)		
Service Directors	$116,844	$145,113
Director, National Center for Preventive Health	99,628	145,113
Physician and Dentist Base and Longevity Schedule*		
Physician Grade	$97,987	$143,725
Dentist Grade	99,987	143,725
Clinical Podiatrist, Chiropractor, and Optometrist Schedule		
Chief Grade	$99,628	$129,517
Senior Grade	84,697	110,104
Intermediate Grade	71,674	93,175
Full Grade	60,274	78,355
Associate Grade	51,287	65,371
Physician Assistant and Expanded-Function Dental Auxiliary Schedule ****		
Director Grade	$99,628	$129,517
Assistant Director Grade	84,697	110,104
Chief Grade	71,674	93,175
Senior Grade	60,274	78,355
Intermediate Grade	51,287	65,371
Full Grade	41,563	54,028
Associate Grade	35,766	46,494
Junior Grade	30,577	39,748

*This schedule does not apply to the Deputy Under Secretary for Health, the Associate Deputy Under Secretary for Health, Assistant Under Secretaries for Health who are physicians or dentists, Medical Directors, the Assistant Under Secretary for Nursing Programs, or the Director of Nursing Services.

**Pursuant to 38 U.S.C. 7404(d), the rate of basic pay payable to these employees is limited to the rate for level V of the Executive Schedule, which is $145,700.

***Pursuant to section 3 of Public Law 108–445 and 38 U.S.C. 7431, Veterans Health Administration physicians and dentists may also be paid market pay and performance pay.

****Pursuant to section 301(a) of Public Law 102–40, these positions are paid according to the Nurse Schedule in 38 U.S.C. 4107(b), as in effect on August 14, 1990, with subsequent adjustments.

APPENDIX NO. 5

OFFICE OF THE VICE PRESIDENT

The Vice Presidency is a unique office that is neither a part of the executive branch nor a part of the legislative branch, but is attached by the Constitution to the latter. The Vice Presidency performs functions in both the legislative branch (see article I, section 3 of the Constitution) and in the executive branch (see article II, and amendments XII and XXV, of the Constitution, and section 106 of title 3 of the United States Code).

The annual legislative branch appropriations act (see, for example, Public Law 112–74) and the annual financial services and general government appropriations act (see, for example, Public Law 112–74) provide funds for the Vice President to hire employees to assist him in carrying out his legislative and executive functions. Executive branch employees also may be assigned or detailed to the Vice President (see 3 U.S.C. 112) and the Vice President may employ consultants (see 3 U.S.C. 106(a)). The Office of the Vice President (OVP) consists of the aggregation of Vice Presidential employees whose salary is disbursed by the Secretary of the Senate from the Vice President's legislative appropriation, Vice Presidential employees employed with the Vice President's executive appropriation, employees assigned or detailed to the Vice President, and consultants engaged by the Vice President.

The numbers, titles and salaries of OVP personnel change with some frequency. The salaries of Vice Presidential employees whose salary is disbursed by the Secretary of the Senate from the Vice President's legislative appropriation cannot exceed a maximum specified by law (see 2 U.S.C. 60a-1). The salaries of Vice Presidential employees whose salary comes from the Vice President's executive appropriation also cannot exceed a maximum specified by law (see 3 U.S.C. 106). The authority to appoint, administratively determine the pay of, and discharge Vice Presidential employees rests with the Vice President.

The current duty station of all OVP positions is Washington, DC.

○